AF886550

Rethinking *the* Social Sciences *with* **Sam Moyo**

Rethinking *the* Social Sciences *with* **Sam Moyo**

Editors
Praveen Jha
Paris Yeros
Walter Chambati

Tulika Books

Published by
Tulika Books
44 (first floor), Shahpur Jat, New Delhi 110 049, India
www.tulikabooks.in

© This collection, the editors 2020
© Individual articles, respective authors

First edition (hardback) 2020

ISBN: 978-81-939269-4-9

Printed at Chaman Offset, Delhi 110 002

Contents

Tables and Figures

Preface

Sam Moyo entirely deserves a tribute such as this. Apart from the great mind and big heart that he was, Sam was also one of a few in our age to distinguish himself in setting new standards for knowledge production in the social sciences. Some might expect such a feat to require the approval of established centres of learning in the North. But his litmus test was relevance to the tectonic shifts underway in Africa and the South since decolonization. Sam became a leading light in the quest for epistemic sovereignty at a crucial juncture, when Africa and the South as a whole were succumbing to neoliberal adjustment, and when his own country, Zimbabwe, was gaining independence.

Sam belonged to the generation of pan-Africanist intellectuals responsible for defending the gains of liberation and devising strategies of epistemic survival in the midst of structural adjustment. Their epicentre was the Council for the Development of Social Science Research in Africa (CODESRIA), of which Sam eventually became president. He distinguished himself by his relentless drive to build and defend research capacities in Africa, refusing the lure of professional stability and fame abroad. Those who had the good fortune to meet him would affirm that he pursued this mission with flair, generosity and a 'charming inflexibility' on matters of ideology. In 2002, he founded the African Institute for Agrarian Studies (AIAS) in Harare, Zimbabwe against all odds, in the midst of radical land reform and western sanctions.

Sam also forged ahead with the building of new solidarities across the South to recuperate a common front. This he did via CODESRIA, as well the Third World Forum (TWF) and World Forum for Alternatives (WFA) led by Samir Amin, in which he participated over many years. In the 2000s, he also spearheaded the Agrarian South Network (ASN), a new tri-continental initiative with its own research agenda, regular activities and publishing outlet, *Agrarian South: Journal of Political Economy*. Those of us who were closest to him knew that the whole of this work of art was much larger than the sum of its parts: new epistemic standards were being set for generations to come.

This volume brings together friends, comrades and colleagues who interacted with Sam at different moments of his life, and some over a long period of time. Herein are included several contributions published in the special issue of *Agrarian South* devoted to Sam's life and work (Vol. 5, Nos. 2–3, 2016), but mostly new contributions that were presented at the memorial conference held in his honour at Jawaharlal Nehru University, New Delhi, in February 2018, as well as further contributions solicited subsequently. Reflecting the breadth and depth of Sam's global reach and the affection that people had for him, most regions of the world are represented in the volume, with contributors drawn from Africa, Asia, Europe and the Americas. As editors, we gave no specific suggestions to the contributors other than to feel free to write on whatever Sam inspired in them or would like to have read from them. The result – we hope our readers will agree – is a marvellous tribute to brother Sam, and a *sui generis* contribution to the research agenda in contemporary political economy.

The introductory essay by the editors locates Sam's trajectory in the pan-Africanist tradition of political economy, and highlights his contributions to the evolving land, agrarian and national questions at continental level and in his home country. The essay also traces his overall contribution to tri-continental solidarity in the social sciences and the development of a global research agenda. It brings to light Sam's leading role in the frontlines of the struggle for epistemic sovereignty in Africa and the South at a time when neoliberal restructuring set its sights on autonomous knowledge production and when epistemological questions succumbed to a potent 'cultural turn'. Sam fought with great perseverance for autonomous institutions in Africa and the South, and for the integrity of the intellectual traditions produced in the struggles for liberation. He defended an approach to political economy that was homegrown in Africa and fundamentally anti-imperialist, against western intellectual trends, whether materialist or culturalist. This was the vision and mission that defined his pan-Africanism, tri-continental solidarity and cosmopolitanism.

The book is divided in three sections. The first section, entitled 'Epistemic Vision and Contributions', is dedicated to an assessment of Sam's contributions to the social sciences by colleagues who worked closely with him or followed his work over time. Dzodzi Tsikata discusses his institutional contributions and the evolution of his research agenda on the land and agrarian questions. William Martin situates Sam's work as a counter-movement against western-led 'African Studies'. Gladys Lechini brings to light Sam's role in the South–South convergence of social science communities in the 2000s, especially between CODESRIA and the Latin American Council of Social Sciences (CLACSO). Lyn Ossome assesses Sam's contribution to the land and agrarian question in the light of current scholarship in gender studies. Ian Scoones reflects on the application of the Marxist method in Sam's work. Kojo Amanor recuperates Sam's method in environmental studies, and particularly his analysis of the cooptation of the green agenda under structural adjustment. Tendai Murisa closes this first section with a review and assessment of Sam's work on Zimbabwe's land question.

The second section, 'Land, Labour and Agrarian Questions', includes *sui generis* contributions to the research agenda in contemporary political economy. Prabhat Patnaik presents a model for understanding 'income unemployment' in a peripheral workforce devoid of a stable wage relation and underwritten by ongoing primitive accumulation. Arindam Banerjee takes issue with interpretations of the Global Food Crisis post-2006, to argue that a longer food crisis has been evolving due to the generalized income deflation in the South. Archana Prasad focuses on the changing form of expropriation of forest resources through contemporary multilateral agreements which commoditize and cartelize nature via carbon stocks. Smita Gupta analyses the new Land Acquisition Act in India whose provisions enable the exercise of the state's eminent domain to expropriate the lands and resource rights of small and marginal farmers, Adivasis, Dalits and women, among others. Sandeep Chachra reflects on the future of cities in the light of the ongoing agrarian crisis and rural–urban migration in the South. Anamitra Roychowdhury brings the section to a conclusion by examining the character of the unregistered manufacturing sector in India and its ability to provide gainful employment opportunities in the context of rural–urban migration.

The third section, entitled 'Unfinished Dialogues on Revolution and Liberation', takes forward exchanges with Sam that were abruptly suspended by his untimely passing, but which continue to require collective reflection. Samir Amin takes issue with contemporary notions of 'emergence' in the South, and argues that it remains necessary to articulate a new model of industrialization shaped by the renewal of non-capitalist forms of peasant agriculture. Issa Shivji reflects on Sam's contributions to the peasant question, and the forms of accumulation and organization that are necessary for the resolution of the national question. Utsa Patnaik provides insights into Marx's thought on the drain of wealth from peasants and workers in the colonies, and argues that although Marx's analysis remained incomplete, it should not be overlooked or serve as an excuse to omit colonialism and imperialism from the analysis of capitalism. C.P. Chandrasekhar and Jayati Ghosh assess current tendencies in the world economy, arguing that capitalism is disintegrating under its own weight, but without, as yet, spawning sufficient alternatives towards a new order. Erebus Wong, Wen Tiejun, Sit Tsui and Lau Kin Chi defend the ongoing relevance of China's Land Revolution of 1949, and provide insight into how the problem of hyperinflation was resolved by relying on subsistence agriculture and anchoring value in staple grains. Dinesh Abrol focuses on the current challenges in building a peasant–worker alliance in India under a deepening neoliberal policy framework led by right-wing authoritarian populism. Yoichi Mine brings this section to a close by comparing radical activism in the 1970s among Japanese social movements and South Africa's Black Consciousness movement, and traces the trajectories of radicalism in Japan.

We thank the contributors for making such a great effort to put their thoughts on paper and help keep Sam's legacy alive. Sam was steadfast in his conviction that knowledge production is above all a collective endeavour, and that the advance of the intellectual traditions of the South requires systematic solidarity. There is no better way to celebrate his life and work than to plough ahead in the manner that we have done in this book.

We wish to thank also the publishers of *Agrarian South: Journal of Political Economy* for permission to republish the articles by Ian Scoones, Issa Shivji, Tendai Murisa, William Martin and Samir Amin, as well as of *Development and Change* for the article by Dzodzi Tsikata. We also thank Jawaharlal Nehru University, CODESRIA and the Sam Moyo African Institute for Agrarian Studies (SMAIAS) for their support in making possible the 2018 conference in New Delhi. Finally, we thank Steven Mberi at SMAIAS for editorial assistance in compiling this book, and, of course, Indira Chandrasekhar and her team at Tulika Books for accepting this project and bringing it to fruition.

New Delhi, India PRAVEEN JHA
São Paulo, Brazil PARIS YEROS
Harare, Zimbabwe WALTER CHAMBATI

1

The Quest for Epistemic Sovereignty in the South

A Tribute to Sam Moyo

Praveen Jha, Paris Yeros and Walter Chambati

Sam Moyo was heir to the generation of pan-Africanist scholars who laid the intellectual cornerstone of a liberated Africa and inaugurated a new scientific vocation devoted to restoring African civilization to its rightful place. Sam was trained during the apex of this movement in the late 1970s and came of age intellectually when the movement suffered a historic setback, precisely when structural adjustment programmes were to launch an attack on research, teaching and autonomous sources of thinking. Salaries, budgets and personnel were slashed, while the liberation perspective was branded, disrupted and coopted (Mkandawire 1995, 2005; Onimode 1988; Mamdani 2007). Thereafter, neo-liberal adjustment trained its sights on the sources of autonomous knowledge production everywhere, across the South and even in the North.

Sam became a pillar of resistance in the ensuing struggles for epistemic sovereignty – and he was not alone. His main source of strength was the Council for the Development of Social Science Research in Africa (CODESRIA), of which he became vice president (1998–2001) and president (2008–11), as well as a series of global initiatives with a South–South base and perspective: Third World Forum (TWF), in which he participated for many years; World Forum for Alternatives (WFA), of which he became vice president for Southern Africa; and Agrarian South Network, which he founded. At home, in Zimbabwe, he founded the African Institute for Agrarian Studies (AIAS) in 2002, another crucial juncture when the liberation movement was entering a new process of radicalization.

Sam had the rare ability to combine rearguard struggle in defence of existing institutions with vanguard initiatives to build new capacities and solidarities for autonomous research in Africa and the South. Indeed, he had the strong conviction that reconstruction of the social sciences had to be initiated *from* Africa and the South, *for* Africa and the South and the world as a whole. If he was not alone in this, he certainly had a particularly stubborn perseverance in the setting of new epistemic standards for subsequent generations.

In what follows, we trace some of Sam's most important contributions, which continue to require reflection. We, of course, have the benefit of masterful statements on Sam's life and work already penned since his passing.[1] For our part, we wish to bring attention, first, to Sam's trajectory in the pan-Africanist tradition of political economy. This remains important because Sam had an impact on more than one tradition or area of study, such that one runs the risk of losing sight of the pan-Africanist origins of his thought, or even diminishing the pan-Africanist tradition by assimilating it into others. Even if, to date, we do not have proper stock-taking of the character and trajectory of this tradition of political economy, Sam was insistent in recognizing it and conscious of his location within it. We will then bring attention to the significance of Sam's positions on Zimbabwe's land, agrarian and national questions. Aside from the inspiring courage and rigour that he displayed in defending radical land reform, his role was fundamental in restoring land and agrarian questions to the global research agenda. Finally, we will trace Sam's leadership role in the building of tri-continental solidarity towards a global research agenda and identify some epistemological principles that emerge.

The Pan-Africanist Tradition of Political Economy

Sam Moyo was trained in, and later became a protagonist of, a distinct body of thought in political economy which blossomed in the pan-Africanist tradition after independence. Decolonization opened up an unprecedented space for investment in development infrastructure, including in the building of universities and research centres with the potential to establish a home-grown research agenda and train a new generation of intellectuals and development planners. The mission in those euphoric times was nothing less than the total liberation of the continent, accelerated development and civilizational renewal. And although the relationship of pan-Africanist intellectuals with the newly independent states was fraught with tension, this tradition in-the-making embarked on rethinking both African and world history by appropriating principles of political economy on its own terms, largely within historical materialism. In so doing, it came into conflict with the prevailing Eurocentric and economistic canon that exercised hegemony within and without Africa, and imposed concepts drawn from an idealized European or even Asian experience yet with universalistic pretensions. As one of the leading pan-Africanist scholars put it, this was a struggle for 'indigenization of the social sciences', consistent with the struggles for national and regional liberation (Mafeje 1991: 7).

Alongside the various new centres of thought that sprouted in capitals across liberated Africa, from Dar es Salaam to Ibadan and Dakar, there also emerged an identifiably unified continental dynamic in the definition of the research agenda in political economy and its terms of reference. This by no means implied consensus, nor did its emergence supplant Northern and expatriate intellectuals and their own debates (Mkandawire 2005). Nor, indeed, did it gain due world recognition as an autonomous contribution to the social sciences. Yet, this continental dynamic did result in the founding of CODESRIA in 1973, an institution that was to lead the development of the social sciences in Africa through thick and thin and against the increasingly authoritarian tendencies of neo-colonial states. In the decades that followed, CODESRIA would hold the fort against structural adjustment by sustaining a progressive research and training dynamic, and promoting the formation of new centres and networks, across many fields including most notably in gender studies (Mama 2005).

If we do not yet have the benefit of up-to-date stocktaking with regard to the pan-Africanist tradition of political economy, we might attempt to sketch some of its contours at least with respect to Sam's trajectory within it. It would not be an exaggeration to say that Sam was one of the key agents in its survival from one generation to the next in the course of the 'lost decades' of neo-liberal adjustment. He straddled what Mkandawire (1995) identified as the 'second' and 'third' generations of African intellectuals, and made it his mission to create institutions and capacities that could be handed over to subsequent generations. His personal trajectory took him from colonial Zimbabwe first to Sierra Leone in the 1970s, to study for his first degree at Njala University. This was, most significantly, his first exposure to the intellectual trends in liberated Africa (Mabhena Phakamile Moyo 2016), as well as to the very different organization of land and labour relations prevailing there as compared to settler-colonial Africa. From Sierra Leone he would visit his uncle posted at the United Nations Environment Programme (UNEP) in Dakar, where Sam came into contact with luminaries such as Cheikh Anta Diop and Samir Amin. He was also a regular at the Institute for Economic Development and Planning (IDEP), from where Amin, together with Abdalla Bujra, Thandika Mkandawire, Zenebewerke Tadesse, Archie Mafeje, Mahmood Mamdani and others, would embark on the building of CODESRIA, and where the Third World Forum – a pioneering tri-continental network of intellectuals – was also founded. This was precisely the 'baptism of fire' that gave Sam his lifelong epistemological orientation.

Thereafter, Sam spent a short while on postgraduate studies in Canada at the University of Western Ontario, but returned to West Africa for research and teaching, this time to Nigeria, at the Universities of Calabar and Port Harcourt. There, he met the Trinidad-born historian of Africa, David Johnson: a meeting of minds of which Sam always spoke very highly, and which quite possibly was a key moment in opening up the trans-Atlantic dimension of his pan-Africanism and internationalism. Sam returned to Zimbabwe at independence in 1980 and did not leave again for a sustained period of time. He later completed his PhD in the United Kingdom at the University of Northumbria, but he remained fully engaged in nation-building in Zimbabwe at a time when the rest of the continent was heading in another direction.

At home, he was a key figure in the development of the Zimbabwe Institute of Development Studies (ZIDS), where he was reunited with Mkandawire, seconded by CODESRIA. ZIDS was envisioned as an autonomous think tank after independence, convening young and veteran scholars for the building of a new Zimbabwe; Sam led research and policy advocacy related especially to land and agrarian questions. He also founded in 1986, with Yemi Katerere, the Zimbabwe Environmental Research Organization (ZERO), a unique centre for policy advocacy in the national and regional arena. In the 1990s, Sam became a key figure in the development of the Southern African Political Economy Series Trust (SAPES) led by Ibbo Mandaza, and its teaching programme at the Southern African Research Institute for Policy Studies (SARIPS), of which Sam was director.

At a time when the intellectual dynamic at Dar es Salaam was winding down (Tandon, ed. 1982; Shivji 1993), Harare was to provide a second breath to the evolving set of intellectual concerns on the continent, and Sam was fully involved in this (Mandaza, ed. 1986). Harare attracted to its events and conferences such intellectuals as Claude Ake, Samir Amin, Horace Campbell, Mahmood Mamdani, Issa Shivji, Dan Nabudere, Jacques Depelchin, Ben Magubane, Peter Ekeh and Patricia McFadden (Raftopoulos 2016). The founding of the African Association of Political Science (AAPS) added to this momentum. It was precisely in this environment that Sam began to consolidate his approach to the land question, with special insights into the trajectories of land and labour relations in Africa, for which he drew special inspiration from Archie Mafeje, his acknowledged mentor (Moyo 2018).

Yet, in the 1990s, structural adjustment in Zimbabwe took its toll on both the autonomy of ZIDS and academic life. Like so many others, Sam faced the dilemmas presented by the deteriorating conditions for research and teaching at state institutions, and sought sources of strength in CODESRIA as well as new possibilities in non-governmental centres of research, teaching and advocacy, such as SARIPS and ZERO. Nonetheless, this non-governmental terrain was itself unstable and vulnerable to cooptation by donors, of which Sam was all too aware (Moyo, Makumbe and Raftopoulos, eds 2000). Yet, he took the bold step at the turn of the century to build a new institute, AIAS, dedicated to land and agrarian questions in Africa with a pan-Africanist perspective. Such questions were being pronounced 'dead' by intellectual trends all around – by western Marxists and liberals alike, including a slew of neo-Weberians and post-structuralists – at the same time as the pan-Africanist perspective was being coopted by the neo-liberal winds sweeping the reborn African Union and its New Partnership for Africa's Development (NEPAD). CODESRIA itself was not spared the new wave of theoretical approaches and methods, driven above all by a 'cultural turn' that threatened to suffocate the epistemological gains of the past. Sam's initiative to found AIAS at the turn of the millennium was thus a pointed reaffirmation of his convictions.

If the pan-Africanist tradition of political economy had emerged through various concerns in contradistinction to western-inspired Marxism, it was to evolve in the 1990s against the cultural turn. The challenge that this wave presented did not result in disengagement, but renewed rearguard and vanguard struggle. Sam had become vice president of CODESRIA at this stage and was fully engaged in defending the orientation of the institution (Mamdani 2015). And, as if that were not enough, the contradictions escalated at home as well. In February 2000, a mass land occupation movement led by war veterans re-ignited the radicalism of the liberation movement to set off a radical 'fast-track' land reform programme. Western sanctions and prolonged destabilization ensued while western-inspired Marxists and liberals of diverse stripes, culturalists included, closed ranks with imperialist sanctions against land reform. Sam's newborn institute was denied funding and actively de-campaigned by the North Atlantic agencies and settler elements in the region for conducting honest and rigorous research which demonstrated, against the ideological warfare waged, that a real redistributive land reform had taken place in Zimbabwe. But Sam was again to break out of isolation via CODESRIA, eventually even to be elected its president, and via a number of South–South initiatives such as that which led to the Agrarian South Network. These options did not resolve the financial situation of his institute, but provided Sam with intellectual solidarity and a measure of sanity.

The perspective and research agenda that Sam represented could not so easily be suppressed after all. More generally, it is noteworthy that the survival of a pan-Africanist tradition of political economy has depended on its capacity to reflect upon its own contradictions and silences which continued to render it vulnerable to critique and to challenge its liberation credentials, most notably with regard to patriarchy and the gender question. It is here that the liberal-culturalist advance also drew strength in seeking to discredit the anti-imperialist perspective. Sam was one of those who 'recognized the need for embracing critical gender/feminist theory in agrarian studies' (Mbilinyi 2016: 165), and could be counted on for engendering the networks in which he was involved and held high office. Indeed, gender analysis had been a recurrent feature of his work on the land question, even if not backed by robust theory (Moyo 1995a, 2008; see also Ossome, in this volume).

Sam was a good part of the glue that kept it all together, an 'outstanding pillar' of the institutional infrastructure of African social sciences (Mkandawire 2015). He was conscious of the intellectual tradition to which he belonged and confident in its ability to rise up to the challenges of the twenty-first century. He took from his main mentor, Archie Mafeje, his appreciation of the particularity of African social formations, that is, the lineage-based system of social organization, which one way or another survived under the tributary and capitalist modes of production (Mafeje 1991). For Sam, like Mafeje, it was impossible to think of Africa's development without putting the African peasantry at the centre of the national question, including its particular relationship to land through customary tenure. Meanwhile, Sam remained aware of Samir Amin's (1976) insight that Africa's integration in the world economy put systematic pressure on the control that the African peasantry retained over land and labour, whether by the attrition of unequal exchange or waves of land alienation. He also drew from Amin the fuller conceptual elaboration of Africa's three colonial macro-regions, that is, the peasant-based commercial economies of West Africa, the concessionary extractivist economies of Central Africa and the labour reserves of the settler South. This enabled him to develop sophistication in his own analysis of the land, labour and agrarian questions in Africa. Sam drew further inspiration from Issa Shivji (2009a), who remained attentive to the evolving legal basis of customary tenure after independence, insisting that ongoing constitutional changes were directly undermining customary tenure and peasant control over land and labour. Finally, Sam's sustained collaboration in the 1990s and 2000s with feminist scholars such as Patricia McFadden and Rudo Gaidzanwa in Harare, and Zenebewerke Tadesse and Dzodzi Tsikata at CODESRIA, gave him a fuller appreciation of the gendered basis of land and labour relations and their evolution through the three macro-regions.

These threads eventually came together in Sam's bold thesis, published by CODESRIA (Moyo 2008), that under neo-liberal restructuring, the land question in Africa had finally entered a new phase, one of widespread land alienation and conflicts even in non-settler Africa, together with a growing rural–urban land question on account of the agrarian crisis and rural–urban migration. Importantly, he came to this conclusion before the onset of large-scale land grabs, which thereafter spawned a Northern-led publishing industry typically ignorant of the trajectory of thinking on the land question on the continent. Yet, Sam's collaboration in the 2000s with Ben Romadhane, Kojo Amanor, Dessalegn Rahmato, Bernard Founou-Tchuigoua, Abdourahmane Ndiaye, Dzodzi Tsikata, Yakham Diop and many others at CODESRIA took the analysis of the land question – and the political economy tradition itself – to a new level, integrating a whole host of concerns from peasant organizations and sustainable development to labour and gender relations (Moyo and Romadhane, eds 2002; Amanor and Moyo, eds 2008; Founou-Tchuigoua and Ndiaye, eds 2014; Moyo, Tsikata and Diop, eds 2015).

Overall, this body of work suggests that the macro-regional trajectories in Africa have been in transition towards new patterns of accumulation, on account of the new land and resource grabs, the ongoing differentiation in the countryside, and the sustained social reproduction crisis of an expanding labour reserve at the continental level. Such a diagnosis is a wake-up call for development planning and one which requires that the political economy tradition continues to evolve in building alternatives. The same diagnosis is no less a contribution to our understanding of the world economy and its peripheral social formations – the large majority of the world's population – which are constantly being reconfigured across the South. Thanks to this tradition, we have a better understanding *within political economy* of the dynamics of the social reproduction crisis that affects the working people of Africa and the South; the intimate relationship between land, labour and gender in production and reproduction; the requirement that land, agriculture and the environment move to the centre of development alternatives; and, indeed, the imperative that the liberation struggle remains a struggle against imperialism.

Zimbabwe's Land, Agrarian and National Questions

The intellectual dynamic at the continental level synergized with Sam's work on Zimbabwe. Sam returned home after 1980 to devote himself to research and advocacy on the land and agrarian questions. He was a prolific writer – and there was virtually no development issue that was too daunting for him. Over the next twenty years, he delved into the complexities of the land question under settler conditions (Moyo 1987,

1995b), the productivity of large-scale commercial farmers and peasants (Weiner, Moyo, Munslow and O'Keefe 1985), agricultural collectives (Moyo, Sunga and Masuko 1991), the regional environment (Moyo, Sill and O'Keefe 1993; Middleton, O'Keefe and Moyo 1993), gender relations (Moyo 1995a, 2000), democracy (Moyo 1999), land-use change under structural adjustment (Moyo 2000), farm workers (Moyo, Rutherford and Amanor-Wilks 2000), non-governmental organizations (Moyo, Makumbe and Raftopoulos, eds 2000) and social movements (Moyo 2001, 2002).

What distinguished Sam throughout this intellectual trajectory was his insistence that in a settler ex-colony, the land question remained at the heart of both the agrarian and national questions, and, as such, was the point of departure for any alternative development path. This put him on a collision course with the intellectual trends of the 1990s, whose concepts and methods systematically downplayed the land demands of smallholders, while also denying popular aspirations for national liberation. For western Marxists, the agrarian question was now reducible to a mere question 'of labour' (Bernstein 2006), while liberals of various stripes envisioned a future in 'community participation', such as in 'market-led' land reforms or the 'management' of natural resources (see critique in Moyo 2000; and Amanor, in this volume). These intellectual trends served essentially to justify settler domination and preserve the neo-colonial conditions for the benefit of foreign capital and settlers.

The same winds of reaction sought to displace the analysis of the neo-colonial situation by a simplistic dichotomy of 'authoritarianism versus democracy' convenient to all: neo-Gramscians, neo-Weberians, rational choice neo-liberals and post-structuralists. Sam's insistence that settler society had a material basis in the economic monopolies created by colonialism, especially over land, would again bring him into direct conflict. These approaches differed widely across a methodological spectrum ranging from individualism to discourse analysis, yet they all shared a disdain for the analysis of the economic structures of neo-colonial rule. Thus, when land reform took off in 2000, they closed ranks, with hardly any hesitation, behind a 'human rights' agenda in defence of white privilege.

Sam was clear that white supremacy pervaded all aspects of social and cultural life, but also that it had to be defeated as an economic system. His critique of race directly challenged the discourse through which settler monopolies operated. His analysis of settler capitalism took on, first, the 'productivity' myth of white large-scale farming, the sector which had relied on persistent colonial state intervention and recurrent rescue in times of crisis. Such support was never available to the peasantry; much to the contrary, accumulation strategies from below came to be systematically suppressed. Thus, Sam denounced settler 'success' as a product of colonial land dispossession, followed by endless state subsidies, protections and investments in roads and irrigation, and above all, the engineering of a cheap-labour system based on super-exploitation of black labour (Moyo 1987, 1995b). He further pointed out that over half of the large-scale commercial farmland in the 1980s was still lying idle for speculative purposes and not being used productively at all (Weiner *et al.* 1985; Moyo 1995b). Then, in the 1990s, Sam was one of the first to observe that structural adjustment policies provided new accumulation possibilities for settlers (Moyo 2000). They were now able to use underutilized land for game parks catering to the global tourism industry, as well as arable land for 'non-traditional' cash crops for export, such as fresh fruits, vegetables and cut flowers. Again, none of this was accessible to the peasantry.

The second myth that Sam challenged related to the 'passivity' of the peasantry with regard to land. The intellectual tendency in the 1990s was either to deny the existence of peasant demand for land, or otherwise to culturalize it as a regionalized or historically discontinuous anthropological spectacle. In response, Sam elaborated a framework for the analysis of the ebb and flow of peasant land occupations on a national scale after independence (Moyo 2001, 2002; see also Murisa, in this volume). These ranged from 'low-profile but high-intensity land occupations' in 1980–83 on farms abandoned by settlers during the liberation war; to 'low-profile, low-intensity' occupations in 1984–96 on diverse lands, private and state; to 'high-profile but low-intensity' occupations in 1997–98 on settler farms listed for acquisition by state; to the 'high-profile, high-intensity' occupations of 2000, which finally led to large-scale acquisition without compensation of 9 million hectares of large-scale farms in addition to the 4 million hectares hitherto acquired. This analysis turned the tables on those who sought to stigmatize the fast-track land reform of the 2000s as an opportunistic power play by a 'dying' nationalist party devoid of popular content. For those who had downplayed or relativized the land question, the land reform could only be 'unpopular'.

There was a further element which entered the fray in the course of land reform, and that was the aspiring black bourgeoisie which had been effectively shut out by the settler monopolies. For Sam, this only demonstrated how widespread the demand for land actually was, beyond the peasantry. While settler and imperialist discourse labelled the land demands of the emerging bourgeoisie as proof of 'corruption' or an 'anti-poor' policy, he saw the emergence of a black bourgeoisie as an important political fact with legitimacy of its own, and which even presented economic potential within an introverted national accumulation strategy. For

Sam, the character of the black bourgeoisie was not given in advance, and, in fact, depended on the relation of forces with the peasantry. Above all, he considered the peasantry to be the only agent capable of an alternative development path. He insisted that the peasantry remained an 'untested' agent for social transformation despite the historic failure of all other agents, foreign and national capitalists. This explains Sam's lifelong devotion to the analysis of the peasantry, and also explains the class character of his pan-Africanism: either pan-Africanism would be for the peasantry or it would be unable to fulfil its potential. This extended to the South as a whole: it could only claim its rightful place against the North if it heeded the peasant path. Undoubtedly, Sam saw in the Chinese revolution a historical experience that had actually tested the peasantry over time and with unquestionable success.

All this set Sam apart from trends in 'peasant studies' which, from the 1990s onwards, transformed the peasantry into an intellectual curiosity or the object of agroecology thinking. He agreed that imperialism had cornered the peasantry into a petty commodity-producing function; yet, between the formal and real subsumption of labour to capital, there still remained at the turn of the millennium a whole world that refused to go away and needed to be understood. Sam did not adhere to the intellectual trends that emanated from the North even if they gained wide currency in the South; scientific tools would stand or fall on their ability to serve national liberation. And at the millennium, Zimbabwe's re-radicalization was precisely the litmus test. Really-existing capitalism, for Sam, had a peasantry in the middle of it and Africa was in the middle of that! There was no question of wishing the peasantry away or subordinating it to a 'higher' – so-called 'socialist' or 'agroecological' – plan.

His intensive engagement with the land question in Zimbabwe permitted Sam to debunk another series of myths related to the character of the peasantry, which may be summarized as follows. First, the peasantry is embedded in commodity production, but the peasant farm is not a mere business. This makes 'farmers' in Africa and the South substantially different from their supposed counterparts in the North. The peasantry relies on exchange values, but also extensively on the use values extracted from the commons which provide for pasture, wood fuel, water and other natural resources. Second, peasant lands are used not only for production, but also extensively for the reproduction of the household, this being essentially the only social protection system available to the peasantry. This explains why the peasantry persists, even expands, in times of general economic crisis, which otherwise turns so much of capitalist enterprise into dust. Third, both land access and labour mobilization are highly differentiated within the household, which is characterized by a persisting sexual division of labour. Patriarchy and patriliny, which are never the real objects of neo-liberal land or social policies, perpetuate the oppression of women and also provide a systematic subsidy to capital by offsetting the costs of social reproduction on to the shoulders especially of women and children. Fourth, the peasantry is differentiated among the 'rich', 'middle' and 'poor', which are determined by patterns of labour use, land sizes and incomes obtained from outside the farm or agriculture. The poor peasantry, by far the largest agrarian class in Africa and the South, survives by straddling a number of on-farm and off-farm activities across the rural–urban divide and even international borders. Women are generally the poorest of the poor of what is essentially an expanding global labour reserve, reproducing itself under semi-proletarianized conditions by waged and unwaged labour, on-farm or off-farm, productive, unproductive or reproductive. Fifth, and finally, the poor peasantry is where politics of real consequence occurs. Electoral processes and political parties require the countryside for votes, while religious organizations, trade unions, social movements and NGOs dispute the hearts and minds of this semi-proletariat for diverse political projects, often of dubious if not reactionary character.

Where others might have seen in all this an uncouth world, Sam saw in it the only starting point for development and the stabilization of the workforce. This is where development planning, he insisted, needed to focus, by guaranteeing access to land for both production and reproduction in both rural and urban areas, and investing in the technical upgrading of agriculture and rural infrastructure, roads and irrigation for the purpose of accumulation 'from below'. Sam was not fazed by the 'ecological' thinking that could easily be appropriated, or even the 'agroecological' trends that once again turned national liberation into a subset of another cause. He observed the obvious: that the poor peasantry in Africa has always had one foot in agroecology due to the mere fact that its low purchasing power has always made chemical and other inputs inaccessible. What was needed, Sam argued, was a strategy of integration of the home market, together with a national and regional food sovereignty plan, based on qualitatively higher levels of consumption and social reproduction (Moyo 2015). In the case of Zimbabwe, none of this would ever be possible without the overthrow of the settler monopoly. Overall, Sam saw in the peasantry a whole range of developmental potential, including its labour absorption capacity, spontaneous cooperativism, versatility in production, low energy requirements and regard for ecological balance. All these required public support to enable an emergent peasantry to synergize positively with domestic industries and wages, and higher consumption and reproduction standards.

In the 2000s, Sam arguably confronted the most important challenge of his life, the moment of truth for Zimbabwe's land, agrarian and national questions. He had been the central figure in national policy debates on the land question, so he was naturally propelled to the forefront in 1997 when the Government of Zimbabwe (GoZ) listed 1,471 farms for compulsory acquisition. In June 1998, GoZ published a policy framework for land acquisition and resettlement, and an international conference was convened in September with foreign governments, donors and international agencies led by the United Nations Development Programme (UNDP). A spate of land occupations broke out targeting these farms as a demonstration of force. The UNDP conducted a study which counted on Sam's expertise and that of his research team at SARIPS, most notably Prosper Matondi, although the sequence of political events escalated the process of radicalization beyond the niceties of international conferences. The escalation was marked by the refusal of the United Kingdom (UK) government to recognize 'special responsibility' as an ex-colonial power for the costs of land purchase. Meanwhile, trade unions with an urban base but outside the ruling party and war veterans with a rural base but within the ruling party entered a collision course that met its fate in 2000, when a referendum was held for a new constitution which, among other polemical issues, included a clause on compulsory land acquisition without compensation. The constitutional proposal was rejected, leading to the outbreak of mass land occupations in February, and radicalization of the liberation movement and the state apparatus itself (Moyo 2001; Moyo and Yeros 2005a, 2007a, 2007b, 2009, 2011, 2013; Moyo and Chambati, eds 2013).

The internationalization and polarization of the 'Zimbabwe question' that ensued brought to the fore the perennial dilemmas pertaining to structural change in the periphery. In fact, this has been unquestionably the most important case of radicalization in the post-Cold War world, above and beyond the South American experiences. Yet, it also revealed much about the state of the social sciences and the problems of knowledge production, if not also the pitfalls of 'progressive' politics around the world. The social sciences were caught unprepared, having been deeply transformed by neo-liberalism and its culturalist fellow travellers. Whereas just two decades earlier, this would have been analysed as a revolt against neo-colonialism, it was now a mere case of 'authoritarianism', 'bad governance', 'dying nationalism', 'crony capitalism' and 'corruption'. Moreover, research on land reform was either prohibited or conditional: whoever produced data that did not corroborate the Anglo-American line would be branded a 'Mugabe stooge' and denied further funding and publication outlets. Over several years, Sam and the team at AIAS went it alone with very few funds trickling in, fighting to stay out of international quarantine.

Sam maintained his distance from the contradictions and intrigues of the ruling party while remaining a staunch critic of the neoliberal 'opposition'. None of this was an easy road to follow. But he remained available to provide his expertise to anyone who solicited it, in accordance with his own principles. Of the international organizations, aside from UNDP, the World Bank courted him. He also provided his expertise to the Presidential Land Reform Commission (Utete Commision), briefed with the verification of the distributional outcome, and to provincial and civil society dialogues. Moreover, the team at AIAS, which over the years has included a stellar group of young researchers, both employees and associates – namely, Walter Chambati, Tendai Murisa, Dumisani Siziba, Charity Dangwa, Kingstone Mujeyi, Ndabezinhle Nyoni, Wilbert Sadomba, Freedom Mazwi, Rangarirai Muchetu, Steven Mberi and Grasian Mkodzongi – never ceased to produce reports with the little funding that came in, as well as their own master's and doctoral theses on the social and economic outcomes of the land reform. This initial decade-long effort culminated in a world-class publication on agrarian transformation after land reform via a national baseline survey which was conceived and executed by the AIAS team (Moyo *et al.* 2009). This received institutional and research support from the Royal Norwegian Embassy and the Kellogg Foundation. The baseline survey demonstrated in meticulous detail that the land reform had served social justice and historical redress. The research effort extended to a National Working Group supported by CODESRIA, which published a book that Sam co-edited with Walter Chambati (Moyo and Chambati, eds 2013).

Among scholars based in the North, one of the few shining examples of systematic research carried out on the land reform was Ian Scoones and his team at the Institute of Development Studies (IDS) at Sussex. The publication of their work (Scoones *et al.* 2010) marked a *détente* in the research community and the beginning of 'normalization' of research on fast-track land reform. The IDS study was published soon after the AIAS baseline survey and corroborated the findings of the AIAS team. Yet, it also demonstrated that 'truth' was still unobtainable in Africa, requiring Northern validation. Moreover, the trajectory of these publications was starkly different: to this day, it remains a surprise to see references to the AIAS studies even though they have circulated widely in digital format, in contrast to frequent citations made to the IDS study, which was published in book form in the North Atlantic and Southern Africa. Indeed, the first real public recognition of the AIAS team came from a non-specialist of Zimbabwe's affairs, none other than Mahmood Mamdani, in his article

'Lessons of Zimbabwe' published in the *London Review of Books* in December 2008, which caused enormous international outcry and quite possibly set the stage for the subsequent *détente* (Mamdani 2008; Moyo and Yeros 2009).

Much more could be said about the politics of knowledge production. The main specialist journals of agrarian and African studies in the North and others considered 'progressive' generally had great difficulty in recognizing authority in this pan-Africanist tradition of political economy that Sam represented. The *Journal of Agrarian Change* published its very first special issue precisely on the Zimbabwe question, but without including those who were most systematically involved in studying this topic, namely Sam and the AIAS team. As for the *Journal of Peasant Studies*, it was a decade before it took enough interest in Sam's work on Zimbabwe, to the point of inviting him to write on the outcomes of fast-track (Moyo 2011a, 2011b). The *Review of African Political Economy* was not much faster, publishing a joint article years after the onset of fast-track, and another by Sam at the end of the decade (Moyo and Yeros 2007a; Moyo 2011c). Yet another experience was that of *Historical Materialism*, which belatedly published a joint article (Moyo and Yeros 2007b), but also organized a special issue on Africa without any interest in the Zimbabwe experience or the pan-Africanist tradition of political economy. For its part, *Monthly Review* remained silent on the Zimbabwe question throughout this long period, except for an intervention piece in its online magazine edition after the Mamdani episode (Moyo and Yeros 2009). This tough reality formed the backdrop to the decision to found *Agrarian South* in 2012, an independent South–South journal of political economy, by mobilizing the tri-continental networks that were now extensive and deep enough to sustain such an alternative.

It is worth noting, finally, that if the North Atlantic research community was not keen on a radical nationalist land reform in Africa, neither were most social movements of the 'anti-globalization' era. This situation was noted in mid-2000 (Moyo and Yeros 2005). Outside South Africa, whose landless movement supported fast-track, there was no notable support from international trade unionism or even the rising peasant international, *La Via Campesina* (LVC). If the posture of trade unionism could generally be explained by the post-Cold War cooptation of Southern trade unions by the social democratic/liberal trade unionism of the North, what could explain the silence of LVC? The LVC retained an ideological 'black spot' deriving from its commitment to a North–South alliance, as well as from the 'colour blind' left in settler Latin America that has given further ideological substance to the LVC. This explains the pride of place given to agroecology as an ideological and programmatic principle, against the historical fact that peasantries in the twentieth century were the heart and soul of liberation movements. Zimbabwe's land occupation movement, the most important movement post-Cold War, was suddenly off the ideological radar.

Building Tri-Continental Solidarity for a Global Research Agenda

As if Sam's leadership in building institutional and research capacities in Africa and Zimbabwe was not enough for one lifetime, he also forged ahead with a series of initiatives for the building of South–South cooperation. As vice president of CODESRIA in the early 2000s, he represented CODESRIA in Buenos Aires and Havana at meetings held with other organizations from Africa, Asia and Latin America, namely, the Latin American Council of Social Sciences (CLACSO), the African Association of Political Science (AAPS), the Organization for Social Science Research in Eastern and Southern Africa (OSSREA), the Asian Political and International Studies Association (APISA) and the Southeast Asian Conflict Studies Network (SEACSN).With the support of Atilio Boron and Adebayo Olukoshi, the executive secretaries of CLACSO and CODESRIA, respectively, Sam was appointed jointly with Gladys Lechini from CLACSO to draft a comprehensive programme for trilateral South–South cooperation (see Lechini, in this volume). This yielded international conferences, workshops and summer institutes, as well as the publication of books, papers and translations. This was the most important convergence of continental research communities across the South in the 2000s.

Later in the decade, as president of CODESRIA, Sam oversaw the establishment of the Afro-Arab Institute, as well as initiatives for the building of ties with the research communities of China and India (see Tsikata, in this volume). Throughout the 2000s, Sam remained active in the programmes of the Third World Forum (TWF) and the World Forum for Alternatives (WFA) led by Samir Amin, and collaborated in the WFA initiative related to the agrarian question (Herrera and Kin Chi Lau 2015). He also deepened his personal and institutional relationships with intellectuals in China, especially with Wen Tiejun, Sit Tsui, Kin Chi Lau and their research teams at the Universities of Renmin and Southwest; in India, at Jawaharlal Nehru University (JNU), with Praveen Jha, Utsa Patnaik, Prabhat Patnaik, Jayati Ghosh, C.P. Chandrasekhar, Archana Prasad and other faculty members at the Centre for Economic Studies and Planning (CESP) and Centre for Informal Sector and Labour Studies (CISLS), as well as Sandeep Chachra at ActionAid; in Japan, with Yoichi Mine at the Graduate School of Global Studies at Doshisha University; and in Brazil, with Paris Yeros at the Catholic University of Minas Gerais (PUC Minas) and the Federal University of ABC in São Paulo (UFABC), with Marcelo Rosa at Federal Universities in Rio (Fluminense, UFF) and Brasília (UNB), and Francesco Pierri at the Ministry of Agrarian Development (MDA). Sam also maintained strong relationships with faculty members and institutions in the United States, especially with Bill Martin at the State University of New York at Binghamton and Beverly Silver at Johns Hopkins University in Baltimore.

Alongside his CODESRIA work, Sam began to stitch together what would eventually become the Agrarian South Network (ASN), drawing from all the above networks. A key ally on the continent was Issa Shivji, who supported Sam in his efforts to build the AIAS network, having founded Hakiardhi, a land rights advocacy organization in Tanzania on whose advisory committee Sam also served, in 1994. They shared a deep appreciation of the land question, the need to defend the radical pan-Africanist perspective, and the disposition to create South–South alliances. The first milestone was the launch of an annual South–South Summer School programme in 2009 in Harare, which was to become the soul of the network. This is where current research and ideas have been debated annually among a group of young and veteran scholars, together with activists from social movements. Many of the participants returned year after year to create a cumulative collective learning experience. The Summer School has relied on the South–South partners mentioned above, especially Praveen Jha from India and Paris Yeros from Brasil, but its centre of gravity has remained in Africa, among associates including Issa Shivji, Ng'wanza Kamata, Marjorie Mbilinyi, and younger researchers and activists from the University of Dar es Salaam and Hakiardhi; Dzodzi Tsikata, Kojo Amanor and postgraduate students from the University of Ghana; Lungisile Ntsebeza, Horman Chitonge and Fred Hendricks from the Universities of Cape Town and Rhodes in South Africa, plus activists from the Trust for Community Outreach and Education (TCOE), especially Mercia Andrews.

Another marker in the building of the network has been the 'Reclaiming' trilogy of tri-continental publications, produced on the basis of research initiatives launched by AIAS at its inception in 2002. The first tri-continental research initiative sought to assess the growth of rural social movements under neo-liberalism across the South and to situate within it the experience of Zimbabwe. The result was *Reclaiming the Land: The Resurgence of Rural Movements in Africa, Asia and Latina America* (Moyo and Yeros, eds 2005), a comparative book on rural social movements across the three continents, the first of its kind since the onset of neo-liberalism. Two conclusions from the book were noteworthy: first, that the deepening agrarian crisis and rural–urban migration experienced under neo-liberalism had not put an end to the land and agrarian questions but rather they had aggravated them; second, that the emergence of rural movements under neo-liberalism was widespread, and these had become the organizing centres of the semi-proletarianized peasantry and workers retrenched from mines and urban areas.

A second tri-continental research project was launched in 2007, now focused on the new nationalisms that were emerging across the South, often linked to rural movements. Again, Zimbabwe's experience called for broader comparative work, given that several experiences of radicalization were on the rise and were grappling with similar dilemmas. This comparative project resulted in the publication of *Reclaiming the Nation: The Return of the National Question in Africa, Asia and Latin America* (Moyo and Yeros, eds 2011), which again reached some noteworthy conclusions: first, that under neo-liberalism, global integration and national disintegration were two sides of the same coin; second, that the differentiation of the trajectories of states in the South was advanced, with some managing to 'emerge' and even restabilize temporarily under comprador conditions, while others succumbed to fragmentation or foreign occupation and a handful of small peripheral states entered a period of radicalization. Again, this book had no equal at the time.

A third tri-continental project was launched at the end of the decade, focusing on imperialism, primitive accumulation and land grabs. Issa Shivji's book, *Accumulation in an African Periphery* (2009b), had already set the tone. In fact, this set of concerns yielded a number of ever-more close research collaborations and publications with colleagues at JNU. Sam published a book with Utsa Patnaik in 2011 with a preface by Issa Shivji, entitled *The Agrarian Question in the Neoliberal Era* (Patnaik and Moyo, eds 2011); over the following years, the work of Utsa Patnaik and Prabhat Patnaik would become a major reference for Sam (see Patnaik and Patnaik 2017). In addition, Sam co-authored a number of articles on African agriculture and global issues with Praveen Jha and Paris Yeros, ranging from contemporary imperialism and the agrarian question (Moyo, Yeros and Jha 2012; Moyo, Jha and Yeros 2013, 2016), to global labour reserves (Jha, Moyo and Yeros 2017), to the peasantry in Africa (Moyo, Yeros and Jha 2018). Two of these appeared in books dedicated to the life and work of Utsa Patnaik and Prabhat Patnaik. Sam was snatched away from us in 2015 during a conference at JNU, just as this reinforced tri-continental relationship was gathering steam.

The final book of the 'Reclaiming' trilogy was published posthumously and with great delay in 2019, entitled *Reclaiming Africa: Scramble and Resistance in the 21st Century* (Moyo, Jha and Yeros, eds 2019). It was the result of probably the most important collaborative and sustained effort in the South to assess the new scramble for Africa's land. Unlike other initiatives, this one sought to avoid the pitfalls of problematic theoretical approaches to imperialism and primitive accumulation and of the liberal-institutionalist 'food regime' theories emanating from the North, which had received prior critical attention (Moyo and Yeros 2005; Moyo, Yeros and Jha 2012; Yeros 2012). The more detailed empirical focus of the book was on the newly 'emergent' players among the semi-peripheral countries of the South and on a number of national experiences in Africa.

This whole experience of annual Summer Schools and tri-continental collaboration made for a substantial and growing network, again the only one of its kind in the world. Perhaps most importantly, a number of young scholars who participated regularly in the Summer School have completed their postgraduate studies and gone on to publish important research which arguably bears the hallmark of the School! In so far as this is the case, we may certainly speak of a 'school of thought' being cultivated. Apart from the in-house AIAS team mentioned earlier, others long associated with the Summer School completed their doctoral theses during these years to become examples of excellence, including no less than Lyn Ossome, Ricado Jacobs, Rama Salla Dieng, Manish Kumar and Santosh Kumar.

Finally, the founding of *Agrarian South: Journal of Political Economy* in 2012 was another milestone. Published in New Delhi by the Centre for Agrarian Research and Education for South (CARES), which is managed by Sandeep Chachra, and Sage Publications India, Sam was its founding editor-in-chief. The journal synergized with the Summer School to provide a publication outlet for young and veteran scholars involved in the proceedings of the network, but also for scholars worldwide and especially those based in regions of the South. The journal adopted a tri-continental format for its editorial team, and has given voice to research concerns that either do not appear in Northern journals or are subject to approaches that are distant from the intellectual traditions of the South. Its inaugural editorial statement expressed the difference in tone and substance:

> [T]he agrarian question continues to evolve. It certainly remains a question of national sovereignty, under conditions of a new scramble. It still concerns the joining of the hammer and the sickle; but both have now mutated. The land question itself has taken on new meanings. And it is, more emphatically than ever before, a question of gender equity and ecological sustainability. (Editorial 2012: 9)

Half a century after generalized political decolonization, one is still hard pressed to find a tri-continental journal of this sort. It is possibly the only one currently in operation with these characteristics, that is, a scientific research journal with a tri-continental editorial format, committed to building tri-continental solidarity and advancing the intellectual traditions of the South.

Principles of Epistemic Sovereignty

We would be remiss if we desisted from drawing larger epistemological conclusions from Sam's trajectory, and the experiences that we have shared as friends, colleagues and comrades. By way of conclusion, we indicate briefly a set of principles which emerge from our mode of knowledge production.

Some time ago, Paulin Hountondji (1990: 9) remarked that 'in our countries, scientific activity remains basically extraverted, alienated, dependent on an international division of labour that tends to make scientific invention a monopoly of the North, while confining Southern countries to the importing and application of these inventions'. He went on to indicate 'thirteen indices of scientific dependence', all of which have been quite germane to our own struggle for epistemic sovereignty. Most of these have been addressed above in one way or another, and for the most part, Sam's lifelong work certainly receives a high score! More recently, some further reflections have been offered by Mahmood Mamdani, Issa Shivji and Sabelo Ndlovu-Gatsheni.

Mamdani has traced the evolution of knowledge production in Africa – the main location of Sam's intellectual formation – and made a distinction between the 'public intellectual' of CODESRIA and the 'scholar' with which CODESRIA, in Mamdani's view, has had trouble reconciling itself. The two are said to be 'different persona': the former working 'closer to the ground' and the latter having 'universalist aspirations' (Mamdani 2016: 79). The latter is distinct, he suggests, by addressing the 'epistemological dimension of decolonization', which is 'focused on the categories with which we make, unmake and remake, and thereby apprehend, the world. It is intimately tied to our notions of what is human, what is particular and what is universal' (ibid.: 79). This debate, Mamdani laments, has not found room in the CODESRIA of the public intellectual, the type who 'swore loyalty' to political economy. And although he admits that there is no hard and fast distinction between the two persona, and that, anyway, the neo-liberal wave transformed the public intellectual into a cog in the chain, he suggests that the 'public intellectual' of the past was unable to delve into scholarly epistemological questions, understood as those concerning 'discourse and representation'.

This stream of thought would require lengthy unpacking, but suffice it to note here that such a distinction has been questioned by Issa Shivji (2018). While Shivji agrees that the 'public intellectual' of today is an intellectual organic to neo-liberalism – governments, university bureaucracies, corporate media and social media – he suggests that the intellectuals that formed the basis of what has been described here as the pan-Africanist tradition of political economy, including those associated with CODESRIA, were not polarized by the above distinction. The fundamental question was how to engage in ideological struggle in defence of the interests of the oppressed and exploited classes. This brought many 'closer to the ground', but by no means was it contrary to 'focusing on the categories with which we make, unmake and remake, and thereby apprehend, the world'. We might add that the question thus posed by Shivji has required full engagement with issues of discourse and representation, which after all have always been inherent to the 'critique of political economy', in Marx's terms, despite the known limitations of the Eurocentric and economistic canon.

Sam, for one, never turned his back on questions of discourse and representation. He engaged with them on his own terms, not those imposed by the west or the cultural turn. Sam's work on settler colonialism in Zimbabwe was entirely devoted to debunking the mythologies of white supremacy. The real question was one of method. He was clear that the critique of discourse and representation could not simply be detached from the material conditions and aspirations of Africa's working people; doing so would mean to bandwagon to a liberal platform, which again was the preferred terrain of imperialism (see Amanor, in this volume). At the same time, Sam had no doubt that he and those from whom he drew inspiration were proper 'scholars' in Mamdani's sense, that is, committed to unmasking the universalist pretensions of the west and seeking to define what was particular about Africa, and even the South (see Scoones and Martin, in this volume). He also remained organic to popular causes; indeed, there was no more sophisticated an exponent of the land occupation cause in Zimbabwe than Sam himself.

Ndlovu-Gatsheni has added to these reflections with an extensive statement on 'epistemic freedom' in Africa, which he defines as follows:

> Epistemic freedom is different from academic freedom. Academic freedom speaks to institutional autonomy of universities and rights to express diverse ideas including those critical of authorities and political leaders. Epistemic freedom is much broader and deeper. It speaks to cognitive justice; it draws our attention to the content of what it is that

> we are free to express and on whose terms . . . [it] is about democratizing 'knowledge' from current rendition in the singular into its plural known as 'knowledges'. (Ndlovu-Gatsheni 2018: 4)

There are two problems with this conceptualization. First, epistemic freedom thus defined does not address the material conditions of knowledge production which exercise systematic influence over what 'we are free to express and on whose terms'. These are precisely the material conditions denied most emphatically by neo-liberal restructuring. The question of cognitive justice, therefore, must be founded on a struggle for the establishment of autonomous and viable scientific infrastructure. This, after all, was Sam's lifelong mission. The challenge remains one of control of knowledge production, which in turn is a question not of epistemic freedom as such but of *epistemic sovereignty*.

Second, apart from the material conditions of cognitive justice, there is also its content. For it is quite normal for content to go missing even when material conditions are favourable. This, after all, is the situation in centres of knowledge production in the North, and, to a lesser extent, in the semi-peripheral and settler countries of the South. Cognitive justice still requires being 'closer to the ground', organic to liberation struggles and respectful of the intellectual traditions which they have spawned. For it is commonplace for liberation struggles to be idealized and appropriated by new theoretical trends that emanate from the academies of the North, only to be fed back to the South, most easily through settler states. The point of departure (or 'standpoint') cannot but be the body of thought produced over time by the liberation struggles. As such, neither romantic 'epistemologies of the South' (dos Santos 2014) nor culturalized 'decolonial' rediscoveries of the modern world (Mignolo 2007; Grosfoguel 2007) are sufficient to the task.

The difference between epistemic freedom and sovereignty is not in the detail. What emerges from Sam's lifelong vision and struggle are some concrete principles. At a most basic material level, the exercise of sovereignty over knowledge production requires autonomous capacity for teaching, research and publication; that is, autonomous scientific infrastructure. This implies the defence of publicly and adequately funded centres of higher learning in the South, as well as the breaking of monopolies in the publication industry that restrict the flow of ideas from South to North.

At an ideological level, there is the requirement of sovereignty over the trajectories of the intellectual traditions of the South, especially of pan-Africanism and the Bandung experience. Sovereignty in this sense is fundamental to the advance and renewal of these traditions in the twenty-first century, and to guarding against what Jacques Depelchin (2004) has termed the syndromes of 'discovery' and 'abolition'. This type of sovereignty has some further requirements. One is the acknowledgment of collective authorship or acknowledgment of one's intellectual precursors, which is in itself an act of defence of authorship against appropriation. There is also the requirement of staying anchored in the analysis of the material conditions of the modern world. If our task as intellectuals is to 'interpret the world to change it', there is no escape from historical materialism. This must be kept alive by being put to the service of anti-imperialist struggle and liberation.

Finally, there is the requirement of building solidarities across the South to reinforce the capacity to contest collectively the Eurocentricity of the social sciences and to hone skills for the analysis of all regions of the South, comparatively and collaboratively. If obtaining universality remains the fundamental historic task, and if this requires ascertaining particularity, both are fundamentally comparative and collaborative exercises. It is also on the basis of solid South–South solidarity that strong bridges can be built with scholarship in the North. Sam's rare feat was to establish the conditions for a tri-continental solidarity whose centre of gravity remained in Africa.

His even greater feat was to put all this into motion without making personal enemies. One might recall Engels' eulogy to Marx at his graveside: 'I make bold to say that, though he may have had many opponents, he had hardly one personal enemy.'[2] This surely applies to brother Sam. May he rest in peace.

We sincerely thank Dzodzi Tsikata and Issa Shivji for their insightful comments on an earlier draft.

Notes

1. See contributions to the commemorative *CODESRIA Newsletter*, 28 November 2015, https://www.codesria.org/spip.php?article2489&lang=en; the articles in the Special Issue of *Agrarian South: Journal of Political Economy*, 'Remembering Sam Moyo: Intellectual Formation and Contributions' (2016, 5 [2–3]), several of which are reprinted in this volume; and Tsikata (2017), also reprinted herein.
2. Frederick Engels' speech at the grave of Karl Marx, Highgate Cemetery, London, 17 March 1883, available at https://www.marxists.org/archive/marx/works/1883/death/burial.htm, accessed 4 November 2019.

References

Amanor, Kojo Sebastian and Sam Moyo, eds (2008), *Land and Sustainable Development in Africa*, London and New York: Zed Books.

Amin, Samir (1976), 'Unequal Development', *Monthly Review*, New York.

Bernstein, Henry (2006), 'Is There an Agrarian Question in the 21st Century?' *Canadian Journal of Development Studies*, 27 (4): 449–60.

Depelchin, Jacques (2004), *Silences in African history: Between the syndromes of discovery and abolition*, Dar es Salaam: Mkuki Na Nyota Publishers.

dos Santos, Boaventura (2014), *Epistemologies of the South: Justice against Epistemicide*, Boulder, CO, and London: Paradigm.

Editorial (2012), 'The Agrarian Question: Past, Present and Future', *Agrarian South: Journal of Political Economy*, 1 (1), 1–10.

Founou-Tchuigoua, Bernard and Abdourahmane Ndiaye, eds (2014), *Réponses radicales aux crises agraires et rurales africaines*, Dakar: CODESRIA.

Herera, Rémy and Kin Chi Lau, eds (2015), *The Struggle for Food Sovereignty: Alternative Development and the Renewal of Peasant Societies Today*, London: Pluto Press.

Hountondji, Paulin (1990), 'Scientific Dependence in Africa Today', *Research in African Literatures*, 21 (3), 5–15.

Grosfoguel, Ramón (2007), 'The Epistemic Decolonial Turn', *Cultural Studies*, 21 (2–3), 211–23.

Jha, Praveen, Sam Moyo and Paris Yeros (2017), 'Capitalism and "Labour Reserves": A Note', in C.P. Chandrasekhar and Jayati Ghosh, eds, *Interpreting the World to Change It: Essays for Prabhat Patnaik*, New Delhi: Tulika Books: 205–37.

Mafeje, Archie (1991), *The Theory and Ethnography of African Social Formations: The Case of the Interlacustrine Kingdoms*, Dakar: CODESRIA.

Mama, Amina (2005), 'Gender Studies for Africa's Transformation', in Thandika Mkandawire, ed., *African Intellectuals: Rethinking Politics, Language, Gender and Development*, Dakar, London and New York: CODESRIA and Zed Books: 94–116.

Mamdani, Mahmood (2007), *Scholars in the Marketplace: The Dilemmas of Neo-Liberal Reform at Makerere University, 1989–2005*, Dakar: CODESRIA.

——— (2008), 'Lessons of Zimbabwe', *London Review of Books*, 30 (23), https://www.lrb.co.uk/v30/n23/mahmood-mamdani/lessons-of-zimbabwe, accessed 2 November 2019: 17–21.

——— (2015), 'A Tribute to Sam Moyo', *CODESRIA Newsletter*, https://www.codesria.org/spip.php?article2491&lang=en, accessed 21 October 2019.

——— (2016), 'Between the Public Intellectual and the Scholar: Decolonization and Some Post-Independence Initiatives in African Higher Education', *Inter-Asia Cultural Studies*, 17 (1): 68–83.

Mandaza, Ibbo, ed. (1986), *Zimbabwe: The Political Economy of Transition, 1980–1986*, Dakar: CODESRIA.

Mbilinyi, Marjorie (2016), 'Debating Land and Agrarian Issues from a Gender Perspective', *Agrarian South: Journal of Political Economy*, 5 (2–3): 164–86.

Middleton, Neil, Philip O'Keefe and Sam Moyo (1993), *The Tears of the Crocodile: From Rio to Reality in the Developing World*, London and Boulder, CO: Pluto Press.

Mignolo, Walter D. (2007), 'Delinking: The Rhetoric of Modernity, the Logic of Coloniality and the Grammar of De-coloniality', *Cultural Studies*, 21 (2–3): 449–514.

Mkandawire, Thandika (1995), 'Three Generations of African Academics: A Note', *Transformations*, 28: 75–83.

——— (2005), 'African Intellectuals and Nationalism', in Thandika Mkandawire, ed., *African Intellectuals: Rethinking Politics, Language, Gender and Development*, Dakar, London and New York: CODESRIA and Zed Books: 10–55.

——— (2015), 'Sam Moyo', *CODESRIA Newsletter*, https://www.codesria.org/spip.php?article2492&lang=en, accessed 21 October 2019.

Moyo, Mabhena Phakamile (2016), 'A Family Perspective on Sam Moyo's Intellectual Development', *Agrarian South: Journal of Political Economy*, 5 (2–3): 131–37.

Moyo, Sam (1987), 'The Land Question', in Ibbo Mandaza, ed., *Zimbabwe: The Political Economy of Transition 1980–1986*, Dakar: CODESRIA: 165–202.

——— (1995a), 'A Gendered Perspective on the Land Question', *SAFERE*, 1 (1): 13–31.
——— (1995b), *The Land Question in Zimbabwe*, Harare: SAPES Books.
——— (1999), *Land and Democracy in Zimbabwe*, Monograph Series, Harare: SAPES Books.
——— (2000), *Land Reform and Structural Adjustment in Zimbabwe: Land Use Change in the Mashonaland Provinces*, Uppsala: Nordiska Afrikainstitutet.
——— (2001), 'The Land Occupation Movement and Democratization in Zimbabwe: Contradictions of Neoliberalism', *Millennium: Journal of International Studies*, 30 (2): 311–30.
——— (2002), 'The Interactions of Market and Compulsory Land Acquisition Process with Social Action in Zimbabwe's Land Reform', in Ibbo Mandaza and Dani W. Nabudere, eds, *Pan-Africanism and Integration in Africa*, Harare: SAPES Books: 300–39.
——— (2008), *African Land Questions, Agrarian Transitions and the State: Contradictions of Neo-Liberal Land Reforms*, Dakar: CODESRIA.
——— (2011a), 'Three Decades of Agrarian Land Reform in Zimbabwe', *The Journal of Peasant Studies*, 38 (3): 493–531.
——— (2011b), 'Changing Agrarian Relations after Redistributive Land Reform in Zimbabwe', *The Journal of Peasant Studies*, 38 (5): 939–66.
——— (2011c), 'Land Concentration and Accumulation after Redistributive Reform in Post-Settler Zimbabwe', *Review of African Political Economy*, 38 (128): 257–76.
——— (2015), 'Rebuilding African Peasantries: Inalienability of Land Rights and Collective Food Sovereignty in Southern Africa', in Rémy Herrera and Kin Chi Lau, eds, *The Struggle for Food Sovereignty: Alternative Development and the Renewal of Peasant Societies Today*, London: Pluto Press: 56–82.
——— (2018), 'Debating the African Land Question with Archie Mafeje', *Agrarian South: Journal of Political Economy*, 7 (2): 211–33.
Moyo, Sam and Walter Chambati, eds (2013), *Land and Agrarian Reform in Zimbabwe: Beyond White-Settler Capitalism*, Dakar and Harare: CODESRIA and AIAS.
Moyo, Sam, Walter Chambati, Tendai Murisa, Dumisani Siziba, Charity Dangwa, Kingstone Mujeyi and Ndabezinhle Nyoni (2009), *Fast-Track Land Reform Baseline Survey in Zimbabwe: Trends and Tendencies, 2005/06*, Harare: AIAS.
Moyo, Sam, Praveen Jha and Paris Yeros (2013), 'The Classical Agrarian Question: Myth, Reality and Relevance Today', *Agrarian South: Journal of Political Economy*, 2 (1), 93–119.
——— (2016), 'The Agrarian Question and Trajectories of Economic Transformation: A Perspective from the South', in E.S. Reinert, Jayati Ghosh and Rainer Kattel, eds, *Handbook of Alternative Theories of Economic Development* Northampton: Edward Elgar: 487–503
Moyo, Sam, Praveen Jha and Paris Yeros, eds (2019), *Reclaiming Africa: Scramble and Resistance in the 21st Century*, Singapore: Springer.
Moyo, Sam, John Makumbe and Brian Raftopoulos, eds (2000), *NGOs, the State and Politics in Zimbabwe*, Harare: SAPES Trust.
Moyo, Sam and Ben Romadhane, eds (2002), *Peasant Organizations and Democratization in Africa*, Dakar: CODESRIA.
Moyo, Sam, Blair Rutherford and Dede Amanor-Wilks (2000), 'Land Reform and Changing Social Relations for Farm Workers in Zimbabwe', *Review of African Political Economy*, 27 (84): 181–202.
Moyo, Sam, Michael Sill and Phil O'Keefe (1993), *The Southern African Environment: Profiles of the SADC Countries*, London: Earthscan Publications Ltd.
Moyo, Sam, Ishmael Sunga and Louis Masuko (1991), 'Agricultural Collective Co-operation:

A Case Study of the Socio-Economic Viability of the Makoni District Union of Cooperatives', *ZIDS Consultancy Reports Series*, No. 21, Harare.

Moyo, Sam, Dzodzi Tsikata and Yakham Diop, eds (2015), *Land in the Struggles for Citizenship in Africa*, Dakar: CODESRIA.

Moyo, Sam and Paris Yeros (2005a), 'Land Occupations and Land Reform in Zimbabwe: Towards the National Democratic Revolution', in Sam Moyo and Paris Yeros, eds, *Reclaiming the Land: The Resurgence of Rural Movements in Africa, Asia and Latin America*, London and Cape Town: Zed Books and David Philip: 165–205.

——— (2005b), 'The Resurgence of Rural Movements under Neoliberalism', in Sam Moyo and Paris Yeros, eds, *Reclaiming the Land: The Resurgence of Rural Movements in Africa, Asia and Latin America*, London and Cape Town: Zed Books and David Philip: 1–64.

——— (2007a), 'The Radicalized State: Zimbabwe's Interrupted Revolution', *Review of African Political Economy*, 34 (111): 103–21.

——— (2007b), 'The Zimbabwe Question and the Two Lefts', *Historical Materialism*, 15 (3): 171–204.

——— (2009), 'Zimbabwe Ten Years On: Results and prospects', *Monthly Review Online*, 10 February, http://mrzine.monthlyreview.org/2009/my100209.html, accessed 31 October 2019; republished in *Pambazuka News*, 12 February, https://www.pambazuka.org/governance/zimbabwe-ten-years-results-and-prospects, accessed 31 October 2019.

——— (2011), 'After Zimbabwe: State, Nation and Region in Africa',' in Sam Moyo and Paris Yeros, eds, *Reclaiming the Nation: The Return of the National Question in Africa, Asia and Latin America*, London: Pluto Press: 78–102.

——— (2013), 'The Zimbabwe Model: Radicalization, Reform and Resistance', in Sam Moyo and Walter Chambati, eds, *Land and Agrarian Reform in Zimbabwe: Beyond White-Settler Capitalism*, Dakar: CODESRIA: 331–58.

Moyo, Sam and Paris Yeros, eds (2005), *Reclaiming the Land: The Resurgence of Rural Movements in Africa, Asia and Latin America*, London and Cape Town: Zed Books and David Philip.

——— (2011), *Reclaiming the Nation: The Return of the National Question in Africa, Asia and Latin America,* London: Pluto Press.

Moyo, Sam, Paris Yeros and Praveen Jha (2012), 'Imperialism and Primitive Accumulation: Notes on the New Scramble for Africa', *Agrarian South: Journal of Political Economy*, 1 (2): 181–203.

——— (2018), 'Peasant Farming in Sub-Saharan Africa: Contemporary Trajectories and Prospects', in Arindam Banerjee and C.P. Chandrasekhar, eds, *Dispossession, Deprivation and Development: Essays for Utsa Patnaik*, New Delhi: Tulika Books: 10–36.

Ndlovu-Gatsheni, Sabelo J. (2018), *Epistemic Freedom in Africa: Deprovincialization and Decolonization*, London and New York: Routledge.

Onimode, Bade (1988), *A Political Economy of the African Crisis*, London: Zed Books.

Patnaik, Utsa and Sam Moyo, eds (2011), *The Agrarian Question in the Neoliberal Era: Primitive Accumulation and the Peasantry*, with a preface by Issa G. Shivji, Cape Town, Dakar, Nairobi, Oxford: Pambazuka Press.

Patnaik, Utsa and Prabhat Patnaik (2017), *A Theory of Imperialism*, New York: Columbia University Press.

Raftopoulos, Brian (2016), 'Zimbabwe Institute of Development Studies (ZIDS): The Early Context of Sam Moyo's Intellectual Development', *Agrarian South: Journal of Political Economy*, 5 (2–3): 187–201.

Scoones, Ian, Nelson Marongwe, Blasio Mavedzenge, Jacob Mahenene, Felix Murimbarimba and Chrispen Sukume (2010), *Zimbabwe's Land Reform: Myths and Realities*, London, Harare, Rochester, Auckland Park: James Currey, Weaver Press, Boydell and Brewer, Jacana Media.

Shivji, Issa G. (1993), *Intellectuals at the Hill: Essays and Talks, 1969–1993*, Dar es Salaam: Dar es Salaam University Press.

——— (2009a), *Where is Uhuru? Reflections on the Struggle for Democracy in Africa*, edited by Godwin R. Murunda, Cape Town, Dakar, Nairobi and Oxford: Pambazuka Press.

——— (2009b), *Accumulation in an African Periphery: A Theoretical Framework*, Dar es Salaam: Mkukina Nyota.

——— (2018), 'The Metamorphosis of the Revolutionary Intellectual', *Agrarian South: Journal of Political Economy*, 7 (3), 394–400.

Tandon, Yash, ed. (1982), *University of Dar es Salaam Debate on Class, State and Imperialism*, Dar es Salaam: Tanzania Publishing House.

Tsikata, Dzodzi (2017), 'Sam Moyo: A Life of Prodigious Scholarship, Institution Building and Strategic Activitism', *Development and Change*, 48 (5), 1154–67.

Weiner, Dan, Sam Moyo, Barry Munslow and Phil O'Keefe (1985), 'Land Use and Agricultural Productivity in Zimbabwe', *The Journal of Modern African Studies*, 23 (2): 251–85.

Yeros, Paris (2012), 'Book Review of Henry Bernstein's *Class Dynamics of Agrarian Change* (2010)', *Agrarian South: Journal of Political Economy*, 1 (3), 341–46.

PART ONE

Epistemic Vision and Contributions

2

Sam Moyo

A Life of Prodigious Scholarship, Institution Building and Strategic Activism[1]

Dzodzi Tsikata

The car accident that took Sam Moyo's life in Delhi on 22 November 2015, and injured his comrades Paris Yeros and Marcelo Rosa, cut short a scholar at the height of his powers. Working together with a group of like-minded colleagues, Sam had finally built the foundations of a vibrant tri-continental network that could hold his dreams: the Agrarian South Network. He was in Delhi at a conference on 'Labour Questions in the Global South', hosted by Praveen Jha, professor at Jawaharlal Nehru University and one of his two closest intellectual partners – the other, of course, being Paris Yeros. The conference, like earlier gatherings in Sao Paulo and Brasilia, was an opportunity to coordinate meetings of the Network and its journal, *Agrarian South: Journal of Political Economy*. As it turned out, a meeting of the journal's editorial board was Sam's last activity before the accident.

While the outpourings of grief at the news of his passing partly reflected the shocking nature of the event, discussions in different media at the time, and more recently, were united by the recognition of Sam's immense gifts and contributions as a scholar, public intellectual and institution builder. They were also expressions of profound loss and appreciation of his unique ability to bring people together and inspire them to throw themselves into worthwhile projects, such as theorizing land and agrarian questions in Africa, developing methodologies for research on land redistribution in his beloved Zimbabwe, or consolidating a research and learning organization that he was building or developing. Throughout an intellectual career that spanned decades and produced a massive body of work, Sam consistently championed the rights of Africa's smallholders as well as its landless and dispossessed communities, and chronicled the struggles of agrarian social movements for equitable land rights. He followed up his research with intensive engagements with policy makers, civil society organizations and research networks, as well as social movements, and was much in demand in Africa and beyond in these capacities.

In this essay, I discuss Sam Moyo's politics and his knowledge production as two equally important strands in his life. While his achievements in each of these spheres were significant, the combination of the two lent a monumental quality to his work and highlighted the strengths he brought to his endeavours: intellectual clarity and depth, hard work, stubborn determination, a huge appetite for life and friendship, and charisma in large doses. He had a way with people irrespective of class, race, gender and generational differences, and while certain that his positions were non-negotiable, he was always personable and persuasive in argument, consistently displaying what Praveen Jha has described as his 'charming inflexibility on matters of principle'.

Sam Moyo's Life and Politics

Sam's birth and childhood in colonial Zimbabwe, his sojourns in Sierra Leone and Nigeria, and his return to Zimbabwe in the 1980s as a researcher in the newly established Zimbabwe Institute of Development Studies (ZIDS), were all important influences on his life and achievements. Brought up in the black township of Highfield by a trade unionist father and a mother who was one of the first black women to work in broadcasting in colonial Zimbabwe, he was a Zimbabwe African People's Union (ZAPU) Youth League activist from an early age, enduring a short stint in jail even before he was a teenager (M. Moyo 2016). This history of struggle shaped his view of post-colonial land and labour questions in settler Africa, and influenced his career choices, his research interests and his political stances. After high school in Zimbabwe, he gained a scholarship to study at Njala University in Sierra Leone, graduating with a BA in education and geography in 1976. He then went to Canada for postgraduate studies, earning an MA in geography from the University of Western Ontario in 1979. After several years of study while working, he was awarded a PhD in Rural Development and Environmental Management from the University of Northumbria in the United Kingdom in 1994 (M. Moyo 2016; Amanor-Wilks 2016).

Whilst in Sierra Leone, he often spent holidays with relatives in Dakar; he later had two stints in Nigeria to conduct thesis research and then to teach at the Universities of Calabar and Port Harcourt. All these experiences left an indelible mark on Sam; they cemented his pan-African sensibility, gave him a strong appreciation of West Africa's distinct colonial and post-colonial trajectories, and a love for its cuisine and dress.

Most importantly, they brought him into first contact with the Council for the Development of Social Science Research in Africa (CODESRIA), established in 1973 by a small group of directors of African social science research institutions under the leadership of Samir Amin. CODESRIA drew prominent intellectuals in exile such as Archie Mafeje, Thandika Mkandawire, Mahmood Mamdani and Zenebeworke Tadesse to its nurturing fold. Having become an active participant in CODESRIA from the 1980s, Sam coordinated several of its working groups. As one of only a handful of scholars involved in research on agrarian and land issues in this period, he became very important to CODESRIA's efforts to build knowledge in this area. He joined already established scholars in the field such as Archie Mafeje, Dessalegn Rahmato and Mahmoud Ben Romdhane, and went on to make important interventions in land debates in Africa. In 1998, he was elected vice-president of CODESRIA for three years, becoming president of the organization a decade later, between 2008 and 2011. It was during his tenure that CODESRIA established the African–Arab Advanced Institute to deepen intellectual understanding and challenge the divides between North Africa and sub-Saharan Africa, as well as the China–Africa and Africa–India initiatives which broadened intellectual exchanges within the global South. He brought his leadership gifts to an organization enjoying a period of growth and consolidation after crisis. In CODESRIA, Sam found a home that became increasingly vital for his very survival, particularly in a turbulent period in Zimbabwe during which his positions on the land reforms fractured his intellectual and personal relations with some of his closest collaborators of the past, and complicated his relations with the Zimbabwe African National Union–Patriotic Front (ZANU–PF) government.

In spite of his long-standing consistent critique of government policy shifts on the land question – which, as he pointed out, had from 1990 privileged the creation of a cadre of large and small black capitalist farmers, in keeping with its embrace of neo-liberal economic policies while ignoring the interests of the rural and urban landless and poor peasants in rural areas (S. Moyo 1995, 2000) – Sam's relations with Zimbabwe's Ministry of Agriculture and the President's Office were mutually respectful. Anecdotal evidence points to requests for his advice on a range of issues over the years, which he honoured, as well as offers of farmlands and high-level government appointments, which he declined. At the same time, like many who were critical of government policies, he suffered his fair share of intimidation. In May 2008, while he was in Accra at the meeting of a CODESRIA multinational working group, he received news that some unknown persons had broken into his house and trashed his study. This targeted attack on the space of his intellectual production had the hallmarks of an intelligence warning, although this could not be verified.

Sam's strong relationship with CODESRIA and significant actors within it had been forged early in his academic career. On his return to Zimbabwe after a stint as lecturer in Nigeria in the 1980s, Sam and several other young researchers such as Brian Raftopoulos, Yemi Katerere and Rudo Gaidzanwa were hired by the embryonic Zimbabwe Institute of Development Studies, conceived by the Zimbabwe state under the leadership of Ibbo Mandaza, then permanent secretary in the Ministry of Manpower Planning and Development. It was established with the support of the then executive secretary of CODESRIA, Abdala Bujra, and of Thandika Mkandawire, who was seconded from CODESRIA (Raftopoulos 2016). ZIDS, which was part of the post-colonial emancipatory project in Zimbabwe, was to provide a counterweight to the domination of knowledge production by white scholars and a history of discrimination at the University of Rhodesia against black students pursuing postgraduate training and subjects such as the natural sciences and economics. It was also to respond to demands to decolonize the academy and ensure the substantive participation of black scholars on the faculty and in administration. By all accounts, ZIDS played a critical part in Sam's formation as a scholar in the traditions of Marxist political economy (Martin 2017; Raftopoulos 2016).

The connection with CODESRIA put ZIDS at the centre of African intellectual production; it brought its scholars into the orbit of leading African social scientists and gave them access to some of the key persons and debates in CODESRIA in this period. CODESRIA's early success owed much to the work of individual scholars from important hubs of Africa's post-colonial knowledge production, such as the universities of Dar es Salaam, Makerere, Ibadan, Ghana, Ahmadu Bello and Cheikh Anta Diop. Several of these individuals also became members of another CODESRIA-supported organization, the African Association of Political Science (AAPS), based in Harare. The young scholars who came to work at ZIDS thus had the benefit of a vibrant network of radical scholars whose formidable intellect and commitment to an emancipatory project in knowledge production has continued to inspire generations of scholars.

Sam worked in ZIDS for over a decade. These were productive years during which he cemented his research interest in the agrarian and land questions of Zimbabwe and Africa, rising to the rank of research professor in the 1990s, when ZIDS was absorbed into the University of Zimbabwe. His work in this period laid the groundwork for his distinctive analysis of land and agrarian issues in Zimbabwe. An important piece of work in this regard is a monograph from 1995 entitled *The Land Question in Zimbabwe*, considered by many to be a seminal contribution, which provides a compass for understanding what came to pass under the fast-track land reforms and the farmland invasions (S. Moyo 1995).[2] This was also when Sam and his colleague and friend, Yemi Katerere, established the Zimbabwe Environmental Research Organization (ZERO) devoted to environmental questions, an important research interest that continued to be a red thread in his scholarship. A collection of SADC (Southern African Development Community) country profiles, *The Southern African Environment*, which he edited with Phil O'Keefe and Michael Sill (S. Moyo *et al.* 1993), is an example of the work he and colleagues at ZERO were engaged in. In that book, environmental issues were framed within a sustainability approach, taking a community perspective that highlighted the ways in which productive systems affected agrarian livelihoods. This was an explicit departure from the productivity and stewardship perspectives on sustainability, and was in keeping with Sam's prioritization of the lives of small peasants. The years at ZIDS were also when he established a family life, married Dede Amanor-Wilks and brought up five daughters who became his pride and joy (Amanor-Wilks 2016).

On leaving ZIDS – whose fortunes began to wane because of flagging state commitment – he joined the Southern Africa Regional Institute for Policy Studies (SARIPS), founded by Ibbo Mandaza as a project of his Southern Africa Political Economy Series Trust (SAPES Trust). As director of SARIPS, Sam filled a critical intellectual leadership and mentorship role in which he thrived. Scores of students from the southern African region were awarded post-graduate degrees at SARIPS. Together with other members of the faculty such as Patricia McFadden, Sam fashioned a curriculum in critical policy studies which enabled students to engage with African scholarship that was not much read in mainstream universities across Africa. As this period also coincided with the crises in higher education in Africa, SARIPS provided a welcome alternative for students and scholars wanting to escape academic environments that were often in survival mode, churning out students with few opportunities for critical learning. Although SARIPS is now defunct, members of the cadre it contributed to producing thrive in research and policy positions, making important contributions to the search for solutions to Africa's problems.

In 2002, Sam established the African Institute of Agrarian Studies (AIAS), recently renamed as the Sam Moyo African Institute of Agrarian Studies (SMAIAS) to commemorate his life and work. It was to be his last institutional home. This most ambitious project, a research and policy advocacy organization, consolidated his earlier efforts and signalled his maturation as one of Africa's foremost intellectuals of agrarian and land issues, something of a 'fundi',[3] as a mutual friend once described him to me. In addition to a prodigious amount of scholarship and research output, Sam continued to supervise and advise numerous postgraduate students from universities across the globe, and was in high demand as a keynote speaker at conferences, and as consultant to several African governments and regional and sub-regional organizations. He threw his energies into the Agrarian South Network (ASN), which, from small beginnings, now brings together over 50 members actively involved in agrarian research and teaching, policy advocacy and social movement work in Africa, Latin America and Asia. The ASN has three core, interconnected projects – *Agrarian South: Journal of Political Economy*, the International Agrarian Summer School, and research and publications on contemporary issues of agrarian transformation. Its tangible outputs to date are two books, several volumes of the journal, and seven annual meetings of the Summer School, which is arguably its most vibrant and visible undertaking – a space to engage with heterodox perspectives, to debate and test ideas about the trajectories of agrarian change.

Some of the emblematic debates within the ASN have been generated by Sam's dense body of work with its rich theoretical and empirical insights. These include whether there is a land question in settler Africa or only a labour question, the salience and applicability of the concept of re-peasantization, and the nature of agrarian social movements in Africa. Such debates are essential to the Network's mandate to build epistemologies of the global South, and to create an epistemic community on land and agrarian change. In the second part of this essay, I reflect on three strands of Sam's contributions: the land and agrarian questions of Zimbabwe and the rest of Africa; the scramble for land in Africa, Asia and Latin America; and agrarian social movements of the global South.

Three Contributions

On Land and Agrarian Change in Zimbabwe and Africa

Sam's work on Zimbabwe is praised by several scholars for its empirical rigour (Johnson 2015; Mamdani 2008; Scoones 2017). Scoones's reflections on Sam's method shed light on his contributions. He notes,

> the combination of detailed empirical investigation, and deep knowledge of the technical and practical aspects of agricultural production and farming livelihoods, with big picture political economy analysis, and wider theorization, is especially important and reflects a tradition in political economy that goes back to Marx's original discussion of method in Grundrisse. (Scoones 2017: 2)

Beyond methodological rigour, Sam showed great courage in his robust engagement with Zimbabwe's land reforms. Building on his earlier research (S. Moyo 1986, 1995, 2011a, 2011b), he charted a course of independent research that eschewed sensationalism and illuminated the scale and significance of land redistribution represented by the fast-track land reform programme, which saw over 200,000 Zimbabwean households acquiring land for their livelihoods. This was, for a long time, a very lonely undertaking which incurred the disapproval of the different sides of the debates on Zimbabwe's land reforms. However, Sam was much respected and admired in the wider community of progressive intellectuals within the global South for his consistency and the quality of the evidence he produced to back his positions. Murisa (2017) notes that without this work, the story of the land reforms would not have been comprehensively understood. This is a view shared by some of those who disagreed with, and continue to critique, Sam's positions on the Zimbabwe land reforms (Raftopoulos 2016). A long-term advocate of land reforms, Sam expected such processes to address historical dispossession, fostering accumulation from below to resolve the social reproduction challenges of the small peasantry and the rural and urban poor, and to promote the broader democratization of Zimbabwe. This was his consistent grid for assessing the Zimbabwe land reforms. In this, he also chronicled the agency and autonomy of war veterans and rural social movements. He found, based on empirical studies, that the fast-track land reforms had resulted in a massive redistribution of land that had benefited mostly rural people and changed the structure of the agrarian system in Zimbabwe. Previously dominated by large-scale commercial farmers, the system was now more equitable in creating one of the conditions for broad-based transformation that could address poverty, inequalities and citizenship deficits – although, in drawing this conclusion, Sam did not turn a blind eye to instances of patronage, illegalities and corruption (S. Moyo and Chambati 2013; S. Moyo and Yeros 2005a, 2007a, 2007b, 2009, 2011; Murisa 2017; Scoones 2017). This pitted him against scholars who saw the fast-track land reforms as simply a regime-survival strategy, and preferred to focus on the authoritarian nationalism of ZANU–PF and its long-term implications for Zimbabwean politics (Moore 2003; Raftopoulos 2003, 2016; Sachikonye 2003).[4]

Over long periods when there was little policy interest, Sam and a few other scholars kept Africa's land and agrarian questions alive. While not comparable to his work on Zimbabwe, Sam's insights from Zimbabwe had a positive influence on his work on Africa's land and agrarian questions. This was evident in the book *Land in the Struggles for Citizenship in Africa* that he co-edited with me and Yakham Diop (S. Moyo, Tsikata and Diop, eds 2016), and the monograph he produced before CODESRIA launched the Multinational Working Group which produced that book (S. Moyo 2008) – although both publications ranged over issues not always explicitly discussed in the Zimbabwe work. In the introduction to the co-edited volume (S. Moyo, Tsikata and Diop 2016), much of which he wrote, Sam tackled some of the key debates about agrarian and land issues across Africa. First was the question of whether a land question existed outside settler Africa. The great Archie Mafeje himself had argued that in countries which had not experienced settler colonization and widespread land expropriation, there was no significant land question; instead, there was an unresolved agrarian question (Mafeje 1999). Based on studies of agriculture outside settler Africa that had identified the common challenges to include the marginalization of the poor (and particularly the marginalization of women from access to land) and the growing problem of landlessness alongside land concentration, we argued that there were agrarian questions of both land and labour in small-holder Africa (S. Moyo, Tsikata and Diop 2016). With over 65 per cent of Africans still working in agriculture, addressing these problems comprehensively would require land redistribution, strengthening of agrarian productive systems, promotion of industrialization and addressing the challenges of urbanization. Even in countries where agriculture contributes less than 10 per cent of the gross domestic product (GDP), such as South Africa, Mauritius and Nigeria, there are critical land and agrarian questions.

The insistence that there were land questions in small-holder Africa is linked with Sam's earlier work on agrarian change in Zimbabwe, in which he and Yeros had identified re-peasantization and semi-proletarianization as two of the processes of agrarian transformation occurring under neo-liberalism (S. Moyo 2008; S. Moyo and Yeros 2005a). Their analysis also critiqued an influential strand in the agrarian literature which argued that, because of the agrarian crisis under neo-liberalism, droves of peasants were leaving the countryside and their agriculture-based livelihoods behind. This was theorized as a process of de-agrarianization (Bryceson, Kay and Mooij 2000). While this drew welcome attention to the deep crises in agrarian livelihoods and the responses of farming populations in parts of Africa, the notion of de-agrarianization was widely contested. Many in the field argued that agrarian livelihood activities had always been diversified, and included off-farm and non-agricultural elements combined in different ways depending on the perceived opportunities and risks. S. Moyo and Yeros (2005a) argued that one response to agrarian crises has been the expansion of wage work among smallholders who continued to engage in self-employment and self-provisioning as a process of semi-proletarianization, which was neither new nor linear (see also Mafeje 2003). In support of this position, other studies have observed that the countryside across Africa is home to labour which is less dependent on earnings from agriculture, but also not easily absorbed within the non-farm economy. Even in countries with advanced agrarian transitions, such as South Africa, rural peoples' strategies for survival straddle rural and urban spaces, combining formal and informal sources of income, agricultural self-provisioning and state-sponsored social protection (Du Toit and Neves 2014).

S. Moyo and Yeros (2005a) had also observed the growing number of urban dwellers returning to the countryside to take up agrarian livelihood activities, a process they conceptualized as 're-peasantization'. There have been calls for an examination of the wider applicability of this concept. As I have argued elsewhere, this is because it is still unclear how widespread and sustained the process is, under what conditions it occurs, and what it represents in agrarian futures (Tsikata 2015). In Zimbabwe, the mixed profile of new small and middle peasants, which includes war veterans, retired officers of the Zimbabwe armed forces, teachers and other professionals, as well as ex-farm labourers, points to a complex agrarian structure in which actors are connected and resourced in ways not usual for small peasants. Beyond Zimbabwe, studies of agricultural commercialization have observed cases of return to agrarian livelihood activities by a range of urban-based workers in Ghana, Kenya and Zambia, three countries with very different agrarian histories (Hall, Scoones and Tsikata 2017). In describing contract farmers in southwestern Togo, Gardini (2012) argues that several of these are not poor smallholders, but rural and urban ex-migrants with savings to invest in land and commercial farming. Hecht has termed this development a 'new rurality', in which rural households are 'largely semi-proletarianized, semi-globalized and increasingly semi-urban' (Hecht 2014: 878, cited in Fairbairn *et al.* 2014: 659). There is no question, however, that the work of Sam Moyo and Paris Yeros demonstrates significant differences between the responses of the peasantry, and those of the rural and urban landless and poor, to the changing conditions in agrarian political economies – responses that need consistent and systematic mapping and analysis.

Explaining the Third Scramble for Land in Africa

A few years ago, civil society groups from the developing world expressed alarm about land grabbing. This was occasioned by a spate of large-scale land acquisitions by transnational corporations and governments from Europe, the Americas, Asia and the Middle East as a response to the global financial, food and energy crises from around 2007. It resulted in a frenzy of intellectual activity. One strand mapped the land grabs around the world, and provided a tool for collecting and updating the data about acquisitions (Anseeuw *et al.* 2013). A second strand comprised studies that identified what were called drivers of land grabbing – the list of drivers increasing, with some in dispute, as time went by (Borras and Franco 2010; Cotula *et al.* 2009; Kachika 2010). For example, the idea that land grabs only happened to countries with weak land regulatory mechanisms was challenged with evidence from Latin America, where Brazil was in the paradoxical position of being both a participant in and at the receiving end of large-scale land acquisitions (Borras *et al.* 2012). Soon, there was a proliferation of case studies of large-scale commercial land acquisitions, examining their implications for local livelihood activities and posing questions about promised and delivered benefits, land tenure and common property resources, employment and responses to dispossession. Some highlighted class and gender differences in effects and responses (Doss, Summerfield and Tsikata 2014; Hall, Scoones and Tsikata, eds 2015). While the land-grabbing literature frenzy has subsided and some of its participants have moved on in response to a call for a second stage of studies focusing more broadly on processes of agrarian change, particularly patterns of land and agricultural commercialization (Edelman 2013; Oya 2013), its influence on the research landscape will remain for a long time. To learn its lessons, it is useful to examine what Sam Moyo, Paris Yeros and Praveen Jha wrote about it.

In a 2012 article entitled 'Imperialism and Primitive Accumulation: Notes on the New Scramble for Africa' (Moyo, Yeros and Jha 2012), Sam and his collaborators took a historical approach that characterized what was going on as a third scramble for land in Africa, to be distinguished from colonial acquisitions, especially in settler Africa, and significant land dispossessions of the structural adjustment years for mining and other extractive industries, commercial agriculture, tourism and infrastructure. Their most important argument was to draw a connection between primitive accumulation and imperialism, while highlighting the changing character of capital's march from mercantilism to monopoly capitalism which had moved from an industrial stage to one of financialization (ibid. 2012). Fairbairn's analysis of the implications of financialization of capital for land markets is a fascinating account of this stage of monopoly capital identified by Sam and his colleagues as being at the heart of the third scramble for land (Fairbairn 2014). Their discussion clearly showed the limitations of the early debates about land grabbing, and demonstrated the importance of research that illuminates the challenges of Africa's failed agrarian transitions and links the current situation to questions about Africa's agrarian past and futures.

Valorizing Agrarian Social Movements

One of the highlights of a one-day colloquium to commemorate Sam Moyo's life and work during the Agrarian Summer School of January 2016 was a panel to mark a decade since the publication of the book *Reclaiming the Land: The Resurgence of Rural Movements in Africa, Asia and Latin America* (S. Moyo and Yeros, eds 2005). Introducing the book's fourteen chapters, which chronicle the struggles of rural social movements across three continents, its editors challenge the dominant wisdom about the disappearance of the peasantry, drawing attention to the fact that the most progressive and militant social movements in the world are based in the countryside. On the other hand, they point out that this was a position that required qualification and critical engagement with rural movements, noting the wide range of such social movements, from the more organized and recognized in parts of Latin America to embryonic, diffuse and spontaneous land occupation movements in Ghana, Malawi and India. As they note, rural movements can be distinguished by ideology, strategy and tactics, even as they have a shared social basis in the semi-proletarianized peasantry, landless proletarians and urban unemployed (S. Moyo and Yeros 2005b).

This introductory chapter situates rural social movements in a wide-ranging discussion of the contexts in which they have been shaped over the years in the periphery by the industrial revolution in Europe, two world wars, the anti-colonial struggles and the current conjuncture of financialization of capital. All these processes have resulted in the globalization of the agro-food system and a crisis of dependency and underdevelopment in the periphery. This approach enabled Moyo and Yeros to link rural social movements with the unresolved land and agrarian questions, as well as the national question in ex-colonies in Africa, Asia and Latin America, and to shift the debate away from the crises of reproduction facing the peasantry to their struggles. As they point out, the activities of rural social movements are often misunderstood or underestimated because of analyses that do not take their conditions of existence and reproduction into account. While some of these issues have also been raised by Sam in his CODESRIA monograph (S. Moyo 2008), the comparative approach to social movements in *Reclaiming the Land* is particularly useful. The book is a testament to the importance of the tri-continental knowledge project of Sam and his colleagues. At the same time, the schematic nature of the discussion suggests that there is much work to be done on theorizing the diversity of social movements. Sam's observation about the shallowness of scholarship on rural social movements almost a decade ago (S. Moyo 2008) remains valid. In the ASN, there are ongoing efforts to continue this work.

The Future of Sam Moyo's Project

The small group which coordinates the ASN and serves as editorial collective to the journal is united by its determination to take this project forward and ensure its growth and vitality. Under the leadership of Issa G. Shivji, one of Sam's old comrades from CODESRIA who has been acting as honorary executive director of SMAIAS, Joshua Nyoni, chair of the SMAIAS Trust Board, and Walter Chambati, deputy executive director of SMAIAS, who worked very closely with Sam for many years and was involved in many of the surveys carried out by the institute, the Agrarian Summer School of January 2016 was one of the best attended, most productive and intense. A long-standing gap in the work of the ASN – gender relations and agrarian change – took centre stage. At the School, Sam's absence was palpable and was felt in both the intellectual and the social programmes. It was sad that after many starts and stops, one of the issues to which he was committed as necessary for a full appreciation of agrarian change was being discussed in a number of sessions without his input. The debates that broke out about urban land questions in settler colonies and the gender relations of agrarian change showed very clearly that the spirit of vigorous debate and contestation would remain a key part of the Network. The social segment of the programme was rescued by the generosity of Beatrice Mtetwa, human rights lawyer and Sam's life partner of his last decade, who invited the entire school to dinner at her home and provided a live band. The various plans that were made – for books, conferences, more issues of the journal – are all on course. A vibrant and productive Network would be a most fitting way to honour Sam Moyo's life and work, and secure his legacy as a gifted and tenacious intellectual and champion of the rights of the small peasantry and the rural and urban poor of the global South.

This essay was published earlier in *Development and Change,* 48 (5): 1154–67. DOI: 10.1111/dech.12335 © 2017 International Institute of Social Studies.

Notes

[1] This essay has benefited from the funeral brochure produced by the Moyo family, a commemorative CODESRIA Bulletin, a recent essay in *Pambazuka* by Dede Amanor-Wilks (www.pambazuka.org/pan-africanism/memories-sam-moyo-one-year-tribute), and some of the contributions to a special issue of *Agrarian South* (5 [2–3], 2017) on Sam Moyo's life and work.

[2] The book had been preceded by an article with the same title published in 1986.

[3] Derived from *umfindisi* (a teacher), from the Nguni family of languages, meaning a master craftsman, expert or genius.

[4] Sam's positions have been sharply criticized on the basis that he did not sufficiently acknowledge the human rights abuses and suffering accompanying the fast-track land reforms; see, for example, Jacobs and Mundy (2009) and a rebuttal by David Johnson (2009).

References

Amanor-Wilks, D. (2016), 'Memories of Sam Moyo: One-Year Tribute', www.networkideas.org/whats-new/2016/11/memories-of-sam-moyo-one-year-tribute/, accessed 3 January 2017.

Anseeuw, W., J. Lay, P. Messerli, M. Giger and M. Taylor (2013), 'Creating a Public Tool to Assess and Promote Transparency in Global Land Deals: The Experience of the Land Matrix', *The Journal of Peasant Studies*, 40 (3): 521–30.

Borras, S. and J. Franco (2010), 'Towards a Broader View of the Politics of Global Land Grab: Rethinking Land Issues, Reframing Resistance', ICAS Working Paper Series No. 001, Amsterdam: Transnational Institute, in association with Initiatives in Critical Agrarian Studies (ICAS) and Land Deal Politics Initiative (LDPI).

Borras, J., J. Franco, S. Gomez, C. Kay and M. Spoor (2012), 'Land Grabbing in Latin America and the Caribbean', *The Journal of Peasant Studies*, 39 (3–4): 845–72.

Bryceson, D.F., C. Kay and J. Mooij (2000), 'Disappearing Peasantries? Rural Labour in Codes of Conduct in African Horticulture', *World Development*, 31 (9): 1511–26.

Cotula, L., S. Vermeulen, R. Leonard and J. Keeley (2009), *Land Grab or Development Opportunity? Agricultural Investment and International Land Deals in Africa*, London: IIED and Rome: FAO and IFAD.

Doss, C., G. Summerfield and D. Tsikata (2014), 'Land, Gender, and Food Security', *Feminist Economics*, 20 (1): 1–23.

Du Toit, A. and D. Neves (2014), 'The Government of Poverty and the Arts of Survival: Mobile and Recombinant Strategies at the Margins of the South African Economy', *The Journal of Peasant Studies*, 41 (5): 833–53.

Edelman, M. (2013), 'Messy Hectare: Questions about the Epistemology of Land Grabbing Data', *The Journal of Peasant Studies*, 40 (3): 485–501.

Fairbairn, M. (2014), '"Like Gold with Yield": Evolving Intersections between Farmland and Finance', *The Journal of Peasant Studies*, 41 (5): 777–95.

Fairbairn, M., J. Fox, S. Ryan Isakson, M. Levien, N. Peluso, S. Razavi, I. Scoones and K. Sivaramakrishnan (2014), 'Introduction: New Directions in Agrarian Political Economy', *The Journal of Peasant Studies*, 41 (5): 653–66.

Gardini, M. (2012), 'Land Transactions and Chieftaincies in South-Western Togo', *Africa Spectrum*, 1: 51–72.

Hall R., I. Scoones and D. Tsikata (2017), 'Plantations, Outgrowers and Commercial Farming in Africa: Agricultural Commercialization and Implications for Agrarian Change', *The Journal of Peasant Studies*, 44 (3): 515–37.

Hall, R., I. Scoones and D. Tsikata, eds (2015), *Africa's Land Rush: Implications for Rural Livelihoods and Agrarian Change*, Martlesham: Boydell and Brewer Ltd.

Hecht, S.B. (2014), 'Forests Lost and Found in Tropical Latin America: The Woodland "Green Revolution"', *The Journal of Peasant Studies*, 41 (5): 877–909.

Jacobs, S. and J. Mundy, eds (2009), 'Reflections on Mahmood Mamdani's "Lessons of Zimbabwe"', *Concerned African Scholars Bulletin 82*, http://concernedafricascholars.org/ docs/acasbulletin82.pdf, accessed 27 June 2016.

Johnson, D. (2009), 'Mamdani, Moyo and "Deep Thinkers" on Zimbabwe', *Pambazuka News*, 12 February, www.pambazuka.org/governance/mamdani-moyo-and-%E2%80%98deepthinkers%E2%80%99-zimbabwe

——— (2015), 'Nigeria to Zimbabwe: Remembering Sam Moyo', Dakar: CODESRIA, www.codesria.org/spip.php?article2503&lang=en, accessed 27 June 2016.

Kachika, T. (2010), 'Land Grabbing in Africa: A Review of the Impacts and the Possible Policy Responses', Oxford: Oxfam International.

Mafeje, A. (1999), 'Imperatives and Options for Agricultural Development in Africa: Peasant or Capitalist Revolution?', unpublished.

——— (2003), 'The Agrarian Question, Access to Land and Peasant Responses in Sub-Sahara Africa', UNRISD Programme Papers on Civil Society and Social Movements, Geneva: United Nations Research Institute for Social Development.

Mamdani, M. (2008), 'Lessons of Zimbabwe: Mugabe in Context', *London Review of Books*, 30 (23–24): 17–21.

Martin, W. (2017), 'Sam Moyo and the Struggle for Intellectual Decolonization', *Agrarian South: Journal of Political Economy*, 5 (2–3), https://doi.org/10.1177/2277976016682080, accessed 20 April 2017.

Moore, D. (2003), 'Zimbabwe's Triple Crisis: Primitive Accumulation, Nation-State Formation and Democratization in the Age of Neo-Liberal Globalization', *African Studies Quarterly*, 7 (2–3): 33–51.

Moyo, M. (2016), 'A Family Perspective of Sam Moyo's Intellectual Development', *Agrarian South: Journal of Political Economy*, 5 (2–3).

Moyo, S. (1986), 'The Land Question', in I. Mandaza, ed., *Zimbabwe: The Political Economy of Transition, 1980–1986*, Dakar: CODESRIA: 165–202.

——— (1995), *The Land Question in Zimbabwe*, Harare: SAPES Books.

——— (2000), *Land Reform under Structural Adjustment: Land Use Changes in Mashonaland Provinces*, Uppsala: Nordiska Afrikainstitutet.

——— (2008), *African Land Questions, Agrarian Transitions and the State: Contradictions of Neoliberal Land Reforms*, Green Book Series, Dakar: CODESRIA.

——— (2011a), 'Changing Agrarian Relations after Redistributive Land Reform in Zimbabwe', *The Journal of Peasant Studies*, 38 (5): 907–34.

——— (2011b), 'Three Decades of Agrarian Reform in Zimbabwe', *The Journal of Peasant Studies*, 38 (3): 493–531.

Moyo, S. and W. Chambati (2013), 'Introduction', in S. Moyo and W. Chambati, eds, *Land and Agrarian Reform in Zimbabwe: Beyond White Settler Capitalism*, Harare: AIAS and Dakar: CODESRIA: 1–27.

Moyo, S., P. O'Keefe and M. Sill (1993), *The Southern African Environment: Profiles of the SADC Countries,* London: Earthscan Publications Ltd.

Moyo, S., D. Tsikata and Y. Diop (2016), 'Introduction: Africa's Diverse and Changing Land Questions', in S. Moyo, D. Tsikata and Y. Diop, eds, *Land in the Struggles for Citizenship in Africa*, Dakar: CODESRIA Books: 1–34.

Moyo, S., D. Tsikata and Y. Diop, eds (2016), *Land in the Struggles for Citizenship in Africa*, Dakar: CODESRIA Books.

Moyo, S. and P. Yeros (2005a), 'Land Occupations and Land Reform in Zimbabwe: Towards the National Democratic Revolution?', in S. Moyo and P. Yeros, eds, *Reclaiming the Land: The Resurgence of Rural Movements in Africa, Asia and Latin America*, London: Zed Books and Cape Town: David Philip: 165–208.

——— (2005b) 'Resurgence of Rural Movements under Neoliberalism', in S. Moyo and P. Yeros, eds, *Reclaiming the Land: The Resurgence of Rural Movements in Africa, Asia and Latin America*, London: Zed Books and Cape Town: David Philip: 8–64.

——— (2007a), 'The Radicalized State: Zimbabwe's Interrupted Revolution', *Review of African Political Economy*, 111: 103–21.

——— (2007b), 'The Zimbabwe Question and the Two Lefts', *Historical Materialism*, 15 (3): 171–204.

——— (2009), 'Zimbabwe Ten Years On: Results and Prospects', *MRzine*, 10 February, http://mrzine.monthlyreview.org/2009/my100209.html, accessed 27 June 2016.

——— (2011), 'The Fall and Rise of the National Question', in S. Moyo and P. Yeros, eds, *Reclaiming the Nation: The Return of the National Question in Africa, Asia and Latin America*, London: Pluto Press: 3–28.

Moyo, S. and P. Yeros, eds (2005), *Reclaiming the Land: The Resurgence of Rural Movements in Africa, Asia and Latin America*. London: Zed Books and Cape Town: David Philip.

Moyo, S., P. Yeros and P. Jha (2012), 'Imperialism and Primitive Accumulation: Notes on the New Scramble for Africa', *Agrarian South: Journal of Political Economy*, 1 (2): 181–203.

Murisa, T. (2017), 'Prospects for Equitable Land Reform in Zimbabwe: Revisiting Sam Moyo's Work on the Land Question', *Agrarian South: Journal of Political Economy*, 5 (2–3), https://doi.org/10.1177/2277976016682083, accessed 14 May 2017.

Oya, C. (2013), 'Methodological Reflections on "Land Grab" Databases and "Land Grab" Literature "Rush"', *The Journal of Peasant Studies*, 40 (3): 503–20.

Raftopoulos, B. (2003), 'The State in Crisis: Authoritarian Nationalism, Selective Citizenship and Distortions of Democracy in Zimbabwe', in A. Hammar, B. Raftopoulos and S. Jensen, eds, *Zimbabwe's Unfinished Business: Rethinking Land, State and Nation in the Context of Crisis*, Harare: Weaver Press: 217–42.

——— (2016), 'Zimbabwe Institute of Development Studies (ZIDS): The Early Context for Sam Moyo's Intellectual Development', *Agrarian South: Journal of Political Economy* 5 (2–3).

Sachikonye, L. (2003), 'From "Growth with Equity" to "Fast Track" Reform: Zimbabwe's Land Question', *Review of African Political Economy*, 30 (96): 227–40.

Scoones, I. (2017), 'Livelihoods, Land and Political Economy: Reflections on Sam Moyo's Research Methodology', *Agrarian South: Journal of Political Economy*, 5 (2–3), https://doi.org/10.1177/2277976016683750, accessed 14 May 2017.

Tsikata, D. (2015), 'The Social Relations of Agrarian Change', IIED Working Paper, London: IIED, http://pubs.iied.org/pdfs/17278IIED.pdf, accessed 14 May 2017.

3

Sam Moyo and the Struggle for Intellectual Decolonization

William G. Martin

Sam Moyo was blessed with rare, rare gifts: a sparkling and generous intelligence emanating from a radiant persona. It was a combination he shared madly with friends and colleagues across many continents. News of his parting led to an immediate outpouring of testimonies to an extraordinary life, from Bella Matambanadzo's (2015: 11) thrilling account of his impishly brilliant childhood in the townships, to David Johnson's (2015) vivid depiction of his dazzling young scholar days in exile, to his fellow scholars' many renditions of his brilliance, inspiration and ability to forge a global network in pursuit of a more equitable, African-rooted existence.[1] No one who crossed his path could doubt that here was a compelling intellectual leader. Indeed, Sam's life has much to teach us about efforts to decolonize the production of knowledge in and about Africa. Tracing his passage not only renders sharply major epochs and inequalities in the study of Africa, such an exercise also points towards the possibility of disrupting and replacing the coloniality that structures our intellectual work. It is this legacy, among the many he left, that I want to address here.

One would not know of this struggle from the dominant Northern scholarship on the production of knowledge, which largely remains focused on the self-possessed problems of the divide between the natural sciences and the humanities, the need for crossing the boundaries of western disciplines, and, more belatedly, the process of appropriating those excluded by gender, sexuality, ethnicity, race and the west's focus on the 'Other'. Even in the latter field, there is little probing of the distribution of resources and institutional power that structure the global polarization of higher education and research.

Far along the margins of the dominant disciplines, western scholars of Africa, the 'Africanists',[2] have, on rare occasions, at least noted the issue. Over forty years ago, Immanuel Wallerstein (1974: 9–10), the leading Africanist, sociologist and world-systems scholar, argued that objectivity in the production of knowledge would only obtain under conditions of equal resources across the North and South. Few social scientists picked up the challenge that such observations raise; it would be only in the 1990s and later that serious studies on North–South inequities in the study of Africa would emerge, largely from black scholars.[3]

Work on the history and inequalities in the study of Africa was not central to Sam's agenda. Yet, to attend a summer school in Harare, visit his African Institute for Agrarian Studies (AIAS) or read the journal *Agrarian South* was to witness concretely a growing network that offered an alternative to the self-enclosed schools of African Studies. Remarkably absent was the global North; one did not find senior representatives of the Euro-American managerial class of African Studies. Less noticed was a new aim: to move beyond long-standing calls to create independent African institutions and reach out with formal links to Asia and Latin America. Something new was afoot, breaking with past patterns of how and where the knowledge of African economies, cultures and political systems were produced and consumed. Even the focus on local land struggles was a rupture: this subject had been long abandoned by scholars of 'development'. Loudly proclaimed was an alternative formulation: the necessity of focusing on problems, data and theory posed not by the paragons from the North, but by the scholars and people of Africa and of the global South.

The Colonial Construction of African Studies

Zimbabwe could easily claim to be the homeland of African Studies, which traces its lineage back to 1938 and the establishment of the Rhodes-Livingstone Institute (RLI) in the then sister colony of Northern Rhodesia. There was no question whom the RLI served: it was chartered in the service of the settler state and mining companies, with direct funding from the Northern Rhodesian government, the British South African Company, Rhodesia Railways and a half-dozen mining companies. Its first director, Godfrey Wilson, reported to its trustees that the RLI research mission was 'systematic analysis' of 'social problems of urgent practical interest' (Wilson 1937; see also Tembo, n.d.). Ethnology could provide, it was trumpeted, an understanding of increasingly disruptive native subjects, and, more specifically, the reasons for the massive strikes on the copper belt mines. RLI was but one node in a growing colonial network, with close relations with the International African Institute in London (founded in 1926), and the evolving school for African Studies at University of Cape Town (UCT), established in 1920 with government funding (van der Merwe 1979: 62).[4]

Indeed, these nodes were so deeply part of the hubris of British and settler rule that few remarked upon the colonial hierarchies of their conception, staffing and research findings. At the end of World War II, it was blithely assumed by victors in the war that settler and colonial rule would continue, and new regional research institutes would be established in East and West Africa – the East African Institute of Social Research in Makerere (1948) and the West African Institute of Social and Economic Research in Ibadan (1950).[5] Such hopes were disrupted by the unruly winds of change, and as African states emerged, British scholars retreated to their mother country or the white dominions, taking their funding, journals and scholarship with them. What was not anticipated was the reconstruction of the study of Africa from above as the far, far wealthier US academy usurped British leadership. African and American initiatives would henceforth lead to a new era in how and where knowledge of Africa was produced.

Independence and Decolonization? The Africanist Enterprise and the African Response

This was most apparent in the US core of the Africanist enterprise. In the 1920s and 1930s, American foundations emerged as major supporters of British scholarship on Africa. A fellow white settler state, South Africa became the focus for this effort, with US funds flowing to the Institute of Race Relations, the Carnegie Commission on the Poor White Problem in South Africa (Grosskopf *et al.* 1932), and hundreds of visits of South African scholars and officials to the United States. In the 1950s, US foundations led a charge to move beyond funding British initiatives, such as the *Journal of African History*, to the creation in the United States of multiple federally funded African Studies centres.[6] Americans would do, it was proclaimed, what European colonizers had not done: promote development and the training of African students in modernity. It was the golden age of academic Africanists: funding chased Euro-American scholars all over the planet, multi-million-dollar grants established new institutes, new journals flourished, every major US research university had its array of Africanist positions and students flocked to the field.

Conceptions of development and their application to Africa by US scholars reigned supreme. Africanists in the jet age became 'academic tourists' (Ochwada 1996; Zeleza 1983), flying across the Atlantic to conduct their studies, collate local resources and theses, and return home to publish monographs in the service of progress and modernization.

Propelled by nationalist movements and extensive state investment in higher education, African scholars countered by setting up their own institutions, journals and schools (especially notable in Ibadan, Dar es Salaam and Kenya). This led to continental associations, of which the Council for the Development of Social Science Research in Africa (CODESRIA), founded in 1973, and the nurturing of Sam's generation of new and rambunctious students, were the most notable. The task was, simply stated, a radical one: to seize control of developmental prospects from Northern scholars, governments and institutions. As a summary, signal collection titled it, 'Our Continent, Our Future' (Mkandawire and Soludo 1999).

Academic tourism and the response to it pointed to a fundamental polarization of knowledge production across the North–South divide. Americans might promise development but it would be on their terms – as the rise of the US Africanist enterprise generated the centralization of journals, publishers and lucrative teaching positions in the North. A patron–client division of labour was promoted, with concepts, models and theory to be generated in the North and applied to empirical data collected in the South. Research organized and conducted by Africans was largely invisible in the North; African-authored or published journals and books were rarely read in the North and even more rarely cited. There were few tenured Africans at African Studies centres, the African Studies Association or as teachers in US classrooms (beyond African languages and culture).

These divisions became more entrenched in the 1980s as structural adjustment weakened the drive to establish self-reliant centres of knowledge production on the continent. At the behest of the World Bank, which argued that returns were higher for basic education and that Africa really did not need state universities, funding for higher education was sharply reduced. Efforts to decolonize knowledge production through independent research and training became increasingly a struggle against privatization and the market (Mamdani 2007). Expectations that the victory of the national liberation movements would deliver more radical challenges to the epistemic, institutional and paradigmatic domination of the North failed to be sustained into the 1990s.

Under these conditions, Africa's independent journals and institutes began to close and scholars were increasingly unable to sustain themselves and their families. The evaluation of those who had fostered the creation of regional and continental research networks and organizations in the 1960s and '70s made for dismal reading. Mkandawire (2005: 28) reported an epoch of 'disenchantment and disillusionment', Tadesse (1999) charted African institutes passing from 'Euphoria to Gloom', and Zeleza referenced a massive intellectual brain drain as 20,000 highly educated Africans moved to the North every year in the post-1990 period (see West 2002), devastating the intergenerational transfer of skills and knowledge on the continent.

The withdrawal of funding for African universities and their replacement by external non-governmental organizations (NGOs) and private universities further diminished the possibilities of self-reliant knowledge production, as noted by many scholars.[7] Those who had worked most assiduously to chart the path towards autonomous, local knowledge production reported regularly on unfulfilled promises (Hountondji 1990: 10, 2009: 8–9). Even CODESRIA (2012: 20) concluded in its most recent strategic plan that 'African universities do not feature prominently in the global rankings of universities, and knowledge produced by Africa, even allowing for the under-counting it suffers from, is marginal in terms of the volume'. And the divide between the continent and the North seemed to many as fixed as ever. As Mkandawire (2011: 25) recently put it, '[a]ny student of Africa is confronted by two research communities that rarely interact'.

As conditions worsened in the 1990s, a small number of senior African scholars (predominantly male) moved North, often under political pressure. As Mamdani put it, 'when the going got rough, we got going across borders' (Mamdani, ed. 1993, cited in Mkandawire 2005: 33). Positions opened up in the United States in particular, following the Afrocentric, US student protests of the late 1980s and early 1990s, which often denounced the colonial staffing and scholarship of African Studies centres. While these positions were not numerous, they were notable additions to tenured faculty and US centres, including Michael Chege (University of Florida), Mamadou Diouf (University of Michigan), Toyin Falola (University of Texas at Austin), Amina Mama (Mills College), Mahmood Mamdani (Columbia University), Micere Mugo (Cornell to Syracuse), Achille Mbembe (Columbia) and Tiyambe Zeleza (Trent, University of Illinois), among others. This crossing of the continental divide created new possibilities, as in Mamdani's support of African scholars in New York and his subsequent rebuilding effort as director of the Makerere Institute of Social Research. For its part, CODESRIA (2014) launched a new programme to expand the links of African scholars in the diaspora with African universities.

Zimbabwe, Decolonization and the Moyo Counter-movement

It was precisely in this epoch of gloom and rare resources that Sam Moyo sought to sustain intellectual and institutional innovations that would challenge the centralization of knowledge production in Europe and America. Sam knew the system well. Like a previous Southern African cohort before him – one need only mention A.C. Jordan, the UCT's first African PhD in 1957, who was forced into exile in the United States in 1961, and his friend Archie Mafeje, exiled from UCT and the country in the late 1960s (Hendricks 2008) – settler colonialism had forced Sam into exile in search of higher education. But there he did not remain. In 1983, after teaching and working in West Africa, he returned to Zimbabwe. Despite being offered employment in the North, he would stay in Zimbabwe.

Advances after independence in 1980 had been sharp, wide-ranging and, in many areas, effective. Lively efforts to transform the colonial inheritance spanned from the production of new African-centred primary education texts to locally driven research at the University of Zimbabwe and the Zimbabwe Institute of Development Studies (ZIDS), among other centres. Economic growth was matched by expanding investment across the educational and health sectors. These gains were reversed after the government entered into agreements with the World Bank and, in 1991, signed a stand-by loan arrangement with the International Monetary Fund (IMF). A standard package of adjustment policies was subsequently applied (such as budget cuts to the education and health sectors, deregulation of commodity and labour markets, trade liberalization and tax cuts). Increasing indebtedness and an economic downturn followed, paralleling development elsewhere across the continent.

Zimbabwe in the 1990s was thus hardly an auspicious location for radical initiatives, with students and scholars heading North and South. But Sam pushed forward, moving from research at ZIDS (1983–95), through his years at the Southern Africa Regional Institute for Policy Studies (1995–2001), to his founding of the AIAS, in 2002. The institute would remain the centre of his work thereafter, an effort that took place outside the university and its disciplinary and institutional constraints – but offset, to be sure, by lack of university infrastructure and support. By the end of the first decade of this new century, these efforts took definitive shape and direction, marking a notable movement in the attempt to continue to decolonize advanced research on and about the continent.

As a concept, 'decolonization' surfaces regularly. In the hands of Fanon and Cabral, among others, it marked revolutionary expectations. State or 'flag' independence and the forging of a territorial, national identity often underwrote, however, a process that shaded into promotions of 'Africanization' and 'authenticity'. These uses and abuses of 'decolonization' by state elites have underpinned a deeper and richer investigation of the concept in the most recent period, tracing how formal independence permitted the continuation of colonial hierarchies and domination in the production of knowledge. As charted above, while 'coloniality' as a concept most often references racial, labour and gender hierarchies in its Latin American context, the production of knowledge regarding Africa in the post-independence period has been sharply marked by global North–South (or core–periphery) hierarchies that reach far beyond national inequalities, and, if anything, have become more marked in recent decades due to structural adjustment.

Tracing out the continuing colonial nature of knowledge production has been most frequently conducted by African philosophers, often with close attention to epistemological concerns (Hountondji 2009; Mbembe 2015; Wiredu 1998). For those labouring in the social sciences, more mundane material concerns have imposed themselves – and it is here, in often unobserved fashion, that Sam and fellow travellers charted new ground in the neo-liberal era. These myriad efforts can be illustrated in three areas: (i) defining and conceptualizing African research problems; (ii) creating self-directed centres of training, research and publication; and, most problematically, (iii) recasting relationships among intellectuals, the state and post-colonial social movements.

Beyond Academic Tourism: Whose Problems, Concepts, Methods?

In her novel *A Small Place*, Jamaica Kincaid (2000) unveils, step by step, how modernity and independence have failed to alter colonial relationships: the rich fly into international hotels and resorts in the Caribbean, and are served and entertained by labouring locals. Academic tourism in the post-colonial era exhibited a similar division of wealth and labour: academic wealth was withdrawn to core zones, with Northern scholars, in common parlance, travelling to the South to collect data using local informants. As with multinational corporations, activities of the brain were to be retained in the mother country while brawn was supplied by ex-colonial subjects. Even after decades of independence, as Hountondji (1990: 7) puts it, 'scientific and technological activity, as practised in Africa today, is just as "extroverted", as externally oriented, as is economic activity'. Scholars from the North were to centralize model- and theory-building, which was then applied to the South.

Moyo's work, subtly but directly, moved against this framework. This took place most critically in the very selection of the research problem, which was dictated by local priorities as opposed to the research agenda of the North. In a period when leading scholars of development had long assumed that urbanization and capital would wipe out rural areas, Sam placed the agrarian question at the centre of contemporary anti-capitalist struggles. This generated much debate, from the very name of the institute, to the case he and his colleagues made for the relevance of the agrarian peoples and struggles today. Seen from the North, the agrarian problem was a historical artefact, a concern of pre-industrial or, at best, early industrial societies. Zimbabwe's land struggles, from this standpoint, were historical oddities at best and historical retreats at worst. And they were, accordingly, most easily explained through conceptions of corrupt, neo-patrimonial elites and failed states – depictions facilitated, to be sure, by the actions of the Mugabe government.

Seen from Harare, however, land struggles were hardly blockages to the course of development, but central aspects of countering colonial dispossession and contemporary poverty and inequality. If of little interest to scholars and journals in Europe and America, land was of overwhelming interest to local students, local scholars, local policy makers and local audiences – not least of all the landless, land-poor and farm workers embroiled in a major social struggle. Seen from the North, by contrast, land grabs across Africa were analysed from the conception of crisis in the North, which was to be resolved by a crudely reductionist conception of primitive accumulation in the South. There was little room in that conception for Southern problems and agency as in Zimbabwe, which received very little attention.

Centralizing land in the twenty-first century also led to keen methodological and conceptual innovations, following directly from the difficulties of applying concepts and theory predicated on the historical paths of core states. This was most evident in the debate over the contemporary relevance of the agrarian question.[8] While one might claim that peasant life in the North disappeared with development, such developments in the North proceeded through colonial plunder and the commodification of rural life elsewhere. Agrarian issues might disappear in the richer zones of the world; in the South, they were created in the age of European expansion and endured in the post-colonial age.

The conceptual and epistemological assumptions of such an account are rarely traced out. As Connell (2007, 2011) has argued at length, models of development of core states and cultures were constructed on the bedrock of colonialism – and thus necessarily fail when applied to the South. Epistemologically, 'the society of the periphery comes to be understood as an imperfect extension of metropolitan modernity' (Connell 2011: 108). To argue otherwise requires insight and inventiveness, and much objection from the North. Awkward as they might seem, concepts such as 'semi-proletarianization' and 'repeasantization' that Sam and his colleagues deployed pointed towards distinctly regional processes tied to, but distinct from, core class and accumulation processes. These terms also suggested that emancipatory projects may be agrarian projects, a vision very different indeed from those projected from core academic zones of the capitalist world. Movement along these lines was very much a part of a growing effort to break with conceptions generated in, and appropriate to, the North, and construct alternative subject matters, concepts and emancipatory possibilities.

Decolonizing Education, Research and Publications

Colonial powers and educators were quite clear: advanced research and training would take place in the universities of the North. The continent's best students would be sent there, and research projects and teams would originate from there; post-World War II regional research institutes would be headed by scholars dispatched from the mother country (or apartheid South Africa).

State independence and US hegemony reshaped but did not fundamentally alter this understanding, which was based on vast disparities in resources and institutional power. Indeed, publication in Northern journals became in short order the privileged location for assessing value, tenure and promotion. As continental associations and institutions advanced in the post-colonial period, a long struggle ensued to reorient the training of young scholars, centres of research and publication outlets. This proceeded in large part hidden behind the North–South divide, with rich universities in the North complacently secure in their hubris, while new intellectual collectives, programmes and institutes emerged in Ibadan, Dar es Salaam and Dakar, among others. If the absence of African authors in Northern journals was noted by many, it was mentioned by few; at a conference in the mid-1990s, a past progressive Africanist editor of the *Journal of African History* spoke on the issue, saying that he had attempted to break this pattern by heavily recruiting African authors, but without success. Senior African authors in the room mentioned the reasons: unbeknown to the North, they had organized an informal boycott of the journal at the time.

Sam grew up as a student in this international complex, moving from Zimbabwe to North America to receive his postgraduate degree. Moreover, he came of age as a scholar in the wake of the full-scale attack waged by structural adjusters against higher education and research on the continent. Yet, from his earliest days after his return home, Sam sought out avenues with fellow scholars to promote local students and local research. In this, his effort followed long-standing continental initiatives, most notably those by CODESRIA, where Sam was successively an executive member (1995–97), vice president (1998–2002) and president (2009–11). Against the advice of his seniors, at times, he sought out and promoted young scholars, a practice that was extensively advanced with the founding of the AIAS in 2002.

The summer schools organized by AIAS, like all the above initiatives, reached out not to the North, but to scholars struggling with similar concerns in the region and the continent. This imperative followed through to publications, an area long stratified by the global academic division of labour. To find an academic audience has long meant, for many, finding a European or North American journal audience and addressing the problems they pose, the concepts they value and the theoretical tradition they represent. This puts scholars concerned with locally defined research agendas, and developing alternative conceptions and theory, with few avenues to publish their research, forcing them all too often to locate their work within the Northern Africanist or area studies framework that speaks to the intellectual and practical needs of the North.

This research complex created colonial lines of communication: while scholars in Europe and North America had conversations with each other, African scholars were pressed into vertical engagements, looking North (Hountondji 1990: 11–12). In recent years, this colonial division of labour has worsened. As one recent quantitative study notes, Africa's share of journal output has steadily declined over the last several decades, and African-based scholars' publications in leading Northern Africanist journals has been falling as well, despite an increasing number of submissions by African scholars to these journals (Briggs and Weathers 2016: 466).

Breaking out of this trap would require journals grounded in local experiences and needs, and that foster conversations among African scholars. *Agrarian South*, with admittedly thin resources like most continental journals,[9] moved in this direction with support from fellow African scholars and institutions. Just how stark a contrast this presents is indicated by the editorial boards of journals in agrarian studies.

In 2015, the editorial boards of the so-called leading journals in the field were completely without a *single* board member in Africa and composed almost wholly of scholars resident in the North (85 per cent for the *Journal of Peasant Studies*, 100 per cent for *Agrarian Change*). *Agrarian South*'s editorial board, by contrast, had not a single member resident in the North. Even more strikingly, its board, beyond Sam, had 50 per cent of its members from Asia, 25 per cent from Latin America and 25 per cent from Africa. If decolonization means self-definition and self-ownership, the lesson could not be clearer.

In this domain, Moyo and his colleagues also moved significantly beyond attempts to create a community bound by regional or continental boundaries, as had been common in the twentieth-century response by African scholars. In a period when everyone was celebrating transnationalism, Sam practised it from within his local setting, reaching out to Asia and Latin America. This also spoke to the decline of the unbridled power of the North, and the emergence of a much more multi-polar world that opened up relationships across the South. The summer schools were similarly tri-continental affairs, with participation from the federal universities of Brasília and the ABC region in Brazil, and the Jawaharlal Nehru University in India. Regional partners included Rhodes University and the UCT (South Africa), and the University of Dar es Salaam in Tanzania.

Movements and Decolonization

One of the great challenges posed in both the North and the South in the wake of the 1960s' revolts has been the post-colonial relationship among social movements, intellectuals and the state. For most of the twentieth century, social movements generally, and independence movements specifically, were focused on capturing state power. In both the United States and much of Africa, however, electoral victories in the 1960s by the leaders of civil rights and independence movements did little to improve the lives of their peoples. Fanon's (2004: 116 passim) assessment of nationalist leaders would prove prophetic: the new governments and new parties would become, increasingly, instruments of coercion and anti-democratic. Expectations that the armed national liberation movements would lead to a more democratic decolonization would prove illusory. A long-standing dilemma was reinforced: how might decolonization and equality be pursued without being appropriated and corrupted by state power and party politics?

Zimbabwe was no exception to this dilemma, with intellectuals increasingly divided between those supportive of the new state and those, over time, more aligned with opposition parties. The explosion of land occupations after 2000 polarized these two groups and their followers. On one side stood a growing phalanx of 'international leftists and liberals',[10] united in their criticism of the regime's authoritarianism and cronyism and supportive of human rights and civil society (Bond and Saunders 2005; Campbell 2003; Ranger 2005). Land reform, from this perspective, was often reduced to the act of a desperate and brutal regime, destined to destroy the nation's agricultural sector and eventually its entire economy. At another pole stood local intellectuals sympathetic to the regime who stressed external imperialist pressures, and opposition parties' affiliations with white farmers and structural adjustment (Moyo and Yeros 2007; Ndlovu-Gatsheni 2013; Raftopoulos 2006).

Sam was committed to land reform and struggling against domination from the North. Yet, he rejected the polarization dictated by electoral politics, and avoided involvement in party politics and intrigues that could compromise intellectual autonomy. His primary concern and research interest – in contrast to much of the external left, urban opposition party supporters and intellectuals directly tied to and benefiting from the government – were with the possibility of land occupation delivering a more just rural order. (Offered a farm himself, Sam declined.) This stance came at great cost. Extensive research reports by Sam and his colleagues of much greater equity produced by land occupations than expected were regularly denounced or, more commonly, ignored by those living in richer climes.[11] At the 2011 CODESRIA General Assembly in Rabat, Sam was virulently denounced as a regime apologist by Moeletsi Mbeki and others; a notable few, such as Mamdani, countered the charge then and later.[12]

It would be a mistake to cast this as merely a personal political decision. For, the dilemma it addresses remains: how do post-independence intellectuals reject service to organs of the party and state, and engage social change from below? This is even more pressing today, as mass movements – in both urban township and rural land struggles across the South – refuse to be channelled as in the past into party political work. Complicating the challenge even further is the 'uncivil' and often violent defence of the commons and its collective ownership, from land through public resources to public goods, including education. These challenges move us very far beyond the simple verities of decolonization in the 1960s and 1970s, making Sam's and his colleagues' choices rich examples to consider indeed.

Steadfast in the Interregnum

In this, as in so many areas, Sam left us no model, no ideal type, no framework to implement a new stage of decolonization. Sam was no angel, as friends could all attest. Life around Sam involved vigorous arguments, disappointments and debate. The summer schools were a focus for this, as charges of gender, generational and regional disparities and inequalities among those present were raised, contested and confronted. Debates erupted – and often continued in the journal – over the localization or importation of concepts and methods from the North; the endurance of colonial patriarchal discourses and analyses in participants' work and institutions; and the need for greater democracy across generational, regional and intercontinental participants. None of these were resolved – they remain before us, a legacy of Sam's life and work. And here, moving forward, we would be well served to remember and practise Sam's generosity and good spirits – his ability to eat and drink and dance and celebrate with his friends after each conference, summer school and gathering. His love of a party – if not the political kind – was legendary.

And so the effort goes forward, often in difficult times and locations for many, as Sam knew so well. Here, too, Sam provides guidance, steadfast and unshakeable as he was in the face of insults and constraints, advancing with remarkable grace and good humour. Sam's many friends can at such moments call up his memory. In this spirit, I call up another Sam story: while checking in late at night at the hotel for a major, heavily-funded, international conference on land grabs, Sam, after long travel from Zimbabwe and without dollars in hand, was told that he was assigned to share a room with an unknown student. While I watched, rather stunned, Sam simply acquiesced; this was common treatment. More on point, another black scholar pulled out his US visa card and separately booked Sam a room. When I awoke, I turned to the young African American woman manning the hotel registration desk and asked: 'Are all the whites in rooms by themselves, and African scholars and students sharing rooms? Is that how it works?' She replied: 'Yes, of course.' Sam was unfazed. The work and conversations, surely with Sam's guidance and blessings, continue.

This article was originally published in *Agrarian South: Journal of Political Economy*, Vol. 5, Nos. 2–3, 2016. Copyright 2016 © Centre for Agrarian Research and Education for South (CARES), New Delhi. All rights reserved. Reproduced with the permission of the copyright holders and the publishers, SAGE Publications India Pvt. Ltd, New Delhi.

Keen insight and guidance provided by David Johnson and Zenebework Tadesse is very gratefully acknowledged, as are comments and suggestions from participants at the Colloquium in Memory of Professor Sam Moyo, 18 January 2016, Harare. The views and errors are of course the author's and reflect his location.

Notes

1 See, among others, the collection of tributes in Matambanadzo (2015).

2 'Africanists' here refers to Northern, self-identified scholars of continental Africa, a group solidified by organizations such as the US African Studies Association.

3 See, among others, Depelchin (2005), Zeleza (1997), Connell (2011: 103–35) and Martin and West (1999).

4 In 1919, the Royal Anthropological Institute pressured the South African government to form an ethnological bureau, a project seconded by the Coleman Committee, and to 'show a real and adequate interest . . . in the problems whose solution is necessary for the future safe development of a country in which white and black are to live side by side' (Levy 1971). The dominance of anthropological investigation of the troubling 'native problem' is indicated in headships of A.R. Radcliffe-Brown (1920–25), Isaac Schapera (1935–50) and Monica Wilson (1952–73).

5 The passage of the 1940 Colonial and Welfare Development Act provided for generous state-officer salaries for the European scholars staffing the regional institutes in West, Central and East Africa (Gluckman 1945: 3). As the founder of the East African Institute, Dr Audrey Richards (via the RLI, Johannesburg and London) noted, '[t]he Institute will cooperate as closely as possible with government research departments' (Richards 1951: 152). For a comparative history, see Mbalibulha (2014).

6 The following paragraph draws upon Martin (2011).

7 As Mkandawire (2011: 21), among others, recounts, the transition of research

and funding from universities to contractual work for NGOs 'is producing a type of knowledge that is rarely useful to Africans, either because it is hidden from them in confidential reports or it is in not easily understood languages. Reports by donors and the scribbling of their consultants enjoy little credibility in African circles which tend to hold them in poorly concealed contempt. . . . To sustain the charade and complicity, locals must feign ignorance so as to attend the lucrative "capacity building" workshops. This process has poisoned relationships between visiting scholars and the local academic community, turning the former researcher into the peripatetic consultant or the academic tourist. These may be stereotypes and intentionally so, but they are not caricatures. The encounter between these two communities is no longer at the senior common room or seminar room but in hotel lobbies or resort areas where workshops are often held. To the experts, the local scholar became some kind of informed native or what is nowadays referred to as "local".'

See also Shivji (2007). For US Africanists, contractual military research funding served to offset falling state support; see Martin and McQuade (2014).

8 See Bernstein (2004) on the demise of the agrarian question, and the response by Moyo, Jha and Yeros (2013).

9 It must be mentioned that the main journals in the North have far greater funding to sustain their operations and generate far greater profits. The academic publisher Elsevier, which owns a majority of the prestigious academic journals, is reported to have higher operating profits than Apple; see Schmitt (2014).

10 See the summary and the use of the term in Ndlovu-Gatsheni (2013: 181), as well as Moyo and Yeros (2007) and Raftopoulos (2006).

11 The most publicized discussion, predictably, took place in the North, initiated by Mamdani (2003) in the pages of the *London Review of Books*, and followed by David Johnson (2016), Alexander, Scarnecchia *et al.* (2009), Campbell (2008) and Jacobs and Mundy, eds (2009).

12 Mamdani spoke on the stage at the time; see also Johnson (2016).

References

Alexander, Jocelyn, Timothy Scarnecchia, *et al.* (2009), 'Letter: Lessons of Zimbabwe', *London Review of Books*, 31 (1), www.lrb.co.uk/v31/n01/letters, accessed 12 March 2016.

Bernstein, Henry (2004), '"Changing before our very eyes": Agrarian questions and the politics of land in capitalism today', *Journal of Agrarian Change*, 4 (1–2): 190–225, doi:10.1111/j.1471-0366.2004.00078.x

Bond, Patrick and Richard Saunders (2005), 'Labor, the State, and the Struggle for a Democratic Zimbabwe', *Monthly Review* 57 (7), www.monthlyreview.org/2005/12/01/labor-the-state-and-the-strugglefor-a-democratic-zimbabwe/, accessed 12 March 2016.

Briggs, Ryan C. and Scott Weathers (2016), 'Gender and Location in African Politics Scholarship: The Other White Man's Burden?' *African Affairs*, 115 (460): 466–89, doi:10.1093/afraf/adw009

Campbell, Horace (2003), *Reclaiming Zimbabwe: The Exhaustion of the Patriarchal Model of Liberation*, Trenton, NJ: Africa World Press.

——— (2008), 'Mamdani, Mugabe and the African Scholarly Community', *Pambazuka News*, 18 December, www.pambazuka.org/resources/mamdani-mugabe-and-african-scholarlycommunity, accessed 12 March 2016.

Connell, Raewyn (2007), *Southern Theory: The Global Dynamics of Knowledge in Social Science*, Cambridge: Polity Press.

——— (2011), *Confronting Equality: Gender, Knowledge and Global Change*, Cambridge: Polity Press.

CODESRIA (2012), *Strategic Plan, 2012–2016*, www.codesria.org/IMG/pdf/codesria_strategic-plan_2012-2016.pdf, accessed 12 March 2016.

——— (2014), *CODESRIA Launches a New Programme: African Diaspora Support to African Universities*, www.codesria.org/spip.php?article2175, accessed 12 March 2016.

Depelchin, Jacques (2005), *Silences in African History: Between the Syndromes of Discovery and Abolition*, Dar es Salaam: Mkuki na Nyota Publishers.

Fanon, Frantz (2004), *The Wretched of the Earth*, New York: Grove Press.

Gluckman, Max (1945), 'Seven-year Research Plan of the Rhodes-Livingstone Institute of Social Studies in British Central Africa', *Rhodes-Livingstone Journal*, 4: 1–32.

Grosskopf, Johann F.W., Raymond W. Wilcocks, Ernst G. Malherbe, E.R. Mimie, W.A. Murray and J.R. Albertyn (1932), *The Poor White Problem in South Africa: Report of the Carnegie Commission*, Stellenbosch: Proecclesia-Drukkery.

Hendricks, Fred (2008), 'The Mafeje Affair: The University of Cape Town and Apartheid', *African Studies*, 67 (3): 423–51, doi:10.1080/00020180802505061

Hountondji, Paulin (1990), 'Scientific Dependence in Africa Today', *Research in African Literatures*, 21 (3): 5–15.

——— (2009), 'Knowledge of Africa, Knowledge by Africans: Two Perspectives on African Studies', *RCCS Annual Review*, 1, September: 1–11.

Jacobs, Sean and Jacob Mundy, eds (2009), 'Reflections on Mahmood Mamdani's "Lessons of Zimbabwe"', special issue of the *ACAS Bulletin*, No. 82, http://concernedafricascholars.org/docs/ acasbulletin82.pdf, accessed 12 March 2016.

Johnson, David (2015), 'Nigeria to Zimbabwe: Remembering Sam Moyo', *Pambazuka News*, 6 December: 754, http://pambazuka.org/en/category/features/96156, accessed 12 March 2016.

——— (2016), 'Mamdani, Moyo and "Deep Thinkers" on Zimbabwe', www.pambazuka.org/governance/mamdani-moyoand-%E2%80%98deep-thinkers%E2%80%99-zimbabwe, accessed 12 March 2016.

Kincaid, Jamaica (2000), *A Small Place*, New York: Farrar, Straus and Giroux.

Levy, Leah (1971), *The School of African Studies, UCT*, Cape Town: UCT Library.

Mamdani, Mahmood (2003), 'Lessons of Zimbabwe', *London Review of Books*, 30 (23): 17–21.

——— (2007), *Scholars in the Marketplace: The Dilemmas of Neo-Liberal Reform at Makerere University, 1989–2005*, Dakar: CODESRIA.

Mamdani, Mahmood, ed. (1993), *The Intelligentsia, the State and Social Movements in Africa*, Dakar: CODESRIA.

Martin, William G. (2011), 'The Rise of African Studies (USA) and the Transnational Study of Africa', *African Studies Review*, 54 (1): 59–83, doi:10.1353/ arw.2011.0003

Martin, William G. and Brendan Innis McQuade (2014), 'Militarizing – And Marginalizing? – African Studies USA', *Review of African Political Economy*, 41 (141): 1–17.

Martin, William G. and Michael O. West (1999), *Out of One, Many Africas: Reconstructing the Study and Meaning of Africa*, Urbana, IL: University of Illinois Press.

Matambanadzo, Bella (2015), 'An Ode in Memory of Chimusoro Sam Moyo', *CODESRIA Bulletin*, 3–4: 11.

Mbalibulha, Stanley Baluku Bakahinga (2014), 'The history of Makerere Institute of Social Research (MISR) and Her Place in the Study of the Social Sciences in Africa', *Journal of Higher Education in Africa*, 11 (1–2): 121–42.

Mbembe, Achille (2015), 'Decolonizing Knowledge and the Question of the Archive', http://wiser.wits.ac.za/system/files/ Achille%20Mbembe%20-%20Decolonizing%20

Knowledge%20and%20the%20Question%20of%20the%20Archive.pdf, accessed 12 March 2016.
Mkandawire, Thandika (2005), 'African Intellectuals and Nationalism', in T. Mkandawire, ed., *African Intellectuals: Rethinking Politics, Language, Gender and Development: Africa in the New Millennium*, London and Dakar: Zed Books and CODESRIA: 10–35.
——— (2011), 'Running while Others Walk: Knowledge and the Challenge of Africa's Development' *Africa Development*, 36 (2): 1–36.
Mkandawire, Thandika and Charles C. Soludo (1999), *Our Continent, Our Future: African Perspectives on Structural Adjustment*, Trenton, NJ: Africa World.
Moyo, Sam, Praveen Jha and Paris Yeros (2013), 'The classical agrarian question: Myth, reality and relevance today', *Agrarian South: Journal of Political Economy*, 2 (1): 93–119, doi:10.1177/2277976013477224
Moyo, Sam and Paris Yeros (2007), 'Intervention: The Zimbabwe Question and the Two Lefts', *Historical Materialism*, 15 (3): 171–204, doi:10.1163/ 156920607X225924
Ndlovu-Gatsheni, Sabelo J. (2013), *Coloniality of Power in Postcolonial Africa: Myths of decolonization*, Dakar: CODESRIA.
Ochwada, Hannington (1996), 'African Studies: A Re-Assessment of Academic Tourism since 1960', *Africa Development*, 21 (4): 123–40.
Raftopoulos, Brian (2006), 'The Zimbabwean Crisis and the Challenges for the Left', *Journal of Southern African Studies*, 32 (2): 203–19.
Ranger, Terence (2005), 'The Uses and Abuses of History in Zimbabwe', in Mai Palmberg and Ranka Primorac, eds, *Skinning the Skunk – Facing Zimbabwean Futures*, Uppsala: Nordiska Afrikainstitutet: 7–15.
Richards, Audrey (1951), 'East African Institute of Social Research', *Sudan Notes and Records*, 32 (1): 151–53.
Schmitt, Jason (2014), 'Academic Journals: The Most Profitable Obsolete Technology in History', *Huffington Post*, 23 December, www.huffingtonpost.com/jason-schmitt/academic-journals-themos_1_b_6368204.html, accessed 12 March 2016
Shivji, Issa G. (2007), *Silences in NGO Discourse: The Role and Future of NGOs in Africa*, Nairobi: Fahamu.
Tadesse, Zenebework (1999), 'From Euphoria to Gloom? Navigating the Murky Waters of African Academic Institutions', in William G. Martin and Michael O. West, eds, *Out of One, Many Africas: Restructuring the Study and Meaning of Africa*, Urbana, IL: University of Illinois Press: 145–54.
Tembo, Alfred (n.d.), 'The Rhodes-Livingstone Institute and Interdisciplinary Research in Northern Rhodesia (Zambia), 1937–1964', *Strategic Review for Southern Africa*, 36 (1): 90–99.
van der Merwe, Nikolaas (1979), 'African Studies', in Alan Lennox-Short and David Welsh, eds, *UCT at 150*, Cape Town: David Philip: 62–66.
Wallerstein, Immanuel (1974), *The Modern World-System*, New York: Academic Press.
West, Michael O. (2002), 'Like a River: The Million Man March and the Black Nationalist Tradition in the United States', *Journal of Historical Sociology*, 12 (1): 81–100, doi:10.1111/1467-6443.00081
Wilson, Godfrey (1937), 'Memorandum to the Trustees of the Rhodes-Livinstone Institute, 7 November 1937', UCT Archives, BC880, B 4.11, Correspondence, Rhodes Livingstone Institute.
Wiredu, Kwasi (1998), 'Toward Decolonizing African Philosophy and Religion', *African Studies Quarterly*, 1 (4): 17–46.
Zeleza, Tiyambe (1983), 'African History: The Rise and Decline of Academic Tourism', *Ufahamau*, 13 (1), 9–42.
——— (1997), *Manufacturing African Studies and Crises*, Dakar: CODESRIA.

4

Working with Sam Moyo, An African Voice from the South

Gladys T. Lechini

I met Sam Moyo in Buenos Aires in September 2002, on the occasion of a conference organized by the Latin American Council of Social Sciences (CLACSO), 'New Challenges in Peace and Conflict Studies: What Role for the Third World'. More than twenty scholars from the South – from countries of Asia, Africa and Latin America – gathered in Argentina to discuss South–South cooperation. The consultative process was anchored in the leading social science research networks based in the three regions, and it involved CLACSO, the Council for the Development of Social Science Research in Africa (CODESRIA), the African Association of Political Science (AAPS), the Organization for Social Science Research in Eastern and Southern Africa (OSSREA), the Asian Political and International Studies Association (APISA), and the Southeast Asian Conflict Studies Network (SEACSN).

At that time, Sam had created the African Institute for Agrarian Studies (AIAS) in Harare, and was its first executive director. He was also vice president of CODESRIA. I was professor of international relations at the National University of Rosario, Argentina, and a researcher at the National Council of Scientific and Technical Research (CONICET) on issues related to South–South cooperation and international politics of Latin America and Africa.

For both of us, as well as for the scholars attending the seminar coming from the South, 'the South' was a comprehensive and elusive concept. It comprised a group of developing countries belonging to the periphery which shared similar situations of vulnerability and similar challenges. The idea of being colonized, of having been the object of colonization, of being 'the other' was a subtle link, a common identification among all the participants seeking to cooperate, to increase mutual knowledge and to share intellectual agendas and experiences.

We also discovered that despite certain analogous situations, our countries did not constitute a homogeneous group, for they had their specificities: particular local contexts and different socio-economic, political and cultural characteristics, apart from the heritage deriving from diverse colonialist powers of the North. Our academic and personal exchanges were a reflection of our common, while also diverse, experiences and realities. Furthermore, they revealed a certain lack of knowledge of the other and sometimes wrong basic assumptions. At the same time, we discovered that we had walked parallel paths without being aware that horizontal cooperation could make a difference, if we could bring together our particular regional historical backgrounds.

Although almost everybody at that intercontinental meeting had some personal experiences of South–South cooperation, the relationship with the North–South axis, though asymmetrical, was to a certain extent daily bread. This could explain why we all agreed that South–South cooperation was neither natural nor spontaneous. Quite on the contrary, it rowed against the current. This recognition explained why it was so urgent and imperative to promote links amongst us and our academic institutions, to change this uncomfortable and unfair situation.

Within this context, one year later, on the occasion of CLACSO's General Assembly in October 2003, Sam and I met again in Havana. At that time, I was academic coordinator of CLACSO's South–South programme. A special retreat was organized to outline the collaborative principles that could be adopted to advance with cooperation. In Cuba, we had more time to share and exchange ideas and perceptions concerning the 'South' and our respective regions through our participation in different workshops and panels, but mainly because Sam in the name of CODESRIA and I on behalf of CLACSO had to produce the draft of a new comprehensive programme on trilateral South–South cooperation, to be presented to the donors attending the Assembly.

We both agreed that South–South cooperation referred to a political cooperation aimed at strengthening bilateral relations between countries in the periphery and at building coalitions in multilateral fora so as to gain power to negotiate together in favour of our own interests. At the hard core is the belief in the possibility of building up a cooperative consciousness to face common problems through gaining wider margins of manoeuvre. South–South cooperation is a political construction that, because of its nature and main assumptions, requires a certain type of likemindedness.

Sam created a particular synergy with people around, with his clear ideas and strong beliefs. *La lucha continúa* (the struggle continues) was a phrase he repeated in Spanish each time he was with Latin American colleagues, to show his strong desire for change at the domestic and global levels and his endless fight against colonialism, neo-colonialism and imperialism.

The encounter in Havana was the beginning of a strong and enriching friendship, and an intellectual challenge, as we shared the same academic interests, philosophical points of view and concern for the people of our regions. This meeting was also the seed of the above-mentioned programme on South–South cooperation through which we worked together for about five years. The basic objective was to reorient the theoretical and methodological frameworks of the dominant development discourses and improve the organization of Southern research infrastructures.

On the one hand, there was awareness of the increasing dissatisfaction with mainstream social sciences due to their incapacity to contribute towards explaining and proposing solutions to enduring social problems in the South. The Gulbenkian Report in 1996, emphasizing the need to reorient the social sciences in general and to foster cooperative efforts between the North and South, was seen as an important landmark. Consequently, since the year 2000, a series of consultations to initiate and improve coordination between scholars in the South has been launched with the participation of key research networks in the three regions.

On the other hand, some factors were detected to explain the lack of connections among scholars in the South: isolation, lack of resources and knowledge of each other's academic production; the existence of different traditions of intellectual work, which are not always easy to coordinate; limited capacity to make visible the research output at the international level; weak multilingual communication and dissemination infrastructures; and last but not least, the importance of a long-established tradition of an asymmetrical relationship between the North and the South, whereby the former provides the theoretical and methodological orientations and the latter supplies the raw data. Although there were common global socio-political trends present in Latin America, Africa and Asia, the efforts were dispersed, and there was an urgent need to organize inter-regional academic spaces to discuss local, regional and global problems as seen from the South.

Sam had sound experience in preparing and writing projects, and I learnt a lot from interacting with him and working elbow to elbow. For me, it was a foundational moment to assist and participate in the renaissance of a new period of academic cooperation between scholars of the South, channelled through relevant institutions of the three regions with support led by the Swedish International Development Cooperation Agency (SIDA), and with full respect for the research agenda developed in the South. It meant to put theory into practice and see how it worked.

The issues arising from Havana were structured in a multi-year project named 'The Africa–Asia–Latin America Scholarly Collaborative Program', and were presented in December 2003 in Dakar, within the framework of a *grande-finale* conference and celebration of the thirtieth anniversary of CODESRIA. The main drivers were CLACSO and CODESRIA under Atilio Boron and Adebayo Olukoshi, as secretaries of the respective organizations.

The objective of such a collaborative enterprise was to improve the production and dissemination of relevant knowledge in the South – by means of various joint academic activities – and to create an authoritative Southern voice in international scholarly and policy debates on critical issues. The purpose was to enable scholars from across the South to engage in a joint reflection on three broad issues that were considered to be central to their regions: democracy, social movements and governance in the South; rethinking development at the national, regional and global levels; and international hegemony and the countries of the South.

Although no single, regionally undifferentiated 'Southern' viewpoint exists, the profound intellectual meaning of this project was to pull together and synthesize the diverse 'culturally' grounded outlooks and experiences in the South, so as to develop insights and perspectives relevant to the concerns of our countries. At every turn in this project, efforts were made to apply a holistic approach to capture the political, economic, social and cultural components of the different issues that were covered, and doing so with attention to history and context.

The basic activities of the South–South collaborative programme included: (i) the adequate handling of research activities involving social scientists in the various countries of the three regions; (ii) the organization of international conferences, workshops and summer institutes; (iii) the publication of books and papers, and the translation of the resulting body of literature into languages relevant to the scientific and policy communities in the various regions.

During the first phase of the project (2004–07), when I worked closely with Sam, comparative research and international conferences were held with the presentation of grounded analytical papers. This material – related to the three main research themes above and focusing on a specific sub-theme – was then discussed at three international conferences, one in each continent every year. Meetings were held in Cairo, Caracas, Kuala Lumpur, Dakar, Costa Rica, Accra and Saigon, among others.

One summer institute was implemented each year – in Havana (2005), Dakar (2006) and Kuala Lumpur (2007) – to train younger scholars on diverse Southern perspectives and to expose them to varied contexts, thus enabling them to overcome the narrowness of local discourses and scientific practices. Conference proceedings were published in book form, monographs or special issues, and electronic dissemination of selected papers was promoted through tailormade websites.

In the meantime, CLACSO translated and published several of Sam Moyo's works, such as the one he co-edited with Paris Yeros, *Reclaiming the Land: The Resurgence of Rural Movements in Africa, Asia and Latin America* (*Recuperando La Tierra: El Resurgimiento de Movimientos Rurales en África, Asia y América Latina*, Buenos Aires, 2008). Two years earlier, and as a result of an international conference, Atilio Boron and I had co-edited a book titled *Politics and Social Movements in an Hegemonic World* – with a Spanish and an English edition, published by CLACSO in 2006 – to which Sam contributed a chapter, 'The Land Question and the Peasantry in Southern Africa'.

Amidst this intellectual euphoria and physical mobility of attending intercontinental seminars, Sam and I met frequently and shared precious time together, working on and planning the steps that followed, until I left CLACSO's South–South programme in 2008. We last met in 2007, in Belo Horizonte, Brazil, at the Catholic University of Minas Gerais (PUC Minas), on the occasion of the organization of a new book, *Reclaiming the Nation: The Return of the National Question in Africa, Asia and Latin America*, which Sam co-edited with Paris Yeros, published in 2011.

I found Sam's spirit and soul in November 2016, when I was lecturing in New Delhi. There I met Professor Archana Prasad, director of the Centre for Informal Sector and Labour Studies at Jawaharlal Nehru University, who had received the sad news of the car accident, and we shared our sorrow for his early demise.

This is my humble tribute to a great friend and an outstanding scholar. As a friend, he was a nice person, always smiling, ready to help others and enjoy life. As a colleague and as an intellectual, he was an icon on issues related to political economy, and to land and agrarian studies in Africa. He will always be with us through his work and intellectual legacy.

5

The Agrarian Question of Gendered Labour in Sam Moyo's Scholarship

Lyn Ossome

Agrarian Questions in the South

There is a poignant introductory paragraph in the editorial carried in the inaugural issue of *Agrarian South: Journal of Political Economy* – whose founding editor-in-chief was Sam Moyo – which clearly outlines a statement of the problem facing agrarian societies in transition today. It is worth citing it in its entirety as it frames with urgency the crisis of social reproduction in the global agrarian South, which this essay explores in relation to Moyo's work:

> [A]griculture and ecological sustainability have been the basis of all historical civilizations. This is no less true of our contemporary world system, despite the capitalist industrial, informational and biotechnological revolutions that have transformed agriculture and nature on a world scale. What is different in the contemporary world system, beyond its truly planetary scope and its necessary centre–periphery structure, is the range of functions that agriculture, land and other natural resources are called upon to perform. These extend from servicing the profit requirements of monopolistic firms and financial speculators to meeting planetary food needs, supplying raw materials, producing energy, releasing labour, absorbing carbon and providing space for industrial and service activities, as well as for the residential and reproductive imperatives of the world's population; this includes its poorest layers, that half of humanity *reduced to a labour reserve and reproduced largely by unwaged labour,* especially of women and children. (Editorial 2012: 1; emphasis added)

The debates of the Agrarian South Network over the course of a decade, preceded by earlier debates and scholarly interventions (Moyo and Yeros, eds 2005, 2011), have managed to recast debates about the global South in relation to the agrarian and national questions, and firmly in solidarity with the peasant path. Much of the earlier thinking on these questions has drawn lessons and insights from Zimbabwe's experience with land and agrarian reforms. The culmination of these debates is a trenchant critique of the industrialization myth, and the political and ideological limitations of the Eurocentric and economistic tendencies that have sustained it, not least within Marxian political economy. The critique appeared in an article in which Moyo, Jha and Yeros (2013) elaborated the social and political implications of setting aside the national question and its land and peasant components, which had in fact been the basis of the classical agrarian question. They laid out the basis for re-engagement with earlier debates that had been 'more organic to the peasant struggles of the Third World, for whom backwardness was seen as a dynamic process intrinsic to imperialism and industrialization as an aspect of a larger strategic objective: *national liberation*' (ibid.: 96; emphasis added).

Analysis of the character of peasant organizations that lead agrarian struggles has also been a core building block in Moyo's work. In his analytical framework, 'the social base of peasant organization, and their class- and gender-based identities, are critical for understanding the political economic basis of peasant household structuration at the micro and macro levels' (Moyo 2002: 11). His empirical studies of peasant organizations highlight the exclusion of poorer peasants, landless labourers and women from the development of project-based organizations, and, therefore, from the material benefits that could be derived from them, because they do not in the first place possess land, water rights or cash to finance their participation in projects. He considers, for instance, that those who do not produce commodity surpluses have tended not to be members of market associations. Interlocking memberships and leadership of peasant associations have thus tended to concentrate access to resources among a few, and therefore to provide the basis for class and social differentiation of the peasantry, rather than merely accentuate the different cultural and social identities of the peasantry (ibid.: 12).

A significant question arises in relation to the historical mission and capacity of peasant organizations to promote political and economic changes that are driven by their class vision rather than cultural interests: can peasant organizations pursue a national project for social justice or even a nationalist project to develop capitalist farming? The study by Moyo (2002) showed that the ethnographic basis of peasant leadership and its patriarchal grounding reproduced male dominance in peasant associations' leadership in general, and even encroached upon the leadership ranks of predominantly women's peasant organizations. Furthermore, women-based and women-dominated peasant organizations tended to be developed around the margins of the mainstream rural economic and political system, focusing on marginal income generation projects mostly initiated by the state, NGOs and donors. Few women's peasant organizations were found to have 'an articulated autonomous and empowering gender-sensitive or feminist ideology: [t]heir economic strategy tends not to be politically articulated' (ibid.: 13).

This concern with depoliticization of the 'fragments' of the nation retains centrality in Moyo's work and later emerges as key in their conceptualization of the national question, of which gender equity is a core dimension:

> The collapse of the Soviet Union and the exuberance of finance capital managed the unthinkable: to take the national question off the global agenda. . . . Yet, just as the national question would lose its economic thrust and its political bearings, the deeper organic forces of social change and resistance would build back up against parasitic development, racism and militarism, to demand all the unresolved issues of the past and more: participatory democracy, indigenous rights, racial equality, gender equality, agrarian reform, urban reform . . . sustainable development, control over natural resources, food sovereignty, the freedom to develop the forces of production on the basis of internal needs. . . . These are now the parameters of the new national question. (Moyo and Yeros, eds 2011: 11–12)

The path to national liberation was viewed as historically constrained by land monopolies that concentrated economic, political and economic power, and constrained the peasantry. The process of unleashing these forces raises a set of contemporary agrarian questions which both critique and move beyond the classical agrarian question (AQ) and its attendant burden of transition in the putative backwardness/industrialization axiom. The antithesis of the backwardness debate in relation to the South is that the AQ cannot but remain grounded in a critique of its relation with monopoly capital and its militarism, and its social, political and environmental consequences (ibid.: 98) that are fundamentally related to the necessity of *liberation*:

> The key difference between the AQs of industrialization and liberation is that the latter has articulated with unprecedented clarity and conviction the requirement of *sovereign* industrialization, or the safeguarding of the capacity to determine one's own external relations and

> internal balances. Moreover, by its very logic, it has enabled the posing of new agrarian questions in a universal way, namely gender equity and ecological sustainability – these being the dimensions that have most defined the contemporary AQ – as well as the incipient debate on 'regional integration'. Thus, the AQ of liberation has been the common thread between the classical and contemporary AQs . . . [N]either gender equity, nor ecological sustainability, nor autonomous regional integration can be expected to progress under the tutelage of monopoly capitalism. (Ibid.: 103–04; emphasis in original)

This essay focuses on the development and various elaborations of the question of gender equity in Moyo's work, and its culmination as an AQ (as outlined above). I begin below by examining this evolution conceptually (though not genealogically), and mainly through a conceptual framework that is extensively debated within and in reference to Sam's work – that of semi-proletarianization. Here, I also locate the conceptual development of the gendered labour question within the social and political context of rural land struggles through which the question of gender equity also encounters its sharpest contraction, located within the peasantry. Lastly, I briefly outline the contours of feminist scholarship within the aegis of the *Agrarian South* school and, more broadly, elaborated as the agrarian question of gendered labour (Mbilinyi 2016; Tsikata 2016; Prasad 2016; Naidu and Ossome 2016; Ossome and Naidu 2019). The concluding section is a summary and tribute in light of the legacy of Sam Moyo's agrarian scholarship and the significance of his theoretical praxis.

Conceptual/Theoretical Underpinnings of Gendered Labour

The concept of semi-proletarianization of agrarian labour finds extensive elaboration across Moyo's work. The semi-proletarian thesis in classical Marxist theory derives from an analysis of the separation of rural producers from land and the emergence of a class of 'free' wage labourers, which are considered the hallmarks of capitalist development. This assumption of full proletarianization was, however, shown to bear little semblance to reality. In Southern Africa, for instance, a system instead of circular migration between rural labour reserves and the urban capitalist sector produced a class of semi-proletarianized peasants whose livelihoods depended on a combination of wage and non-wage income sources (Zhan and Scully 2018; Arrighi 1970). This anomaly, Zhan and Scully (2018) point out, was elaborated through the semi-proletarian thesis, which argued that conditions in which rural households earn income from both farming and labour migration are in the best interests of capital because the non-wage agricultural income subsidizes part of the cost of labour reproduction, allowing employers to pay lower wages (Burawoy 1976; Meillassoux 1972; Wolpe 1972; Wallerstein 1983). However, beyond the internal workings of the colonial political economy, semi-proletarianization reflects, according to Wallerstein (1983) and Moyo and Yeros, eds (2005), uneven development in the capitalist world-system, with it being most prevalent in peripheral and semi-peripheral countries.

Inquiring into the socio-economic and political dynamics of underdevelopment in the course of neo-liberal restructuring, Moyo and Yeros (2005) find that socio-economically and contrary to dominant claims (see Bernstein 2004), 'the peasantry has not entirely "disappeared", but that semi-proletarianization has continued to absorb the costs of social reproduction, as these have been systematically expelled by capitalism' (Moyo and Yeros, eds 2005: 9; see also Johnson 2004; Bryceson 2000). Their identification of a political question (later elaborated in a national question) inherent to semi-proletarianization – symptomatic of the disarticulated pattern of accumulation (Amin 1976; de Janvry 1981) – is a key departure from earlier theorizations, in that they consider that:

> the diversity of rural movements that have emerged share the same social basis in the semi-proletarianized peasantry, landless proletarians and urban unemployed [as] militant on land and agrarian reform, most often employing the land occupation tactic; and, in the most organized of cases . . . have become the leading forces of opposition to neoliberalism and the neo-colonial state . . . [T]the nucleus of anti-imperialist politics today . . . is to be found in the countrysides of the periphery. (Moyo and Yeros, eds 2005: 9)

In a recent significant study of long-term urban residents who combine proletarian and peasant forms of livelihood in the city (with no intention or desire to return to the countryside), Ricardo Jacobs (2018) confirms the political nature of land struggles, viewing the significance of land as not just a means of livelihood but as an object of political struggle. Alongside, semi-proletarianization has been the conceptual development of the notion of re-peasantization, an assertion that the peasant path is not only 'the central arc of struggles but also the bearer of the solution to contemporary economic, ecological and food crises (Moyo and Yeros, eds 2005; McMichael 2013, cited in Jacobs 2018: 887). Feminist agrarian scholars have complemented and critically extended these debates, elaborating the different dimensions of the gendered nature of semi-proletarianization and proletarianization in the context of agrarian transformation under neo-liberalism (Prasad 2016), and the ways in which gender inequity functions as a contradiction to the peasant path to agrarian transformation (Naidu and Ossome 2016). These latter sets of debates are elaborated below in the third section of this essay.

The feminist debates are driven by the question of exploitative labour relations that produce impoverished worker and peasant households, for whose sustenance land or wages alone are insufficient. This leads, in turn, to conditions of exploitation and self-exploitation by rural reproducers whose labour depends on continued access to land, and who become, under these immiserating conditions, the primary subjects of land and agrarian reforms. This may be presented as a broader structural question: from where does the motive force for agrarian reform and land redistribution emerge? To the extent that semi-proletarianization at its core implies a reproduction deficit, or crisis of social reproduction, or the 'reproductive limits' of 'nature, the current system of agriculture, and historical capitalism' (*Agrarian South*, Editorial 2012: 1), how might it be posed as a gender question in the trajectory of agrarian transformation – that is, in relation to the 'reproductive limits' of capitalism?

Locating the semi-proletarianization thesis in the feminist analysis of agrarian households and gendered labour is further possible through its conceptual framing in relation to the issues that necessitate social reproduction under capitalism. Dickinson and Russell (1986), using Marxian methodology, outline the social and economic dimensions of the social reproduction process as such. Each mode of production has within it a distinctive mode for the reproduction of labour power, and under capitalism, the social reproduction process is importantly and distinctively shaped by the special qualities of labour power itself. First, of all the commodities appearing in the marketplace, labour power is the only commodity that is inseparable from its human agency, and due to this embodiment, it can never fully be alienated from its seller. Productive consumption is as such a central concern to the labourer: labour power actively resists its own consumption (ibid.). The second peculiarity is expressed in the relative indeterminateness of the value of labour power; that is, the social and historical element which enters into the constitution of its value. The working class is reproduced at a socially and historically established standard of living, with the possibility of incorporating new needs, undoing old ones and changing the value of labour (ibid.). The third peculiarity of labour power is that it is the only commodity that itself cannot be produced capitalistically, that is, on the basis of wage labour and extraction of surplus value: there are no capitalist enterprises and no portion of total social capital devoted to, and which specialize in, the production of the living labourer whose capacity to labour is then purchased as an input to the manufacture of other commodities. It is unique in that, of all commodities under developed capitalism, its production and reproduction is antithetical to capitalist forms of organization, and as such remains external to the sphere of surplus value production. This peculiarity establishes the radical separation in modern capitalism of the sphere of production of commodities from the sphere of reproduction of labour power. This separation is grounded in the distinction between productive and individual consumption, both of which are carried out by the labourer in different social locations with vastly different consequences (ibid.).

It is thus in the reproductive sphere where the worker 'belongs to himself' that 'he performs his necessary vital functions outside of production' (Marx 2011: 625–26). Capital is therefore forced to rely on the working class undertaking something that cannot be included under commodity production proper, but is nevertheless vital to it. Given capitalism's structural features, reproduction of labour power is externalized into a variety of historically specific, putatively non-capitalist institutions and agencies. The household, in its patterns of infinite consumption, forms the social locus of individual consumption involving constant acquisition, transformation, consumption and, hence, annihilation of the necessities of life. The separation of economy and household, of productive and individual consumption, coupled with the mediation of reproduction through labour markets, establishes severe contradictions and tensions between these two locations of the proletariat.

Accumulation is dependent on the supply and regeneration of labour, while the maintenance of the household is dependent on the capacity of the economy to generate employment opportunities and wages at levels which allow for individual consumption. Apart from the market (realm of productive consumption) and the family/household (where exchange values are converted to use values), sensitivity to the fractures, limitations and asymmetrical dependencies possible between economy and households foreground another major reproductive institution in contemporary society – the state and its social policies. It is in the latter that processes of land and agrarian transformation find concrete expression in feminist political economy analyses of the state in relation to the crisis of social reproduction. This is partly a critique of the neo-classical assumption of separation of spheres – of the public/private, household/state, production/reproduction – based on insights that state intervention into the household sphere is, in fact, historical. As Moyo, drawing on Mafeje, shows, the legal basis for the creation of private property and new systems of land allocation and land administration had already been established during the last decade of colonialism, leading to a partial ouster of the relatively egalitarian and socially grounded household lineage-based land tenure system (Moyo 2018).

The peasantry, then, whose persistence is in part explained as an incomplete agrarian transition under colonial capitalism, strides both countryside and urban industry, and compels a rearticulation of the AQ to the contradictions borne by its differentiation along lines of class, ethnicity, caste, generation and gender, produced by exploitative processes of capital accumulation. These differences, while empirically manifesting from below, were a core legacy of the colonial bifurcation of the state and its attendant identitarian legacies (Mamdani 1996) that redirected claims and distribution of resources along the fragmentations on which the colonial state had stabilized its rule, and which most African post-colonial states inherited wholesale, due to constraints imposed externally (imperialism and globalization) and internally in the process of consolidating a nationalist agenda. While racial discrimination in land ownership patterns had retreated to the domain of civil society (such as via the Africanization agenda), ethnicity and gender remained unresolved and firmly embedded within the customary domains where they had been shaped and instrumentalized by indirect rulership.

The questions of land, labour and the peasantry which preoccupy Moyo's work become, as already suggested, most pronounced when processes of social reproduction go into crisis. Colonial capitalism and its attendant labour question – that is, primitive accumulation and dispossession of the peasantry in order to compel it towards the service of colonial capitalist production – produce the land question in the colonies, albeit with different articulations between settler and non-settler countries. The magnitude of land and labour questions in the colonies, the extent to which they structurally altered those societies, were at the core determined by the extent of alienation of productive labour from its sources of reproduction, conditions of which invariably compelled the debates towards a resolution that measured inequality on the basis of failure to maximize productive forces requisite for industrialization. A significant body of left agrarian scholarship influenced the conceptual trajectory of this question in Moyo's work.

Mafeje's (1991) arguments, for instance, which rejected dominant liberal and neo-liberal Africanist and Eurocentric readings of the sources of Africa's failed agrarian transition, bore similarity to Moyo's intervention in the debates on land and labour relations, agrarian class formation processes, and the development of capitalist property relations. Through an ethnographic approach, Mafeje was able to shift analysis of agrarian production systems (of non-settler territories in Africa) downwards to account for land and labour relations in the smallest units of production, which, he argued, were not fundamentally altered by colonialism and capitalist penetration. His argument in this regard is that

> the absence of substantive forms of tributary modes of production, in most of precolonial Africa, as well as the failure of colonialism and capitalism to fully disrupt these pre-existing social formation, albeit their subjection to widespread political and economic domination, led to the persistence of autonomous household agricultural producers with full control over their land and labour. The exploitation of such households at the level of exchange had shaped the trajectory of limited accumulation in non-settler Africa. (Mafeje 1991, 2003, cited in Moyo 2018: 213)

The agency, access and control of land attributed to household economies of subsistence and petty-commodity production have, however, been a source of considerable debate (see Mamdani 1987; Mafeje 1999; Moyo 2003) regarding the relevance of the land question today. For Mamdani, like Mafeje, the land question is real but does not exist everywhere. Their argument, based on the existence and functioning of customary land tenure systems in most African countries, is that because the majority of peasants and small-scale farmers reside on customary land that is under state control with rights made through customary tenure arrangements, a large portion of the peasantry appears to be in efficient occupation of land. Moyo (2003), in a counter-argument, considers conflicts that continually reassert a land question, pointing to ongoing and persistent land wrangles and conflicts emanating from unequal access, control and use of land, and 'distortion of land tenure systems and agrarian class differentiation in the context of growing land concentration in customary tenure regimes', or Communal Areas (ibid.: 10). Moreover, he argues, the majority of poor peasants are still discriminated on grounds of gender, race, class, age and ethnicity. As such, the context of agrarian issues is critical and the key to understanding the nature and character of land issues in Africa, meaning that the land question should be perceived and comprehended in the context of uneven agrarian relations based upon one's ownership of land as a primary means of production and survival (Moyo 2003, 2007).

As such, Moyo (2018) concedes that, while the current scale of land alienation in non-settler Africa has indeed not led to extensive landlessness, let alone full-scale proletarianization, it nonetheless represents a diffuse but socially significant degree of land concentration which forebodes critical changes in agrarian relations despite the persistence of 'independent' household landholdings and production (Moyo 2018: 223). Thus, despite the fact that the land–property–wage labour relationship had not been universally extended throughout non-settler Africa, it has become evident that various forms of land inequalities and struggles over access to land are becoming politically significant enough to weaken the lineage-based household land tenure system (Moyo 2018; Moyo and Yeros, eds 2005). These concerns warranted Moyo's conclusion that 'a land question, *based upon unequal access to land and social marginalization* had emerged' (Moyo 2018: 223, emphasis added; Moyo 2008). Both these questions of access and marginalization are at the core of contemporary attempts to theorize gendered labour; that is, why the reproductive labour that is mainly (although not exclusively) performed by women remains unrecognized, unpaid, exploitative and self-exploitative, and removed from circuits (indeed the possibility) of accumulation. Is it possible to think of development on a national scale when underlying processes of production and reproduction are undermined by inequalities that present fundamental contradictions for the peasantry's march in revolutionary form?

The Agrarian Question of Gendered Labour

In a 2018 article on what they term 'agrarian Marxism', Levien, Watts and Hairong observe that much of the recent empirically grounded theorizing on social reproduction 'has been explicitly or implicitly situated within urban and post-industrial northern horizons, with comparatively little recent scholarship on the relationship between social reproduction and agrarian change in the South' (Levien, Watts and Hairong 2018: 872–73). This, of course, is a circumscribed view, given the foregoing debates which evidence an extended engagement with this issue through the social, political and economic dimensions of the agrarian question (AQ). Below, I deal with more contemporary interventions into the debate through scholarship that has unfolded primarily within the pages of the journal *Agrarian South*, and which attempts to develop a conceptual framing for what might be termed as an AQ of gendered labour. This, in articulation with other contemporary agrarian questions including land, ecology and regional integration, also constitutes the basis for ongoing debates on national sovereignty and liberation. Furthermore, as Tsikata (2016) notes, analyses of long-term processes of structural change benefit from engaging the literature on gender, land and agrarian issues, which spans decades of basic and policy research, and includes the gendered impacts of colonial and post-colonial land commercialization and tenure reforms, particularly on changing rules of access to land, and gendered processes which have deepened land concentration, the dispossession of smallholders, tenure insecurities and land conflicts in sub-Saharan Africa.

A question that any notion which claims to critique capitalism must grapple with is that of *accumulation*. The difficulty (for western feminists) in this regard arose from the orthodox left's acceptance of the capitalist division between private housework (reproductive work) and public productive (wage) work, and the challenge they posed to this division of labour and definitions of 'work' and 'non-work'. In the ensuing debates, feminists attempted to show that the housewife and her labour are not outside the process of surplus value production but constitute the very foundation upon which this process can begin (Dalla Costa and James 1972), and challenged the idea that women are only 'oppressed' – arguing that as capital is able to command the unpaid labour of the wife as well as the paid labour of the wage labourer, it is impossible to understand the exploitation of wage labour without understanding the exploitation of non-wage labour. It is one thing to claim an exploitative relationship between the household and capital, as earlier texts did. It is quite another to demonstrate 'beyond the instincts for self-preservation' (Marx 2011: 625–26) that labour power is socially produced through processes that impoverish women, alienate them and extract surplus value for the capitalist. The ineffectiveness of these earlier strategies against exploitation thus partly exposes the limits of its conceptual framing.[1] In other words, what is it that lends reproductive labour to the structural workings of capitalism? And, for our purposes in this essay, what is it that lends gendered labour to an agrarian question?

A number of questions might further be posed in this regard: what exactly are the gendered dimensions of the AQ? And what is the nature of exploitation of the surplus populace whose labour is increasingly irrelevant to capitalism, but which nonetheless retains centrality in the reproduction of capitalist forces of production? Women constitute a part of the surplus population, but are also still labourers. What does it mean to be both part of surplus labour yet integral to the reproduction of that surplus (Ossome and Naidu 2019)? Labour, in general, has been talked about as factory wage labour (the capital–labour relation). Domestic labour is not governed by the capital–wage relation but is nonetheless essential to it, even though on its own it may not be sufficient for the surplus population, which survives because of other forms of labour that continue to exist (petty-commodity production, peasant, domestic). The peasant farm in this regard continues to be integral, if not much more important in the past few decades (when it seemed that the main objective was to push everyone into capitalist forms of production). Labouring here is not to be understood (only) in the Marxian sense, but in terms of labouring to survive. The agrarian economy does not disappear, but is really intertwined with the capitalist sector. Furthermore, capitalism needs only a certain amount of unemployed labour, but we have much more than that. Because this population does not survive entirely on wages but brings in all of the other forms of labour, they continue to be integral to the understanding of the AQ. The reproduction of this surplus population exploits an existing structure of gender inequality and exploitation historically produced in the process of capitalist accumulation (ibid.). Maria Mies (2014: 177) similarly locates the relationship between national liberation and women's liberation in the existing international division of labour and its relation to a particular sexual division of labour.

Utsa Patnaik (2012) elaborates with clarity a structural framing of the problem, pointing to the 'reproductive limits' mentioned earlier. She critiques the 'absolute immiserization' that has accompanied the renewed dominance of finance capital and its attempt to control land, minerals, and other primary resources in the global South through the promotion of an economic 'discipline' of domestic fiscal contraction, free trade and free capital flows (Patnaik: 250–51). This new process of primitive accumulation and accompanying immiserization, she argues, does not simply signify greater inequality (ibid.): unlike the European colonizing migrant of yesteryear, today's displaced peasants and displaced workers of the South simply have nowhere to go. In the competition they face with capital over land and resources, they pose the question of sovereignty of food and natural resources. To us, then, the contemporary AQ of gendered labour necessarily addresses itself to Patnaik's (2012) elaboration of the limits of accumulation, and Mies's (2014) conceptualization of gendered labour, which she refers to as the 'last colony' for the accumulation process.

The prism of subsistence economies and the gendered labour regimes therein, which are highly predicated upon the free, exploitative and self-exploitative labour performed by rural women on a daily and generational basis, present the peasantry as a contradictory social force in the course of agrarian transformation processes in the South. Even when gender is taken into account (normatively, through guarantees of women's rights to land), this incorporation cannot proceed in isolation from the conditions of the global economy. That is, women might have land which they do not actually cultivate due to, for instance, insufficient support for agriculture and the failures or insufficiency of state provisioning. It may not be possible for women to escape the trap of poverty and immiseration simply because they have access to land. The failure to address the question of reproductive labour (the agrarian question of gendered labour) thus renders land reforms incomplete (Naidu and Ossome 2016: 70–71). Ultimately, there is a need to address the question of social reproduction in the process of land reforms. In this regard, we view the failure of land and agrarian reforms as critical to understanding not only capitalism's exploitative tendencies in relation to women's reproductive labour, but also, ironically, as a commentary on the continued relevance of land in the process of household reproduction (ibid.).

The question of addressing gender inequities in land and agrarian reforms is posed by feminists through their analysis of gendered labour, as a political question. The conceptual underpinnings of the AQ of gendered labour has been aided by the thinking that has gone into clarifying the political significance of the peasantry in the current conjuncture of our struggles against neoliberal capitalism. The significant insights drawn from analyses of land reforms, and the rearticulation of the classical agrarian question to account for issues such as gender, ecology and imperialism, are both historical legacies of capital's exploitative tendencies and contemporary questions that democratizing states must address in their claims for sovereignty. This reflects Shivji, who, in conversation with Sam Moyo, outlines some conceptual underpinnings which he insists we must deal with in a new, concrete situation: first, the category of 'the peasant', in its analytical and empirical dimensions; second, the relationship between the peasant question and the national question; third, the form and character of accumulation in the agrarian sector; and fourth, the social agency for transformation and forms of its organization (Shivji 2016: 158, and in this volume). The review of debates in this chapter has attempted to bring to life the broad, if still rudimentary, dimension of an AQ of gendered labour, by highlighting the contributions to these foregoing concerns in relation to the scholarship and theoretical praxis of Sam Moyo, who, until the very end, remained committed to the liberation of African people.

Conclusion

Sam Moyo, like many of his contemporaries, rejected economic determinism and sought to understand Africa's development trajectory on the basis of its own historical terms; hence his ability to reassert the continued relevance of an agrarian question in much of the global South. By critiquing the linear-stagist classical trajectory of capitalist development, this contemporary assertion of an AQ allows us to pose in new ways the unresolved questions of land, gender equity and ecological sustainability. Just as significantly, the works of Moyo, his collaborators and interlocutors have created conceptual and analytical space for feminist agrarian scholars of the South to move beyond the social/cultural and economic concern with questions of household labour, towards a broader articulation that merges with the major political questions of our time – that of national sovereignty as the basis of the unfinished business of liberation. Without a doubt, my own collaborative work on the AQ of gendered labour has found its greatest expression in the course of sustained debates with fellow comrades in the tri-continental alliance of the Agrarian South Network, in whose founding more than a decade ago, Sam Moyo and his visionary scholarship was instrumental.

Note

1 For instance, Mies (1986) writes that, as a strategy to overthrow capitalism, the 'Wages for Housework' campaign was launched in 1972. Many women in Europe and Canada were mobilized by this campaign, and a lively discussion took place about the prospects of this strategy. Eventually, the campaign petered out because several questions inherent in it could not be solved, such as: the problem that 'wages for housework' would not end the isolation and atomization of housewives; or that the total generalization of wage labour would not necessarily lead to an overthrow of capitalism but rather to a totalization of alienation and commodity production; or the question of who would pay the wages for housework: the capitalists, the state or the husband?

References

Amin, S. (1976), *Unequal Exchange,* translated by Brian Pearce, Brighton: Harvester.

Arrighi, G. (1970), 'International Corporations, Labor Aristocracies, and Economic Development in Tropical Africa', in R.I. Rhodes, ed., *Imperialism and Underdevelopment: A Reader,* New York and London: Monthly Review Press, 220–67.

Bernstein, H. (2004), 'Changing Before Our Very Eyes: Agrarian Questions and the Politics of Land in Capitalism Today', *Journal of Agrarian Change*, 4 (1–2): 190–225.

Bryceson, D.F. (2000), 'Peasant Theories and Smallholder Policies: Past and Present', in J.E. Mooij, D.F. Bryceson and C. Kay, eds, *Disappearing Peasantries? Rural Labour in Africa, Asia and Latin America*, London: Intermediate Technology Publications: 299–324.

Burawoy, M. (1976), 'The Functions and Reproduction of Migrant Labor: Comparative Material from Southern Africa and the United States,' *American Journal of Sociology*, 81 (5): 1050–87.

Dalla, C.M. and S. James (1972), *The Power of Women and the Subversion of the Community*, Bristol: Falling Wall Press.

de Janvry, A. (1981), *The Agrarian Question and Reformism in Latin America*, Baltimore, MD and London: Johns Hopkins University Press.

Dickinson, J. and B. Rusell (1986), 'Introduction: The Structure of Reproduction in Capitalist Societies', in J. Dickinson and B. Russell, eds, *Family, Economy and The State: Social Reproduction under Capitalism*, New York: St. Martin's Press: 1–20.

Editorial (2012), 'The Agrarian Question: Past, Present and Future', *Agrarian South: Journal of Political Economy*, 1 (1): 1–10.

Jacobs, R. (2018), 'An Urban Proletariat with Peasant Characteristics: Land Occupation and Livestock Raising in South Africa', *The Journal of Peasant Studies*, 45 (5–6): 884–903.

Johnson, H. (2004), 'Subsistence and Control: The Persistence of the Peasantry in the Developing World', *Undercurrent*, 1 (1): 55–65.

Levien, M., M. Watts and Y. Hairong (2018), 'Agrarian Marxism', *The Journal of Peasant Studies,* 45 (5–6): 853–83.

Mafeje, A. (1991), 'African Households and Prospects for Agricultural Revival in sub-Saharan Africa', CODESRIA Working Paper No. 1/91, Dakar.

——— (1999), 'Imperatives and Options for Agricultural Development in Africa: Peasant or Capitalist Revolution?', unpublished.

——— (2003), 'The Agrarian Question, Access to Land and Peasant Responses in sub-Saharan Africa, UNRISD Civil Society and Social Movements Programme Paper No. 5.

Mamdani, M. (1987), 'Extreme but Not Exceptional: Towards an Analysis of the Agrarian Question in Uganda,' *Journal of Peasant Studies,* 14 (2): 195–225.

——— (1996), *Citizen and Subject: Contemporary Africa and the Legacy of Late Colonialism*, Princeton, NJ: Princeton University Press.

Mbilinyi, M. (2016), 'Debating Land and Agrarian Issues from a Gender Perspective', *Agrarian South: Journal of Political Economy*, 5 (2–3): 164–86.

McMichael, P. (2013), *Food Regimes and Agrarian Questions: Agrarian Change and Peasant Studies Series*, Halifax and Winnipeg: Fernwood Publishing.

Meillassoux, C. (1972), 'From Reproduction to Production,' *Economy and Society*, 1 (1): 93–105.

Mies, M. ([1986] 2014), *Patriarchy and Accumulation on a World Scale: Women in the International Division of Labour*, London: Zed Books.

Moyo, S. (2002), 'Peasant Organizations and Rural Civil Society in Africa: An Introduction', in M.B. Romdhane and S. Moyo, eds, *Peasant Organizations and the Democratization Process in Africa*, Dakar: CODESRIA: 1–26.

——— (2003), 'The Land Question in Africa: Research Perspectives and Questions', paper presented at CODESRIA conference on 'Land Reform, the Agrarian Question and Nationalism' in Gaborone, Botswana, 18–19 October 2003 and Dakar, Senegal, 8–11 December 2003.

——— (2007), 'The Land Question in Southern Africa: A Comparative Review', in L. Ntsebeza and R. Hall, eds, *The Land Question in South Africa: The Challenge of Transformation and Redistribution*, Cape Town: Human Sciences Research Council Press: 60–84.

——— (2008), 'African Land Questions, Agrarian Transitions and the State: Contradictions of Neoliberal Land Reforms', *CODESRIA Green Book Series*, Dakar: CODESRIA.

——— (2018), 'Debating the African Land Question with Archie Mafeje', *Agrarian South: Journal of Political Economy*, 7 (2): 211–33.

Moyo, S. and P. Yeros, eds (2005), *Reclaiming the Land: The Resurgence of Rural Movements in Africa, Asia and Latin America*, London: Zed Books.

——— (2011), *Reclaiming the Nation: The Return of the National Question in Africa, Asia and Latin America*, London: Pluto Press.

Moyo, S., P. Jha and P. Yeros (2013), 'The Classical Agrarian Question: Myth, Reality and Relevance Today', *Agrarian South: Journal of Political Economy*, 2 (1): 93–119.

Naidu, S. and L. Ossome (2016), 'Social Reproduction and the Agrarian Question of Women's Labour in India', *Agrarian South: Journal of Political Economy*, 5 (1): 50–76.

Ossome, L. and S. Naidu (2019), 'The Agrarian Question of Gendered Labour,' in P. Jha, W. Chambati and L. Ossome, eds, *Labour Questions in the Global South*, New Delhi: Springer.

Patnaik, U. (2012), 'Some Aspects of the Contemporary Agrarian Question', *Agrarian South: Journal of Political Economy,* 1 (3): 233–54.

Prasad, A. (2016), 'Adivasi Women, Agrarian Change and Forms of Labour in Neo-Liberal India', *Agrarian South: Journal of Political Economy*, 5 (1): 20–49.

Shivji, I. (2016), 'In Conversation with Sam', *Agrarian South: Journal of Political Economy*, 5 (2–3): 158–63.

Shivji, I.G., S. Moyo, W. Ncube and D. Gunby (1998), 'Draft National Land Policy for the Government of Zimbabwe', Discussion Paper, Harare: FAO and Ministry of Lands and Agriculture.

Tsikata, D. (2016), 'Gender, Land Tenure and Agrarian Production Systems in Sub-Saharan Africa', *Agrarian South: Journal of Political Economy*, 5 (1), 1–19.

Wallerstein, I. (1983), *Historical Capitalism*. London: Verso.

Wolpe, H. (1972), 'Capitalism and Cheap Labour-Power in South Africa: From Segregation to Apartheid,' *Economy and Society*, 1 (4): 425–56.

Zhan, S. and B. Scully (2018), 'From South Africa to China: land, migrant labour and the semi-proletarian thesis revisited', *The Journal of Peasant Studies*, 45 (5–6): 1018–38.

6

Livelihoods, Land and Political Economy

Reflections on Sam Moyo's Research Methodology

Ian Scoones

Why Methods Matter

Sam Moyo is best known as an agrarian political economist with major contributions on the land issue in Zimbabwe and, more broadly, post-colonial agrarian change. Having been trained as a geographer, he also spent considerable time focusing on environmental issues. This combination is important when reflecting on his massively important contributions and, in particular, his methodological approach. Throughout his life's work, Sam combined wider theorization of the structural political economy features of agrarian change with on-the-ground empirical studies, examining the differentiated practices and processes in agrarian settings. His focus ranged from detailed studies of livelihoods, farming practice and agricultural production, to land use and environmental change, to historically informed interpretations of political dynamics. The scope, breadth and impact of his work are highly impressive.

In this essay, I want to focus on the methodological lessons that we can learn from Sam's scholarship. I want to argue that the combination of detailed empirical investigation, deep knowledge of the technical and practical aspects of agricultural production and farming livelihoods, and big picture political economy analysis with wider theorization is especially important, as this reflects a tradition in political economy that goes back to Karl Marx's original discussion of method in the *Grundrisse* (Marx 1973). Such an approach is often lost in many contemporary applications, which fail to sustain the important tension and dialectical debate between diverse empirical realities and wider theorization of the emergent processes of change. In looking back on Sam's work, I argue that we can learn a lot from his applications, in ways that will continue to be important for new generations of scholars and activists eager to engage with the legacy of his work.

The next section of this essay lays out, selectively, Sam's research career and briefly traces his methodological journey over several decades. This highlights the move from geography and environmental studies to agrarian political economy, and how a productive conversation emerged between different disciplinary perspectives. The subsequent section reflects on method in political economy, drawing in particular on Marx's explications in the *Grundrisse* and Stuart Hall's interpretations of these (Hall 2003). I suggest that Sam's work offers a fine example of the application of these ideas in practice. The final two sections talk about some examples from Sam's work on Zimbabwe's land reform, highlighting the power of such a methodological stance and how it throws up debates about both interpretation and political action.

In the conclusion, I attempt to summarize my interpretation of Sam's methodological approach to agrarian political economy, arguing that deep engagement in particular contexts, when combined with wider theorization around political implications, provides both an analytically rigorous approach and an opportunity for political positioning, in ways that combines evidence with action. Sam not only was robust and thorough in his theorization, collection of empirical data and wider analysis, but also was engaged as a critical activist-scholar in struggles that have not disappeared with his passing. Future generations of scholar-activists engaged in land and agrarian struggles in Africa and beyond would do well to reflect on Sam's methodological approach, learn from it and extend it to new contexts.

Tracing a Methodological Journey

Sam started out as a geographer with a keen interest in environmental issues. His undergraduate studies were at Njala University College at the University of Sierra Leone. He graduated in 1976 with a BA in education and geography. He went on to get an MA in geography from the University of Western Ontario in Canada in 1979.[1] Returning to Zimbabwe after independence, he worked at the Zimbabwe Institute for Development Studies (ZIDS), conducting research on a range of topics linked to land and rural development, and publishing an important paper in 1984 on land use and productivity (Moyo *et al.* 1984). Based on his growing body of work on land reforms in Zimbabwe, he did a PhD in rural development and environmental management at the University of Northumbria in the United Kingdom, graduating in 1994.

Working with the Zimbabwe Environment Research Organization

(ZERO), he published on a range of environmental themes (Moyo *et al.* 1991; Moyo, O'Keefe and Middleton 1993; Moyo, O'Keefe and Sill 1993). His work on NGOs and social movements followed, situating his interest in the social dynamics of agrarian change (e.g., Moyo, Makumbe and Raftopolous 2000). By then, he had moved to the Southern Africa Political and Economic Series (SAPES) Trust and the Southern Africa Regional Institute for Policy Studies (SARIPS), where he became more immersed in political economy debates and analysis. Outside Zimbabwe, of course, his work with the Council for the Development of Social Science Research in Africa (CODESRIA) was influential, and in 2009 he became the Council's president.

Sam's classic book, *The Land Question in Zimbabwe*, published in the mid-1990s, was based substantially on his thesis work, combining detailed fieldwork with wider analysis of the land question (Moyo 1995). It was the first major work on land in many years since earlier classics reflecting on the colonial context (e.g., Palmer 1977). This set the terms for his subsequent work as well as the wider debate through the latter part of the 1990s, when he became increasingly engaged in the politics and policy of land in Zimbabwe (e.g., Moyo 1998, 2000a, 2000b). With the major land reform from 2000, Sam's work was in the spotlight and his views were widely sought. In this period, his scholarship perhaps best exemplified the approach highlighted in the introduction: his background in geography combined with wider theorization of political change following agrarian upheaval. There were heated debates among scholars on how to interpret the political transition of the early 2000s (e.g., Yeros 2002; Moore 2004; Raftopolous 2006; Moyo and Yeros 2007a, 2007b; among others), highlighting the fracturing of 'left' positions in this period. But beyond the somewhat rarefied discussions in the pages of *Historical Materialism* and elsewhere, Sam and his colleagues were also engaged in much more grounded, empirical work.

The major district-level study that was published in 2009 (Moyo *et al.* 2009) was set in place several years before, soon after the establishment of the African Institute for Agrarian Studies (AIAS) in 2002. This was a hugely important, large empirical survey of new land reform settlements across the country, and complemented work being done in particular regions (Scoones *et al.* 2010; Matondi 2012). At the same time, drawing on both his wider political economy analysis and this growing set of data, Sam worked on policy-oriented engagements, particularly with the World Bank, on the implications of the land reform for the agricultural sector (e.g., Moyo and Sukume 2006; Moyo and Binswanger 2011). This illustrated Sam's ability to span the worlds of theory and practice, making use of empirical data to forward important interpretations of change.

His in-depth evaluations of Zimbabwe's land reform appeared in print in a series of significant articles in *The Journal of Peasant Studies* and *Review of African Political Economy* (Moyo 2011a, 2011b, 2011c), each becoming a vital reference point and presenting extensive data combined with wider theorization. His edited book with Walter Chambati, *Land and Agrarian Reform in Zimbabwe: Beyond White Settler Capitalism* provided an opportunity to pull together in one place a broader array of works, much of it supported and supervised by Sam – and again this contribution soon became a classic (Moyo and Chambati 2013). The Zimbabwe case also, in turn, contributed to wider debates in agrarian studies about how to interpret the contemporary conjuncture, with Sam's insights underpinning important contributions to this journal (Moyo, Jha and Yeros 2012, 2013).

Over forty years, then, Sam's scholarship moved from one focused on land use and environmental change to one much more deeply inspired by Marxist political economy, allowing a nuanced and effective analysis of the fast-changing dynamics of agrarian challenges, particularly of Zimbabwe. I first engaged with Sam and his work in the late 1980s as I was starting out on my PhD in Zimbabwe. I had close contact with his work with ZERO, given our mutual interest in environmental issues. I commented on his thesis draft in the 1990s and learned much, but, like many, I was not engaged in a more fundamental debate about land until the 2000s, when radical shifts in the agrarian structure occurred and no one could ignore what was happening.

It was in this period that I learned much from Sam, and our debates about how to interpret what was happening became more intense. We both agreed and disagreed, and these discussions often, at root, reflected different methodological stances. Through Sam's influence, over time, we converged: I saw the importance of the wider political economy analysis that he advocated, while I insisted on retaining the located, site-specific approach to the analysis of people in places, which, because of his training in geography, he also appreciated. We both agreed fervently that detailed empirical information about what was happening, where and to whom was essential if a more mature debate on Zimbabwe's land reform was to evolve and inform both policy and public commentary, and we spent many hours sharing findings from our various studies.

Methods for Understanding the Political Economy of Agrarian Change

How, then, can we learn from Sam's work to think about methods for understanding the political economy of agrarian change? As already mentioned, a good starting point is Marx's treatise on method in political economy, the *Grundrisse* (Marx 1973). In order to understand the processes of agrarian change – production, consumption, reproduction, exchange, and the processes of accumulation, investment and social differentiation that follow – we must, following Henry Bernstein (2010), ask some fairly basic questions: who owns what, who does what with it, who gets what and what do they do with it? Answers to these empirical questions can then reveal wider interpretations of agrarian change and allow us to define categories and processes in relation to what is happening in particular places at particular times.

This is essentially the argument of Marx in the *Grundrisse*: that a critical political economy approach exposes the 'rich totality of many determinations and relations' and so exposes a 'concrete' understanding, which appears through iterations between conceptual abstractions and detailed empirical observation. '[T]he concrete is concrete because it is the concentration of many determinations, hence unity of the diverse' (Marx 1973: 100–01). To avoid 'a chaotic conception of the whole', a dialectical method is advocated. This, he states, moves

> analytically towards ever more simple concepts, from the imagined concrete towards ever thinner abstractions until I had arrived at the simplest determinations. From there, the journey would have to be retraced until I had finally arrived at the population again, but this time not as a chaotic conception of a whole, but as a rich totality of many determinations and relations. (Ibid.: 100)

According to Stuart Hall (2003: 118), in his interpretation of Marx's 1857 Introduction, 'to penetrate a structure as dense and overlaid with false representations as the capitalist mode of production, we need concepts more fundamentally dialectical in character'. Hall continues:

> [T]he concept of a 'differentiated unity' is a methodological and theoretical key to this text, and to Marx's method as a whole. This means that, in the examination of any phenomenon or relation, we must comprehend *both* its internal structure – what it is in its differentiatedness – as well as those other structures to which it is coupled and with which it forms some more inclusive totality. Both the specificities and the connections – the complex unities of structures – have to be demonstrated by the concrete analysis of concrete relations and conjunctions. If relations are mutually articulated, but remain specified by their difference, this articulation, and the determinate conditions on which it rests, has to be demonstrated. It cannot be conjured out of thin air according to some essentialist dialectical law. Differentiated unities are also therefore,

> in the Marxian sense, *concrete*. The method thus retains the concrete empirical reference as a privileged and undissolved 'moment' within a theoretical analysis without thereby making it 'empiricist': the concrete analysis of concrete situations. (Ibid.: 127; emphasis in original)

How, then, does such a method for political economy operate, combining an empirical stance with a theorization of 'the concrete', the result of multiple determinations and relations? According to Marx, 'the abstract determinations lead towards a reproduction of the concrete by way of thought' (quoted in ibid.: 129). Hall explains, 'thought accomplishes such a clarification by decomposing simple, unified categories into the real, contradictory, antagonistic relations which compose them' (ibid.). He continues, 'Marx's "historical epistemology," then, maps the mutual articulation of historical movement and theoretical reflection, not as a simple identity but as differentiations within a unity' (ibid.: 137). Hall, in turn, argues that: 'Marx's method depends on identifying two dialectically related but discontinuous levels: the contradictory, antagonistic "real relations" which sustain the reproductive processes of capitalism and the "phenomenal forms" in which the contradictions appear as "equalized"' (ibid: 140). This, he states, '*not only* lays bare the "real relations" behind their "phenomenal forms" but does so in a way which *also* reveals as a contradictory and antagonistic necessary content what, on the surface of the system, appears only as a "phenomenal form"' (ibid: 141; emphasis in original).

While presented in somewhat abstract terms, I would argue that this was exactly Sam's methodological stance. He was no 'vulgar' political economist, only interested in deterministic, historical 'laws', nor a simplistic 'structuralist', uninterested in the 'multiple determinations and relations' of complex realities. He was always interested in exactly the sophisticated dialectic that Marx describes, and which Hall interprets as the core feature of method in political economy. Such an approach to political economy allows for engagement with the diversity of livelihood strategies, production practices and social arrangements across sites, while at the same time understanding longer-term livelihood trajectories and their structural conditioning and shaping. It also focuses attention on the political and economic alliances being forged between different classes, and so the structuring of the wider political economy.

As Henry Bernstein (2010: 209) argues, a movement between the specifics of diverse livelihood contexts and the wider 'abstractions and tendencies' associated with a relational and dynamic understanding of class offer vital insights into longer-term processes of social differentiation and agrarian change. This, in turn, must include perspectives on gender, ethnicity and other dimensions of difference often missed out in classical Marxist analysis. It was this combination of approaches that made Sam's work so powerful and his scholarship so impressive, and, as already argued, emerged from his cross-disciplinary engagements in the social sciences. Of course, he knew his physical geography and agronomy too, and so the underlying determinants of 'the material' bases of change were always incorporated in his perspectives.

Reflecting now on our many conversations over the years, Sam was always critical of the 'livelihoods approach' that I have advocated (Scoones 1998, 2009). In the terms elaborated above, I was clearly too focused on the 'multiple determinations and relations' – the detailed specificities of everyday life – rather than the wider 'concrete' features that allowed an interpretation in relation to wider processes of change. Sam, instead, always defended an analysis that encouraged a dialogue between diverse empirical contexts and wider structural interpretations. He made good use of a comparative survey method, and his detailed fieldwork across sites helped expose the 'multiple determinations' very effectively. His wider theorization of agrarian change drew out broader 'concrete' understandings, making use of the analytical categories of Marxism. My critique was always that a survey method sometimes failed to engage with all such 'determinations and relations', and so ignored particularity and nuance, requiring a deeper ethnographic perspective in combination. Equally, a theorization that focused too much on class as a defining characteristic perhaps missed other dimensions of 'the concrete' – whether gender or ethnicity – that provided insights into wider dynamics of change.

Over time, and highly influenced by Sam's work, our perspectives converged. My reflection, (auto)-critique and extension of the livelihoods approaches of the 1990s (Scoones 2015a) drew on exactly this argument, inspired by Sam and others. Locality, place, context and the specific, textured understandings of differentiated livelihood strategies and their changes are all vital, but are merely descriptive without a wider appreciation of political economy and structural forces of power and politics that intersect with them. Pathways of change are always co-constructed in this way. As with Sam's work, greater analytical power and more effective, generalizable arguments can emerge through an interaction of deep empiricism and intelligent theorization. Theory cannot exist in a vacuum, though, as it never stands up to scrutiny without being rooted, engaged and supported by empirical foundations.

Dialogue and Debate: Interpreting Land Reform in Zimbabwe

In this section, I want to share two examples of where empirical insights and theoretical frames combined to result in divergent interpretations. In one case, my view differed from that of Sam to a degree, while in the other, Sam's work directly informed a change in my perspective. Both examples highlight how methodological choices are important, and why sustaining the dialogue between field realities and wider theorization is vital.

The first example relates to the interpretation of Zimbabwe's land invasions from the late 1990s, accelerating in 2000–01. These took place across the country and resulted in the invasion of large tracts of farmland owned mostly by white farmers – the now famed *jambanja* period. This was read by some as a chaotic, violent confrontation organized by the party-state following the constitutional referendum in 2000. In such a reading, the invasions were coordinated, deliberate and supported by state forces, including the army and security services, as part of a desperate attempt to reassert power, being challenged by the rising force of the opposition – the Movement for Democratic Change party (Hammar, Raftopoulos and Jensen, eds 2003; Raftopoulos and Phimister 2004). The invaders were cast as 'cronies', agents of the party-state, and the land reform, therefore, was seen as an illegitimate 'grab' by politically connected elites (Zamchiya 2013).

By contrast, others argued that this was the result of a new revolutionary social movement emerging from the grassroots, and responding to liberation war demands for the redistribution of land as well as genuine demands from peasant farmers living in cramped Communal Areas. The invasions of 2000–01 were, it was argued, a continuation of other protests and land invasions in previous years, organized by local people with the support of the war veterans, confronting the state and a white land-owning elite head on (Moyo 2001; Moyo and Yeros, eds 2005). This became, according to these commentators, a cross-class mobilization that involved the state on its terms, allowing the facilitation of a wider involvement beyond disenfranchised peasants to include the middle class and the political-business elite. The result was a political compromise within the 'fast-track' programme that accommodated diverse interests, across different types of resettlement models, from villagized to self-contained A1 models, to medium-scale A2 farms and large-scale A2 farms (Moyo and Chambati, eds 2013).

In these two versions of the land invasion period, theorizations of the political character of land reform differed dramatically. In one, the land reform was the result of a corrupt, failing state and party, exercising its power ruthlessly and violently; in the other, a popular movement transformed into a cross-class accommodation between citizens and the state, responding to genuine demands.

In this instance, my view has been that theory – and with this particular political positions – ran ahead of the empirical realities. In practice, both interpretations had some elements of truth embedded in them, but neither was sufficient to explain such a dramatic period in Zimbabwe's history. The problem with much of the discussion of the *jambanja* period is that it often proceeds without attention to the empirical realities on the ground, or, if cases are referred to, they are single instances, often outliers, whether the Svosve invasions of the late 1990s (Magure 2015) or particular contexts of a certain site (cf. Marongwe 2003; Zamchiya 2011, 2013). Too much discussion of this period is coloured by intense political emotion and extremely distorted media reportage (Willems 2004). There was not much research going on in the rural areas in 2000–01, as it was very volatile, sometimes dangerous, and so empirical grounding was limited and the crucial tension for political economy analysis was lost.

Our work in Masvingo from this period showed a much more variegated picture, reflecting both narratives (Chaumba, Scoones and Wolmer 2003a, 2003b; Scoones *et al.* 2010; Scoones *et al.* 2012). It varied massively farm by farm and over time. Early invasions may have been quite spontaneous, led in some cases by farm workers who knew the area; later, others joined, including war veterans, who organized people into 'base camps'; later still, they may have garnered assistance from the state and security forces, including support for planning as well as food and logistics. Across sixteen sites, we did not find a single pattern, making it difficult to interpret the process. Indeed, both narratives applied in different places at different times.

Attention to the empirical realities, I would argue, forces us to temper interpretations and sometimes to accept that no singular explanation will do. Interpretations of conjunctures emerge from diverse threads, and piecing these together requires attention not only to the bigger picture but also to the complex, sometimes contradictory, realities on the ground (cf. Li 2014). Our understanding of the bigger story has only slowly emerged over time. Here, the argument for a hedged compromise involving diverse cross-class alliances seems appropriate. But again, this is different in different places: for example, deals struck in the Lowveld sugar estates have been very different to those in the core resettlement areas of Masvingo province, and different again to areas where high-value commercial contract agriculture grew, as in the parts of Mashonaland through the tobacco boom (Scoones 2012, 2015b, 2016; Scoones *et al.* 2012; Scoones *et al.* 2018).

My second example relates to the broader interpretation of the politics of the land reform in Zimbabwe. Here Sam's work – with Paris Yeros, Walter Chambati and many others – has been vitally important. While I do not subscribe to a singular interpretation, as in the particular case of the *jambanja* moment, making sense of the period since 2000 does require the wider theorization that Sam and colleagues have offered. In the 2000s, many of us spent a huge amount of time and effort on detailed empirical studies. Large datasets were amassed, asking very basic questions about what was happening, to whom and where. Data on production, investment, patterns of accumulation and reproduction added to a rich picture of the post-land reform scene. This emerged from the district studies of AIAS, led by Sam (Moyo *et al.* 2009); from our work in Masvingo (Scoones *et al.* 2010), and subsequently Mvurwi in Mashonaland (Sukume *et al.* 2015) and Matobo in Matabeleland; and from studies led by Prosper Matondi and the Ruzivo Trust (Matondi 2012). Together, these added up to an impressive body of qualitative and quantitative data that could confront some of the oft-repeated 'myths' about the land reform. Since then, our early insights have been added to substantially extending the geographic scope, deepening the focal areas and on occasions challenging some of the findings (e.g., Murisa 2011; Chambati 2011; Mutopo 2011; Zamchiya 2011, 2013; Mkodzongi 2013; Chigumira 2014; Chiweshe 2014; among many others).

While these studies answered important empirical questions, few added up to a wider interpretation. This was an important – and legitimate – critique of our earlier work (Rutherford 2012), a view echoed in a different way by Sam in our many conversations. He argued that we were getting stuck in the detail and not seeing the wood for the trees. We needed to understand not just what was happening in particular villages, but also in the wider political economy, including geopolitical pressures affecting flows of finance and capital, in the context of 'sanctions'. We could not understand the relations of A1 and A2 farmers simply in terms of exchanges of tractors; these had to be seen in relation to cross-class alliances and the ways patronage networks from the state influenced outcomes. Further, we had to understand how a large mass of people on the land with different affiliations and alliances, as well as class positions, were in turn influencing the state and party.

In other words, Sam and others were urging us to link our empirical work with a wider political economy theorization, exploring more broadly what this meant for agrarian change, and not only in Zimbabwe. This was a vitally important encouragement to engage with exactly what Marx offered in the *Grundrisse*, as a guide to method in political economy.

The book on Zimbabwe as a post-settler economy (Moyo and Chambati, eds 2013) and a number of other publications (Moyo 2007, 2008; Moyo and Yeros, eds 2011) began to lay out Sam's interpretation. It was sadly an unfinished work, but allows us glimpses of what he was thinking. Continuing to engage with these ideas, and extending them in new ways that engage fully with the hugely complex and varied empirical realities will be an important legacy of Sam's work.

Methodological Lessons from Engaging with Land Reform in Zimbabwe

What, then, do we take from these reflections on methodology from engaging with Sam's research, especially on land in Zimbabwe?

First, and perhaps most obviously, empirical detail really matters. Whether from surveys, case studies, biographies or deeply immersive ethnographic engagements, the data that highlight the texture, nuance and variation of what is happening are vital. Using mixed methods, combining quantitative and qualitative insights, is essential. This is not just the formulaic approaches of the standard consultancy with a rushed survey and a focus group or two providing the data, but requires deeper, engaged work that allows confidence in the material produced. Such work becomes especially powerful if carried out over a long time, to get a sense of temporal dynamics, and over space in multiple locations, to get a sense of spatial variability. Comparative analysis over time and space can in turn add to our depth of understanding. Context, contingency and conjuncture are, as the examples above vividly show, vital features of any dynamic situation, and essential for grasping what is happening. Sam's work, especially with the impressive team at AIAS, showed all these features of empirical methodology and a commitment to fieldwork in particular places over time, even when funding was very short.

Data that accumulate as solid evidence are essential when confronting contested issues. Having reliable and robust data is the core of a strategy for influencing change. It may not result in a simple narrative and may add layers of complexity, but it provides the grounds on which challenges to existing policies, or media and academic commentary can be made. In the period from 2000, when the global media and many academic colleagues railed against the land reforms in Zimbabwe, without having done any recent empirical work and with scant attention to any that had been produced, having a solid basis to develop arguments and counter misinterpretations was important.[2] In this, the work of a growing group of committed scholars in Zimbabwe, with Sam central to this network, was essential.

Second, without wider theorization, it is impossible to make sense of the diversity, variety and general confusion that much empirical work throws up. Single cases are insufficient and theorization must emerge from engagement with diverse sources. Theory that is grounded and robust must engage with the 'many determinations and relations' defining the 'concrete', while at the same time avoiding a 'chaotic conception of the whole'. To reiterate Marx's point above, 'the concrete is concrete because it is the concentration of many determinations, hence unity of the diverse'. For Sam, an analysis centred on class but sensitive to other axes of difference, including gender, was at the core. But empirical contexts meant that static class assignations were inadequate, and a sophisticated, fluid interpretation, appropriate to the southern African context, had to emerge. Thus, 'real relations' informed what Stuart Hall (2003) calls the 'differentiated unity' of analytical phenomena such as class. Linked to a located understanding of class relations and struggle, Sam's work articulated a wider understanding of finance and capital in the context of globalization, within an unequal, evolving post-colonial world order. These broader assessments, inspired by the likes of Samir Amin (1972, 1978) and Giovanni Arrighi (1994), for example, in turn informed more micro-analyses of particular places and processes.

As I hope this essay has shown, Sam was deeply committed to both these elements of method in political economy, and deployed them effectively in combination, one dialectically informing the other. The key lessons from Sam's work were to keep both strands of thought and action alive and in dialogue. For him, both the geographer and political economist were ever-present. The lesson for us all is this: neither to disappear into grand theory nor into micro-empirical detail, but capture them both, holding them in tension. Sam's impressive approach combined a sustained commitment to fieldwork, to people and places – a direct result of his training in geography, and his ability to theorize the political economy of land, emerging from his engagement with radical scholars rooted in agrarian struggles around the world. It is a rare skill to observe in one person and across such an impressive career, but a skill that is essential and one we can all learn from Sam's work.

Rigour in method arises from keeping these tensions in play, always being reflexive about how evidence is constructed and for what purposes. Big surveys, micro case studies and wider political analysis can all come together, but only with a really deep sense of how connections are made and how each informs the other. This was Sam's great skill.

Conclusion

Sam's methodological stance was mature and sophisticated. It was often not directly articulated as he engaged across such a wide range, but reflecting back on an impressive forty-year career, tragically cut short, we can see the influences and how these combined so effectively.

An appreciation of context, spatial difference and comparative insights, and a commitment to sustained empirical fieldwork comes from human geography; at least the kind taught in places avoiding the worst excesses of the post-structuralist turn. From his PhD, through the range of outputs in the 1990s, to the crucially important AIAS district studies in the 2000s (now being repeated), a solid commitment to detailed empirical study is highly evident in Sam's massive corpus. But, as I have shown, this was not all. This background of empirical work could only be made sense of through wider theorizing of how 'concrete' features of class, gender, social relations, capital, labour and political formation created such diversity and variation. And rather than theorizing in a vacuum, as sadly too many do, Sam and his colleagues were able to challenge simplistic theories drawn from elsewhere and make them real for a Zimbabwean context.

Knowledge – especially in the context of a field as contested as land in Zimbabwe – is inevitably political. This means rigour in methodology is especially important, as challenge comes from all sides. Sam was, of course, positioned normatively and politically around a commitment to land reform, a stance he made clear long before the land reforms of the 2000s. As a public intellectual and a policy actor operating on an international stage, especially through his association with CODESRIA, Sam's research came under special scrutiny. This meant that being explicit about how data are collected, how theories are constructed and how findings are presented was essential. It meant 'speaking truth to power', even when this was uncomfortable. Uncovering patronage, illegal dealings and corrupt practice threw a sharp light on the land reform, but was balanced with a wider assessment of the land reform as a positive and long overdue move that benefited many, and provided the opportunity to set in train a process of agrarian reform that, with qualifications, addressed poverty, inequality and social justice. You could disagree with some of Sam's analyses and interpretations – and sometimes I did – but you could not doubt the integrity of the work and the dedication with which it was put together. This was not sloppy, casual research masquerading as scholarship with conclusions already formulated, but thorough, perceptive and profound research that his critics could not counter in substantive terms.

Sam's formidable, enquiring mind, his dedication to extreme hard work and his methodological approach – never formulaic, sometimes rather eclectic, but rooted in a rounded interpretation of method for political economy, as I have argued here – all contributed to a massively important body of work that will influence Zimbabwe and the region more widely for many years to come. One of his major commitments was to support a next generation of African agrarian studies scholars, and he did this with generosity and enthusiasm. Hopefully, some of his students, and their students in turn, will take lessons from Sam's remarkable journey, as I have, and think not only about the findings of his scholarship, but also the way it was conducted and its sophisticated methodological approach, which combined different approaches to understanding both the empirical realities of 'multiple determinations and relations' and also structural features of 'the concrete' in a rigorous, enlightening way.

This article was originally published in *Agrarian South: Journal of Political Economy*, Vol. 5, Nos. 2–3, 2016. Copyright 2016 © Centre for Agrarian Research and Education for South (CARES), New Delhi. All rights reserved. Reproduced with the permission of the copyright holders and the publishers, SAGE Publications India Pvt. Ltd, New Delhi.

Notes

1 See a summary CV at http://our-global-u.org/oguorg/en/?wpfb_dl=427, accessed 18 October 2016.

2 This was perhaps most extreme in the depths of Zimbabwe's economic crisis in the late 2000s. Mahmood Mamdani's 2008 piece for the *London Review of Books*, 'Lessons of Zimbabwe', for example, led to a collective signed letter from a group of academics: http://concernedafricascholars.org/reflectionson-mahmood-mamdanis-lessons-of-zimbabwe/, accessed 18 October 2016.

References

Amin, S. (1972), 'Underdevelopment and Dependence in Black Africa: Origins and Contemporary Forms', *The Journal of Modern African Studies*, 10 (4): 503–24.

——— (1978), 'Unequal Development: An Essay on the Social Formations of Peripheral Capitalism', *Science and Society*, 42 (2): 219–22.

Arrighi, G. (1994), *The Long Twentieth Century: Money, Power, and the Origins of Our Times*, London: Verso.

Bernstein, H. (2010), *Class Dynamics of Agrarian Change*, Virginia: Kumarian Press.

Chambati, W. (2011), 'Restructuring of Agrarian Labour Relations after Fast Track Land Reform in Zimbabwe', *Journal of Peasant Studies*, 38 (5): 1047–68.

Chaumba, J., I. Scoones and W. Wolmer (2003a), 'From *Jambanja* to Planning: The Reassertion of Technocracy in Land Reform in South-Eastern Zimbabwe?', *The Journal of Modern African Studies*, 41 (4): 533–54.

——— (2003b), 'New Politics, New Livelihoods: Agrarian Change in Zimbabwe', *Review of African Political Economy,* 30 (98): 585–608.

Chigumira, E. (2014), 'Re-Peasantization under Fast Track Land Reform: Implications for Livelihood and Landscape Change', unpublished PhD thesis, University of Oregon, Sanyati district, Zimbabwe.

Chiweshe, M.K. (2014), *Understanding Social and Solidarity Economy in Emergent Communities: Lessons from Post-Fast Track Land Reform Farms in Mazowe, Zimbabwe*, Geneva: UNRISD.

Hall, S. (2003), 'Marx's Notes on Method: A "Reading" of the "1857 Introduction"', *Cultural Studies*, 17 (2): 113–49.

Hammar, A., B. Raftopoulos and S. Jensen, eds (2003), *Zimbabwe's Unfinished Business: Rethinking Land, State and Nation in the Context of Crisis*, Harare: Weaver Press.

Li, T.M. (2014), *Land's End: Capitalist Relations on an Indigenous Frontier*, Durham, NC: Duke University Press.

Magure, B. (2015), 'Polarization and Transformation in Zimbabwe: Social Movements, Strategy Dilemmas and Change', *Journal of Contemporary African Studies*, 33 (3): 415–18.

Marongwe, N. (2003), 'Farm Occupations and Occupiers in the New Politics of Land in Zimbabwe', in A. Hammar, B. Raftopoulos and S. Jensen, eds, *Zimbabwe's Unfinished Business: Rethinking Land, State and Nation in the Context of Crisis*, Harare: Weaver Press: 155–90.

Marx, K. (1973), *Grundrisse*, Harmondsworth: Penguin.

Matondi, P.B. (2012), *Zimbabwe's Fast-Track Land Reform*, London: Zed Press.

Mkodzongi, G. (2013), 'Fast Tracking Land Reform and Rural Livelihoods in Mashonaland West Province of Zimbabwe: Opportunities and Constraints, 2000–2013', unpublished PhD thesis, University of Edinburgh.

Moore, D. (2004), 'Marxism and Marxist Intellectuals in Schizophrenic Zimbabwe: How Many Rights for Zimbabwe's Left? A Comment', *Historical Materialism*, 12 (4): 405–25.

Moyo, S. (1995), *The Land Question in Zimbabwe*, Harare: SAPES Books.

——— (1998), *The Land Acquisition Process in Zimbabwe 1997/8: Socioeconomic and Political Impacts*, UNDP/SAPES Policy Monograph Series No. 1, Harare: SAPES.

——— (2000a), *Land Reform under Structural Adjustment in Zimbabwe: Land Use Change in the Mashonaland Provinces*, Uppsala: Nordic Africa Institute.

——— (2000b), 'The Political Economy of Land Acquisition in Zimbabwe, 1990–1999', *Journal of Southern African Studies*, 26 (1): 5–28.

——— (2001), 'The Land Occupation Movement and Democratization in Zimbabwe: Contradictions of Neoliberalism', *Millennium: Journal of International Studies*, 30 (2): 311–30.

——— (2007), 'Land In the Political Economy of African Development: Alternative Strategies for Reform', *Africa Development*, 32 (4): 1–34.

——— (2008), *The Land Question, the State and Agrarian Transition: Contradictions of Neoliberal Reforms*, Dakar: CODESRIA.

——— (2011a), 'Three Decades of Agrarian Reform in Zimbabwe: Redistributive Outcome?', *Journal of Peasant Studies*, 38 (3): 493–31.

——— (2011b), 'Changing Agrarian Relations after Redistributive Land Reform in Zimbabwe', *Journal of Peasant Studies*, 38 (5): 907–34.

——— (2011c), 'Land concentration and accumulation by dispossession: Redistributive reform in post settler Zimbabwe', *Review of African Political Economy*, 38 (128): 257–76.

Moyo, S. and H. Binswanger (2011), 'Agricultural Growth Trends', draft paper commissioned by and prepared for the World Bank, Harare: World Bank.

Moyo, S., W. Chambati, T. Murisa, D. Siziba, C. Dangwa, K. Mujeyi and N. Nyoni (2009), *Fast Track Land Reform Baseline Survey in Zimbabwe: Trends and Tendencies, 2005/06*, Harare: African Institute of Agrarian Studies.

Moyo, S., P. Jha and P. Yeros (2012), 'Imperialism and Primitive Accumulation: Notes on the New Scramble for Africa', *Agrarian South: Journal of Political Economy*, 1 (1): 181–204.

——— (2013), 'The Classical Question in Agrarian Question: Myth, Reality and Relevance Today', *Agrarian South: Journal of Political Economy*, 2 (1): 93–119.

Moyo, S., J. Makumbe and B. Raftopolous (2000), *NGOs, the State and Politics in Zimbabwe*, Harare: SAPES Books.

Moyo, S., P. O'Keefe and N. Middleton (1993), *Tears of the Crocodile: From Rio to Reality in the Developing World*, London: Pluto Press.

Moyo, S., P. O'Keefe and M. Sill (1993), *The Southern African Environment: Profiles of SADC Countries*, London: Earthscan.

Moyo, S., P. Robinson, Y. Katerere, S. Stevenson and D. Gumbo (1991), *Zimbabwe's Environmental Dilemma: Balancing Resources Inequities*, Harare: ZERO.

Moyo, S. and C. Sukume (2006), 'Agricultural Growth and Land Reform in Zimbabwe: Assessment and Recovery Options', Report No. 31699-ZW, Harare: World Bank.

Moyo, S., D. Weiner, P. O'Keefe and B. Munslow (1984), 'Land Use and Productivity in Zimbabwe', *Journal of Modern African Studies*, 23 (2): 251–85.

Moyo, S. and P. Yeros (2007a), 'The Radicalized State: Zimbabwe's Interrupted Revolution', *Review of African Political Economy*, 34 (111): 103–21.

——— (2007b), 'The Zimbabwe Question and the Two Lefts', *Historical Materialism*, 15 (3), 171–204.

Moyo, S. and W. Chambati, eds (2013), *Land and Agrarian Reform in Zimbabwe: Beyond White-Settler Capitalism*, Dakar: Council for the Development of Social Science Research in Africa (CODESRIA).

Moyo, S. and P. Yeros, eds (2005), *Reclaiming the Land: The Resurgence of Rural Movements in Africa, Asia and Latin America*, London: Zed Books.

——— (2011), *Reclaiming the Nation: The Return of the National Question in Africa, Asia and Latin America*, London: Pluto Press.

Murisa, T. (2011), 'Local Farmer Groups and Collective Action within Fast Track Land Reform in Zimbabwe', *Journal of Peasant Studies*, 38 (5): 1145–66.

Mutopo, P. (2011), 'Women's Struggles to Access and Control Land and Livelihoods after Fast Track Land Reform in Mwenezi District, Zimbabwe', *Journal of Peasant Studies*, 38 (5): 1021–46.

Palmer, R.H. (1977), *Land and Racial Domination in Rhodesia*, London: Heinemann Educational Publishers.

Raftopoulos, B. (2006), 'The Zimbabwean Crisis and the Challenges for the Left', *Journal of Southern African Studies*, 32 (2): 203–19.

Raftopoulos, B. and I. Phimister (2004), 'Zimbabwe Now: The Political Economy of Crisis and Coercion', *Historical Materialism*, 12 (4): 355–82.

Rutherford, B. (2012), 'Shifting the Debate on Land Reform, Poverty and Inequality in Zimbabwe: An Engagement with Zimbabwe's Land Reform: Myths and Realities', *Journal of Contemporary African Studies*, 30 (1): 147–57.

Scoones, I. (1998), 'Sustainable Rural Livelihoods: A Framework for Analysis', IDS Working Paper No. 72, Brighton: Institute of Development Studies.

——— (2009), 'Livelihoods Perspectives and Rural Development', *Journal of Peasant Studies*, 36 (1): 171–96.

——— (2012), 'Livelihoods after Land Reform in Zimbabwe: Understanding Processes of Rural Differentiation', *Journal of Agrarian Change*, 12 (4): 503–27.

——— (2015a), *Sustainable Livelihoods and Rural Development*, Halifax/Rugby: Fernwood Press/Practical Action Publishing.

——— (2015b), 'Zimbabwe's Land Reform: New Political Dynamics in the Countryside', *Review of African Political Economy*, 42 (144): 190–205.

——— (2016), 'Land Reform, Livelihoods and the Politics of Agrarian Change in Zimbabwe', in A.A. Pallotti and C. Tornimbeni, eds, *State, Land And Democracy in Southern Africa*, London: Routledge: 127–48.

Scoones, I., J. Chaumba, B. Mavedzenge and W. Wolmer (2012), 'The New Politics of

Zimbabwe's Lowveld: Struggles over Land at the Margins', *African Affairs*, 111 (445): 527–50.

Scoones, I., N. Marongwe, B. Mavedzenge, F. Murimbarimba, J. Mahenehene and C. Sukume (2010), *Zimbabwe's Land Reform: Myths and Realities*, Oxford, Harare and Johannesburg: James Currey, Weaver Press and Jacana.

Scoones, I., B. Mavedzenge, F. Murimbarimba and C. Sukume (2018), 'Tobacco, Contract Farming and Agrarian Change in Zimbabwe', *Journal of Agrarian Change*, 18: 22–42.

Sukume, C., B. Mavedzenge, F. Murimbarimba and I. Scoones (2015), 'Space, Markets and Employment in Agricultural Development: Zimbabwe Country Report', Research Report No. 46, Capet Town: PLAAS.

Willems, W. (2004), 'Peasant Demonstrators, Violent Invaders: Representations of Land in the Zimbabwean Press', *World Development*, 32 (10): 1767–83.

Yeros, P. (2002), 'Zimbabwe and the Dilemmas of the Left', *Historical Materialism*, 10 (2): 3–15.

Zamchiya, P. (2011), 'A Synopsis of Land and Agrarian Change in Chipinge District, Zimbabwe', *Journal of Peasant Studies*, 38 (5): 1093–22.

——— (2013), 'The Role of Politics and State Practices in Shaping Rural Differentiation: A Study of Resettled Small-Scale Farmers in South-Eastern Zimbabwe', *Journal of Southern African Studies*, 39 (4): 937–53.

7

Green Grabbing and Political Class Lobbies

Revisiting Land Reform under Structural Adjustment in Zimbabwe

Kojo S. Amanor

In 2012, *The Journal of Peasant Studies* published an issue dedicated to 'green grabbing', with an introduction by Fairhead, Leach and Scoones titled 'Green Grabbing: A New Appropriation of Nature?' In this essay, the authors defined green grabbing as the appropriation of land and trade in natural resources on global markets that is justified by reference to environmental concerns. The concept of green grabbing advanced by them has some similarities with Sam Moyo's 1994 study, *Land Reform under Structural Adjustment in Zimbabwe*. In this work, Moyo analysed the rise of new markets for wildlife, natural resources, tourism and horticultural products in Zimbabwe, and explored how these served to reframe the land question in Zimbabwe through a process of market commodification.

Moyo focused on the impact of economic liberalization policies on the administration of land, and the regulation and deregulation of natural resources in the face of increasing 'transnational regulation of the use of nature or the environment' (Moyo 1994: 25). This describes a period before the implementation of the fast-track land reform, when donor-prescribed market-based reforms dominated land policies in Zimbabwe, and before the formal support extended by the state for land occupation resulted in the imposition of sanctions by the United States and the European Union in 2002, which in effect curtailed the neo-liberal project in Zimbabwe. Moyo was critical of the policies implemented by the Zimbabwean government under structural adjustment as effecting an appropriation of natural resources by the wealthy at the expense of the rural poor, and investigated the coalition of political interests shaping and taking advantage of the opportunities created by liberalized markets.

Moyo analysed the structural adjustment programme in Zimbabwe through a framework rooted in political economy and regional economy.

He examined how the commodification of natural resources and the opening up of new frontiers for natural resource extraction affected the distribution of land and land policies. He explored the penetration of capitalism into various regions of Zimbabwe with unequal development, including intensively exploited commercial farming areas, densely settled Communal Areas and less developed frontier areas, which included wildlife parks set aside for ecotourism.

Fairhead, Leach and Scoones (2012) derive their conception of green grabbing from Harvey's (2003) reworking of Marx's concept of primary or primitive accumulation as 'accumulation through dispossession'. This is combined with the Foucauldian analysis of policy processes, with a heavy emphasis on the central significance of linkages between science and policy in creating the commodification of natural resources. This science–policy nexus displaces a deeper analysis of the relationship between economic restructuring policies, the global expansion of transnational corporations, and the role these firms play in opening up the natural resource sectors in developing countries to global markets. This is replaced with the narratives of science–policy (development) actors within the environmental sector, who are seen as creating new societal and policy values that transform and commoditize natural resources and land.

Similarities in these two works include notions of the commodification of natural resources related to new forms of valuation, and new non-state actors intervening in and shaping this process of commodification. Beyond this, there are significant differences in approach which relate to theoretical frameworks. Moyo used a political economy framework which grounds the changing policy frameworks within the material realities of the Zimbabwean economy and its position in the global economy. He examined the class interests and coalitions that influenced and reacted to policy, and the dialectical interaction between ideology, class, social differentiation and processes of capitalist accumulation. Fairhead, Leach and Scoones (2012) combine political economy with Foucauldian discourse theory and actor network theory, and focus on science–policy discourse as the main force creating new values and markets.

This essay interrogates the theoretical framings in these two works with the intention of examining the significance of political economy and postmodernism to understanding environmental policy processes and capital accumulation in natural resource sectors. It is concerned with the relationship between Marxist political economy and postmodern discourse theory, and between economy, discourse, class and ideology. It also highlights the original contribution of Sam Moyo's work to understanding environmental and land policy processes under neo-liberalism, and the relationship between economic forms, ideology, class influence and political lobbying within the policy process.

The first section below provides a summary of the theoretical framing of green grabbing. This is followed by a critique of its framing of the role of science–policy in natural resource commodification, through reflections on both the role of historical materialism in political economy, and the role of transnational capital and corporate sectors in the commodification of nature. The third section examines Moyo's framing of environmental policy and the land question in Zimbabwe, focusing on the relationship between material factors, ideology and class alliances, and the political and economic interests that drive state policy.

Framing Green Grabbing

Fairhead, Leach and Scoones (2012) define green grabbing as a process through which large tracts of land are acquired for more efficient farming while at the same time alleviating pressures on forest resources. In this commercial deal, the transfer of land is 'intended to serve "green" ends – whether through biodiversity conservation, biocarbon sequestration, the protection of ecosystems services, ecotourism or "offsets" related to any and all of these' (ibid.: 239). The appropriation of nature involves the transfer of ownership, user rights and control over resources that were once privately or publicly owned from the poor into the hands of the powerful. Referring back to some of their earlier works, Fairhead, Leach and Scoones argue that green grabbing builds upon colonial and neo-colonial environmental narratives that justify the alienation of natural resources from rural people to protect the environment as exclusive parks and forest reserves, or to halt destructive local practices through regulation (Leach and Mearns 1996; Fairhead and Leach 1998; Keeley and Scoones 2003). Green grabbing also involves new forms of commodification and valuation, and the participation of a wide range of new actors and alliances in environmental policy, ranging from pension funds, venture capitalists and commodity traders, to consultants, green activists and 'anxious consumers'.

The conception of green grabbing draws on Harvey's (2003) theory of 'accumulation by dispossession' with its four elements of:

1. Privatization of public assets and common resources, which includes the sale of, or contracting out of, the management of forest reserves, game parks and grazing land to private companies.
2. Financialization, which involves setting property values on nature through costing the financial value of the environment, environmental services and environmental degradation. Notions of value

related to payment for services create opportunities for the financialization of nature and are 'linked to the circulation of capital in new economic systems' (Fairhead, Leach and Scoones 2012: 244). Thus, forests have potential for carbon storage and carbon trading, biofuel production, funding from reduced emissions from deforestation and degradation, biodiversity funding, and tourism.
3. Management and manipulation of crises, which lock environments into the booms and busts of financial markets. The crisis of indebtedness forces developing countries into the prescriptions of international financial institutions, which have included market liberalization and structural adjustment.
4. State redistribution from people to corporate interests that arise from fiscal policies to attract foreign and private sector investors, which include debt for nature swaps.

Fairhead, Leach and Scoones (2012) append the relationship between the 'science–policy world' and the operation of markets on to this framework of 'accumulation by dispossession', thus shifting the analysis firmly to policy discourse theory:

> A key analytic perspective in this collection is to explore the relationship between the science–policy world that establishes these commodities and the operation of the markets, and their tangible effects on agrarian settings. Thus science–policy discourses have produced carbon as a commodity, shaped forests as 'otherwise disappearing', given value to biodiversity and cast biofuels as sustainable. These moves in turn suggest a Foucauldian knowledge/power relation in the production of scarcity (Mehta 2011), loss (Fairhead and Leach 2003) and repair (Leach *et al.* 2013). Markets in these discursive commodities have therefore emerged from complex encounters between science, technology and politics, and it is the interactions between such discursive and political-economic relations that must be at the centre of any analysis. (Fairhead, Leach and Scoones 2012: 241).

Discourse Theory, Political Economy, Idealism and Historical Materialism

Although inspired by Harvey's political economy, Fairhead, Leach and Scoones' recourse to a postmodernist discourse framework inverts the theoretical basis of Marxist political economy. It replaces a dialectical approach rooted in historical materialism with an idealistic framework in which economic value is not produced by the social relations of production and the position of labour in production, but by a science–policy discourse that produces commodities out of natural resources through new framings that mobilize social actors.

Mavroudeas (2006) argues that, although Marxism recognizes the social construction of subjects, it bases this on the social division of labour and class interests. In contrast, postmodernism attributes primacy to the subjective and 'applies a discursive conception of social dimensions that has little bearing on the material condition of life' (ibid.: 13), in which politics is understood to be a struggle for power and hegemony which is superimposed upon the economy rather than occurring in a dialectical interaction. Class relations are replaced by networks of individuals and institutions. These create alliances for the production of knowledge that reconstruct social and cultural values, and transform the norms and values of material production. The labour theory of value is replaced by social values and knowledge generation (ibid.).

Postmodernist analysis of policy processes has little concern to root the process of appropriation and commodification of natural resources and land in real-life material conditions. It identifies science–policy discourses as major transformers of markets and the creators of new forms of commodification. But since the context of these new commodification processes are economic liberalization and globalization, there is clearly a relationship between science–policy discourses and the expansion of market competition and global investments that needs to be addressed. This concerns the nature of the relationship between science policy, the expansion of activities of transnational corporations throughout the world and neo-liberal economic reforms.

The origins of the neo-liberal order can be traced back to the immediate post-war period in which the United States emerged as the dominant western power bailing out the war-exhausted European nations through the Marshal Plan. In contrast with the colonial European powers, the US state was not interested in carving out an empire based on geographically limited colonial boundaries; rather, it wanted to facilitate a global free-trade order in which US multinational corporations could range freely and dominate global markets. These ambitions were hampered by the emergence of the Soviet bloc, and by radical nationalistic governments that attempted to control their own economies and natural resources and did not always side with the US in the Cold War. International development became a major strategy through which the United States sought to win influence within the former colonial world, realign the institutional structures of nation-states with US objectives, and curb the influences of the Soviet Union (Lantham 2011). When the ideology of international development proved to be ineffective, the United States used military means to overthrow intransigent regimes. During the 1950s, this went well beyond containing communism. The United States schemed to bring about *coup d'états* in Iran when the Mosaddegh-led government nationalized the oil industry, and in Guatemala when the Alliance for Progress introduced a land reform programme that redistributed estates acquired by the United Fruit Company, a US multinational corporation (ibid.). In this period, the US government intervened internationally in the interests of US multinational corporations. By the 1970s, these military interventions expanded in ambition with the coup in Chile against the socially progressive Allende government, which brought Pinochet to power with advisors from the University of Chicago students of Milton Friedman, who implemented the first experiment in neo-liberal government (Klein 2007).

Beyond the military might of the US state internationally intervening to support the interests of US corporations, corporate organizations and wealthy billionaires have also organized lobbies to further their interests within the state and society. Hertel-Fernandez (2019) focuses on three major groupings set up to achieve these objectives: America for Prosperity (AFP) established by the Koch Brothers, the American Legislative Exchange Council (ALEC) and the State Policy Network (SPN). He shows that since the 1970s, conservative capitalists have sought to build influential lobby groups which seek to promote research and media commentary that supports right-wing ideologies, influences political candidates, and encourages elected officials to introduce new legislation in support of the political interests of these groups. They even create model bills that legislators can use for drafting new legislation. The common agenda of all these groups is to support cuts to government spending and regulation, reduce taxation on the rich, and weaken labour unions. These kinds of influences are not only limited to right-wing politics and the Republican Party; corporate interests also work to win influence within social democratic, liberal-oriented parties. The most influential of these currently is the Democratic Alliance, a network of wealthy Americans (including George Soros) who promote centre–left priorities within the Democratic party and civil society, fund what they consider to be worthy progressive organizations, and address what they consider to be the main threats to American free enterprise (Hertel-Fernandez, Skocpol and Sclar 2018).

The strategy for organizing the political influence of the Koch Network has been outlined by Richard Fink, the chief executive officer of Koch Companies Public Sector PLC, which provides legal, government, philanthropy and community relations services to Koch companies. Building his framework on Hayek's theory of the structure of production, Fink writes:

> Instead of the transformation of natural resources to intermediate goods to products that add value to consumers, the model, which I call the Structure of Social Change, deals with the discovery, adaptation, and implementation of ideas into change that increases the wellbeing of citizens. Although the model helps to explain many forms of social change, I will focus here on the type I know best – change that results from the formation of public policy. . . . When we apply this model to the realm of ideas and social change, at the higher stages we have the investment in the intellectual raw materials, that is, the exploration and production of abstract concepts and theories. In the public policy arena, these still come primarily (though not exclusively) from the research done by scholars at our universities. At the higher stages in the Structure of Social Change model, ideas are often unintelligible to the layperson and seemingly unrelated to real-world problems. To have consequences, ideas need to be transformed into a more practical or useable form.
>
> In the middle stages, ideas are applied to a relevant context and moulded into solutions needed for real-world problems. This is the work of the think tanks and policy institutions. Without these organizations, theory or abstract thought would have less value and less impact on our society. But while the think tanks excel at developing new policy and articulating its benefits, they are less able to implement change. Citizen activist or implementation groups are needed in the final stage to take the policy ideas from the think tanks and translate them into proposals that citizens can understand and act upon. These groups are also able to build diverse coalitions of individual citizens and special interest groups needed to press for the implementation of policy change.
>
> We at the Koch Foundation find that the Structure of Social Change model helps us to understand the distinct roles of universities, think tanks, and activist groups in the transformation of ideas into action. (Fink 2012: 3–4)

What is most significant here is that this mirrors the framework of actor networks described by Fairhead, Leach and Scoones (2012), except that the driving force is not science–policy agents, but the corporate sector and wealthy billionaires who financially support and organize academics, think tanks and civil society activists to carry out their bidding and generate the narratives that support their economic and political interests. The transformations in society are not wrought by science–policy discourses, but the organization of these forces to create ideological pressures for political and policy changes, alongside political lobbying for legislative change and the financial support of political candidates who are willing to represent the main interests of the wealthy.

During the 1970s, the unity of state and corporate sectors drew closer as major developments occurred in public sector research in universities in information technology and biotechnology. This created the potential for new forms of accumulation. While several academics working in these fields established their own private companies and were able to build economic empires, such as Bill Gates with Microsoft, many of these initiatives were taken over by existing multinational corporations. Takeovers became a major mode of acquiring new technologies, moving into new sectors and establishing control over economic sectors. The creation of new legislation by the state on intellectual property rights became an important mode of establishing private control over these new sectors (that is, information technology, agricultural biotechnology and pharmaceuticals). By the early 1980s, corporate lobbies began to create pressure within policy circles to privatize the public sector land grant system, as the commercial potentials of biotechnology became evident. In the agricultural sector, the influential 1982 Report of the Rockefeller Foundation and Office of Science and Technology (1982) criticized the lack of cutting-edge research within public research, and emphasized the need for closer ties between university and commercial industry. Buttel (1991: 49) comments that, during this period, 'there was an important shift in the perception, if not the reality, of the land grant's predominant clientele having begun to shift from farmers to private-firms'. These shifts have transformed the notion of research from public service into a commercial commodity. Fuglie *et al.* (2012) estimate that by the early 2000s, 76 per cent of research and development in the crop, seed and biotechnology sectors was controlled by eight transnational companies; 76 per cent of all US patents issued for crop cultivars were registered by six companies; and five companies accounted for 74 per cent of research and development on agricultural chemicals. This erosion of public research in the US was accompanied by similar developments throughout the world, including in Africa, where the existing structures of national agricultural research from the 1960s had been based on the US model.

International agricultural research agencies came under increasing pressure from the 1970s to serve the interests of agribusiness (Gerlach 2008; George 1976; Dinham and Hines 1983). Reflecting on the commodification of seeds, Erna Bennet, one of the early pioneers of genetic conservation who worked at the Food and Agriculture Organization (FAO), comments:

> Corporate manoeuvres to take over the genetic resources of agricultural crops entered their present phase with the Plant Breeders' Rights legislation of 1962. This legislation *conferred marketing rights not on plant breeders as its authors falsely suggest, but on the companies employing plant breeders*. This move marked the onset of a massive privatization which saw plant breeding transformed, in the course of a single decade, from a largely public service to a heavily privatized industry increasingly tied to giant agro-chemical corporations. . . . Since the 1970s, the corporate take-over of a field long associated with the public sector and relatively small local enterprises has proceeded at breakneck pace. In the late 1970s and 1980s, pressure began to grow around patenting and intellectual property rights (IPRs), and the battle, already worldwide, became intense. (Bennet 2002: 4; emphasis added)

Bennet is very clear that the appropriation of seeds was brought about by corporate takeover of public science through privatization and through legislation on intellectual property rights that enabled the corporations to appropriate the knowledge of plant breeders. The commodification of seeds was carried out through appropriation of the social labour of plant breeders as privately hired labour, and by legislation recognizing the right to appropriate and commodify seeds. It was not carried out by plant breeders as autonomous entities independent of corporate firms and by the public production of knowledge outside of corporate-controlled research.

In the developing countries, this process of privatizing the public agricultural research sector was achieved through the conditionalities attached to financial loans from western powers, associated with the restructuring structural adjustment of the IMF (International Monetary Fund). This came to replace the use of *coup d'état*s to bring about regime change and open up markets for US multinational corporations. The world economic recession had a severe impact on African economies, and by the early 1980s, many states sought economic relief from the IMF. Arrighi (2002) argues that the internal economic crises within the African state were compounded by the external monetarist policies that the United States designed to address the impact of the world recession on its national economy. During the 1960s and 1970s, the United States had been the major source of direct investment in Africa. However, by the 1980s, the US began to compete for capital worldwide, emerging as the world's largest debtor nation. This redirection of capital flows to the US reflated demand and investment there, while deflating it in other nations throughout the world. This was accompanied by the outsourcing of manufacturing in sectors that US corporations no longer found profitable to emerging industrial countries with large sources of cheap labour, of which China was the largest market. This exacerbated the economic crisis in African countries that had become heavily debt-ridden during the 1970s, when large amounts of cheap loans were available. The increasing scarcity of capital intensified the burden of debt servicing and the cost of gaining access to new loans. The structural adjustment policies with their emphasis on promoting international investment and rolling back public services forced the African states to open up their economies to global market competition. This effectively ended attempts to build import substitution industries nurtured by the state, and led to an emphasis on the export of natural resources as the main avenue through which the state and national enterprises could gain access to foreign exchange. Thus, natural resources became a prime sector within the restructuring of the economy, and decentralized environmental management emerged as a major field in working out new forms of neo-liberal governance and destabilizing state control over the economy through notions of civil society and community participation. Transnational corporations and capitalist investors have been a major force pressurizing for these developments, taking over the more valuable state corporations, and mobilizing social activists and intellectuals to provide the ideological justifications for these developments. Thus, science–policy discourses belong to the realm of ideological justifications rather than being creators of new forms of commodification, and it is rather the appropriation of public technology by private corporations and their ability to pressurize states into introducing new legislations that bring about the new forms of commodification.

Land Reform under Structural Adjustment in Zimbabwe

Moyo's *Land Reform under Structural Adjustment* (1994) was concerned with the tensions in Zimbabwe between the historical legacies of a national liberation movement, in which a central concern was redressing the injustices of the land question and of white-settler agriculture, and the structural adjustment programme with its concern of opening up Zimbabwe to global market competition. Under structural adjustment, the framing of the land question was transformed into one concerned with finding market-based solutions to land distribution. Moyo's work focused not only on the economic, social and political context of land reform in Zimbabwe, but also on the impact of structural adjustment on the commodification and appropriation of land. It traced the relationship between the development of new export crops and emerging property rights and privatization of land, and new forms of rural land and commodity markets.

Moyo examined the dynamics of these new land uses and land

redistribution in three distinct areas: marginal lands, highly productive large-scale commercial farming areas and within the densely populated Communal Areas. He categorized the non-state land users into corporate interests (including transnational corporations, tourist and wildlife investors and banks), large-scale commercial farmers (including the established class of white farmers and newly emerging class of black commercial farmers), smallholder farmers within the Communal Areas, and the landless poor.

Moyo argued that during trade liberalization of the 1980s, agricultural market deregulation and agricultural export promotion had far-reaching institutional effects on land administration, and on access to land and natural resources. The need to generate foreign exchange income and the depressed state of manufacturing in Zimbabwe led to promotion by the state of new markets in wildlife management, tourism-related sectors, horticultural and livestock exports including ostriches. The expansion of these new land sectors was influenced by privatization of state forest land, wildlife reserves and common property resources. This transformed the notions of property in marginalized lands in the communal and large-scale commercial farming areas, but also in state lands under parks, forests and wildlife reserves. These changing land-use values transformed economic activities:

> Various players, ranging from LSCF [large-scale commercial farms] farmers, parastatal managers, indigenous non-farming business people and local authority income-generating managers to Communal Area communities and environmental NGO group project members, have, during the 1990s in particular, begun to place greater value on non-agricultural land use. Such uses include wildlife ranching, the creation of private or community nature and recreation parks, ostrich farming, forest and woodland plantations etc. (Moyo 1994: 62)

The structural adjustment reforms were reflected in official discourses on land redistribution policy, which shifted from concern regarding the relative efficiency of different scales of farmers on class and racial basis, to more macroeconomic concerns related to foreign exchange earnings, returns on financial investment and environmental benefits. Land uses that optimized foreign currency returns were given special priority and their success in bringing in foreign earnings was crucial to their further promotion. Land-use policy discourses promoted these new land uses, suggesting that cropping and livestock activities in both the large-scale commercial farms and Communal Areas were inferior to wildlife and tourism land use, and that, in the lower rainfall areas, maintaining land under indigenous woodlands was more productive than other land uses.

The allocation of large amounts of land to wildlife by the Government of Zimbabwe and by commercial farmers compounded the inequalities in access to land, favoured the redistribution of privatized public lands to commercial users within these new export sectors, and stalled land redistribution to the poor. However, smallholders were not completely excluded from this process, and as national private and transnational corporations grew in scale, they began to create new 'business linkages' and sub-contracting relations with other land users. NGOs were also active in mobilizing smallholder participation in these schemes, effectively extending the process of land and natural resource commodification into Communal Areas. For instance, the Community Management Programme for Indigenous Resources (Campfire) sought to extend wildlife management and tree plantations into Communal Areas, and advocated for wildlife resource management as yielding better incomes than low-yield grain cropping. Campfire sought to promote commercial use of the Communal Areas woodlands for livestock management at the expense of livestock grazing, which effectively appropriated common rangeland. It arranged joint ventures with private operators to facilitate the conversion of land. Most of the Campfire programmes depended upon access to the tourism and wildlife markets through middlemen and sub-contractors. This 'linkages strategy' sought to forge economic relations between the dominant white and transnational businesses and smaller black businesses, with the aim of counteracting radical demands for land redistribution among smallholders and aspiring black commercial farmers, while expanding the terrain for the commodification of natural resources and the expansion of natural resource markets. Linkages with white farmer associations and corporate groups also provided smaller farmers and black businesses with the benefits of their corporate lobbying of government. Moyo (1994: 157) recorded one of the justifications of The Ostrich Producers Association of Zimbabwe (TOPAZ) for its linkages with the white-dominated CFU (Commercial Farmers Union) thus: 'TOPAZ needed the CFU for its expertise, its lobbying skills and its clout in international marketing for our long-term future.' Political lobbying of the state by commercial interests played an important part in influencing land policy in Zimbabwe: '[t]he close scrutiny, support and lobbying of large-scale landed domestic and external financial interests has been crucial to this model of land reform with little land redistribution' (ibid.: 165). While these types of activities are seen in the good governance framework as being central to civil society participation, Moyo argued that: 'Far from creating civil society space for democratic participation, this form of "societal corporatism" created conditions for narrowly-based, class and racially-founded commercial land user associations and their allies to continuously derive the major gains from macro-economic, sectoral and land policy changes (ibid.: 149).

Moyo noted that the Zimbabwean state was able to achieve political compliance and relative peace despite very mediocre redistribution of land. This was accomplished by deft political manoeuvrings, which included: piecemeal land distribution as acts of appeasement; radical posturing and threats to carry out comprehensive radical land redistribution in the future; and overlooking the informal land occupations that had begun to occur. Nevertheless, the official discourses and validations of these new land uses were highly contested by the landless poor and 'black elites', who characterized them as 'ideological tools' used by the white commercial farm sector to legitimize existing patterns of landownership and control. The increasing commodification of land and natural resources under structural adjustment only served to fuel popular demands for land redistribution, which intensified as market prices placed the price of land beyond the reach of the rural poor. Eventually, the increasing wealth disparities and restraints on formal land redistribution due to economic liberalization policies spiralled out of hand into 'a populist land acquisition process forced upon government by strong elements in the rural party in 1997' (ibid.:164).

Conclusion

In Moyo's work, three distinct elements can be seen at play. The first constitutes the weaknesses of the Zimbabwean economy, leading to the structural adjustment programme and an emphasis on export-oriented production, external finances and natural resources. The second consists of the various programmes and policies and the ideological justifications for these, which correspond to the policy discourses. The third element comprises political lobbying and alliances, which are dominated by the corporate sector and transnational capital. This third element is decisive in shaping the direction of policy implementation. Moyo pointed out that this element is frequently overlooked in studies of the post-colonial state, since it is often assumed that statist objectives inhibit the participation of farmers and business organizations in constructive economic policy. This third element also brings into the political arena a host of new actors advocating for policy change, linking smallholder producers to corporate production strategies and serving the interests of the corporate sector.

In contrast, this field of corporate influence and lobbying is woefully neglected in postmodern studies. For instance, in *The Anti-Politics Machine*, James Ferguson goes to great pains to disassociate the operations of a bureaucratic state from economic interests, and rejects notions that the state exists to implement dominant class-based economic interests related to capital accumulation (Ferguson 1994). He asserts that development is about entrenching state power rather than state economic control. Development is about squashing political challenges to the system by 'reposing political questions on land, resources, jobs, or wages as technical "problems"' (ibid.: 270). He argues that the power of the state emerges unintentionally, as the working out of complex and unacknowledged structures of knowledge in interaction with local social and cultural factors. Further, that the state is neither the source of power nor the projection of an interested ruling group, but a 'relay or point of coordination and multiplication of power relations' (ibid.: 272). Ferguson then draws a divide between western states, in which the state plays a vital role in developing techniques for disciplining the bodies and optimizing the capacities of its citizens to be productive, healthy and vital, and the state 'in a country like Lesotho', where the state does not have the capacity to centralize 'social engineering' but only to refer citizens through bureaucratic channels. In recent years, the western state has been seen to be increasingly dysfunctional, imposing an agenda of austerity upon its citizens while facilitating the appropriation of public resources by wealthy individuals and the concentration of wealth in the hands of a very small minority. While this has led to an appreciation of 'accumulation by dispossession' on the one hand, it has also led to the growth of studies that show how powerful corporate interests have successfully intervened within the political landscape and how these interests remain deliberately hidden from public view (Hertel-Fernandez 2019; Page, Seawright and Lacombe 2018; Mayer 2016).

By atomizing the state as a political entity concerned with the workings of knowledge and neglecting its economic roles, postmodernists reaffirm the hidden nature of the influence of corporate capital. By focusing on science–policy and knowledge as the main instigator of the commodification of knowledge, postmodernists neglect the most significant aspects of economic liberalism: the appropriation of social welfare sectors, public knowledge and common resources, and their transformation into privately owned commodities that can be accumulated by transnational corporations; and the refashioning of property laws through state and international legislation to facilitate, legitimate and stabilize this appropriation. While Marxist political economy is accused of being 'teleological' and 'economically determinist', the emphasis in postmodernism on knowledge–power discourses is far more totalizing, hegemonic and one-dimensional.

The interplay of economic factors, technical policy discourses and ideology, and political lobbying by corporate interests in Zimbabwe analysed by Moyo in the 1990s reveals a much more subtle analysis grounded in real-world economies and economic processes. The contradictions between an economic model rooted in market liberalism, export-oriented growth through natural resources, and governance systems that claimed to support land reform, popular aspirations and civil society mobilization, ultimately unravelled. The export sectors failed to achieve sufficient economic growth and social redistribution to mask the inequalities involved in the process, as donors failed to provide sufficient aid and relief to carry through the ideology of market-oriented land reform. This ultimately led to a change of direction in the dominant political party for survival. This phase of the neoliberal project collapsed in Zimbabwe in the late 1990s. But the dynamics outlined by Moyo of the commodification of natural resources in new frontiers transforming the value of land; the privatization of public lands; the mobilization of NGOs and farmers' associations to promote new commodification of nature among smallholders by transnational interests and donor funding; the building of business linkages and sub-contracting between corporate interests and smallholders; and the lobbying of government by big capital – all these resound with contemporary land issues in Africa. They point to the origins of present-day land grabbing within the process of structural adjustment and economic liberalization of the 1980s and 1990s and expansion of transnational capital.

References

Arrighi, G. (2002), 'The African Crisis: World Systemic and Regional Aspects', *New Left Review,* 15 May–June: 5–36.

Bennet, E. (2002), 'The Summit-to-Summit Merry-Go-Round', *Seedling*, Grain Publications, July: 3–10.

Buttel, F. (1991), 'The Restructuring of the America Public Agricultural Research and Extension Technology Transfer System: Implications for Agricultural Extension', in W.M. Rivera and D.J. Gustafson, eds, *Agricultural Extension: Worldwide Institutional Evolution and Forces for Change*, Amsterdam: Elsevier: 43–56.

Dinham, B. and C. Hines (1983), *Agribusiness in Africa*, London: Earth Resources Research Ltd.

Fairhead, J. and M. Leach (1998), *Reframing Deforestation: Global Analysis and Local Realities: Studies in West Africa*, London: Routledge.

Fairhead, J., M. Leach and I. Scoones (2012), 'Green Grabbing: A New Appropriation of Nature?', *Journal of Peasant Studies*, 39 (2): 237–61.

Ferguson, J. (1994), *The Anti-Politics Machine: Development, Depoliticization and Bureaucratic Power in Lesotho*, Minneapolis: University of Minnesota Press.

Fink, R. (2012), 'The Structure of Social Change', https://archive.org/details/TheStructureOfSocialChangeLibertyGuideRichardFinkKoch, accessed 25 August 2019.

Fuglie, K., H. Paul, K. John and S. David (2012), 'Rising Concentration in Agricultural Input Industries Influences New Farm Technologies', Amber Waves, United States Department of Agriculture Economic Research Services, 3 December, https://www.ers.usda.gov/amber-waves/2012/december/rising-concentration-in-agricultural-inputindustries-influences-new-technologies, accessed 10 September 2019.

George, S. (1976), *How the Other Half Dies: The Real Reason for World Hunger*, Harmondsworth: Penguin Books.

Gerlach, C. (2008), 'Illusions of Global Governance: Transnational Agribusiness Inside the UN', in A. Nutzenadel and F. Trentman, eds, *Food and Globalization: Consumption, Markets and Politics in the Modern World*, Oxford: Berg: 193–211.

Harvey, D. (2003), *The New Imperialism*, Oxford: Oxford University Press.

Hertel-Fernandez, A. (2019), *State Capture: How Conservative Activists, Big Businesses, and Wealthy Donors Reshaped the American States – and the Nation*, Oxford: Oxford University Press.

Hertel-Fernandez, A., T. Skocpol and J. Sclar (2018), 'When Political Mega-Donors Join Forces: How the Koch Network and the Democratic Alliance Influence Organized US Politics on the Right and Left', *Studies in American Political Development*, 32 (2): 127–65.

Keeley, J. and I. Scoones (2003), *Understanding Environmental Policy Processes: Cases from Africa*, London: Earthscan.

Klein, N. (2007), *Shock Doctrine*, New York: Metropolitan Books.

Latham, M.E. (2011), *The Right Kind of Revolution: Modernization, Development, and US Foreign Policy from the Cold War to Present*, Ithaca, NY: Cornell University Press.

Leach, M. and R. Mearns (1996), *The Lie of the Land*, London: James Curry.

Mavroudeas, S. (2006), 'A History of Contemporary Political Economy and Postmodernism', *Review of Radical Political Economy*, 38 (4): 499–518.

Mayer, J. (2016) *Dark Money: The Hidden History of the Billionaires Behind the Rise of the Radical Right*, New York: Anchor Books.

Moyo, S. (1994), *Land Reform under Structural Adjustment in Zimbabwe*, Uppsala: Scandinavian African Institute.

Page, B.I., J. Seawright and M.J. Lacombe (2018), *Billionaires and Stealth Politics*, Chicago: University of Chicago Press.

Rockefeller Foundation and Office of Science and Technology Policy (1982), *Science for Agriculture*, New York: Rockefeller Foundation.

8

Prospects for Equitable Land Reform in Zimbabwe

Revisiting Sam Moyo's Work on the Land Question

Tendai Murisa

In 2003, the Government of Zimbabwe (GoZ) officially adopted the Fast-Track Land Reform Programme (FTLRP). The story of the FTLRP will, undoubtedly, never be complete without discussing the contributions of Sam Moyo. Up until the time of his death, Moyo significantly contributed towards an improved understanding of what probably stands out as one of the most difficult moments of Zimbabwe's post-independence history. Indeed, the programme had been vilified by many as a part of the Zimbabwe African National Union Patriotic Front's (ZANU-PF) attempts at retaining power and also as 'the end of development'. One can also argue that were it not for Sam Moyo's various writings (e.g., Moyo 2001, 2004, 2005), his collaborative work (Moyo and Chambati, eds 2013; Moyo, Helliker and Murisa, eds 2008; Moyo *et al.* 2009) and those of others (Scoones *et al.* 2010), the story of land reform would not have been comprehensively understood.

Yet, thirteen years later, the FTLRP has not been completed. There are many outstanding issues, such as clarifying the position on compensation and the methodology thereof, multiple farm ownership and incoherence around land tenure. In this essay, I will discuss the significance of Sam Moyo's contribution to land reform in Zimbabwe, and how it influenced the intellectual and policy debates. Instead of only celebrating Sam (which is important), I will also focus on identifying some of the outstanding issues that need urgent scholarly intervention, such as land tenure issues in fast-track areas, as part of an approach to help mobilize the desperately required financing mechanisms to spur agricultural production. Sam was cognizant of these issues; he had started tracking their development and significance as far back as 2007, in what he called the 'normalization process' (Moyo 2007, 2013). The main objective of this essay is to ensure that the contributions made by Sam are properly understood, in so far as they help in advancing a much more comprehensive understanding of Zimbabwe's national question.

Sam Moyo and Zimbabwe's Land Question

Sam Moyo will be remembered as a brave and highly productive scholar who, in the face of seemingly organized voices against his work, preferred to stand on principle instead of political expediency, or even to satisfy donor agendas. His writings covered most of the post-independence land reform initiatives in Zimbabwe (Moyo 1986, 1995, 1998, 2001, 2005, 2013). Although it is very difficult to pigeonhole Sam, it is perhaps safe to say that his name became synonymous with the land question especially in the post-2000 period, and very few discussions could be held on this subject without referring to his work or having him in attendance. He also made important contributions to the study of the environment, broader rural development and civil society.

It is important to note at the very outset that Moyo was first a nationalist and above all concerned with the national question, that is, the economic and political processes that would lead to liberation from the neo-colonial trap into which Zimbabwe had entered since 1980. He belonged among those who combined academic prowess with engagement in practical initiatives. Amongst his many national duties, he was a member of the short-lived 'Team Zimbabwe',[1] a joint initiative of the Commercial Farmers' Union (CFU), the finance sector and land policy experts to find an amicable solution to the land issue, and to keep donors and the government engaged on the possibilities of funding land reform (Selby 2006: 32). This initiative was established at a time when ZANU-PF and President Mugabe, through his speeches and stance, were quickly moving towards a more radical land reform. Moyo was also involved with the Presidential Land Reform Commission (PLRC), headed by the former Secretary of State, Charles Utete. In fact, what is commonly referred to as 'Volume 2' was developed under his intellectual supervision and guidance. Immediately after the PLRC, Sam Moyo, as head of the African Institute for Agrarian Studies (AIAS), worked closely with the Ministry of Lands in carrying out Provincial Dialogues on Land Reform.

Sam Moyo argued strongly that the agrarian question was at the centre of the national question. Like many other former settler colonies, Zimbabwe's agrarian question could not be resolved without addressing the land question. Sam's scholarship was dedicated to the resolution of this question, without romanticizing any particular farm model over another, but focusing instead on how to disentangle Zimbabwe from the web of neo-colonial existence into a truly functional and articulated economy with sufficient linkages between the rural and the urban. He also saw the potential of a genuine land redistribution process to contribute to democracy. Like many other progressive rural development scholars (see, for instance, Necosmoss 1993; Veltmeyer 2005; Warriner 1955), Sam Moyo also subscribed to the idea that land reform that prioritized smallholders and farm workers would broaden participation in agricultural commodity markets, ensure rural social reproduction and contribute towards an expanded and more equitable formal economy, beyond the minority white-dominated large-scale commercial farm sector. He was passionate about gender and farm workers' questions (see Moyo, Rutherford and Amanor-Wilks 2000). He also devoted scholarly attention to interpreting the significance of the demands for land from below.

Sam Moyo's seminal book, aptly titled *The Land Question in Zimbabwe* (1995), provided a most comprehensive understanding of the multiple dimensions of the land issue. He argued that there were five dimensions to Zimbabwe's contemporary land question that required urgent policy attention, as described in Table 1. In terms of distribution, the majority (83 per cent) of the black population was resident in Communal Areas and had to contend with declining quality of land, diminishing land-sizes, overpopulation and insecure usufruct to customary lands. Meanwhile, there were approximately 6,000 white-owned, large-scale commercial farms on 15,500,000 hectares, or 39 per cent of Zimbabwe's arable land, and 8,500 African small-scale commercial farmers on 1,400,000 hectares or 4 per cent. Moyo showed that over 66 per cent of the Communal Areas had excess populations of more than double their assessed carrying capacity.

At the time of independence, the Communal Areas were characterized by high levels of landlessness, which became manifest through increasing population density and declining average farm size. As families grew, the male head would be forced to sub-divide his portion of arable land for his male sons, who in turn would do the same when their own male children came of age. This negatively affected the social reproduction capacities of many rural households. The communal lands had on average over twenty-five persons per square kilometre, contrasted with nine persons per square kilometre on commercial land of superior quality. The average landholding size was 3.8 hectares in areas with average family sizes of six (Moyo 1995: 166). The restricted land resource base limited the spontaneity and efficiency required for sustainable social reproduction at the household level (ibid.: 167).

Moyo argued that the envisaged land reform programme should be seen as part of an economic policy of broadening accumulation from

Table 1 ***The Dimensions of Zimbabwe's Land Question***

Dimension of land question	*Issues to be resolved*
Land distribution	Inequitable and unjust access to land
	Limited rights/access for majority blacks
	Costly and cumbersome transfers of land
Land utilization	Speculative underutilization of land in freehold areas (studies carried out by World Bank and others had shown that LSCF were on average using only one-third of their farms)
	Unsustainable use in overcrowded areas
	Coercive regulations in some tenures
Land tenure	Insecurity of some tenures
	Discriminatory protection systems
	Overcentralized regulations
	Weak rights for women (especially in customary areas)
Land administration	Coercive and centralized approach
	Poor representation of majority
	Unclear separation of duties between traditional authority and decentralized structures of government
Land adjudication	Biased towards markets and state sectors
	No restitution/victims' compensation
	Merged powers of local courts/authorities

Source: Compiled by the author from various writings of Sam Moyo.

below and, in the process, resolving the challenges of social reproduction. He was also alert to the fact that any land reform would have to dilute the power or influence of large-scale commercial agriculture as part of the broader democratization processes. Thus, for Moyo, land reform had to resolve three challenges: historical dispossession, economic empowerment and deepening of democratization. He was to later state that 'land reform was meant to redress historical settler–colonial land dispossession and the related racial and foreign domination, as well as the class-based agrarian inequalities which minority rule promoted' (Moyo 2013: 29).

Sam Moyo on Mobilization and Land Reform

Moyo also emphasized the significance of rural and informal politics in the changing political economy of the land question (Yeros

2002: 123). Critical issues raised by him regarding rural politics and land occupations include, first, the inability of formal, urban-based, donor-dependent civic organizations to tap and articulate systematically the rural grievances of smallholders engaged in petty-commodity production and the wage economy. Second, he noted the existence of a fragmented land occupation movement which emerged in the euphoria of independence and evolved through various phases of intensity and visibility.

Moyo was not alone in raising the issue of land occupations; others such as Ranger (1985), Alexander (1993, 2003, 2006) and Marongwe (2002) have made similar observations of land occupation (squatting) as a tactic of attaining land. However, it was the interpretation of the land occupations of 2000 that led to acrimonious debate. They all argued that land-needy rural households used a variety of methods to acquire land, which included land occupation (squatting), natural resource poaching and fence-cutting (Alexander 2003: 87; Moyo 2001: 313). The tactics used by land-hungry peasants varied according to the natural region (NR): in the drier parts (NR IV and V), the tactics entailed 'poach grazing' (Alexander 2003: 85), while in the wetter areas (NR I–III), they involved land occupations. People turned to the local party structures to demand specific pieces of land on the basis of historical claims (Moyana 1984).

But in terms of the organization of these demands for land, Moyo (2001: 312) states that, empirically, a land occupation movement that was not necessarily organized on a national level but which shared common grievances had existed since the pre-independence period across the country. These land occupations remained the single most important and visible strategy of advocacy for radical land reform (ibid.: 313). The essence of the movement had been the same since 1980, and the tactic of land occupation had been used to gain access to land in various tenure categories, including white-owned commercial land, state land and communal lands (ibid.: 314). The occupations went through different phases of intensity throughout the post-independence period. Accordingly, land occupation or squatting tended to become an organized community strategy, and state-owned lands increasingly became a 'soft target' for occupation, especially in Matabeleland and Manicaland, where forests and parks have been predominant (Moyo 2003: 68).

Moyo (2001: 313) proceeded to develop a periodization of the land occupations, composed of four phases. The first phase, from 1980 to 1983, was one of 'low-profile but high-intensity land occupations'. During this time, there were widespread land occupations which received substantial support from local and state elites with links to the ruling party. However, these occupations remained hidden from the public in terms of media coverage. The media were more focused on the wildcat strikes taking place in urban areas and participating in the euphoria of independence. The central government tolerated the occupations as long as they were on abandoned farms, but disapproved of occupation of utilized commercial farmland. As independence progressed and the initial equity thrust of land distribution tapered off, because of the increasing disinterest in land reform within the ruling political party and the fiscal crises of the state, a rift began to grow between ZANU-PF and its rural base.

The second phase, from 1984 to 1996, was one of 'low-profile and low-intensity occupations', and it took place in a context of dwindling resources for land resettlement, alongside economic liberalization which resulted in loss of jobs in urban areas and mines (ibid.: 318). Moyo made an important connection between economic policy and land reform. In his 2000 book, *Land Reform under Structural Adjustment*, he argued that the Economic Structural Adjustment Programme (ESAP) in Zimbabwe had created incentives for large-scale commercial farmers to diversify into other land-use patterns, such as wildlife ranching and new export crops, but had not adequately brought smallholders into these circuits of production and accumulation, leading instead to growing inequality. ESAP had also created a disincentive for land reform under the 'willing-buyer–willing-seller' model, given that it created a boom in large-scale agriculture and thus an incentive to keep land.

During this period, there was a shift in the treatment of land occupiers ('squatters'). Those occupying white-owned farms were evicted and described as 'undisciplined and criminal elements who intended to frustrate the agricultural industry and resettlement process' (Alexander 2003: 90). In 1985, the Cabinet assigned the Minister of Local Government the responsibility to 'deal' with 'squatters' and rapidly instituted several changes which included the establishment of 'squatter control' committees in every district council (ibid.: 89).

The effectiveness of land occupations declined during this period of 'low-profile, low-intensity' occupations, as vacant land became scarce and resettlement schemes filled up. The government used forced evictions to restrain land occupations, especially during the transition to the liberalized economic policy framework. The brutality with which these evictions were carried out by police and farmers alike was reminiscent of the colonial era (Moyo 2001). In 1986, the Minister of Local Government stressed that land grabbers would be removed and that no squatter would be allocated land (Alexander 2003: 89).

The third phase, from 1997 to 1998, was one of 'high-profile and low-intensity land occupations'. The designation of 1,471 white-owned farms by GoZ in 1998 and, subsequently, the delisting of the majority of farms due to legal contestations, were followed by a spate of occupations, mostly on the originally designated farms, throughout the country. These land occupations that followed received wide media coverage (hence 'high profile') and were initially viewed as a form of political demonstration to symbolize the level of demand for land.

The occupations during this third phase occurred in waves, starting with about thirty cases in 1997, mostly on farms that had been identified for compulsory acquisition (Moyo 2001). Ten more land occupations occurred in Mashonaland East, within Goromonzi district. In Matabeleland, 200 families occupied about four farms in the Nyamandlovu area, apparently where twenty-five out of the twenty-six earlier designated farms had been delisted by GoZ as unsuitable for resettlement (Larsson Lidén 2000; Marongwe 2002: 23). In a high-profile case, the Svosve people of Marondera in Mashonaland East occupied four farms in June 1998, and received support from some government officials. The group, led by Chief Svosve and war veterans, approached Igava, Daskop and Homepark farms in Marondera and informed the owners of their intention to take over, based on their historical claim to the land. This was followed by the actual movement of villagers into these farms with their belongings, within five days of their giving notice of intention to occupy. In Masvingo province, thirty-six war veterans occupied the Agricultural and Rural Development Authority (ARDA) Mkwasine Estate (owned by the state) in Chiredzi district, while some 700 people led by war veterans occupied Longdale Farm, 15 kilometres south of Masvingo (*Daily News* 1999; Marongwe 2002: 23). Further nationwide occupations were carried out by thousands of people who were mainly communal and resettlement area farmers, retrenched workers and war veterans (Yeros 2002: 241). Knight (1998: 13) aptly captured this moment: 'land invasion followed land invasion becoming almost a national movement'. The occupations spread to Guruve, Makonde, Macheke, Hurungwe and Odzi (Yeros 2002: 241). Unlike in past phases of land occupation, most of the land occupied in this phase was white-owned commercial land.

The first two decades of independence were indeed characterized by the growth of the land movement across classes and regions. As the land occupations were proving successful, the numbers began to swell and the membership broadened (Moyo 2001: 315). While in the 1980s and the first half of the 1990s, the movement was essentially composed of the rural landless and poor, in the late 1990s, it began to incorporate retrenched workers from the urban and mining areas (Yeros 2002: 244).

In the process, Moyo (2001, 2005) helped unpack the process of rural mobilization, power relations and social relations of production. He tracked mobilizations for land in terms of the material demands and the class category of those making those demands, and, contrary to what others have argued, he did not seek to romanticize the peasantry but rather engaged critically in an effort to understand their agency. His interpretation of the land movement, especially his views on the similarities between the land movement pre-2000 and post-2000, has been subject to intense debate. Moyo (2001) argued that the essence of land occupations has been the same since independence: the overriding grievances spurring demands for land reform remained; the land movement was still made up of landless rural people and urban unemployed; and the manner of mobilization and leadership had been the same since 1980. Furthermore, since 1980, the state remained ambivalent about land occupations. In the early years (1981–83), the state used a strategy of formalizing land occupations, while it preferred to use squatter-control committees to contain land occupations in the mid-1980s.

On the other hand, Hammar, Raftopolous and Jensen (eds 2003), Sachikonye (2005) and Marongwe (2002) argued that there was no continuation or similarity between the pre-2000 and post-2000 land occupations, largely because of the changed role of the state. Selby (2006) argued that, while prior to 2000 the state mostly aligned itself with large-scale commercial farmers and opposed land occupations, after the February 2000 referendum on the government's constitutional reform proposal, which was defeated and which included *inter alia* a clause on the right to expropriate land, the state seemed to be the main instigator of the land occupations. Moore (2003) and Alexander (2003) portrayed the post-2000 land occupations and fast-track programme as a response on the part of ZANU-PF to the referendum defeat. For instance, Moore (2003) described the defeat as 'the straw that started to break the ZANU(PF) camel's back', and posited this as a direct catalyst for the Third Chimurenga or liberation struggle, now by means of fast-track land reform (Moore 2001: 255). Scholars such as Sachikonye (2005), Moore (2001) and Raftopolous (2003) at that time reduced 'fast-track' to a mere regime-survival strategy. However, their analysis did not adequately include the motivations of those among the land occupiers, especially their socio-economic context and the significance of land to rural social reproduction.

Selby's (2006) assertion that the state was the main instigator of the land occupations overlooks grassroots-based forms of mobilization and the role of war veterans in land occupations. However, Moyo (2011a) cautioned against conflating war veterans as a part of the ZANU-PF machinery without comprehensively analysing the relationship between the two. Those opposed to land reform privileged the political factors, especially the regime-survival imperative, at the expense of the colonial history of land alienation, the difficulties of redistributing land within the Lancaster House Agreement which sealed independence, the failure of the willing-buyer–willing-seller model to effectively redistribute land, and the impact of structural adjustment, especially the loss of urban wage jobs and intensification of rural poverty. Even the first phase of land reform was dismissed as largely benefiting ZANU-PF elites, without acknowledging evaluations which showed the positive outcomes of land reform (Cusworth and Walker 1988; Kinsey 1999).

Sadomba (2008)[2] has noted that land occupations did not really stop between 1999 and 2000; in some parts of the country, political elites convinced the rural people desirous of land to wait first for the outcomes of the Donor Conference, in progress at the time, and then the constitutional reform process, in which it was envisaged that the new dispensation would allow the state to redistribute land quickly. The 'no' vote was translated as meaning denial of land reform through the legitimate process.

Sam Moyo collaborated with many scholars, but perhaps it is his joint work with Paris Yeros in their 2005 book, *Reclaiming the Land: The Resurgence of Rural Movements in Africa, Asia and Latin America* that remains seminal in many respects, especially the manner in which they analysed Zimbabwe's land reform within a global South context. In the process, they helped to debunk myths regarding the possibility of development via the liberalization project of the Washington Consensus. They demonstrated how the failure of structural adjustment programmes across the entire global South yielded land occupations by the marginalized peasantry. *Reclaiming the Land* (Moyo and Yeros, eds 2005), on land occupations across the global South and the different types of peasant-based movements such as the Movimento Sem Terra (MST) in Brazil, the Landless People's Movement (LPM) in South Africa and that of the war veterans in Zimbabwe, was instrumental in creating connections between seemingly disparate and disconnected struggles for land. In response, the African Union hastened the process of developing Land Policy Guidelines for its member states, and the World Bank increased its investments towards policy dialogues on land.

The book recognized the local and global significance of these land occupations, arguing that they are 'the most important challenge to the neo-colonial state in Africa under neo-liberalism' (Moyo and Yeros, eds 2005: 165). To their credit – and this is missing in many discussions on land reform – Moyo and Yeros acknowledged the agency of rural dwellers through land occupations as possibly the only remaining force of resistance to the market philosophy of resource management, although its ideology has not been adequately developed to wage a sustained campaign against the state.

Moyo on the FTLPR

Sam Moyo did not romanticize the land occupations; he spent time in the field talking to land occupiers and also engaging the state in terms of understanding their response. When GoZ officially announced the FTLRP in 2001, he began to make calls for a more effective state to be at the centre of the process of land reform. He argued that the FTLRP had been negatively affected by the absence of an effective mechanism for coordinating and ensuring the implementation of numerous multisectoral land reform functions (Moyo 2004). He noted that land administration and management systems, information systems and skills required to coordinate the functions at the various levels of government were under-resourced (ibid.). Mechanisms for resolving conflicts between various levels of government remained ineffective, while the management of conflicts between settlers, landowners and government officials over land matters was poorly coordinated. It is no wonder, therefore, that the FTLRP became synonymous with chaos and corruption to many. In fact Moyo, in one of his most recent articles on land, also identified corruption as one of the biggest challenges to the effective resolution of outstanding issues. He argued: 'the FTLRP allocation process was not free from corruption. In particular, the A2 scheme entailed jumping application queues to gain better capitalized plot (e.g. with irrigation facilities) and "whole farms" and unsubstantiated plans to justify access to larger sized plots, using "pseudo-legal" administrative loopholes' (Moyo 2013: 37). In our field surveys (as part of the AIAS), we came across many cases where political elites, state officials and private citizens with connections had gained temporary but free use of the underutilized state farms, and some of the lands acquired by the state but not unallocated.

Despite the evident challenges of land administration, Moyo argued that the outcome of fast-track had been significantly redistributive: of the 15 million hectares of land which, in 1980, were controlled by about 6,000 white farmers, over 13 million hectares had, by 2009, been formally transferred to over 240,000 families of largely rural origin (Moyo *et al.* 2009), leading to a radically different agrarian structure (Table 2). The fast-track phase alone officially benefited 168.671 families on 9.2 million hectares (Moyo 2013: 42). He also observed that fast-track has led to a net transfer of wealth and power from a racial minority of landed persons to various classes of black people, including mostly previously landless and

Table 2 *Zimbabwe's New Agrarian Structure*

Farm class	Land tenure	Farms/Households		Area		
		Numbers	% of total	Hectares (million hectares)	% of total	Farm size (hectares)
Smallholder	Communal	1,100,000	81.2	16.400	49.9	15
	Old resettlement	75,000	5.5	3.667	11.2	49
	A1	145,800	10.8	5.759	17.5	40
	Sub-total	*1,321,000*	*97.6*	*25.286*	*78.6*	*20*
Small- to medium-scale commercial (SSCF)	Old SSCF	8,500	0.6	1.400	4.3	165
	Small A2	22,700	1.7	3.000	9.1	133.9
	Sub-total	*31,200*	*2.3*	*4.400*	*13.4*	*142*
Large-scale commercial (LSCF)	Medium–large A2	217	0.03	0.509	1.6	2,345
	Black LSCF	956	0.07	0.531	1.6	555
	White LSCF	198	0.01	0.117	0.4	593
	Sub-total	*1,371*	*0.11*	*1.157*	*3.5*	*844*
Corporate estates	Corporates	20	0.001	0.806	2.5	40,320
	Conservancies	8	0.001	0.247	0.8	30,875
	Parastatals	106	0.01	0.296	0.9	2,788
	Institutions	113	0.01	0.146	0.4	1,289
	Sub-total	*247*	*0.022*	*1.495*	*4.5*	*6,051*
Total		1,353,818	100	32.338	100	

Source: Moyo (2011b).

land-poor classes and a substantial number of low-income, wage-earning and unemployed workers, as well as various categories of the petty bourgeoisie (ibid.: 44). Fast-track also substantially reduced the overall land concentration and expanded the numbers of those involved in farming.

Together with others (see, for instance, Murisa 2009; Scoones *et al.* 2010), Moyo observed that most of the beneficiaries of fast-track came from rural areas, being largely peasants from the Communal Areas, with a few coming from the farm-worker population in large-scale commercial farms, while about 25 per cent were from the urban areas (Moyo *et al.* 2009). One of the most important claims that Moyo made was that fast-track land reform has undermined the class logic of settler-colonial agrarian relations, founded on monopoly control over land which deprived peasants of land-based social reproduction and compelled cheap agrarian labour supplies (Moyo 2013: 60–61). Based on his claim, one can then argue that fast-track land reform has ushered in a new set of agrarian labour and production relations, barring any changes that could be effected in the future.

Outstanding Land Tenure Reforms

Although I can never speak on behalf of Sam Moyo with authority, my suspicion is that among many other things he would have wanted to see resolved is the question of land tenure in the aftermath of fast-track land reform. Prior to fast-track, the state redistributed land through three resettlement models – 'A', 'B' and 'C'. The most common resettlement types were Model A and Model B. The former offered individualized plots averaging 5 hectares per household and provided for common grazing lands, while the latter entailed the formation of cooperatives. The majority of those who were offered land for resettlement were settled within the Model A scheme, which replicated the pattern and conditions of the Native Land Husbandry Act of 1951, which had been designed to promote limited individual ownership and production for Africans. In terms of land tenure, the beneficiaries' claim to land was based on state-issued, annually renewable permits that provided very little security (Gaidzanwa 1981). The state had basically used the resettlement programme to acquire land from the freehold sector, and to cancel title to it and expand state ownership (Cheater 1990: 197). Table 3 provides a summary of the evolution of land tenure regimes in Zimbabwe.

The onset of fast-track also saw the extinguishing of most private property rights in agricultural land and the broadening of the effective occupation and use/ownership of the redistributed land through socially differentiated forms of land tenure (Moyo 2013: 45). The GoZ commit-

Table 3 *Types of Land Tenure Arrangements in Zimbabwe since Independence*

Sector	Type of Tenure	Rights	Administrative Arrangements	Security
LSCF *	Freehold tenure based on surveying, mapping and lodged with the Deeds registry	Secure rights Land used as collateral Use of courts to protect rights	Individual responsibility Local authority's collection of unit tax Intensive conservation areas	Secure in a normal situation, but insecure in a context of demand for land based on historical circumstances
SSCF **	Freehold tenure as above	Secure rights and land may be used as collateral	Individual responsibility Local authority's collection of unit tax	Problems of inheritance and fragmentation because of pressures for access to land
Resettlement (old)	Permit system then revised into leaseholds	Rights of the authorities are prioritized than those of the settlers	State through MoLGRUD**** and now traditional leaders	Highly insecure because of the ministerial powers which allows for expulsion
Communal Area	Customary tenure	Usufruct rights Private use of arable land and shared commons Land can be taken without recourse to courts	Traditional leaders (chiefs, headmen, etc.) Local authorities through VIDCOs# and WADCOs## State through its statutory agents	Secure in principle, but land cannot be used as collateral
State Land	State land	Leasing, licensing, statutory allocations	State administers land through its own parastatals	Secure for the state but not so for individuals when the lease period comes to an end
A1	Offer letter issued by Minister of MoLARR***	Insecure rights Seem usufruct rights with promise of leaseholds	State and traditional leaders contesting to govern	Highly insecure as the situation on the ground is still fluid
A2	Offer letter issued by Minister of MoLARR***	Promises of leaseholds Highly insecure	Individual State and traditional leaders contesting to govern	Highly insecure as the situation on the ground is still fluid

* Large-scale Commercial Farms. ** Small-scale Commercial Farms. ***Ministry of Lands, Agriculture and Rural Resettlement. ****Ministry of Local Government and Rural Development. # Village Development Committees. ## Ward Development Committees.
Source: Moyo (2004).

ted to a new tenure system of permits held in perpetuity for A1 plots and 99-year leases for A2 plots. Thus, on paper, the land tenure issue has been resolved: A1 beneficiaries will be issued with the permits, while A2 beneficiaries will be issued with 99-year leases. However, in practice, it remains outstanding for a variety of issues. Less than 5 per cent of the beneficiaries have been issued these signed documents. Many of the former large-scale commercial farmers are still to be compensated, or to agree to terms with the GoZ on how they will hand over title.

The GoZ justified the extinguishing of private property of land and introduction of permissory and leasehold tenure as a safeguard against land concentration (interviews with officials from Ministry of Lands, September and March 2007). The insecurities derive from the fact that the state has, with a stroke of the pen, cancelled freehold land without attendant consultations and compensation for the actual land, raising the question of what would stop it from doing the same with permits and leases, especially since it now owns the land (based on submissions made at an AIAS Policy Review Dialogue on Land Tenure, August 2007). Furthermore, the GoZ has not clarified the institutional arrangements for administration of the new land tenure system. The Land Board that was introduced in 2000 remains largely inactive and is based within the Ministry of Lands instead of having an autonomous structure that would enable it to interact with the Ministry of Land as an equal.

During the initial stages of resettlement, land beneficiaries were issued with an 'offer letter' representing official recognition of the right over land. However, this offer letter did not provide adequate security to new landholders. Clause 7 of the letter states that the offer to land can be withdrawn at any time with the government having no obligation to compensate for any improvements that might have been made (World Bank 2006). However, in practice, very few families have been removed from the land that they occupied.

Zimbabwe's agricultural land is now divided into twelve tenure regimes, as shown in Table 2. While the number of land evictions has gone down, questions of improving the productivity of farms loom large. The nexus of production and tenure security needs further investigation at two levels: ensuring that there are optimal farm sizes by introducing deterrent taxes that discourage land hoarding, and creating land tenure instruments acceptable by the financial sector and the broader agro-industry to address the shortage of financing arrangements currently inhibiting productivity. These two issues largely remain unresolved within the fast-track areas and the remaining large-scale commercial sector.

In 2006, GoZ introduced the permit system for A1 farms and

leasehold tenure for A2 farms. According to Ministry sources, the delay in the issuance of permits was caused by legal hurdles in the acquisition of land, and these were only 'resolved' in 2005, when the Constitution was amended to enable the government to nationalize all agricultural land.[3] Prior to the constitutional amendment that nationalized agricultural land, the government could not transfer the ownership of land to the new land beneficiaries because of the appeals against compulsory acquisition lodged by former landowners. The government faced two options: either to respond to every individual appeal, or to come up with legislation that nullified these appeals. In 2005, the state took the latter route, and through Amendment No. 17, precluded the courts from deliberating on matters surrounding compulsory acquisition, although they retained jurisdiction over contests regarding improvements on farms. By the close of 2007, the GoZ had not issued any permits to landholders in A1, while approximately 6 per cent of A2 beneficiaries had been issued leases (Moyo 2007: 2).

The land permit essentially offers partially similar usufruct land rights to those provided under customary tenure, in terms of the nature and breadth of rights to use land for the homestead, cropping, and shared utilization of common grazing and woodland areas (ibid.: 12–13). The permit is registered in the names of both spouses (in the case of married couples) and is offered in perpetuity to the beneficiary household.

There are nuanced differences between the land rights being bestowed in the newly resettled areas and those existing in customary tenure areas (Murisa 2009). In the customary areas, land access and use rights are based on belonging to and membership of a lineage group, while traditional institutions and authority are prominent in the distribution and administration of customary lands. In the newly resettled areas, the A1 permit elevates the role of the state as the initial provider of land and responsible for administrative oversight. The permit is silent on the role of the traditional authority regarding the administration of the land despite the fact that chiefs were mobilized by the state to verify applicants for A1 farms. However, Moyo (2013: 45) was dismissive of these nuanced differences, arguing that the A1 permit provides similar forms of land rights to those provided under the customary tenure. Instead, it is their legal status that differs from their customary area counterparts: in the fast-track areas, the state directly owns such land and controls the land allocation process using criteria which transcend those defined by membership to given 'communities'. Moyo argued that, in effect, the A1 land tenure relationship is 'a vertical legal and social relationship between the state and the families, which is complemented by elements of customary land administration practice' (ibid.). The complexity of the new arrangements and required administration system is quite evident.

The A2 land beneficiaries are being issued with a 99-year lease agreement; as per the government (GoZ 2006: 4), 'the lease provides for an annual rental to be paid to the lessor (state), the leased land to be effectively utilized with due regard to good husbandry and environmental enhancement and protection and bans ceding or subletting of land without the express permission of the lessor's representative'.

The lease requires the beneficiaries to institute basic farm developments, minimum land utilization and recommended natural resources management practices. It requires that the lessee allocate 20 per cent of the land to growing foodgrains or sell 20 per cent of the cattle to the state-owned cold storage company.

The lease is subject to the succession and inheritance laws of the country. The government retains the right to cancel the lease in cases where the lessee has been judged insolvent, or where the lessee either owns or is leasing some other property for agricultural purposes and fails to pay rentals, levies and rates (ibid.: 6). By 2010, less than 1,000 A2 beneficiaries had received the lease contracts.

The Challenges of the New Land Tenure Regimes

The discussion on tenure has been dominated by concerns of financing and investing in agriculture. It has focused on the logic of improving production, tenure security and the tradeability of the A2 lease (see, for instance, Mhishi 2007; Moyo 2007; Richardson 2005). Although Sam Moyo wrote extensively on land tenure (Moyo 2007, 2013), he was careful not to be prescriptive (to a fault); instead, he mostly preferred to discuss the different social, economic and political trajectories that were influencing the preferred tenure regimes. He was clearly concerned about the danger of re-concentration of land if freehold tenure was restored. He spent more time going through the different versions of the lease (A2) and permit (A1), and produced what is probably one of the most credible analyses of the documents.

The jury is still out on whether the new arrangements are permanent and sustainable. Moyo (2007) noted the many strands of arguments that had emerged around land tenure, primarily among market-based actors such as bankers and other agro-industry firms, identified tenure insecurities as an explanation for limited financial investments in the fast-track areas, and made a clear push for the return to freehold tenure as in the large-scale commercial farming sector. At the same time, the GoZ remained mostly ambivalent, preferring to emphasize the legitimacy of the 99-year leases for A2 farmers (commercial) and the permits for A1 farmers (smallholders). Market-based actors have pursued a purely economistic position, arguing that freehold tenure is a superior form of tenure with potential to unlock the desperately needed financial investments for ensuring improved production on the farms. The state, on the other hand, has avoided an overall rush towards freehold tenure and seems to prefer a more gradual approach, by introducing leasehold fees which may end up serving as a form of purchase of the farms. Furthermore, Moyo also argued that the new tenure regimes were more socially legitimate and less insecure as compared to the tenure system that was introduced in the first phase of resettlement (see ibid.).

There is another strand to the argument: the previous farmers still hold the paper titles to the land, which in itself suggests an unresolved contested issue of ownership, especially given some of the legal victories that these farmers have scored at the now defunct Southern African Development Community (SADC) Tribunal. One can also perceive an implicit position on the part of the ZANU-PF state, that is, the need for control: the creation of an independent bourgeoisie on A2 farms and smallholders on A1 farms not beholden to the party is not part of the vision of the ruling elite (see, for instance, Murisa 2013).

The current powers invested in the state lead to a third concern regarding the current tenure regimes: the possibility of state capture. There are fears amongst some of the resettled that a policy shift within government could lead to loss of land amongst the newly resettled in both A1 and A2 areas. The concern about state capture is also directly linked to the democratization concerns raised above: how will land tenure reform contribute to rural democracy? Murisa (2013) has demonstrated how land reform has provided an opportunity for the ZANU-PF government to enhance its control of the rural space and even created new 'traditional' local government authorities. The delays in creating a coherent land administration framework, especially in A1 areas, have led to the emergence or replication of customary land administration structures and norms. While the legal contract, through the permit, seeks to promote a certain form of social relations, it remains inadequately explained and promoted. On the other hand, the introduction of traditional authority without the necessary rule book for what the village heads can and cannot do has contributed to misunderstandings concerning their powers in terms of governing the land. The introduction of the new permissory system has not yet been adequately explained to the beneficiaries. Their understanding of land tenure provisions is currently based on sketchy information from local leaders and government officials, to the extent that some of the beneficiaries we interviewed as part of the AIAS eight-district survey believe that the chiefs have the authority to allocate land or to move them off the land. The situation is compounded by the fact that many of the beneficiaries are from customary areas where a strong relationship exists between traditional structures and land. During interviews with A1 beneficiaries in Goromonzi and Simba, the respondents revealed that they expect traditional leaders to ensure that land and natural resources are being managed properly. Notably, most of the respondents did not see a problem with the expansion of traditional authority into the fast-track resettlement areas.

Connecting the Zimbabwe Debates to Global Discourse

Garret Hardin's 1968 essay, aptly entitled 'The Tragedy of the Commons', played a major role in shaping neoclassical policy prescriptions on land tenure from the 1970s well into the 1980s. In brief, Hardin argued that a shared village grazing pasture would tend to get overused and eventually destroyed because more people utilized the common grazing ground without paying for the cost of maintaining it, a phenomenon known in economics as 'free riding'. This view inspired a variety of land reforms with a general trend towards market-oriented access to, and the privatization of, land through private entitlement. The premise was simple: individualized tenure offers the best certainty in land rights, which provides incentives for sustainable use and facilitates access to credit for investment in agriculture and natural resources, hence contributing to increased productivity and improved natural resource stewardship (Economic Commission for Africa [ECA] 2004: 15). However, the assumptions of the allocative efficiency of freehold tenure have also been challenged; for instance, the World Bank (1991, 1995), in its technical studies on land in Zimbabwe, revealed that land underutilization was mostly practised by large-scale farmers – only 65 per cent of commercial farmland was under productive use.

Meanwhile in Kenya, a study carried out by Rutten (1992) in one of the three Maasai districts, where the individualization of title was pursued through the establishment of group ranches with funding from the World Bank and the UK's Department for International Development (DFID), showed that grazing land had diminished by well over 40 per cent over the period 1982–90, leading to increased vulnerability and destitution of pastoralists, and it had also led to accelerated wanton environmental degradation.

In 2009, the Nobel Peace Prize Committee awarded the prize for economics to the now late Elinor Ostrom, Professor of Development

Economics at Indiana University, together with Professor Oliver E. Williamson. Ostrom was recognized for her work on common property regimes; could this be a signal of a paradigm shift from the Hardin-inspired period? Essentially, Ostrom (1990) argued that far from a tragedy, the commons can be managed from the bottom–up towards shared prosperity, given the right institutions. She forcefully stated that other solutions exist rather than privatization, and that these entail stable institutions of self-government which can be created if certain problems of supply, credibility and monitoring are solved. In terms of land tenure, her argument seems to suggest the rethinking of customary/communal forms of tenure with an adequate institutional framework to address challenges of supply, production and preservations.

The approaches of Hardin and Ostrom to property rights and management have a significant bearing on how the debates on land tenure have evolved in Zimbabwe since 2003. Basically, the debates have been inspired by Hardin, while very limited scholarly attention has been devoted towards exploring ways in which the 99-year lease and the A1 permit can be used to unlock value for agricultural production, except perhaps for Sam Moyo's writing. One of the most influential writers on the right has been Craig Richardson (2005), who has argued that the manner in which land was acquired despoiled agricultural land property rights and that these no longer exist in Zimbabwe. Richardson, and also Mhishi (2007), dismissed the legal basis of introducing new forms of property rights, due to the fact that the land rights of former landowners were undermined and that the redistribution exercise is still under litigation in the courts. Richardson (2005) argued that land reform is the cause of economic decline because of the way it undermined property rights and dampened investor confidence. On the other hand, Moyo argued that the A1 permit and A2 lease offered by the state are formal statutory land rights that should be recognized by banks and other market players (Moyo 2007: 9). However, it is important to remember that land reform has always been a part of the agenda of the state as an attempt to redress the historical settler-colonial land dispossession and the related racial and foreign domination, as well as the class-based agrarian inequalities that minority rule promoted (Moyo 2013: 29). In fact, Moyo (2013) and others have argued that land reform also contributes towards democracy by breaking the monopoly held by white-settler agriculture, including its representative unions (see Murisa 2009).

The above provides a summary of the contradictory, even polarized, positions that have characterized the land tenure reform debates in Zimbabwe. Whilst the state has, at times, seemed unconcerned about the weaknesses inherent in the existing tenure reforms, the weak participation of actors such as banks in the agrarian economy, and also the desire for re-insertion into global commodity and financial circuits, has led the government to make announcements on compensation of former white farmers, creating possibilities to issue freehold title. It is also important to bear in mind that almost all cabinet ministers own at least one farm each and they have an interest in resolving their ownership status whilst still in power, given the contested way in which these farms were acquired.

Conclusion

This essay provides a detailed background to Zimbabwe's land question, and demonstrates how Sam Moyo was central to most of the debates and also how he helped shape land policy. It also discusses land tenure in fast-track areas as an outstanding issue requiring urgent attention to resolve the problem of farm investments and production, and to curtail the powers of the state over farms. There is an implicit shift towards freehold title, especially in A2 farms connected to party elites. Delays in the issuing of leases and permits will not only constrain production on the farms, but perpetuate the state's implicit agenda to ensure some form of control through opaque administration of the leases and permits, which creates uncertainty and room for manipulation of land beneficiaries. The ambivalence on the part of the state has partially contributed to limited investments, thereby hampering a quicker turnaround in terms of agricultural production.

This article was originally published in *Agrarian South: Journal of Political Economy*, Vol. 5, Nos. 2–3, 2016. Copyright 2016 © Centre for Agrarian Research and Education for South (CARES), New Delhi. All rights reserved. Reproduced with the permission of the copyright holders and the publishers, SAGE Publications India Pvt. Ltd, New Delhi.

Notes

1 The leading actors of this initiative were Dr Robbie Mupawose, former Permanent Secretary, Ministry of Agriculture; Greg Brackenbridge, Chairperson, Bankers Association; and Professors Mandivamba Rukuni and Sam Moyo, land policy experts.

2 One of many others to be mentored by Sam Moyo.

3 It seems the GoZ has reconsidered this position and compensation for acquired farms is back on the policy agenda. The Minister of Finance has, on more than one occasion, reassured former farmers that compensation is being organized.

References

Alexander, Jocelyn (1993), 'Things Fall Apart, the Centre Can Hold: Processes of Post-War Political Change in Zimbabwe's Rural Areas', IDS Occasional Paper No. 8, in S.L. Laurids, ed., *Bringing Institutions Back In: The Role of Institutions in Civil Society, State and Economy*, Roskilde: Roskilde University: 131–61.

——— (2003), 'Squatters, Veterans and the State in Zimbabwe', in Amanda Hammar, Brian Raftopoulos and Stig Jensen, eds, *Zimbabwe's Unfinished Business: Rethinking Land, State and Nation in the Context of Crisis*, Harare: Weaver Press: 83–117.

——— (2006), *The Unsettled Land: State-Making and the Politics of Land in Zimbabwe 1893–2003*, Oxford: James Currey Publishers.

Cheater, A. (1990), 'The Ideology of "Communal" Land Tenure in Zimbabwe: Mythogenesis Enacted?', *African Affairs*, 60 (2): 188–206.

Cusworth, J. and J. Walker (1988), 'Land Resettlement in Zimbabwe: A Preliminary Evaluation', Evaluation Report No. EV 434, London: Overseas Development Administration.

Daily News (1999), (Zimbabwe), 15 December.

Economic Commission for Africa (ECA) (2004), *Land tenure systems and their impacts on food security and sustainable development in Africa*, Addis Ababa: ECA.

Gaidzanwa, Rudo B. (1981), *Promised Land*, unpublished MA thesis, Institute of Social Studies, The Hague.

Government of Zimbabwe (GoZ) (2006), *Lease Agreement for the A2 Scheme*, Harare: Government Printers.

Hammar, Amanda, Brian Raftopolous and Stig Jensen, eds (2003), *Zimbabwe's Unfinished Business: Rethinking Land, State and Nation in the Context of Crisis*, Harare: Weaver Press.

Kinsey, B.H. (1999), 'Land Reform, Growth and Equity: Emerging Evidence from Zimbabwe's Resettlement Program', *Journal of Southern African Studies, 25* (2), 173–96.

Knight, R. (1998), 'Zimbabwe's 1998 Land Invasions: An Investigation into the Grassroots Politics of Land Redistribution and Resettlement', unpublished research mimeo.

Larsson Lidén, Lisbeth (2000), 'Democracy Grassroots Movements and Rural Development: Case Studies from Zimbabwe, Zambia and Kerala', unpublished PhD thesis, SLU, Agraria 230.

Marongwe, Nelson (2002), *Conflicts over Land and Other Natural Resources in Zimbabwe*, Harare: ZERO.

Mhishi, Lloyd (2007), 'An Overview of the Legal Aspects of Leasehold Tenure with a Particular Focus on Conveyancing and Land Transfers', paper presented at AIAS Policy Review Dialogue on Land Tenure, 8 August.

Moore, D. (2001), 'Is the Land the Economy and the Economy the Land? Primitive Accumulation in Zimbabwe', *Journal of Contemporary African Studies,* 19 (2), 253–66.

——— (2003), 'Zimbabwe's Triple Crisis: Primitive Accumulation, Nation-State Formation and Democratization in the Age of Neo-Liberal Globalization', *African Studies Quarterly,* 7 (2 and 3), 33–51.

Moyana, Henry (1984), *The Political Economy of Land in Zimbabwe*, Gweru: Mambo Press.

Moyo, Sam (1986), 'The Land Question', in I. Mandaza, ed., *Zimbabwe: The Political Economy of Transition 1980–1986*, Dakar: CODESRIA.

——— (1995), *The Land Question in Zimbabwe*, Gweru: Mambo Press.

——— (1998), *The Land Acquisition Process in Zimbabwe (1997/8)*, Harare: United Nations Development Programme (UNDP).

——— (2001), 'The Land Occupation Movement and Democratization in Zimbabwe: Contradictions of Neoliberalism', *Millennium Journal of International Studies*, 30 (2), 311–30.

——— (2003), 'The Interactions of Market and Compulsory Land Acquisition Process with Social Action in Zimbabwe's Land Reform', in I. Mandaza and D. Nabudere, eds, *Pan Africanism and Integration in Africa*, Harare: SAPES Books.

——— (2004), *Overall Impacts of the Fast Track Land Reform Programme*, AIAS Monograph Series, 02/2004, Harare: AIAS.

——— (2005), 'Land Policy, Poverty Reduction and Public Action in Zimbabwe', ISS/UNDP Land, Poverty and Public Action Policy Paper No. 11, The Hague: ISS.

——— (2007), *Emerging Land Tenure Issues in Zimbabwe*, AIAS Monograph Series, 1, Harare: AIAS.

——— (2011a), 'Changing Agrarian Relations after Redistributive Land Reform in Zimbabwe', *The Journal of Peasant Studies,* 38 (5), 907–34.

——— (2011b), 'Three Decades of Agrarian Reform in Zimbabwe', *Journal of Peasant Studies*, 38 (3), 493–531.

——— (2013), 'Land Reform and Redistribution in Zimbabwe since 1980', in S. Moyo and W. Chambati, eds, *Land and Agrarian Reform in Zimbabwe: Beyond White-Settler Capitalism,* Dakar: CODESRIA: 29–78.

Moyo, S. and W. Chambati (2013), 'Introduction', in S. Moyo and W. Chambati, eds, *Land and Agrarian Reform in Zimbabwe: Beyond White-Settler Capitalism*, Dakar: CODESRIA.

Moyo, Sam, Walter Chambati, Tendai Murisa, Dumisani Siziba, Charity Dangwa, Kingston Mujeyi and Ndabezinhle Nyoni (2009), *Fast Track Land Reform Baseline Survey in Zimbabwe: Trends and Tendencies, 2005–06*, Harare: African Institute of Agrarian Studies.

Moyo, Sam, Kirk Helliker and Tendai Murisa, eds (2008), *Contested Terrain: Land Reform and Civil Society in Contemporary Zimbabwe*, Pietermaritzburg: S&S Publishers.

Moyo, Sam, B. Rutherford and D. Amanor-Wilks (2000), 'Land Reform and Changing Social Relations for Farm Workers in Zimbabwe', *Review of African Political Economy,* 84 (18): 181–202.

Moyo, Sam and Paris Yeros (2005), 'Land Occupations and Land Reform in Zimbabwe: Towards the National Democratic Revolution', in S. Moyo and P. Yeros, eds, *Reclaiming the Land: The Resurgence of Rural Movements in Africa, Asia and Latin America*, London: Zed Books.

Moyo, Sam and Paris Yeros (2013), 'Social Organization in the Aftermath of "Fast Track": An Analysis of Emerging Forms of Local Authority, Platforms of Mobilization and Local Cooperation', in S. Moyo and Walter Chambati, eds, *Land and Agrarian Reform in Zimbabwe: Beyond White Settler Capitalism*, Dakar: CODESRIA.

Moyo, Sam and Paris Yeros, eds (2005), *Reclaiming the Land: The Resurgence of Rural Movements in Africa, Asia and Latin America*, London: Zed Books.

Murisa, Tendai (2009), 'An Analysis of Emerging Forms of Social Organization and Agency in the Newly Restricted Areas of Zimbabwe: The Case of Goromonzi and Zvimba Districts', unpublished PhD thesis, Rhodes University.

——— (2013), 'Social Organization in the Aftermath of "Fast Track": An Analysis of Emerging Forms of Land Authority, Platforms of Mobilization and Local Cooperation', in S. Moyo and W. Chambati, eds, *Land and Agrarian Reform in Zimbabwe: Beyond White-Settler Capitalism*, Dakar: CODESRIA.

Neocosmos, M. (1993), *The Agrarian Question in Southern Africa and Accumulation from Below*, Uppsala: Nordiska Afrika Institutet.

Ostrom, E. (1990), *Governing the Commons: The Evolution of Institutions for Collective Action*, New York: Cambridge University Press.

Raftopolous, Brian (2003), 'The State in Crisis: Authoritarian Nationalism, Selective Citizenship and Distortions of Democracy in Zimbabwe', in A. Hammar, B. Raftopoulos and S. Jensen, eds, *Zimbabwe's Unfinished Business: Rethinking Land, State and Nation in the Context of Crisis*, Harare: Weaver Press: 217–42.

Ranger, Terrence O. (1985), *Peasant Consciousness and Guerrilla War in Zimbabwe,* Harare: Zimbabwe Publishing House.

Richardson, Craig (2005), 'The Loss of Property Rights and the Collapse of Zimbabwe', *Cato Journal*, 25 (3), 541–65.

Rutten, M.M.E.M. (1992), 'Selling Wealth to Buy Poverty: The Process of the Individualization of Land Ownership among the Maasai Pastoralists of Kajiado District, Kenya, 1890–1990', *Fort Lauderdale*, Verlag Breitenbach Saarbrücken: 510.

Sachikonye, Lloyd (2005), 'The Land is the Economy: Revisiting the Land Question', *Africa Security Review*, 14 (3), 31–44.

Sadomba, Wilbert Z. (2008), 'War Veterans in Zimbabwe's Land Occupations: Complexities of a Liberation Movement in an African Post-Colonial Settler Society', unpublished PhD thesis, Wageningen Agricultural University.

Scoones, Ian, Nelson Marongwe, Blasio Mavedzenge, Jacob Mahenehene, Felix Murimbarimba and Chrispen Sukume (2010), *Zimbabwe's Land Reform: Myths and Realities*, Harare: Weaver Press and Oxford: James Currey.

Selby, Angus (2006), 'Commercial Farmers and the State: Interest Group Politics and Land Reform in Zimbabwe', unpublished PhD thesis, University of Oxford.

Veltmeyer, Henry (2005), 'The Dynamics of Land Occupations in Latin America', in S. Moyo and P. Yeros, eds, *Reclaiming the Land: The Resurgence of Rural Movements in Africa, Asia and Latin America*, London: Zed Books: 285–316.

Warriner, Doreen (1955), *Land Reform and Economic Development*, National Bank of Egypt 50th Anniversary Commemoration Lectures, Cairo: National Bank of Egypt.

World Bank (1991), *Zimbabwe: Agriculture Sector Memorandum: Volumes I and II*, Report No. 9429-Zim, Washington, DC: World Bank.

——— (1995), *Zimbabwe: Achieving Shared Growth: Country Economic Memorandum, Volume 1*, Report No. 13540, Washington, DC: World Bank.

——— (2006), *Agricultural Growth and Land Reform in Zimbabwe: Assessment and Recovery Options*, Report No. 31699-ZW, Washington, DC: World Bank.

Yeros, Paris (2002), 'The Political Economy of Civilisation: Peasant-Workers in Zimbabwe and the Neo-Colonial World', unpublished PhD thesis, University of London.

PART TWO

Land, Labour and Agrarian Questions

9

Neoliberalism and Unemployment

Prabhat Patnaik

The neoliberal period has undoubtedly seen a larger extent of unemployment in the Third World than the preceding *dirigiste* period, not just in absolute terms but relative to the size of the workforce. Third World unemployment, of course, is not just open unemployment. Barring a small proportion of the workforce which has full-time employment, almost all others are employed only for a part of the time; very few are openly unemployed. Employment rationing takes the form not of some being fully employed and others being openly unemployed, but of most persons being employed only for a part of the time, which is why we have a plethora of casual employment, part-time employment, intermittent employment and 'disguised unemployment'.

Under these circumstances, it is best if we define unemployment as the inability of a person to earn a 'benchmark' level of real income: those who earn this can be said to be employed, while those who do not can be defined as unemployed. Unemployment, in other words, needs to be defined, and in this essay, it will be defined as what some would call 'income unemployment'.

The greater extent of unemployment in the neoliberal period is not confined only to those belonging to countries where a distinct slowing down of growth has occurred, it also afflicts countries which have experienced much faster growth compared to the earlier *dirigiste* period. And it is not confined only to the recent period of crisis under neoliberalism. It also characterizes neoliberalism even when it was going strong, which of late it has not been doing. In what follows, my implicit focus of analysis will be India, where the growth rate of the gross domestic product (GDP) has doubled even as the rate of growth of employment has halved in the days before the onset of crisis in the neoliberal period, compared to the *dirigiste* era; but what I say on the issue generally, on the basis of the Indian experience, may have a wider relevance to other Third World countries.

Some Determinants of Labour Productivity Growth

For any rate of growth of output, the rate of growth of employment is simply the excess of this rate of growth over the rate of growth of labour productivity.[1] We shall therefore approach the issue of the determinants of employment growth by looking at the determinants of labour productivity growth.

The neoliberal regime is one where the barriers to the introduction of new processes and products have been significantly removed. In fact, since this regime is marked by freer flows of capital, including finance, and of goods and services across country borders, freedom to introduce technological progress becomes an essential feature of such a regime. This fact does not make much of a difference to the agricultural sector where peasant agriculture predominates, and cannot be supplanted by capitalist commercial farming without causing so much displacement and hardship that no government can dare to go in for such supplanting *directly*, at least in contemporary times. Even so, however, there is an attempt to *gradually* supplant peasant agriculture; but this is slow and limited.

In the rest of the economy, technological progress becomes a perpetual phenomenon, including technological progress which entails the substitution of new goods produced by the capitalist sector for the earlier goods produced by the petty production sector. Within the capitalist sector itself, there is a process of perpetual change in the products and the methods of production. This arises both because the Third World economies attempt to 'catch up' with the metropolitan economies with regard to the already existing products and production methods, and also because within the metropolis, too, there is perpetual change in products and methods that is taking place, with new ones coming in to replace the old.

Technological progress in the advanced countries tends to be 'labour-saving', that is, it has the effect of increasing labour productivity. It follows, therefore, that technological progress in the Third World, too, which is essentially derived from that in the metropolis, raises labour productivity. The faster the rate of technological progress, the greater is the rate of growth of labour productivity.

Associated with any rate of growth of the GDP, therefore, there is a certain rate of growth of labour productivity; the higher the GDP growth, the higher is the rate of growth of labour productivity.[2] But there is a second factor also affecting the rate of growth of labour productivity, and this is the share of the rich in total output, for which we shall take the share of economic surplus in output as a proxy.

We can think of goods being ranked in terms of the rapidity of technological change to which they are subject. Wheat and rice will come very low down in such ranking, while supermarkets, smart phones, automobiles and laptops will come much higher. The more unequal the distribution of income, or the higher the proportion of surplus in total output, the greater is the weight of the luxury goods in total output. These are the very goods that are subject to more rapid technological change. Hence, the greater the share of surplus, the higher is the weight of such goods in total output, the higher the rate of technological change and the higher the rate of growth of labour productivity.

Labour productivity growth in a neoliberal Third World economy, therefore, can be seen to depend upon at least two factors: the rate of GDP growth and the proportion of the economic surplus in total output. It increases as either of these two factors increases.

The proportion of surplus in output, however, depends not only on the *level* of labour productivity, but also upon the *level* of the real wage rate. And here we are talking not of the real income per *person* (as mentioned above), but of the real wage rate per *hour of work*. This can be seen to be a more or less constant figure until a substantial amount of the labour reserves has got used up, that is, until the rate of employment, in terms of hours of work of a given intensity, divided by the total workforce, again in terms of hours of work of the same intensity, has reached a certain threshold. If it is below this threshold, then the real wage rate remains unchanged, while if it is above this threshold, then the real wage rate increases in tandem with labour productivity; thenceforth, as the employment rate increases, whatever the share of surplus that had been reached in the economy until then obtains subsequently; there is no tendency for it to rise any further, or to fall.

But if the demand for labour increases faster than the total labour availability (in terms of hours of work), then, *up to* this threshold employment rate, while there is no tendency for the wage rate per hour of work to increase, there will nonetheless be an increase in real income per head of the workforce, as each person will then get to work for a larger number of hours.

A Simple Model

Let us see how we can explain the higher unemployment under neoliberalism with the help of these ideas. For this, we use a simple model.

We assume that the rate of growth of foodgrains output *is given* and the rate of growth of the non-foodgrains sector as being subject to variations. We also assume for simplicity that there is no growth of labour productivity in the foodgrains sector, and whatever growth occurs in labour productivity occurs in the non-foodgrains sector. In such a case, the rate of growth of non-foodgrains output determines at the margin the rate of overall GDP growth; and the rate of growth of labour productivity in the non-foodgrains sector determines the rate of growth of overall labour productivity.

The argument that follows can be more easily comprehended if we assume in addition that the rate of growth of foodgrain output *is the same as the rate of population (and workforce) growth*, which has been more or less the case anyway.

Our earlier discussion about wages and labour productivity growth can be set out in the form of the following two equations, now using only the rate of growth of non-foodgrains output g as the argument in lieu of GDP growth:

$$g_p = (d\beta/dt)/\beta = f(g, 1 - w/\beta) \ \ldots \quad f'_1>0, f'_2>0\ldots \qquad \text{(i)}$$

where g_p denotes the rate of growth of labour productivity and β the labour productivity per man-hour in the non-foodgrains sector; w denotes the real wage rate per man-hour (identical across sectors) in the economy as a whole. *The surplus, it should be noted, does not accrue to the workforce.*

$$(dw/dt)/w = 0 \text{ for } E/N \leq e, \text{ and } w/\beta = (w/\beta)^* \text{ when } E/N>e \qquad \text{(ii)}$$

where E denotes the employment and N the workforce (both in man-hours), e the threshold employment rate when wages start rising, and $(w/\beta)^*$ the level of w/β that would have been reached when E/N reaches e. Finally, we have

$$L_t = L_{0.}e^{nt} \qquad \text{(iii)}$$

which simply postulates that the labour force in natural units (with L.h = N, where h is the standard number of hours of work per period) grows at rate n.

Given our concern, we assume throughout that the *initial state of the economy* is characterized by E/N < e, that is, an employment rate below the threshold (after which wages *per man-hour* start rising), and no food shortage.

Now, a distinction must be drawn between a rise in per capita income of the workforce because of a rise in employment at given wages, and a rise in per capita income because of a rise in the wage rate per man-hour. Whenever the rate of growth of employment, which is given by $(g-g_p)$, exceeds the rate of growth of the workforce, there is an increase in per capita income of the workforce, initially because of the rise in per capita employment, and later because of the rise in the wage rate (when the threshold employment rate has been crossed). But when per capita income of the workforce rises, there is necessarily a rise in per capita food demand. It follows that as long as foodgrain output growth is the same as population growth (we can assume for simplicity that foodgrains are only consumed by the workforce), *there can be no increase in the employment rate* without causing inflation that finance capital abhors and, hence, avoids. As long as foodgrain output grows at the same rate as the workforce, the growth rate of employment must be the same as that of the workforce, for any higher employment would bring food inflation on the agenda.

We can therefore distinguish between two situations: one where the foodgrain constraint is *never reached*. In this case, the rate of growth of employment *always* remains below the rate of growth of the workforce, and the relative size of the labour reserves keeps on increasing. The other is where the foodgrain constraint *is reached*, that is, excess demand is generated in the foodgrain market, at which point the growth rate in the non-foodgrains sector is pulled down through restrictive state policies such as tight money and government expenditure cutbacks. But here, too, instead of the growth rate being tied down *subsequently* to the rate of growth of foodgrain production, once excess demand is generated in the foodgrain market and restrictive policies are followed, the rate of employment growth drops below the rate of workforce growth. Restrictive policies caused by excess demand in the foodgrains market take the economy to a state where foodgrain stocks start piling up.[3]

This second case, too, in other words, is no different from the first one above. In the first, employment growth is less than workforce growth *spontaneously*; in the second, it *becomes less* because the economy hits a foodgrain constraint and then goes downhill. In either case, employment growth drops below the workforce growth, causing growing relative labour reserves.

Even if we assume, *for argument's sake*, that the government does succeed in keeping the economy close to the ceiling imposed by foodgrain output growth, that is, that even when employment growth drops off, the government succeeds in pushing it back up again, even then the long-run growth rate of employment in the economy will still be given *at best* by the rate of growth of foodgrain production, and hence, by assumption, the workforce growth rate. The labour reserves will never get eliminated but will keep growing, maybe not in relative terms but in absolute numbers. *The relative labour reserves, however, will not fall.*

Two conclusions follow from the above. First, the reason why there is a larger labour reserve under the neoliberal *regime* compared to the *dirigiste regime* is two-fold: one, there is the removal of all controls over technological change that had existed earlier; and two, there is a lowering of the rate of growth of foodgrain production because the *dirigiste regime*, as we shall see below, is inherently hostile to peasant agriculture. Second, as long as the rate of growth of foodgrain production does not exceed the rate of population (and hence workforce) growth, there can never be an elimination of labour reserves, which would grow at the very least at the same rate as the workforce growth.

The Fallacy of Faster Growth Overcoming Unemployment

It is sometimes argued that if there is larger unemployment despite higher growth, then what is required for overcoming such unemployment is still higher growth. This appears quite plausible at first sight. But it is clear from the above that this is untrue. If, for instance, there is no increase in foodgrain output growth rate, then an increase in non-foodgrain output growth rate would either still leave larger unemployment than earlier under the *dirigiste* regime (which was generally foodgrain-constrained),[4] or is simply not possible without causing inflation in the economy, which a neoliberal regime is particularly averse to. Its aversion arises from the fact that inflation lowers the real value of financial assets, which is incidentally why there is even talk of having a zero inflation target in a neoliberal economy.

If there is any increase in the growth rate of the non-foodgrain output even in a situation where the foodgrain output is a binding constraint, then that can only happen without inflation – if it is accompanied by such an increase in the growth rate of labour productivity in the non-foodgrain sector that employment growth there does not increase and no excess demand for foodgrains is generated. But this is precisely what does not overcome unemployment. It follows, therefore, that for overcoming unemployment, a mere increase in the growth rate of output of the non-foodgrain sector, is inadequate.

What is required for generating larger employment growth is a *rise* in the foodgrain output growth rate compared to the *dirigiste* period. But even this is only a necessary condition, for, as we have seen earlier, this may simply lead to larger and larger foodgrain stocks being held, or exported, without generating any additional employment at home, other than what is required to sustain the higher foodgrain growth rate itself. But if a larger growth rate in foodgrain production is accompanied by a suitably large growth rate in the output of the non-foodgrain sector, there can be a reduction in the extent of unemployment. The growth in the non-foodgrain sector, however, cannot be made to order; government policy can curtail the growth rate in output, but it cannot increase the growth rate of output. It can, in other words, at best play a permissive role under neoliberalism.

In particular, assuming that the foodgrain sector broadly grows at the same rate as population and there is not much growth in labour productivity within this sector, if the growth rate of non-foodgrain employment does not exceed the growth rate of population (and the workforce), there can be no amelioration in unemployment.

But the question may be raised: even if there is no increase in the growth rate of the foodgrain sector's output, why can't the economy import foodgrains from abroad and export non-foodgrains in return? Why, in other words, should a country grow its own foodgrain requirements? The proponents of neoliberalism, for instance, say in defence of the free flow of goods and services across borders that no country is obliged under free trade to produce its own requirements. What is wrong with this claim?

Even if a country does import foodgrains, it cannot avoid some inflation for at least two reasons. First, the very signal for importing will be given by an upward pressure on prices; second, and more importantly, when a country the size of, say, India, goes to the international market to buy foodgrains, that itself provides a signal for a rise in world market price. It is impossible for India to go to the world market to buy foodgrains without causing a major rise in the spot foodgrains price.

For both these reasons there will be an increase in price; and if money wages are jacked up in response to such inflation (which we have deliberately abstracted from until now), there will be quite a long drawn-out episode of inflation, to the detriment of the interests of globalized finance. Hence, at least large countries, if they have to avoid inflation in food prices, must produce their own food requirements.

Why Does Neoliberalism Ignore Agriculture?

We have assumed so far that the government under neoliberalism is not capable of altering the foodgrain growth rate, that this growth rate is lower than under the *dirigiste* regime, and that this growth rate is not even much higher than the growth rate of population. The question arises: why should this be so? Let us attempt an answer to this question.

One essential feature of neoliberalism is the introduction of freer flows of goods and services, and of capital, including finance, across country-borders. This has major implications: in a world in which we have nation-states but finance is free to move across country-borders with ease, the government of every country must follow policies that are demanded by finance, for otherwise it would leave the country *en masse*, causing a financial crisis. Hence, the ability of any government to pursue policies of its choice is strictly limited.

This has important implications for the economy, which have been much discussed. One obvious implication is that it abridges democracy. Democracy entails that different political formations have different agendas to offer to the electorate, which then chooses between them. But if all of them offer the same agenda – or, worse still, if they offer different agendas before the elections but no matter who gets elected, the same agenda is followed after the elections (thereby not keeping faith with the electorate), the agenda that is to the liking of finance capital – then effectively democracy has been compromised. The sovereignty of the electorate has been effectively replaced by the sovereignty of international finance capital.

But there is a second implication of neoliberalism, and that is to impose a process of primitive accumulation of capital upon the petty production sector, including, above all, peasant agriculture. This is a consequence of the first implication itself, for this is what capital wants, namely the freedom to encroach upon peasant agriculture without the state standing in the way, and such encroachment usually turns out to be constricting for the sector. And in addition, even when encroachment by capital does not *per se* lead to constriction, state withdrawal of support *ipso facto* entails a larger burden upon this sector and hence imposes primitive accumulation of capital.

Primitive accumulation has two aspects: a flow aspect and a stock aspect. The flow aspect relates to the squeeze on the real incomes of the peasants that may be caused by a rise in input prices, a fall in output prices or a rise in the cost of living, or, typically, a combination of all three. The stock aspect relates to the acquisition of the assets of peasant agriculture, notably land, by the capitalist sector either *gratis* or for a fraction of their true value. Sometimes, when what appears as the full 'market price' has been duly paid, the claim that the purchase of land still entails primitive accumulation of capital may come as a surprise. But this is precisely what happens for the following reason.

In pre-capitalist societies, ownership does not exist as a single integral right and does not extend to land as such. It is fragmented into separate claims on the produce from the land by separate groups, each of which enjoys a customary right over it, some in lieu of work and others without work. When the capitalist sector acquires a piece of land, paying for it an amount equal to the capitalized value of the surplus, it may feel that it has paid the full market value *and it would be right, according to the logic of the bourgeois society*. But in fact it has ignored the customary right of the producers over the produce and hence, by extension, upon the land on which the produce is grown, for which it should have paid but has not. This it has done by ignoring the customary rights to streams of income *other than to the surplus.*

Put differently, there would be no primitive accumulation of capital if the capitalist buyers of the land paid the capitalized value of the total output and not the capitalized value of the economic surplus alone. But since they pay only the capitalized value of the surplus, there is primitive accumulation of capital, as the rights of the tenants and labourers have not been recognized in the value of the land. Hence the process of acquisition of land, even by paying what appears to be the 'market value' for it, still amounts to primitive accumulation of capital: it produces a class of free wage labourers who have been stripped of their customary rights.

Primitive accumulation of capital in the flow sense lowers the profitability of peasant agriculture and has an adverse impact on the growth rate of output. In addition, the exposure of the sector to world market prices which fluctuate a great deal enmeshes the peasants in debt. Since neoliberalism insists on inducting the private sector into all areas which had earlier been the preserve of the public sector alone, private banks are inducted into the banking sector. They typically renege on 'priority sector' lending norms, which forces the peasants to turn to non-institutional private credit. The combination of increased debt and more expensive private non-institutional credit results in an increase in debt service payments, which also eats into profitability. Neoliberalism, in short, erodes the profitability of peasant agriculture, which, by lowering the growth rate of foodgrain production, entails a slowing down of employment growth compared to the *dirigiste* period.

An idea of what has been happening to peasant agriculture internationally can be had from cereal production data for the world as a whole.[5] The average annual cereal production for the world as a whole for the triennium 1979–82, divided by the mid-triennium population, gives us a per capita cereal output figure of 355 kgs. For the triennium 1999–2002, exactly the same procedure gives us a per capita cereal output of 343 kgs. And for the triennium 2014–17, we get through similar calculations a figure of 344 kgs. It follows that the per capita cereal output in the world has not gone up for a very long time. What is true of production is also true of availability. Besides, in this period there has also been a diversion of foodgrains towards the production of ethanol. So, per capita consumption must have declined considerably.

Even if the per capita foodgrain consumption in the advanced countries did not increase over this period owing to the increase in per capita real income, that is, even if the income elasticity of demand for foodgrains is close to zero *in the advanced countries*, this is not so for the Third World. In the Third World countries where there was an increase in per capita income, there should have been an increase in per capita consumption of foodgrains, which should have increased the per capita consumption of foodgrains *in the world as a whole*.

The fact that this did not happen suggests that there must have been an income squeeze for vast segments of the world's population, though this gets camouflaged in overall figures. In other words, even though per capita incomes did go up, they must not have done so for the *working people of the Third World*. It follows, therefore, that employment, defined in terms of the 'benchmark' income they earn on average, must not only not have increased, it is likely to have declined. There must have been an increase in the magnitude of 'income unemployment' in the world economy during the period of neoliberalism.

Capitalist Spontaneity and Unemployment

There is a view that while capitalism inflicts primitive accumulation of capital upon the pre-capitalist sector, it also absorbs the displaced petty producers and agricultural labourers from the countryside in the new factories that it establishes. This, however, is untrue. The displaced petty producers from the process of primitive accumulation of capital in Europe were not absorbed by the expanding capitalism in Europe but had to migrate abroad to the 'new world' to make a living for themselves.

The labour requirement of expanding capitalism in Europe was too meagre to absorb the labour reserves that capitalism created in Europe. These reserves ultimately had to emigrate abroad to the temperate regions of white settlement, to countries like the United States, Canada, Australia, New Zealand and South Africa. The migration of tropical populations to these temperate lands was prevented; it remains so to this day (except to the extent wanted by the governments of these countries). But the migration of the populations from other temperate regions was freely allowed, and still is.

In their new habitat, the immigrants snatched land away from the original inhabitants, the Amerindians, and set themselves up as farmers with a reasonable standard of living. It is this fact rather than any so-called agricultural revolution in England or in Europe, as claimed by Arthur Lewis (1978),[6] that explains the higher level of the reservation wage enjoyed by the European workers, both at home when they stayed on and abroad when they emigrated.

During the 'long nineteenth century', according to Lewis, as many as 50 million Europeans migrated to the temperate regions of white settlement. Another estimate suggests that between 1820 and 1913 the annual emigration from Britain was roughly half the annual increase in population that occurred there (U. Patnaik 2012). Migration on such a scale is impossible to imagine today, but it is this which underlay the fact that primitive accumulation in Europe did not create any permanent mass unemployment. There is nothing in the nature of capitalism to prevent such permanent mass unemployment. The fact that it did not happen in Europe was because of these special circumstances that prevailed.

In Third World countries, an earlier process of primitive accumulation of capital had already been carried out by colonialism. Its instruments were primarily the following: there was a 'drain of surplus' from the colony to the metropolis, which entailed a unilateral transfer of a part of surplus without any *quid pro quo*. Additionally, there was a process of 'deindustrialization', which entailed the displacement of local craft producers by the import of machine-made manufactured goods from the metropolis. These two processes added to one another. Their effects combined to produce substantial displacement of petty producers, especially craftsmen who created mass labour reserves.

This is the legacy of colonialism in these countries. They have to absorb not only the displaced petty producers from the current process of primitive accumulation of capital, but also those who had been displaced by the earlier process of primitive accumulation that was carried out over a prolonged period. Now, capitalism in its spontaneity[7] cannot absorb these reserves, because *inter alia* even a *necessary condition for such absorption, namely a rise in per capita foodgrain output, does not obtain under capitalism in its spontaneity (which neoliberalism typifies).*

In fact, there are three conditions whose fulfillment is favourable for the absorption of Third World labour reserves (leaving aside a small reserve army of labour) into capitalist employment. First, there must be greater equality in income distribution, or, putting it in our language, the share of surplus in total income should be kept under control; second, there must be some restraint upon technological change in the capitalist sector; and third, there must be a rate of growth of foodgrain output that clearly exceeds the rate of growth of population. Of these, only the last is a necessary condition in the strict sense.

In the Soviet Union and the Eastern European socialist countries which had overcome unemployment and even systematically experienced labour scarcity, there had been no legacy of vast labour reserves that had been left by colonialism; and World War II had decimated the population as well. Even so, there was control over the introduction of technical change and also far greater equality in income distribution. In the Third World, where the legacy of colonialism has made matters infinitely more difficult, we need the fulfilment of all the three conditions mentioned above to make a dent on mass unemployment.

Neoliberalism reintroduces the spontaneity of capitalism, which had been disrupted by the post-war wave of *dirigiste* development. What is more, it also severely restricts the ability of the state to intervene in the spontaneity of capitalism: the state being a nation-state that cannot stand in the way of the spontaneity of capitalism which is demanded by globalized finance capital. Hence, re-emphasizing peasant agriculture which would stop the process of primitive accumulation of capital and obtain a growth rate of foodgrain output that exceeds population growth, controlling the widening inequality in income and wealth, and restraining the introduction of technological change, are measures which impede the system's immanent tendencies, and are beyond the capacity of the nation-state under neoliberalism. The three propitious conditions for the labour reserves to be used up, therefore, cannot be achieved.

The capacity of neoliberal capitalism, it follows, for achieving full employment, in the sense that every member of the workforce gets employment for a certain 'standard' number of hours, or even for introducing a tightness in the labour market, is severely limited. This objective can be achieved only in an economic regime that goes beyond neoliberal capitalism, and restores to the state its capacity for meaningful and purposive intervention independent of the demands of globalized finance, through the introduction of controls on capital and trade flows, that is, through a process of 'delinking' from the current globalization.

Notes

1 This is strictly true if we take continuous time, but only approximately true with discrete time.

2 Such a relationship has been advanced for the advanced capitalist countries on somewhat different grounds, and is known as the Kaldor-Verdoorn Law; see Kaldor (1966).

3 This is exactly analogous to the boom being truncated by a shortage of labour in Kalecki's model of business cycles. The fact that the boom is so truncated does not mean that subsequently the economy simply grows at the rate of growth of the labour force.

4 For the dynamics of an economy under the *dirigiste* regime, see Kalecki (1972).

5 These computations are based on FAO data.

6 For a critique of Lewis's views on the agricultural revolution, see U. Patnaik and P. Patnaik (2017).

7 'Spontaneity' of capitalism does not refer to *laissez faire*. Within 'spontaneity', I include not only the playing out of a whole lot of immanent tendencies of capitalism, but also state intervention that promotes the playing out of these tendencies. 'Spontaneity' is to be contrasted with state intervention that impedes

or modifies such tendencies, which can happen only under certain special circumstances, such as when the system is facing an existential crisis. The post-war *dirigisme* was such a phase, when the state in the advanced countries, under pressure from the working class, intervened to save the system by checking some of its immanent tendencies; and in Third World countries, capitalism could not establish its hegemony over the newly independent countries. But with neoliberalism, we are back with the 'spontaneity' of the system, with the state accelerating, rather than impeding, its immanent tendencies.

References

Kaldor, N. (1966), *Causes of the Slow Rate of Growth in the United Kingdom*, Cambridge: Cambridge University Press.

Kalecki, M. (1972), 'Problems of Financing Economic Development in a Mixed Economy', in *Selected Essays on the Economic Growth of the Socialist and the Mixed Economies*, Cambridge: Cambridge University Press.

Lewis, W.A. (1978), *The Evolution of the International Economic Order*, Princeton: Princeton University Press.

Patnaik, U. (2012), 'Capitalism and the Production of Poverty', *Social Scienstist*, 40 (1 and 2): 3–20.

Patnaik, U. and Prabhat Patnaik (2017), *A Theory of Imperialism*, New York: Columbia University Press and New Delhi: Tulika Books.

10

The 'Longer Food Crisis' and Consequences for Economic Theory and Policy in the South

Arindam Banerjee

The food question has been placed at the centre of the development discourse with the global food crisis (GFC) that emerged in 2006 and lasted until 2013. The GFC came after a period of a little more than two decades when global food prices had remained 'low and stable', encouraging the economic idea that countries, particularly developing countries, can reliably depend on global food markets for attaining or maintaining their macroeconomic food security. The latter idea, perceived almost as a doctrine, was part of the neoliberal prescription of transforming agriculture towards an export-oriented approach and trade liberalization. It was held that a shift to export crops would raise the income of the agriculturally dependent population, substantially in developing countries, and help in achieving food security at the household level. On the macroeconomic plane, it was expected that the foreign exchange earned through export of agricultural commodities would be more than sufficient to pay for food-import bills. This was one of the implicit assumptions of the multilateral negotiations in the run-up to the World Trade Organization (WTO) agreement in 1995, and persisted for a decade after that. The GFC, however, reinstated the issue of national food sovereignty and security as a core concern globally, but particularly so in the developing world.

The GFC, as understood in terms of the astronomical food prices in world markets, has been diagnosed from various perspectives and theories, identifying several causes in the process. Supply-side factors ranging from drought-led grain production shortages, climate change and rising costs of food production (mainly due to exploding oil prices) have been recognized as important contributory factors of the GFC in the literature (FAO [Food and Agricultural Organization] 2008; IMF [International Monetary Fund] 2008). While, during the period of GFC, the per capita world foodgrain production was increasing at a fair rate, this came after two decades of trend decline; moreover, there was continued diversion of grain to ethanol production in the developed countries, partly reflected in a falling share of their exports in grain production. The latter factor may well have offset the observation by Chand (2008) that the share of oil price rise in the costs of foodgrain production was inadequate for explaining price escalation of the order that actually occurred.

On the demand side, early conjectures identified the rising foodgrain demand from emerging countries such as India and China, where the middle classes were expanding and diversifying their diets, as a major cause of the GFC (IMF 2008). This, too, is not borne out by the trends of per capita foodgrain consumption (PCFC) in emerging countries, except to some extent for China. However, the Chinese rising demand for foodgrains was not so exceptional as to cause the GFC (Banerjee 2011a). On the other hand, the 'biofuel effect' triggered by the rapid expansion of corn-ethanol in the United States seems to have been a central cause for the escalation of grain prices, primarily due to an unusual linkage between oil and grain prices by chains of substitution across sectors (Mitchell 2008; Banerjee 2011b). The US ethanol phenomenon seamlessly transmitted the price spikes to world markets, given the large share of the country in grain exports, especially corn. A significant role in causing volatility in grain markets was that of financial speculation in commodity futures, which defied the rubric of demand and supply (Ghosh 2010).

The GFC has been studied threadbare, as evident from the literature. It caught the attention of policy makers, academics and civil society for its starkness from the middle of the 2000s. More so, the high global prices of foodgrains appeared as a starker reality after the long period of 'low and stable prices' in world grain markets in the 1980s and 1990s. An inspection of the historical data on food production and consumption reveals certain paradoxes between grain production trends and prices even in the period prior to the GFC. This period, therefore, needs to be revisited in order to develop a relatively more precise historical understanding of the food crisis.

The emergence of neoliberalism and structural adjustment policies following the crisis of the 1970s gave rise to a new geo-politics of food, attempting to resolve the incumbent conflict between global capital (represented by transnational food corporations or TNFCs) and sovereign national food policies. Apart from liberalization of cross-border capital flows, the 1980s also witnessed the relaxation of trade rules and the eventual joining of the WTO in 1995 by a large number of developing countries. The emphasis on agriculture in many developing countries shifted to export-oriented production, attempting to take advantage of the world market. The goal of self-sufficiency in food production and attaining macroeconomic food security consequently took a backseat in policy-making in most of the developing world.

This brought back the complexities of the global food system that characterized colonial capitalism in the eighteenth and nineteenth centuries and in the immediate post-World War II period (Friedmann 1990, 1993), but within an altered international political economy. Relocation of production to emerging economies and incorporation of local capital and elites in developing countries into global capital were some of the new paradigms that emerged with neoliberalism. The inner contradictions of development were not manifested as one between nations but as one between globalized capital, including blocs from the developing world, and the masses of workers and petty producers globally. Thus, apart from the global processes which adversely affect food security, the contribution of unequal growth within countries *and income deflation for the majority poor population* also need to be assessed as far as the prevalence of hunger and undernutrition are concerned (McMichael 2009; U. Patnaik 2002a, 2007).

A deeper reflection on the food crisis is thus necessary for at least the following three reasons. First, rather than disparate factors, an integrated approach to international political economy, weaving in major geo-political events, helps in understanding the roots of the food crisis. Second, one is confronted with the question of whether different instances of food crisis in history are mere disconnected events. The specific nature of adjustments and adaptations made in policy responses to past challenges, like the crisis of the 1970s, has much greater implications for the recent behaviour of grain markets than is obvious at first sight. Finally, an examination of the disaggregated cross-country data on food production/consumption for a longer period also reveals that the food crisis may be a much longer phenomenon for the developing world. Such a longer crisis is perfectly compatible with a period of 'low and stable prices' in the world market, something not usually appreciated within the literature. This last point also opens up the question as to whether market price signals are the primary parameters for defining a food crisis.

To capture the historical global processes after World War II and examine the issues mentioned above, this paper undertakes a cross-region analysis of food production and consumption for the period 1960–2015, using data from the United States Department of Agriculture, Foreign Agricultural Service (USDA-FAS) database.[1] Using an economic class analysis of food consumption, it attempts to revisit the history of global food insecurity and comprehend the contemporary political economy of food systems.

The findings of the analysis, particularly for the period between the 1970s' food price spike and the recent GFC, have serious implications for certain theoretical and policy ideas from the perspective of the South. Ideas that dominated the policy debates on trade liberalization and its implications for food security in developing countries during the WTO negotiations may not have been correctly anchored in facts. Similarly, in Marxian political economy, inaccurate readings of the global food question have led to certain conclusions regarding the contemporary agrarian question for the South that may require revisiting.

The next section briefly outlines the theoretical framework within which the disaggregated cross-regional data is analysed. The subsequent section foregrounds the paradoxes which necessitate a fresh look at the data in a disaggregated manner, and this is followed by a section containing a political economy analysis of the data findings and the historical mapping of relevant geo-political events. The final section uses the findings and analysis to revisit two theoretical ideas from the lens of developing countries.

The Theoretical Framework

The development of any country is associated with an improvement and transition of food consumption. This is related to the increase in the income of the population and changing dietary patterns. This is not to discount the influence of geographical and cultural specificities on food habits across different regions in the world, but to recognize the more fundamental relationship between income levels and food consumption.

Yotopoulos (1985) hypothesizes the dietary transitions in any developing society and the role of middle-income classes through his explanation of the modern food–feed competition. With rising income and the expansion of middle-income classes, there is a change in dietary patterns as the population moves to consuming more animal products. This increases the demand for feed from the livestock industry and enhances the competition between food-use and feed-use of grains.

This dietary transition requires an increasing demand for grains in the economy, since direct food-use is always substituted by larger quantities of feedgrains, given that a proportionally higher amount of feed is required to produce animal products that are energy-equivalent to the substituted foodgrain within the human diet. The relationship between income and demand for foodgrains in an economy is captured by the diagram in Appendix 1, where the total demand for foodgrains starts rising at an increasing rate as middle-income classes start demanding animal products. In other words, the income elasticity of foodgrain demand is positive; the higher its value, the faster is the dietary transition accompanying real income increases.

As the dietary transition occurs, there is a gradual increase in foodgrain prices due to higher demand for animal products and the higher price that livestock industry/production can pay for feedgrains. Simultaneously, there is redistribution between food-use and feed-use of grains in favour of the latter. This may not work against the poor population, unless there is simultaneous expansion of the middle-income classes with more and more poor graduating into the middle classes.

The increasing grain consumption in any economy, therefore, represents this dietary transition. Any decline or stagnation in the macroeconomic grain absorption in a country, that is, the presence of a food constraint to development, correspondingly signifies an arrest of this process. This can happen in two situations. First, if the real income declines, there will be a decline in demand for grains. This is consistent with the proposition embodied in the food–feed competition.

There can be a second case where grain demand does not increase or decline even when average real incomes in the economy are rising, a deviation from the above hypothesis, as the income elasticity of grain demand will be negative. Yotopoulos himself noted this in the case of Africa in his period of study, 1965–80. This occurs when the growth of per capita income is highly unequal across the population. If the average real incomes increase primarily as a result of an increase in the income of the richest section of the population and not through any expansion of middle classes or rise in their incomes, there is no significant positive income on grain demand.

The richest sections of the population, having already undergone a dietary transition, does not demand more animal products when their incomes increase, but use their additional incomes for non-food expenditure or for savings. This can happen when the economy is growing along with a rise in average real incomes, but is characterized by a situation of 'mass income deflation' where the incomes of the majority of the population are stagnated or declining. Interestingly, India seems to fit into such a case in recent decades.

Thus, tracking the historical trend of grain absorption in any economy through a normative variable – for example, PCFC – throws light on the existence or non-existence of a food constraint to development. In the presence of such a food constraint, one can further investigate the severity of the food insecurity that the country is subject to, which can vary from high levels of undernutrition to arrested dietary transitions, often leading to malnutrition. It may be mentioned here that the populations in developed countries that have already undergone such a dietary transition, as in North America or Europe, may also be subject to malnutrition due to over-consumption of certain nutrients and unbalanced diets, but that is outside the scope of this essay.

The Paradox of World Grain Markets

In this theoretical context, we will now look at a major paradox that exists with regard to world food prices, particularly since the 1980s. As evident in Figure 1, world food prices in real terms consistently declined after the 1973 peak (oil crisis) for nearly three decades until 2002. As noted earlier, this generated significant optimism within academia and policy makers that the food-supply question had been permanently addressed by technological and organizational leaps in foodgrain cultivation, until that view was abruptly challenged by the food crisis in the new century. This long period of low and stable food prices in the world market was the crucial piece of evidence based on which many developing countries, strongly advised by international financial and multilateral institutions, shifted focus from the goal of food self-sufficiency to export-oriented agriculture. For example, the hypothesis that a shift to commercial export

Figure 1 ***FAO Food Price Index (FPI), 1961–2018***

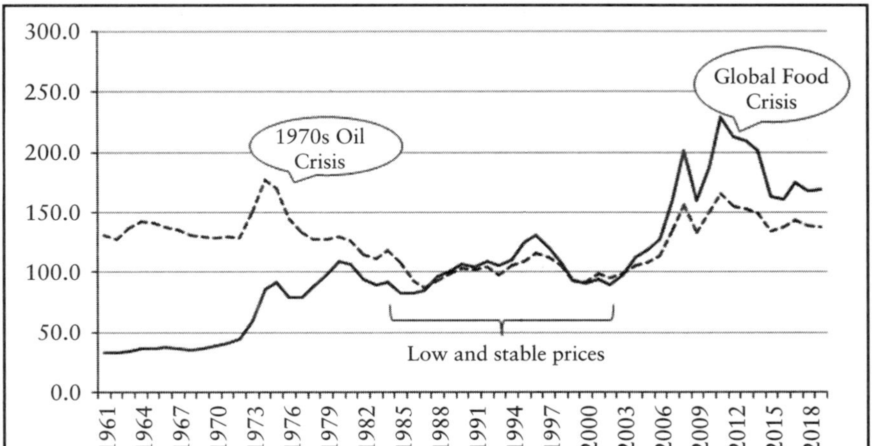

Note: The real FPI is the nominal FPI deflated by the World Bank Manufactures Unit Value (MUV) Index.

Source: Food and Agriculture Organization, data available at http://www.fao.org/worldfoodsituation/foodpricesindex/en/, accessed 15 October 2019.

Figure 2 ***World Per Capita Grain Production and Consumption, 1961–2015*** **(kgs)**

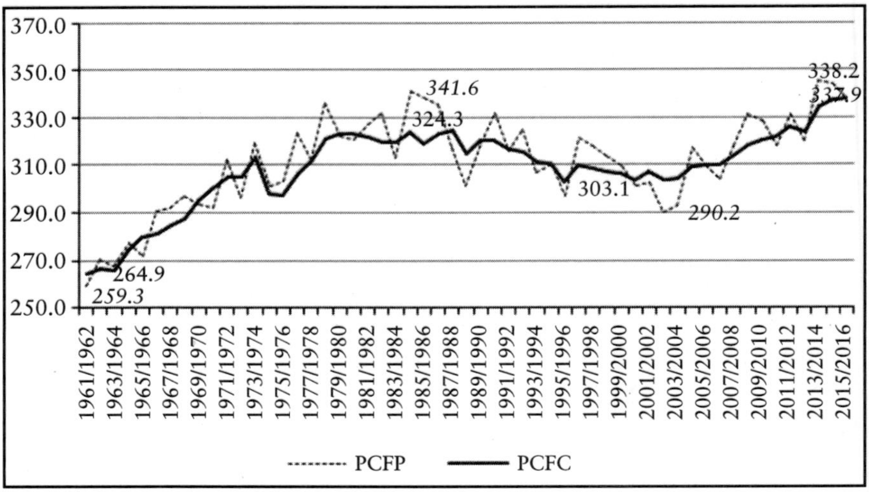

Source: Estimated by the author from USDA, FAS database.

crops and trade liberalization would lead to a clear increase in farmers' incomes is implicitly or explicitly based on the premise that cheap food is available in world (and domestic) markets, and that growing less food for self-consumption is not going to raise the 'cost of living' for farmers (Rao and Gulati 1994; FAO 2003).

An investigation into the trends of foodgrain production, however, casts veritable doubts on this emerging and dominant narrative. Figure 2 shows that between 1961 and 1985, there was a significant advance made in terms of per capita foodgrain production (PCFP) in the world. Various factors played a role in this improvement – often a different set of factors between the developed and developing worlds. The more important observation is the decline of PCFP between 1985 and 2002, from 341.6 kgs to 290.2 kgs. This corresponds largely to the period of low and stable foodgrain prices that we noted earlier. Clearly, foodgrain prices were not keeping 'low and stable' due to unconstrained supplies caused by a permanent 'technical revolution' in agriculture (P. Patnaik 2008).

Similarly, in the period after 2002, when grain prices started rising to culminate in the food crisis, production and supply of grains were increasing throughout. Thus, neither in the period of 'low and stable prices' nor in the later period of GFC were production trends consistent with the movement of grain prices. To unravel this paradox, one needs to look at the consumption or demand side of the grain markets. The world per capita foodgrains consumption (PCFC) declined between 1985 and

2000 from 324.3 kgs to 303.1 kg, creating the downward pressure on prices. After 2000 the trend reversed and the PCFC increased at a rapid pace, particularly during the GFC years. As already discussed earlier, the GFC was more dependent on 'new' demand-side factors like bio-fuels and speculative activities, and not on supply-side factors.[2] This essay does not delve further into the GFC period, but is an attempt to understand specifically the earlier period between 1980 and 2000, when grain prices were unusually stable in spite of declining trends of normative grain production.

The two decades prior to the GFC have been understudied and require an investigation of the factors that affected demand since the 1980s. Further, given that factors which influence grain production and consumption are very different across the developed and the developing world, and also presumably across regions/countries within the two, a disaggregated analysis for the period is essential.

Disaggregating the Historical Lens

For the purpose of disaggregation of trends, we attempt to divide the world into 'Developed' and 'Rest of the World'. The 'Developed' region comprises thirty-one countries from Europe, two from North America, four from Asia and two from Oceania – a total of thirty-nine countries.[3] Needless to say, 'Rest of the World' comprises regions/countries with considerable diversity and requires further disaggregation. This is done through an analysis of the trends in eight geographical regions and investigation into particular countries, wherever relevant and required. The first disaggregation into 'Developed' and 'Rest of the World', however, gives us some major insights into the problem that we have outlined above. In this section we look at developments in the last century, and treat those after 2000 in the subsequent section.

Developed World

In the developed world, the two decades after World War II witnessed a massive technological transformation in agriculture. The TNFCs that emerged in North America and expanded to other regions changed agriculture rapidly in terms of technological improvements, and fundamentally in terms of its organization (McMichael, ed. 1994). Capital accumulation in agriculture progressed briskly by unprecedented vertical integration. As Figure 3 shows, this meant a rapid rise in PCFP in the 1960s and 1970s. This was accompanied by mass demand expansionary policies of the Keynesian policy tradition on both sides of the Atlantic, this having gained dominance as a successful prescription in bringing the world out of the Great Depression of the 1930s. Such welfare-augmenting

Figure 3 *Developed World Per Capita Grain Production and Consumption, 1961–2015* (kgs)

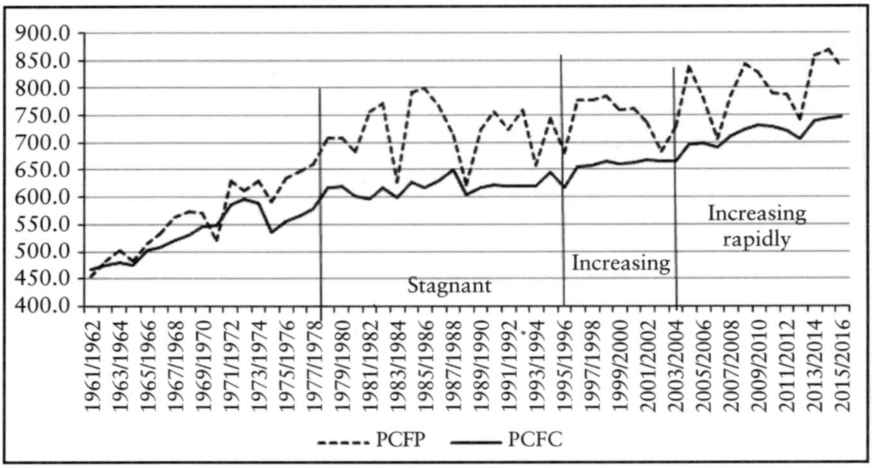

Source: Estimated by the author from USDA-FAS database.

policies were also a result of strong labour movements that emerged in the developed world during the Depression and the subsequent war, and the impending necessity to present capitalism as an acceptable alternative to the ascending socialist system. This meant that the rapid increases in production were matched by expansion of domestic demand for foodgrains during these decades.

During the 1960s and 1970s, the United States, Canada and Australia emerged as net exporters of foodgrains in spite of increase in domestic demand. Eexports increased rapidly in the 1970s, and by the early 1980s the developed world was exporting nearly 20 per cent of its grain production. This, however, was reversed after the late 1980s. Figure 4 exhibits the trends in exports.

It is interesting to note here that this rise in 'net exports' by the developed world was in spite of the fact that a substantial share of grain exports by these countries was to European countries, often financed by post-war reconstruction aid. This continued until the mid-1980s, after which the European continent as a whole became self-sufficient in grain production and also a marginal net-exporter. A significant part of food exports from North America, primarily the United States, was directed as food aid to developing countries, identified as 'dumping' of cheap foodgrains, destroying indigenous food cultivation and creating food-import dependence (Friedmann 1990).

What is important to note from Figure 4 is the stagnation in per

Figure 4 ***Developed World Countries: Net Exports as Percentage of Grain Production, 1961–2015***

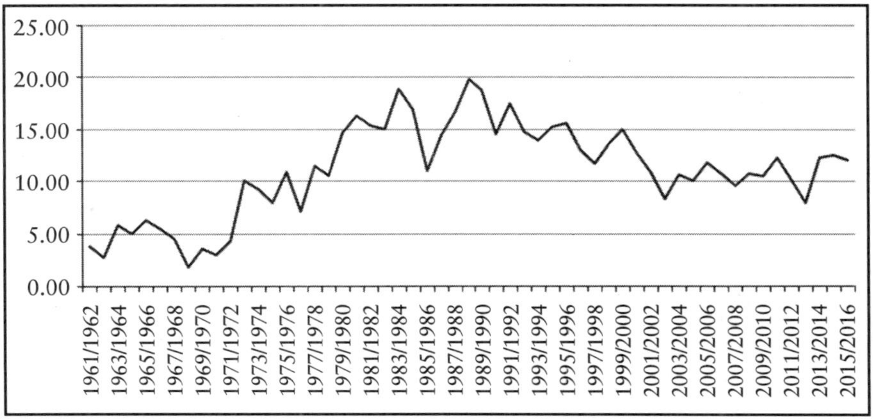

Source: Estimated by the author from USDA-FAS database.

capita consumption of grains between 1978 and 1995. The per capita production of grains actually fell after 1982, but this did not translate into a decline in consumption, primarily due to the reduction in grain exports, as noted above. However, what is to be noted here is that within this period of stagnation, there was a period of decline in PCFC by nearly 30 kgs between 1987 and 1993, owing primarily to a significant decline in grain consumption in developed Europe. The latter trend had some contribution to make towards the decline in world PCFC between the mid-1980s and early 1990s. Beyond 1995 there was a revival of grain consumption, which accelerated after 2003. Clearly, there was no depression in grain consumption in the developed world during the period 1985–2002, when the world as a whole witnessed a decline. In fact, for part of the period there was an increase in grain consumption.

Rest of the World

The 'Rest of the World' consists of the newly liberated ex-colonies in Asia and Africa, Soviet Union or the socialist world, and the Latin American countries, often dependent on the core. In the period after World War II, an era of fresh thinking in economic policies, most ex-colonies and dependent developing countries placed the attainment of food self-sufficiency as a primary policy goal. This was a direct outcome of anti-colonial discourses which recognized the adverse role of free trade, imposed forcefully on the colonies and semi-colonies, in worsening food security as far as the colonial population was concerned. Naturally, this was also a period of protectionism, not leading to autarky but a substantial decoupling of developing countries from international trade. Simultaneously, the 'green revolution' in many Asian countries increased foodgrain production. Accompanied by the introduction of food management systems, the setting up of large publicly-owned companies to manage agricultural production and distribution, together with food-subsidy policies to make grains accessible to poor populations, increased the consumption of foodgrains in these countries.

At the same time, the socialist bloc led by the Soviet Union followed an alternative economic regime, which achieved high food consumption and appreciable nutritional status through the use of heavy grain and meat subsidies. This hastened dietary transition among the population, although this may have been to varied degrees in the different regions within the bloc. The net result of these two sets of policy trends was a secular increase in both PCFP and PCFC in the 'Rest of the World', roughly until the end of the 1970s (Figure 5).

If we look at the trend of PCFC, the first structural break emerged at the beginning of the 1980s, when PCFC growth was arrested and remained stagnant between 250 kgs and 260 kgs over the decade. The following decade of the 1990s witnessed a significant decline in this variable, from around 260 kgs in 1990 to less than 240 kgs by 2000. On the other hand, PCFP was stagnant between 1978 and 1990 and then secularly

Figure 5 ***'Rest of the World' Per Capita Grain Production and Consumption, 1961–2015*** (kgs)

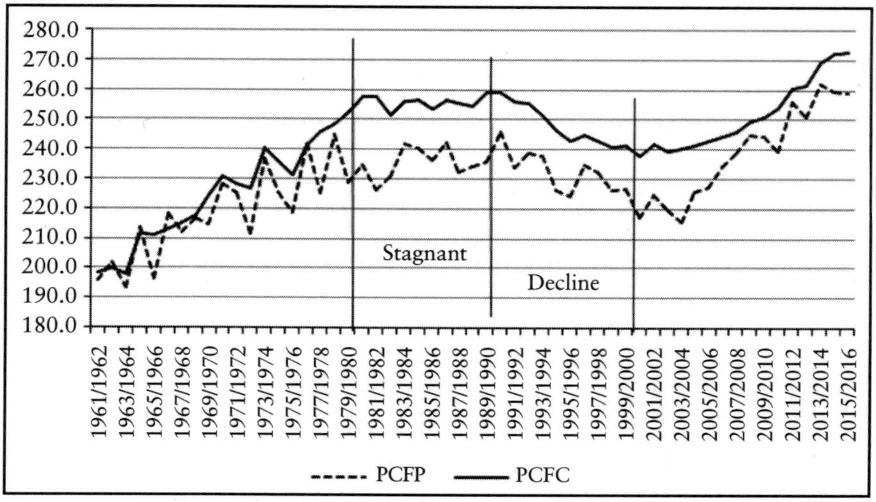

Source: Estimated by the author from USDA, FAS database.

declined between 1990 and 2003. This decline of the food production and consumption variable corresponded with and explained the decline in PCFP and PCFC for the world as a whole (as observed above in Figure 2), particularly from 1990. This was also a period of higher foodgrain import dependence for the developing world.

In the context of the above findings, a further disaggregation of the developing world into different regions helps in identifying the geographical dimension of the decline in grain consumption, and throws light on possible economic or geo-political causes. We look at ten geographical regions or groups of nations, namely, the Caribbean, South America, Central America, West Asia, North Africa, sub-Saharan Africa (SSA), former Soviet Union (FSU),[4] South Asia, East Asia and Southeast Asia.[5] The investigation is largely restricted to the period 1980–2000 (with a few exceptions), when stagnation or a decline in foodgrain consumption occurred in the developing world.[6]

Within these regions, the Caribbean, South America, SSA and West Asia experienced a distinct decline in PCFC in the 1980s. The decline was accompanied by a simultaneous fall in domestic per capita grain production (refer to Figures A2 to A5 in Appendix 3). This is crucial, as many of the countries which adopted structural adjustment programmes (SAPs) in the 1970s and early 1980s attempted to pursue a strategy of competitive commercial agriculture, shifting from the focus away from food self-sufficiency. This meant that much of the policy support and subsidy mechanism adopted for enhancing foodgrain production after decolonization was reversed or gradually downsized. The idea that food security can be maintained by purchasing cheap food from the world markets clearly did not work for most countries in this region. This process of shifting towards export commodities was strongly mediated by TNFCs under corporate and contract farming arrangements and marked the re-entry of global capital in the agriculture of ex-colonies (Watts 1990).

The gradual 'income deflation' that accompanied SAPs with cutbacks in government expenditures and welfare measures ensured stagnation or a decline in macroeconomic foodgrain absorption. Though the average per capita income rose, the income deflation for the majority of the poor reduced demand for foodgrains to an extent that could not be compensated by the additional demand generated by the rich (U. Patnaik 2009). Additionally, the countries in South America were subjected to the economic crisis of the 1980s which followed the liberalization of capital markets in the earlier decade, leading to severe income contraction for the population. The 'Latin American lost decade' is reflected in the substantial decline in the absorption of foodgrains within the economies of the continent.

Table 1 ***Change in PCFC between 1980 and 1990 by Region*** (kg/year)

Region	Change
Central America	9.2
North Africa	29.5
FSU	3.1
South Asia	7.0
East Asia	22.7
Southeast Asia	16.2
Caribbean#	–18.3
South America	–17.0
West Asia*	–26.9
SSA	–2.9

Notes: # The end-year is 1993 until when the decline in PCFC is observed. * The start-year is 1983 from when the decline in PCFC begins.
Source: Estimated by the author from USDA-FAS database.

In the other regions, the 1980s were still witnessing a 'slow to moderate' increase in grain production and consumption, a continuation of trends of the earlier decades (Table 1). The exception here is FSU (Figure A6), which experienced stagnation in grain consumption in the 1980s, though at a level of around 700 kgs per capita per year, comparable to any developed country. The net effect of these changes was the stagnation that we have already observed for the developing world in the 1980s.

The 1990s were more dramatic, as the analysis of these regions reveals. The most significant trend was observed in FSU, where the PCFC declined by a massive 380.5 kgs between 1990 and 1999 (Table 2). There was practically a collapse of foodgrains consumption, almost entirely led by the steep decline in feed consumption by the livestock industries in these countries. This was concomitant with the break-up of the Soviet Union, which fundamentally altered the economic system. The transition to a market system from the erstwhile socialist arrangement was a painful restructuring for these countries, accompanied by a significant trend of decline in population. There was a decline in GDP associated with the transition (U. Patnaik 2002b) and the drastic withdrawal of food subsidies was directly related to high mortality rates, akin to a famine-like situation, something not well-recognized in the literature.

The total decline in demand for foodgrains in the FSU during this period was a gigantic 112.8 million tons.[7] To put this in perspective, the total increase in the world's foodgrain consumption during this period was

Table 2 ***Change in PCFC between 1990 and 2000 by Region*** (kg/year)

Region	Change
Central America	30.3
North Africa	14.2
FSU[@]	–380.5
South Asia	–6.5
East Asia	8.4
Southeast Asia	29.0
Caribbean[#]	27.1
South America	34.3
West Asia	–0.8
SSA	–1.9

Notes: [@] The end-year is 1999 until when the decline in PCFC is observed. [#] The start-year is 1993, from when the increase in PCFC is observed.
Source: Estimated by the author from USDA-FAS database.

148.5 million tons, and the FSU demand collapse compensated for 76 per cent of this. Of course, one needs to recognize that foodgrain production in the FSU region also underwent a significant decline in this period, and it was not the case that this region supplied grains released by the demand collapse to world markets. Nonetheless, there was a significant impact of this phenomenon on world food markets through the disappearance of FSU grain imports. The average annual grain imports by FSU countries in the 1980s was 34.7 million tons, which was 17.3 per cent of the total world trade (all figures based on USDA-FAS database). This ceased to exist in its entirety after 1992. A withdrawal of more than one-sixth of the demand on world foodgrain trade markets undoubtedly played a major role in perpetuating the 'low and stable prices' in global grain markets.

Among the other regions, South Asia, dominated by Indian data, also started experiencing a decline in PCFC in the 1990s. Economic liberalization based on fiscal orthodoxy comprised income deflationary macroeconomic policies and budget cuts in social expenditures. From the second half of the 1990s India witnessed an agrarian crisis which adversely affected rural demand for foodgrains. The export-oriented agricultural strategy adopted by India did not produce favourable results due to a significant decline of commercial crop prices in the world market in the late 1990s (U. Patnaik 2002a). Combined with repeated droughts and downsizing of the public distribution system (PDS) of subsidized food in 1997, foodgrain consumption declined. Between 1996 and 2005, PCFC declined in South Asia by around 11 kgs (Figure A7), the decline of this variable in India being nearly 20 kgs (USDA database).

Within the other developing regions, West Asia and SSA continued to stagnate in terms of grain consumption, while the Caribbean and South America just about recovered from the decline in the earlier decade. North Africa, Central America and Southeast Asia continued to increase their per capita grain consumption, with more dependence on food imports. The logic of attaining food security with the help of cheap food imports seems to have worked for these regions. While the trends in North Africa and Central America did not influence the overall trend in the developing world much due to their relatively smaller populations, the Southeast Asian countries played a more significant role in the reduction of undernutrition with their success in this strategy.

In the case of East Asia, the trends were again dominated by what was happening in China. China does not fit exactly into the SAP strategy of liberalized agricultural trade but maintained strong regulations on food markets. Driven by an expansion of corn outputs and increasing feedgrain consumption by the livestock industry, China witnessed an increase of PCFC from 253 kgs in 1980 to 294 kgs by 1998 (USDA database). Thereafter, owing to declining grain production, there was a slight decline in PCFC until 2005. Much of the supply shock was managed by China by massive de-stocking of foodgrains, and thus the impact on PCFC was minimal.

Looking at all the regions in the 1990s and sometimes a little beyond 2000, one can observe the centrality of the FSU trend in influencing the declining trend in the 'Rest of the World' and also a similar global trend in foodgrains consumption. The decline in PCFC in India was also a significant contributor to the larger trend given the large population size in the country, although this was still a fraction of the FSU contribution. The grain demand collapse in FSU countries and the complete withdrawal of the ex-socialist bloc from world grain markets in terms of import demand were singularly responsible for the global decline in PCFC. The starvation conditions in Russian winters (and in other FSU countries) and the resulting high mortality rates meant that the populations of these countries declined by 10.2 million between 1991 and 2002. Such a major demographic disaster in the 1990s created the conditions for the 'global low and stable food prices', on which a lot of the agricultural policies prescribed by liberalization and SAPs hinged.

To develop a holistic political economy analysis of food insecurity and crisis across the world after World War II, the following observations are crucial. First, in the 1950s and 1960s, there were parallel developments in the developed and the developing world in the wake of decolonization. In the developing world, *dirigiste*, i.e. state-led, economic policies focusing on food self-sufficiency led to the introduction of institutions supporting research, extension and marketing of the produce of small-scale farmers and subsidized food distribution for the poor, among other welfare policies. This witnessed a significant improvement of foodgrain production (with higher crop yields) and consumption in these countries. Simultaneously, there was massive reorganization of agricultural organization and technology using big capital in the North, leading to the emergence of the TNFCs. The process made a few countries major export players in the foodgrains market.

In the 1970s, the oil crisis and resultant economic difficulties led to a juncture where the free trade ideas of neoliberal economic philosophy were gaining ground. In that context, the regulatory agricultural and food management systems of the developing countries were confronted with the interests of big transnational capital controlling world trade in agricultural commodities. The acceptance and introduction of structural adjustments in trade and capital controls in the developing countries marked the resolution of this confrontation in favour of global capital that had emerged from the North.

As shown by the data, this meant a deceleration in foodgrains production, and the volatile commercial crop markets to which farmers were exposed often made their real incomes fall, leading to either reduced or stagnating foodgrains consumption. A structured process of 'income deflation' of the masses, largely small-scale petty producers and informal labour, was set into motion by economic reforms in various regions of the developing world, starting from Latin America. The massive economic restructuring of the socialist world leading to a torturous transition to a market system gave an unprecedented shock to the world demand for foodgrains. Because of these economic and geopolitical processes, foodgrains demand declined faster in the developing world during the 1990s, and this played a major role in keeping world food prices 'low and stable'. The latter condition was then implicitly used by elaborate theoretical propositions to convince more and more developing countries to change their agricultural strategies towards export markets, leaving the goal of attaining food security to the world food markets. Outside the developed countries, the food crisis has a genealogy prior to the GFC, as manifested in declining foodgrains consumption since the mid-1980s – a veritable 'longer food crisis'.

The 'Longer Food Crisis' and Two Theories for the South

Theories in different domains as diverse as Trade Policy and Agrarian Marxism have implicitly or explicitly depended on cheap global supplies of food as a fundamental assumption. In doing so, these theories failed to recognize the 'longer food crisis' that was already prevalent in various parts of the world from the 1980s. In this section, we look at these theories which have significant implications for developing countries of the South.

The Indian debate on trade liberalization for agriculture sheds light on how 'low and stable food prices' in world markets played an important role in theory and policy. The initial negotiations on the WTO agreement on agriculture threw up the question of food security with regard to trade liberalization for agricultural commodities. The dominant argument was that farmers in developing countries would clearly benefit with higher real incomes if they were allowed to grow commercial crops for the export markets where the prices of such crops were generally higher. Such an export-oriented strategy in agriculture was also expected to shift the terms of trade in favour of agriculture (Gulati and Sharma 1994; Rao and Gulati 1994).

Serious concerns were raised regarding the export-oriented agricultural strategy from the perspective of national food self-sufficiency. It was pointed out that a shift to commercial crops would reduce land under food production, and that the implications for domestic food security needed to be treated with caution (Nayyar and Sen 1994). This was all the more important since the neoliberal policies prescribing stringent fiscal discipline would potentially lead to a decline in irrigation and other infrastructural expenditures, and would render 'land' as a fixed resource that cannot be augmented at will. This would potentially recreate the colonial conditions of trade whereby colonies specialized in supplying primary commodities to the metropolitan centres at the expense of their own food self-sufficiency (U. Patnaik 2002a).

Many of these concerns were brushed aside by arguing that India was already self-sufficient in food and that the question of food security was somewhat redundant (see Gulati and Sharma 1994, fn 29). This essentially looks at food security from the supply side and ignores the possibility of foodgrain demand declining due to income deflation among the masses, something already visible in parts of the world due to SAP processes. As noted earlier, the demand for foodgrains actually started declining from the second half of the 1990s, but this was not anticipated by policy makers due to an exclusively supply-side perspective.

But more importantly, the expectation that when farmers shift to export crop cultivation their real incomes would increase, was implicitly based on the assumption that there are adequate supplies of foodgrains in the markets, nationally or internationally. It seems that the only objective basis for such an expectation were the 'low and stable prices' ruling the foodgrain markets since the 1980s. Except that a deeper analysis of this price stability in grain markets, as done here, indicates that it is more of a symptom of declining demand for foodgrains than a positive factor instilling exuberance to free trade arguments.

In fact, the exuberance regarding free trade in foodgrains and other agricultural commodities is well entrenched among the prime multilateral organizations, and cheap food imports have featured prominently in the arguments of 'gains from trade', among other factors. In the FAO report, *State of Food Insecurity in the World*, 2003, the following is stated:

> [I]nternational trade can have a major impact on reducing hunger and poverty in developing countries. Participation in trade allows access to larger markets and opens up opportunities for specialization in production and economies of scale . . . trade provides access to *better and cheaper supplies* (*including food imports*) and may stimulate flows of technology and investment. (FAO 2003: 16; emphasis added)

It is only with the astronomical food prices associated with GFC that the argument regarding necessity of food self-sufficiency in developing countries makes a partial comeback within the literature. Nonetheless, the earlier existence of cheap food supplies in global markets has been usually identified as a positive factor in an uncritical manner, thereby ignoring the 'longer food crisis'.

Agrarian Marxism is the other domain of knowledge where the 'low and stable food prices' at the end of the last millennium seem to have played a more explicit role. The influential thesis developed by Henry Bernstein regarding the (ir-)relevance of the agrarian question under conditions of globalization is an interesting example. Bernstein argues that the classical agrarian question is no more relevant for the developing countries under the twin conditions of 'globalized borderless capital' and the 'New Internationalized Food Regimes' (Bernstein 1996, 2004). The first condition implies that free movement of capital across nations serves as an 'external source of accumulation' for developing countries, something necessary for capitalist development as borne out by the experience of the early industrial countries. With this, the central component of the 'classical agrarian question', that is, the mobilization of surplus from agriculture for industrialization within the boundaries of nations, is rendered redundant. This formulation has been critiqued by scholars from the South.[8]

Here, we are more interested in the second condition, that is, the 'New Internationalized Food Regimes', which plays an equally important role in Bernstein's arguments. The question of 'food sovereignty' formed a core component during the process of 'economic decolonization' for the ex-colonies. The colonial arrangement of free trade had adversely affected food security until the mid-twentieth century in many developing countries. Thus, policy-making in agriculture gave equal attention to increasing food production and consumption domestically, and to raising farmers' incomes and savings. Institutions geared towards subsidized food distribution and technological interventions for raising crop yields went hand in hand in the newly independent countries. In other words, 'food self-sufficiency' constituted an equally important paradigm within the 'agrarian question' in the decolonized South.

Based on Harriet Friedmann's hypothesis on how the food regime has been transformed globally with the emergence of transnational corporations in agriculture, Bernstein argues that stable conditions of agricultural production and consumption have emerged through the operations of private corporate in the world markets. In his 1996 article, 'Agrarian Questions Then and Now', Bernstein writes:

> *[I]nternationalized integration of* national agricultures in the patterns of world production and consumption gave way to increasing *globalization.* The '*transnational restructuring of* agricultural sectors' is accompanied by growing *private* (*corporate*) . . . global regulation of agricultural production, trade, processing and consumption: corporations 'are the major agents . . . to *organize stable conditions of production and consumption* . . . and marketing' on a global scale. (Bernstein 1996: 46; emphasis added)

This assessment of the world food situation appears in the middle of the massive collapse of demand and demographic disaster in the FSU countries undergoing a tumultuous transition to the market system. There is also an inability to comprehend the role of income deflation triggered by SAP policies in various parts of the developing world. The fact that the impact of the collapse of socialism and the advance march of neoliberal policies on global food demand are not accounted for with the seriousness they deserve is evident from Bernstein's later writing on the subject as well. In his 2004 article, '"Changing Before Our Very Eyes": Agrarian Questions and the Politics of Land in Capitalism Today', he writes: 'important "globalizing" tendencies that affect agriculture in capitalism today include new strategies of sourcing by transnational agribusiness; new forms of organization and regulation of global commodity chains for agricultural products' (Bernstein 2004: 201). He goes on to place his conclusion as follows: 'with contemporary "globalization" and the *massive development of the productive forces in (advanced) capitalist agriculture*, the centrality of the "classic" agrarian question to industrialization is no longer significant for international capital. . . . there is no longer an agrarian question of capital on a world scale' (ibid.: 202; emphasis added).

The dominant idea that emerges from the above formulations is that the food question has been largely addressed by the transnational restructuring of agriculture in a global macroeconomic sense. The momentous development of productive forces by vertically integrated corporate agriculture ensured supplies of grain (and other agricultural products) to an extent that seems to have perpetuated stable price conditions in the world food markets. Bernstein's observation that the global food system has come under the hegemony of transnational corporations and the WTO agreement and aggressive patenting of genetic materials to control small to big farmers is undoubtedly a valuable political economy understanding of the current food regime. It is also a fact that a period of stable food prices as long as more than two decades, as witnessed from the 1980s until the 2006 GFC, is a phenomenon that stands out in the history of capitalism.

However, the causality between the rise of TNFCs leading to a consequent 'development of productive forces' and stable grain prices is not borne out by the evidence on global per capita foodgrain production, which exhibited an unambiguous declining trend in 1985–2002. Rather, the price stability in world grain markets was more an illusion created by the instability associated with the break-up of the erstwhile socialist system in the Soviet Union, the income contraction experienced by populations due to the Latin American crisis and the more gradual income deflation processes – which was also tantamount to destabilizing the system of petty production supported by myriad state institutions, brought about by neoliberal economic reforms across a whole range of developing countries in Asia and Africa.

Recognizing the destabilization of various prior economic production systems by neoliberal structural reforms allows us to appreciate the 'longer food crisis' in the developing world and, thereby, to revise the theoretical positions from a 'Southern' perspective. This facilitates the incorporation of the dynamics of neoliberalism in a comprehensive assessment of the challenges of development. With the persistent global economic crisis/stagnation post-2008, and the slew of austerity measures inflicted even on the advanced economies of the North, the lessons of the 'longer food crisis' caused by income deflation/contraction are valuable also for the developed world. These economic lessons are crucial, then, from multiple perspectives: whether in the interest of pro-people, 'rights-based' policy-making, or for the purpose of building and strengthening an emancipatory agrarian politics.

Appendix 1

Figure A1 ***The Food–Feed Competition***

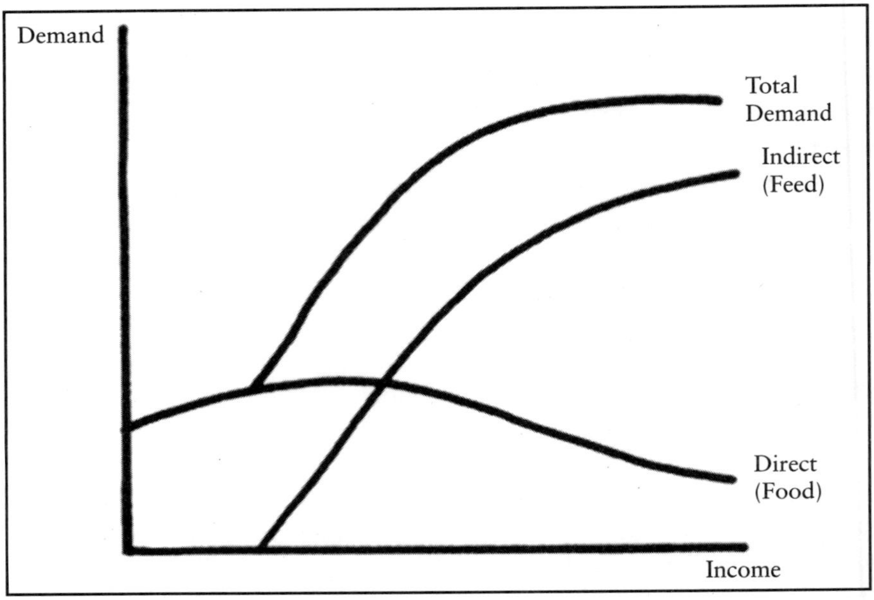

Source: Yotopoulos (1985).

Appendix 2

Table A1 ***List of Developed Countries***

Continent	*List of Developed Countries**
North America	Canada, United States of America
Europe	Austria, Belgium, Bulgaria, Croatia, Cyprus, Czech Republic, Denmark, Estonia, Finland, France, Germany, Greece, Hungary, Iceland, Ireland, Italy, Latvia, Lithuania, Luxembourg, Malta, Netherlands, Norway, Poland, Portugal, Romania, Slovakia, Slovenia, Spain, Sweden, Switzerland, United Kingdom
Asia	Israel, Japan, South Korea, Taiwan
Oceania	Australia, New Zealand

Note: * The list of countries have been drawn on the basis of per capita incomes. Small, island nations and primarily oil-exporting countries have been excluded.

Appendix 3

Figure A2 ***Per Capita Production and Consumption of Foodgrains in the Caribbean: 1980/81–2000/01***

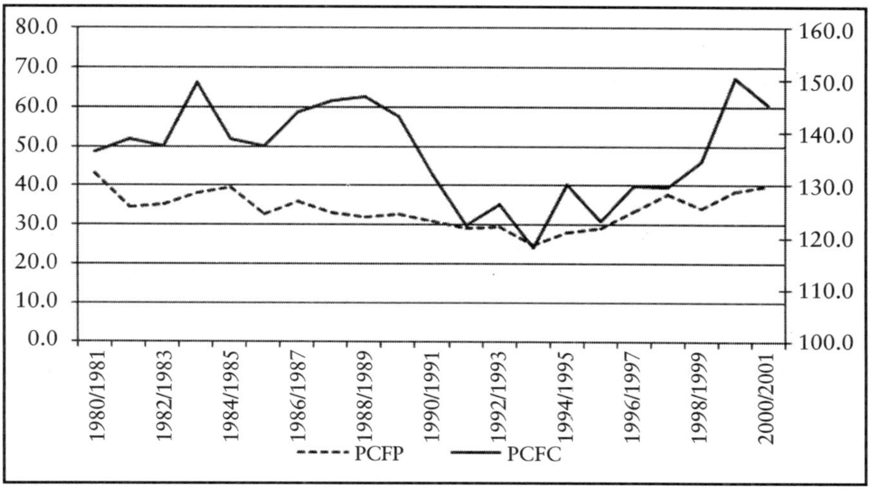

Note: The PCFP is on the LHA and PCFC on the RHA.
Source: Estimated by the author from USDA-FAS database.

Figure A3 ***Per Capita Production and Consumption of Foodgrains in South America: 1980/81–2000/01***

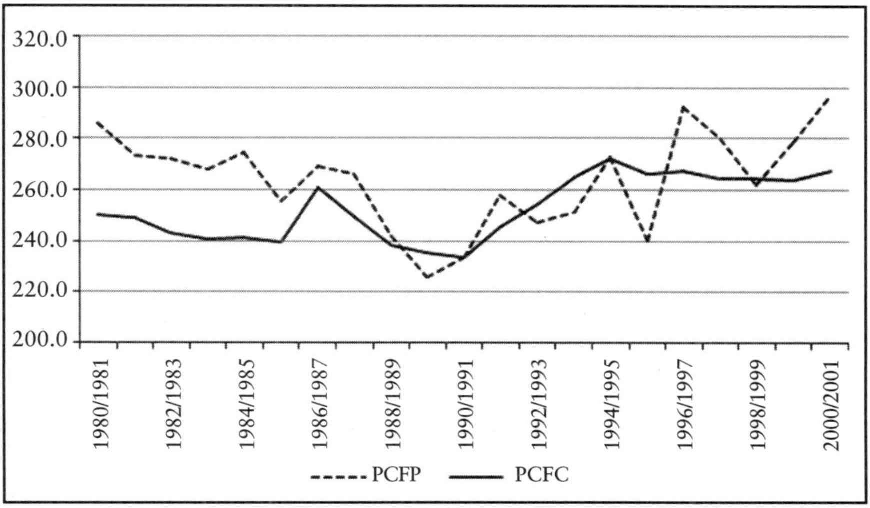

Source: Estimated by the author from USDA-FAS database.

Figure A4 ***Per Capita Production and Consumption of Foodgrains in Sub-Saharan Africa: 1980/81–2000/03***

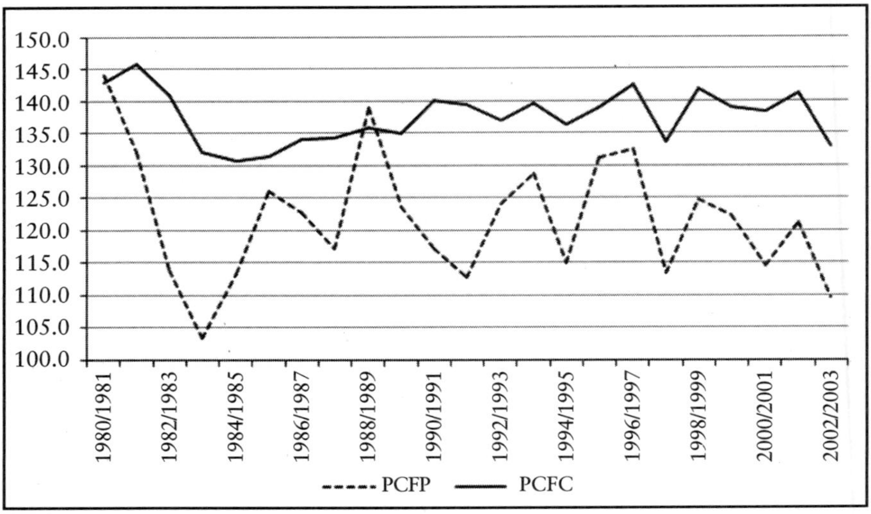

Source: Estimated by the author from USDA-FAS database.

Figure A5 ***Per Capita Production and Consumption of Foodgrains in West Asia: 1980/81–2000/01***

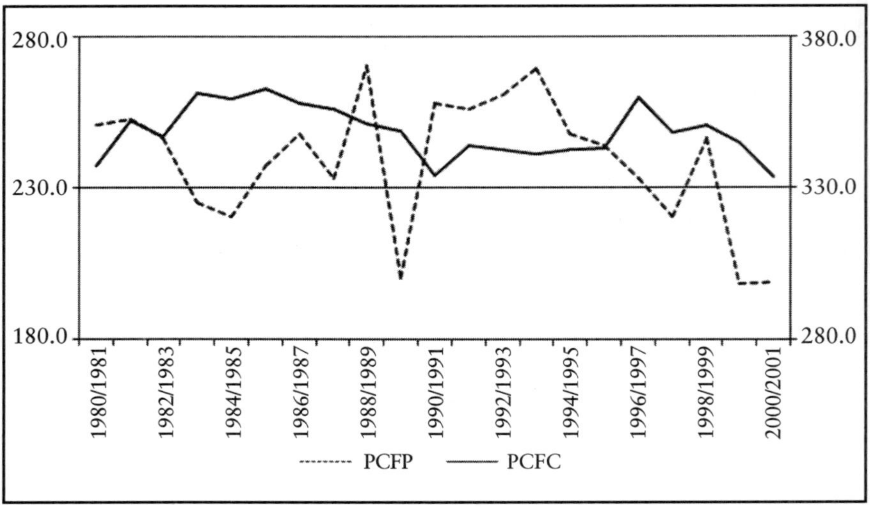

Note: The PCFP is on the LHA and PCFC on the RHA.
Source: Estimated by the author from USDA-FAS database.

Figure A6 ***Per Capita Production and Consumption of Foodgrains in Former Soviet Union: 1980/81–2000/01***

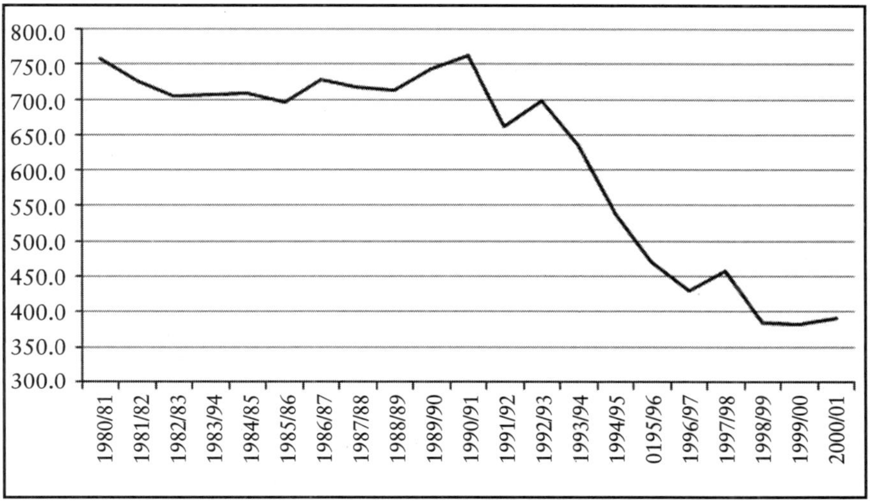

Source: Estimated by the author from USDA-FAS database.

Figure A7 ***Per Capita Production and Consumption of Foodgrains in South Asia: 1980/81–2005/06***

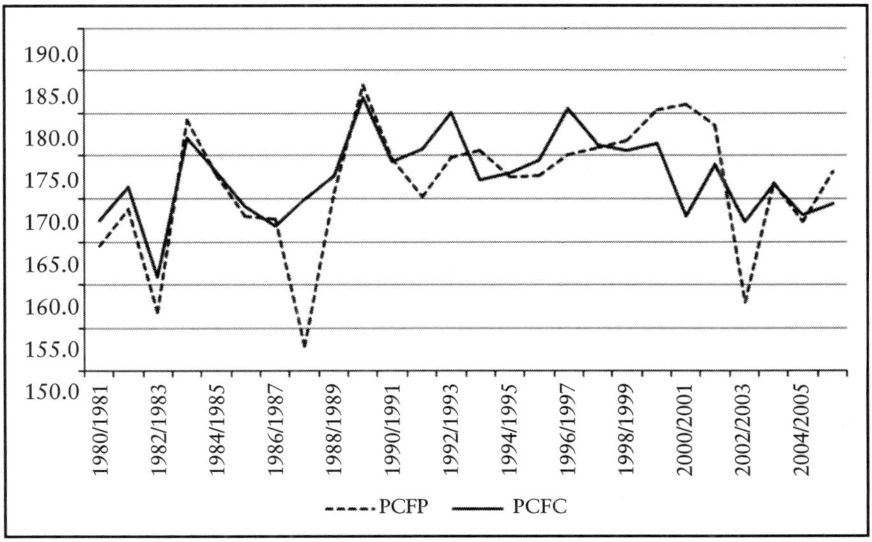

Source: Estimated by the author from USDA-FAS database.

Figure A8 ***Per Capita Production and Consumption of Foodgrains in North Africa:1980/81–2000/01***

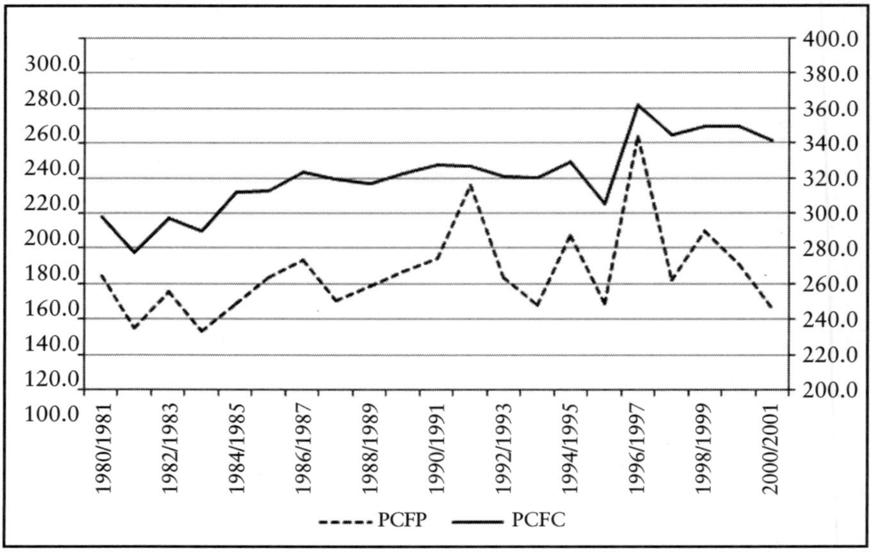

Source: Estimated by the author from USDA-FAS database.

Figure A9 ***Per Capita Production and Consumption of Foodgrains in Central America: 1980/81–2000/01***

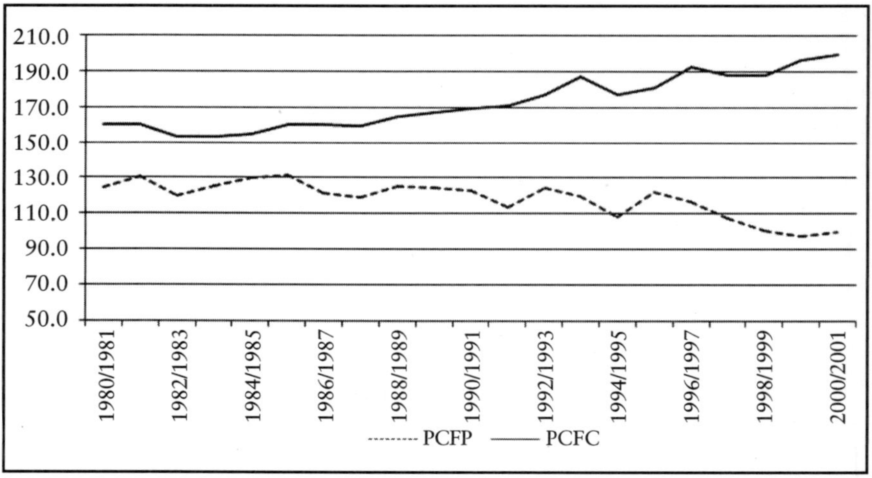

Source: Estimated by the author from USDA-FAS database.

Figure A10 ***Per Capita Production and Consumption of Foodgrains in Southeast Asia: 1980/81–2004/05***

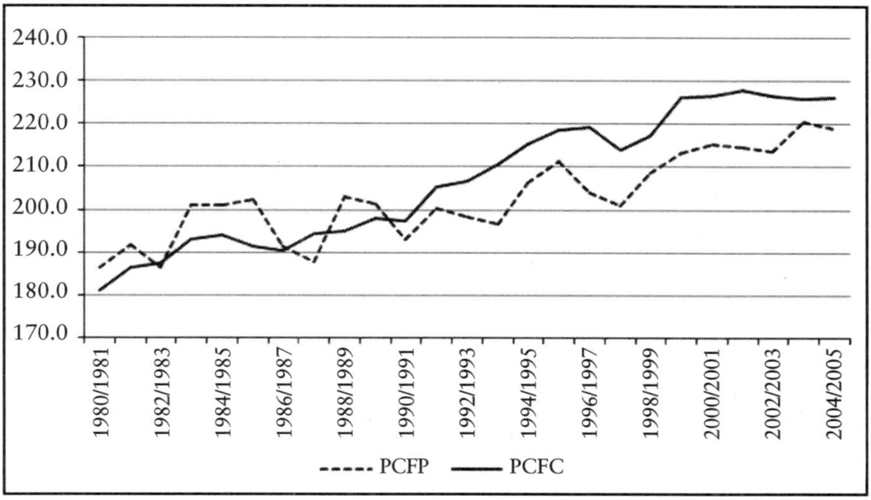

Source: Estimated by the author from USDA-FAS database.

Figure A11 ***Per Capita Production and Consumption of Foodgrains in East Asia: 1980/81–2009/10***

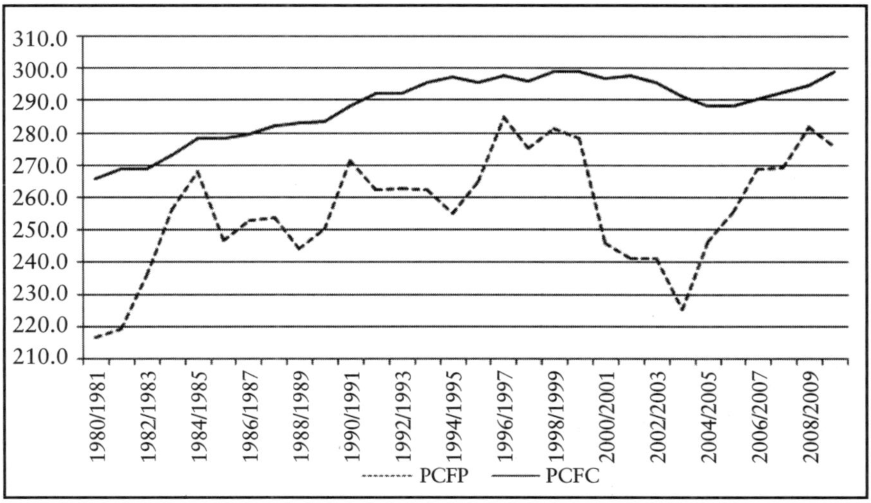

Source: Estimated by the author from USDA-FAS database.

Notes

[1] The data are available at https://apps.fas.usda.gov/psdonline/app/index.html#/app/advQuery, accessed 23 August 2019.

[2] This is not to discount the importance of supply-side factors like climate change or input prices in general or in the long run, but is more of an assessment of the causal factors specifically of the GFC that occurred in 2006–13.

[3] See Appendix 2 for a list of these countries.

[4] The countries comprising this region are the Russian Federation, Azerbaijan, Armenia, Georgia, Moldova, Ukraine, Belarus, Uzbekistan, Kazakhstan, Kyrgyzstan, Tajikistan and Turkmenistan.

[5] The charts plotted for each region are provided in Appendix 3; refer to Figures A2–A11.

[6] The start years for sub-Saharan Africa and West Asia are 1981 and 1983, respectively, when the decline in PCFC begins, and the end-year for FSU is 1999, the year until which the PCFC declines.

[7] One metric ton is equal to 1,000 kgs.

[8] For a comprehensive critique of Bernstein's hypothesis of the redundancy of the classical agrarian question under globalization, see Moyo *et al.* (2013) and Banerjee (2017).

References

Banerjee, A. (2011a), 'Reviewing the Global Food Crisis: Magnitude, Causes, Impact and Policy Options', in B.N. Ghosh, ed., *Global Food Crisis: Contemporary Issues and Policy Options*, United Kingdom: Wisdom Books.

——— (2011b), 'Food, Feed, Fuel: Transforming the Competition for Grain', *Development and Change*, 42 (2): 529–57.

——— (2017), 'Agrarian Crisis and Accumulation in Rural India: Locating the Land Question within the Agrarian Question', in A. D'Costa and A. Chakraborty, eds, *The Land Question in India: State, Dispossession and Capitalist Transition*, Oxford: Oxford University Press.

Bernstein, H. (1996), 'Agrarian Questions Then and Now', *Journal of Peasant Studies*, 24 (1–2), 22–59.

——— (2004), 'Changing Before Our Very Eyes: Agrarian Questions and the Politics of Land in Capitalism Today', *Journal of Agrarian Change,* 4 (1 and 2): 190–225.

Chand, R. (2008), 'The Global Food Crisis: Causes, Severity and Outlook', Review of Agriculture, *Economic and Political Weekly*, 43 (26 and 27).

Food and Agriculture Organization (FAO) (2003), *The State of Food Insecurity in the World 2003: Monitoring Progress towards the World Food Summit and Millennium Development Goals*, Rome: FAO.

——— (2008), *The State of Food Insecurity in the World 2008: High Food Prices and Food Security-Threats and Opportunities*, Rome: FAO.

Friedmann, H. (1990), 'Origins of Third World Food Dependence', in H. Bernstein, B. Crow, M. Mackintosh and C. Martin, eds, *The Food Question: Profits versus People?*, London: Earthscan: 13–31.

——— (1993), 'International Political Economy of Food: A Global Crisis', *New Left Review,* 197: 29–57.

Ghosh, J. (2010), 'The Unnatural Coupling: Food and Global Finance', *Journal of Agrarian Change,* 10 (1), 72–86.

Gulati, A. and A. Sharma (1994), 'Agriculture under GATT: What It Holds for India', *Economic and Political Weekly*, 29 (29).

International Monetary Fund (IMF) (2008), *Food and Fuel Prices: Recent Developments,*

Macroeconomic Impact, and Policy Responses, Report prepared by Fiscal Affairs, Policy Development and Review and Research Departments, IMF.

McMichael, P. (2009), 'A Food Regime Genealogy', *Journal of Peasant Studies,* 36 (1), 139–69.

McMichael, P., ed. (1994), *The Global Restructuring of Agro-Food Systems*, Ithaca: Cornell University Press.

Mitchell, D. (2008), 'A Note on Rising Food Prices', Policy Research Working Paper No. 4682, Development Prospects Group, Washington DC: World Bank.

Moyo, S., P. Jha and P. Yeros (2013), 'The Classical Agrarian Question: Myth, Reality and Relevance Today', *Agrarian South: Journal of Political Economy*, 2 (1), 93–119.

Nayyar, D. and A. Sen (1994), 'International Trade and the Agricultural Sector in India', *Economic and Political Weekly,* 29 (20).

Patnaik, P. (2008), 'The Accumulation Process in the Period of Globalization', *Economic and Political Weekly*, 43 (26 and 27).

Patnaik, U. (2002a), 'Deflation and Déjà Vu: Indian Agriculture in the World Economy', in V.K. Ramachandran and M. Swaminathan, eds, *Agrarian Studies: Essays on Agrarian Relations in Less-Developed Countries*, Delhi: Tulika Books: 111–43.

——— (2002b), 'Agrarian Crisis and Global Deflationism', *Social Scientist*, 30 (1–2).

——— (2007), *The Republic of Hunger and Other Essays*, Delhi: Three Essays Collective and Monmouth: Merlin Press.

——— (2009), 'Origins of the Food Crisis in India and Developing Countries', *Monthly Review*, 61 (3).

Rao, C.H.H. and A. Gulati (1994), 'Indian Agriculture: Emerging Perspectives and Policy Issues', *Economic and Political Weekly*, 29 (53).

Watts, M. (1990), 'Peasants under Contract: Agro-Food Complexes in the Third World', in H. Bernstein., B. Crow., M. Mackintosh and C. Martin, eds, *The Food Question: Profits Versus People?*, London: Earthscan: 13–31.

Yotopoulos, P.A. (1985), 'Middle-income Classes and Food Crises: The "New" Food–Feed Competition', *Economic Development and Cultural Change,* 33 (3): 463–83.

11

Ecological Crisis, Global Capital and the Reinvention of Nature

A Perspective from the Global South

Archana Prasad

The main aim of the study is to show how capitalism resolves its own crisis through the reinvention of nature as capital. Such a process has given rise to a discourse on 'natural capital', which directly pits nature against labour, as discussed in James O'Connor's proposition on the second contradiction of capitalism (O'Connor 1991). However, this view is limited in its understanding because it fails to account for the expropriation of people from their habitat as central to the accumulation process. Under different phases and stages of capitalist development, such alienation assumes diverse forms. In other words, the reinvention of capitalism to stabilize itself after a period of crisis creates its own form of alienation and expropriation (Foster and Clark 2018). This study focuses on the changing form of expropriation of forest resources through multilateral agreements like the REDD (Reducing Emissions from Deforestation and Forest Degradation)-Plus. It is argued that such arrangements represent the latest method of land grab and the cartelization of markets for natural commodities via carbon stocks.

Forest laws have been some of the most oppressive legislations since colonial times and have proved to be the foundation of the control of all non-private resources by the capitalist state. In the case of the global North, E.P. Thompson's study of the English forest laws shows that the forest conflict was, in fact, a conflict between users and exploiters, where 'wealth could be extracted from the territories of the poor, during the phase of capitalist accumulation, provided the number of predatory elites were limited and the state and the law smoothed the way of exploitation' (Thompson 1978: 24). In much of the twentieth century, the forested regions could be described in a similar manner – with one important caveat. The annexation of forested areas in the global South cannot be understood without considering the role of imperialism. This aspect has been missing from even the work of some Marxist ecologists and historians.

For example, historians from the world ecology perspective use Karl Polanyi's approach to argue for the embeddedness of human society within nature, ostensibly countering the so-called dualistic understanding of nature and society which explained the contradictions that arose out of capitalist relations. Thus, Jason Moore argues against the idea that the structures of European imperialism were crucial in the transformation of nature. Instead, he argues for new ways of thinking about capitalism as embedded in the web of life; in other words, capitalism should be seen as a way of organizing nature, and at the same time abstracting both nature and humans as part of a larger ontological process. This view is based on an understanding that both nature and capital are relational and interlocked with each other; and that, therefore, capitalism cannot be seen as having a dominant 'external relationship' with nature. Moore writes:

> Human organizations cannot be reduced to the mythical domain of the society whose arbitrary boundaries obscure the constitutive geo-biological relations of human sociality. In this light, human organizations are at once producers and products of the web of life, understood in its evolving mosaic of diversity. From this perspective capitalism becomes something more than human. It becomes world ecology of power, capital and nature. (Moore 2018: 239)

Such a perspective obscures the processes of accumulation and tends to represent all history as a history of ecological change (Moore 2003). The accent is on the adaptation of capitalism through reordering of nature and human society, where the unpaid work of nature is appropriated by capital. This perspective decentres labour from the discourse by reducing its work as being a part of the 'unpaid work of nature', rather than a source of value creation. Here, nature has more value than labour and, therefore, the role of labour is obscured (Foster and Burkett 2018).

Moreover, Moore does not take into account the problem of 'uneven geographical development', as elucidated, for example, by David Harvey. For Harvey, the problem of uneven development has to be contextualized in the circulation of capital, where the main emphasis is on the way it embeds itself in existing social relations. This process of adaptation results in both dispossession and uneven geographical development (Harvey 2006). The argument that there is 'accumulation by dispossession' is the basis of the survival of capitalism (Harvey 2011). Yet, even here, the analysis is singularly oblivious to the role of the state as a player which acts in the interests of its own bourgeoisie through a regime of control over natural resource use. The character of such a regime is determined by the stage of national and global capitalist development. The debates on climate change also have to be analysed in this larger picture.

A study of the multilateral REDD-Plus regime, which has formed the basis of accumulation from forest-rich regions in the global South, will allow us to relate the emergence of the carbon markets and REDD regimes to the crisis within capitalism, and also reveal the implications of this for nature-dependent people, especially in terms of undervaluation of their work. The first section below historicizes the control of nature in the global North since the process of colonization. The second section provides a contemporary history of the emergence of REDD and REDD-Plus, and shows that the concept of green capitalism emerged after the 1990s in order to resolve the accumulation crisis within world capitalism. The third section carries out a detailed discussion of the REDD-Plus architecture and shows how nature is commodified into a notion of 'natural capital' through a process of financialization. It discusses the emergence and working of carbon markets, especially with respect to the emerging new international division of labour. The fourth section offers some concluding remarks.

The Mastery of Nature

The domination of humans over nature is a long process whose unintended consequences are evident throughout the long period of history. As Engels wrote:

> The mastery over nature, which began with the development of the hand, with labour, widened man's horizon at every new advance. He was continually discovering new, hitherto unknown, properties of natural objects. . . . Let us not, however, flatter ourselves over much on account of our human victories over nature. For each such victory it takes its revenge on us. Each of them, it is true, has in the first place the consequences on which we counted, but in the second and third places it has quite different, unforeseen effects which only too often cancel the first. (Engels [1876] 1950: 10, 18)

Engels states that the main source of the intensification of short-term use is capitalism itself, and, as such, bourgeois social science is preoccupied with the methods of harnessing nature for short-term gains. This insight is not lost on present-day scholars and policy makers and lies at the root of the emerging ecological crisis, which has manifested itself in the rise in the temperature of the earth as well as a discourse on climate change since colonial times (Grove 1998).

There is, first of all, a need to account for the uneven patterns

Table 1 *Long-term Changes in Forest Cover by Region, 1850–2015*

Region	1850 Forest (mha)	2015 Forest (mha)	Change (absolute number, mha)	Change (per cent)
Tropical Africa	792	614	–178	–22
Latin America	1248	932	–316	–25
South and Southeast Asia	533	326	–207	–39
Tropics sub-total	*2573*	*1872*	*–701*	*–27*
North America	768	657	–111	–14
Europe	130	174	44	34
Former USSR	879	857	–22	–3
China	159	208	49	31
North Africa and the Middle East	40	37	–3	–8
East Asia	64	49	–15	–23
Oceania	210	140	–70	–33
Temperate sub-total	*2249*	*2123*	*–126*	*–6*
Global	*4823*	*3995*	*–828*	*–17*

Source: Data adapted from Houghton *et al.* (2017): 464.

of deforestation from the early days of the empire. As shown in Table 1, even though the world lost 828 million hectares of forests in the last century-and-a-half, about half the forested areas were in Latin America, Asia and Africa despite deforestation in the above-mentioned period. If former USSR and China are included, then more than three-fourths of the forests were outside the global North.

This implies that throughout different phases of colonization, the global South continued to consist of forest-rich regions and to provide raw materials for countries of the North. As the data compiled from the Forest Statistics of the Food and Agricultural Organization (FAO) show, by 1961, the countries of Europe and the United States were the largest importing countries of forest products, constituting 77.4 per cent of total imports, and this proportion rose to 83.6 per cent in 2010.[1] This was accompanied by massive displacement of livelihoods and dispossession of people from their habitats, resulting in a growing reserve army of labour. These patterns clearly indicate that accumulation from trade in forest products and other aspects of forest management in the colonies was largely concentrated in the imperialist countries of the global North, and this aspect of the ecological change under capitalism has often been ignored by important scholars such as Moore and Harvey, mentioned above.

A second aspect that is of importance is the role of forests within the colonies themselves. The first wave of colonization after the voyage of Christopher Columbus showed a sharp increase in deforestation and the extension of croplands from 1750 to 1930, with the largest expanse coming westward between the 1860s and 1900. Most of this occurred at the expense of forest and woodlands (Ramankutty and Foley 1999). It could be argued that this expansion proved to be the marginalization of Native Americans and laid the foundations of settler colonialism in the Americas. However, in South America, which was largely a hub of plantation-based exploitation, no significant croplands are detected in the land-use data till the beginning of the twentieth century. This is significant because a major proportion of forestlands remained intact since the ruling classes were largely focused on urban centres. However, regions without settler colonialism faced a different form of deforestation. This largely happened in the form of use of timber wood for setting up infrastructure that could establish colonial domination. A good example of this was the deforestation for railway sleepers in India. Hence, a minimum level of forests had to be maintained in order to make the colony fit for accumulation. This was done through the introduction of the system of 'scientific management', which resulted in multiple forms of expropriation in the colonies (Grove 1998).

Interestingly, this is also the origin of the global climate change discourse, since desiccation was an important part of the forestry discourse since the mid-nineteenth century in French and British colonies (Grove 1995). One explanation for this discourse attributes it to the human and environmental destruction that occurred after the Great Wars in Africa as well as the conflicts in Central Asia (Grove 1998: 35). Hence, it is possible to surmise that crisis situations have often led to climate change discourse. This is evident in several parts of the world, such as South Asia, Southern Africa and parts of the Caribbean; but these discourses were always led by the imperialist European and American states. The United States played an important part in providing markets and investments for tropical timber products, and this led to a fundamental change in forest markets (Tucker 2000). In such a situation, the incorporation of scientists in relations of accumulation was guided by the production of a certain type of science which had some material basis, that is, the increasing contradiction between the depletion of nature and the rising rate of accumulation (Foster 1994). It should be noted that in 1981, Africa, South and Central America, and Asia continued to be the largest exporters of forest products. It is therefore not surprising that the countries of the North showed particular keenness in stressing the importance of arresting deforestation in the global South.

Applying this logic to the global South, one may argue that the climate change discourse was an imperialist strategy to control common lands; but this conclusion would oversimplify the complexity of the processes that go into the reinvention of nature, which is, in turn, essential for the stability of capital and higher rates of accumulation. Though several scholars have pointed to this process from the 1970s onwards, they have rarely linked the phenomenon to a newly emerging international division of labour in the period after the independence of successive states. The Brundtland Commission highlighted the growing inequality between nations and stressed the need to attain sustainability by bridging the inequities between the North and the South. The Commission noted that:

> [t]hrough the ages, people have reached beyond their own borders to obtain essential, valued, or exotic materials. Today's surer communications and larger trade and capital movements have greatly enlarged this process, quickened its pace, and endowed it with far-reaching ecological implications. Thus the pursuit of sustainability requires major changes in international economic relations. (World Commission of Environment and Development 1987 : 60)

In particular, it noted with regard to tropical forests that trade patterns encourage unsustainable practices, and, therefore, international arrangements were needed to ensure trade on the basis of sustainable development in the light of the economic crisis of the 1980s. From this period onwards, that is, after the enactment of the Montreal Protocol of 1987, international arrangements focused on reducing pollution levels and emissions, and the forests were to play an important part in this project.

The Emergence of REDD and REDD-Plus

As is well known, the 1990s saw a surge of finance capitalism in developing countries, with international arrangements being guided by transnational investors. In 1992, the United Nations Framework Convention on Climate Change (UNFCCC) explicitly recognized that developed countries were historically responsible for rising global emissions leading to climate change, but placed the responsibility of the future of the planet on the developing countries, since they housed the maximum proportion of natural resources that would maintain the ecological security of the world. Hence, the developing countries should curtail their emissions by adopting 'sustainable development patterns'. In return, the UNFCCC asked the developed countries to 'provide new and additional financial resources to meet the agreed full costs incurred by developing country Parties. . . .

They shall also provide such financial resources, including for the transfer of technology, needed by the developing country Parties' (United Nations 1992, Article 4 [3]). The mechanism to negotiate this transfer of money and technology would be treaties between 'sovereign states' who would work within the framework of the Montreal Protocol and the UNFCCC.

It should be noted that the UNFCCC was quite clear about its definition of the 'climate system' as encompassing 'the totality of the atmosphere, hydrosphere, biosphere and geosphere and their interactions' (ibid., Article 1 [3]). This implied that every part of nature became a commodity which was assessed in terms of monetary value, thus signalling the big entry of finance capital in natural resource markets, especially with regard to carbon emissions. An important step in this direction was the Kyoto Protocol of 1998 which specifically acknowledged land-use change and deforestation as drivers of increases in greenhouse emissions. In particular, the Kyoto agreement set up monitoring mechanisms to document the removal of carbon sinks through deforestation, and mandated signatory countries to take up afforestation and reforestation programmes (UNFCCC 1998). In return, the Protocol assured the developing countries that they would get the benefit of clean technology to follow a sustainable development path and would also be compensated by the developed countries. Thus, green aid and clean technologies became buzz-words that structured both compliance and incentives for preserving forests in order to decrease the rising temperature of the earth. However, as is evident from the available data, these measures did not yield significant results.

Estimates of the Food and Agricultural Organization (FAO) show that the net forest area lost in the world between 1990 and 2000 was about 8,868,000 hectares. It is significant that more than 7,000 hectares out of this were in Africa and Latin America, with carbon stocks significantly declining in the period between 1990 and 2005. Despite this, Africa, Asia and Latin America continued to have the largest carbon stock, even though their combined proportion declined from 68.3 per cent of total carbon stock in 1990 to 65.3 per cent in 2005 (that is, the year REDD-Plus was initiated).[2] This declining trend, however, did not lead to introspection over the lack of capability of finance to solve the problem of deforestation. Rather, the analysis of policy makers focused more on lack of investments due to 'market failures' and the need to extend inter-governmental efforts. The solution was seen in boosting more private investment in the preservation and creation of carbon stocks so that people would have a stake in the preservation of forests.

In 2005, the Montreal Action Plan formally laid down the REDD guidelines under the agreement negotiated at the 11th Conference of Parties, and thereby defined a forest as 'a minimum area of land of 0.05–1.0 hectare with tree crown cover (or equivalent stocking level) of more than 10–30 per cent with trees with the potential to reach a minimum height of 2–5 metres at maturity in situ' (UNFCCC 2005: 5). It laid out measures to emphasize the mandate of the Kyoto Protocol: 'protection and enhancement of sinks and reservoirs of greenhouse gases not controlled by the Montreal Protocol, taking into account its commitments under relevant international environmental agreements; promotion of sustainable forest management practices, afforestation and reforestation' (UNFCCC 1998, Article 2 [a] ii). In this way, the Action Plan once again redefined the meaning of nature, and also specified the difference between nature created through 'afforestation', or human interventions on lands that did not have forests for the last five decades, and 'natural forests' which provided ecosystem services. The main aim of the Protocol was to set up accounting systems in order to ensure that the natural forests providing ecosystem services could be managed in accordance with the Kyoto Protocol. The REDD secretariat was set up with its main mission being to identify the technical needs of countries of the South for assistance in developing reporting mechanisms on anthropogenic pressures and strategies to alleviate them (The Global Canopy Programme 2008).The Montreal Decisions not only defined forests as a resource in a very specific way, but also created the conditions for its valuation and trade in an open market system.

The instruments of implementation remained almost the same with bilateral arrangements as a major source to assist the countries of the South. Between 2005 and 2008, there was not much headway in reduction of emissions. Because of deforestation, the net emissions came down by a meagre 0.02 per cent, but a major portion of the global South saw increased emissions.[3] Emissions also increased in Northern Europe, and the negotiations were hit by a roadblock over the lack of compensation to 'developing' countries and their 'right to development'. In addition, high-income developed countries faced the challenge of creating a discourse that challenges the 'catch up' strategy and the highly Americanized version of 'development'. The concept of 'green capitalism' was therefore used to marry the contradictory objectives of finding a way to enhance accumulation even while preserving the planetary stability which provided the foundations of capitalism itself. The transition from REDD to REDD-Plus took place in this context.

The Bali Action Plan of 2007 first mooted the idea that REDD-Plus could become a good investment option for the developed nations. It noted that since more than half the world's forests were in the developing countries, the developed countries should make it worthwhile for them to enhance their carbon sinks (UNFCCC 2008: 8–10). The Conference of Parties reached an informal understanding that there was a need to evolve strategies to increase carbon stocks through the preservation of natural forests, rather than having a narrow focus on the mitigation of emissions, thus increasing the scope of international interventions. However, it was only in 2013 that there was a formal agreement on the expansion of REDD under the Warsaw Framework. The Framework agreed that financing REDD-Plus initiatives would include private parties and corporations which would treat the forests as capital and invest through national entities in REDD-Plus projects. This core element was based on the assumption that private finance would pay forest-dependent communities for ecosystem services so that they would not destroy natural forests (UNFCCC 2013). Such an understanding came close on the heels of a UN document titled *Towards a Green Economy*, which held that

> REDD+ mechanisms can provide an important vehicle to drive the green economy transition. Donor pledges to REDD+, including the UNREDD Programme, REDD+ Partnership, Forest Carbon Partnership Facility, the GEF and the Forest Investment Programme among others, currently amount to US$ 5 billion through 2012. As part of ongoing pilots for REDD+, there is mounting evidence that such 'payment for environmental services' holds wider promise not only for climate regulation and biodiversity conservation services, but also to scale up significant resources to communities who are stewards at the landscape level. The Global Environment Facility (GEF) is another important financing vehicle for the green economy that needs to be scaled up and strengthened. (UNEP 2013: 44)

Hence, REDD-Plus became a vehicle for promoting green capitalism in the wake of a severe capitalist crisis and the need to address concerns regarding dipping profits of corporations. One may ask, even if this were the case, why did the countries of the global South accept these arrangements? The answer probably lies in the way the nation-states of the global South were integrated into the larger world economy through increasing debts. Furthermore, with the downward slide in commodity prices in world markets, export-oriented economies faced severe challenges. The adoption of neoliberalism also led to demands for smaller governments and overseas infrastructural investments. The drying up of such investments was one of the main factors for the ruling classes of the global South to accept 'green aid' under REDD-Plus.

The Commodification of Nature

It was not only the case that the concept of 'nature as capital' was incorporated through a process of reinvention, but adjustments in the capitalist structure also necessitated that the corporations and nation-states restructure themselves through complex market and investment processes. This fundamentally changed the relationship between 'finance' and nature that mediated the human–nature–state relationship. Such a change was effected by setting up a completely new institutional arrangement. Though REDD readiness funds had existed ever since the Montreal Action Plan, they were expanded with private participation. The World Bank emerged as one of the key players when the developing and the developed countries requested the Bank to organize the Forest Carbon Partnership Facility (FCPF) as a follow-up to UNFCCC and the Bali Action Plan. The Facility was formed as a partnership between thirty-seven REDD countries with tropical forests, donor countries from developed economies and other observers (including private players to attract investments). This partnership forms the basic structural feature of the REDD-Plus institutional architecture, which consists of the Readiness Fund and the Carbon Fund. The Readiness Fund is for national governments to build up their capabilities to formulate and implement REDD-Plus projects. These were to be made by national governments, who were also to set up their own funding facilities or the national REDD fund. The World Bank provided initial assistance and funding for this activity. The Carbon Fund provides incentives for per ton carbon dioxide reduced by REDD countries through reduction in deforestation and forest degradation under verifiable programmes and standards. These two facilities were meant to attract funds from the developed countries as well as private agencies. The annual report of the FCPF for the year 2016 shows the funds provided by the developed countries.

As can be seen from Table 2, Norway and Germany are the biggest donors for the REDD-Plus project, constituting about 30.6 per cent and 20.8 per cent, respectively, of total donations. This implies that about 51 per cent of the donations came from just two countries. If we take the top six donors, they constitute 80.9 per cent of the total donations, and the Northern European countries constitute about 42.4 per cent of all readiness funds achieved. What is significant is that the money put up by the United States and the United Kingdom is only 4 per cent of the total committed funding. This is also true of the REDD-Plus fund, where maximum donations come from the Northern European countries and Japan. These countries were larger donors than the UNEP (United Nations Environment Programme), UNDP (United Nations Development Programme) and FAO, which were to get contributions from all the signatories of the Kyoto

Table 2 ***FCPF Readiness Fund Donor Contributions as of End-FY 2016*** **(USDM)**

Country	Total	Outstanding*	FY16	FY15	FY14	FY13	FY12	FY11	FY10	FY09
Australia	23.92						6.33	8.06		9.61
Canada	41.36							4.19		
Denmark	58.00								5.8	
European Commission	51.62	1.11			1.36		26.76			
Finland	23.20			3.23		5.27	57.85			9.06
France	110.34						5.19		0.60	4.61
Germany	76.67			23.78	13.91	13.11		26.11		
Italy	5.00							5.00		
Japan	14.00						4.00		5.00	5.00
Netherlands	20.27					7.68	7.68			5.00
Norway	113.06	44.19			38.73			8.80	16.47	5.00
Spain	7.04									7.12
Switzerland	8.21									8.21
United Kingdom	5.76							5.82		
United States of America	9.00					4.00			4.50	0.5
Committed funding	368.88	45.30		27.01	54.00	30.01	31.61	94.88	32.29	53.94

Note: Figures rounded off to two decimal points.
Source: Forest Carbon Parntership Facility (2016): 60.

Protocol and the Paris Agreement. Between 2008 and 2019, a total of US$ 6.15 billion were made available to the United Nations' REDD fund, and only 50 per cent of it was through multilateral organizations.

The second important aspect of the architecture is the setting up of carbon exchanges and markets. There are two types of carbon markets: compliance offset and voluntary offset. Compliance markets are those where the regulated companies have to offset emissions through purchase of companies as per the law of the land. The biggest carbon exchanges for such entities are in Australia and New Zealand, where companies are forced to retire their carbon credits by law. Voluntary carbon markets are open carbon exchanges where companies undertake verifiable carbon audits and retire credits in the open, unregulated market. Some of the biggest carbon exchanges are run by the European Commission and in Tokyo. The state of carbon markets can be seen in Table 3.

Calculations from Table 3 show that between 2011 and 2016,

Table 3 ***Forest Carbon Markets, 2008–16***

Type of finance	Name of finance	2016 (USDM)	All years (USDM)
Market	Voluntary markets	74.2	996.4
	Compliance markets	551.4	1573.9
Non-market	REDD-Plus payments	36.5	218.07
Total		662.1	2788.5

Source: Hamrick *et al.* (2017): 2.

only 35.7 per cent of the investment for carbon markets came from voluntary markets and 10.6 per cent of the investment came from multilateral REDD-Plus funds. The rest of the investment came from compliance markets, pointing to the fact that regulation is essential for even the effective implementation of the 'polluter pays' principle. It also validates the contention that the foundations of REDD and REDD-Plus have been laid by the neoliberal economic regimes.

The third aspect of the REDD-Plus architecture is the integration of academics and NGOs into the carbon credit system, especially as monitors of sovereign governments. The carbon exchange markets are dependent on systems of verification of the quality and quantity of carbon stocks. These verifications are part of an international system of climate change regulation, and, therefore, the academics and agencies are either directly engaged by the donors or are certified by exchanges, as shown in Table 4.

Table 4 illustrates the complex web of global relationships within which national governments, corporations and academia are integrated into a larger framework of capitalist accumulation, thereby making the financialization of nature a reality.

Another important rung of the architecture is the project developer, who not only sets up a carbon sink project but also owns the carbon credits generated from them. The project developer is linked to one of the above-mentioned carbon registries, since the project has to be certified by one of the registries before it gets under way. Most nations signing on to REDD-Plus projects create their own registries, which can also be used by the international mechanism to monitor and assess the state of the carbon market. As the FCPF report states, '[r]egistries are neutral quantitative tools responsive to the informational and infrastructural needs of participants based on laws, rules, practices or guidance. Therefore, it is not the role of the registry provider to make subjective assessments of matters that are better addressed in law, policy or standards' (FCPF 2011: 13). The registry

Table 4 ***Elaboration of Select Carbon Standards and Investment Relationships***

Standard	Organizations	Corporations/Members	Clientele
WBCSD/WRI Standard for Greenhouse Gas Accounting	World Business Council for Sustainable Development (WBCSD)/ World Resources Institute (WRI)	200 big Multinational Corporations WRI is a research organization funded by academic and scientific institutions, funded by private foundations of Intel, Chevron, Walmart, apart from others	Represents investors worth USD 41 trillion in 2017
Verified Carbon Standard (VCS)	Verra, best verification company in environmental finance 2018	Partnership between business leaders largely of the North	An organizations set up by World Economic Forum and WBCSD
ISO 14064	International Standards Organizations	National Standards Organizations from 161 countries	It is just a tandard-setting organization. Premier carbon trading companies like South Pole which is considered the best project developer in the world
Gold Standard	Standard developed by World Wide Fund, HELIO International, South South, North North and clean development mechanism	A consortium of energy and environmental experts supported by World Bank, UNDP, South Pole, Goldman Sachs, and governments of Germany and the US	After VCS this is the biggest and most popular carbon registry. Trading companies like South Pole register their projects here.
The Climate, Community and Biodiversity Standards	Rainforest Alliance, The Nature Conservancy, Conservation International, Wildlife Conservation Society and are registered with VCS database	These are international NGOs funded by Hyundai, Kraft Foundation, Blue Moon Foundation and others	Many energy companies like Biofilica and other national carbon trading companies set up by national governments
Plan Vivo Standard	University of Edinburgh	UK DFID and other European foundations	Largely works through national governments and companies

Source: Information gathered from web pages of different Standards and organizations.

itself becomes the basis for payment for ecosystem services which have been defined in multiple ways. As a report of the World Bank's Global Environmental Facility (2014: 3) states:

> [t]he definition of payment for ecosystem services (PES) varies widely, from narrow market-based definitions with direct transactions between providers and beneficiaries (including schemes where private buyers and sellers arrange voluntary and conditional transactions for the delivery of ecosystem services), to broader schemes in which those who benefit from the ecosystem services pay (usually indirectly) those who provide the services.

However, one basic underlying commonality in all perspectives is that 'payments for any services' need to be 'performance-based' and should increase the efficiency of the production of carbon stock (Bond *et al.* 2009: 33). Both the registry and the monitoring mechanisms were considered essential to determining the transfer of funds. Hence, the PES system is a system that regulates REDD+ finance from top to bottom: if the forest-dependent people do not deliver to the project developer, they do not get paid for the 'services generated'. This also impacts on the assessment of the national jurisdiction which, in turn, is a signatory to multilateral agreements. Hence, the system of monitoring, registry and assessment of performance is key to the networking of various levels of actors under REDD-Plus.

The thirteen countries monitored in Table 5 show that only two countries transferred payments to the last rung of the REDD-Plus architecture, thus revealing the limited role of forest-dependent people and their organizations in the forest finance system. In fact, if we analyse the data more closely, we find that a majority of the funds transferred were retained at the level of the national readiness mechanism, and that actual disbursements for reduction of emissions were relatively small. A recent study of the relationship between performance and funding shows that REDD-Plus finance was willing to bear the costs of restoration of forest cover in deforested regions, but the funding came down dramatically once the cover was restored. Table 6 reviews the REDD-Plus finance data per metric ton of emission reduction in ten countries.

Table 6 is clear that the rate of funding decreases dramatically once the forest cover is restored and the emissions begin to be controlled through carbon stock production. This is seen in all cases, and is especially true of the Democratic Republic of Congo, Brazil and Columbia, which receive the highest amount of REDD-Plus funds. But the authors of the study also note, significantly, that differences in funding are linked to the

Table 5 *Different Flows of Payment for Thirteen REDD-Plus Countries*

Country	Total committed funds (USDM)	Percentage of flows from one stage to the next		
		From fund to 1st recipient	From 1st to 2nd recipient	From 2nd to 3rd recipient
Brazil	1545.1	91	40.1	0
Colombia	33.34	47	86.4	0
Democratic Republic of Congo	264.3	57	4.8	0
Ecuador	22.2	76	12.5	0
Ethiopia	39.8	33	0.0	0
Ghana	98.2	30	5.6	0
Indonesia	756.6	49	0.0	0
Liberia	47.2	31	47.5	0
Mexico	451	5	More than received	0
Peru	147.6	46	0.4	0
PNG	45.3	56	8.3	0
Tanzania	93.6	81	82.6	0.96
Vietnam	84.3	60	83.2	20.1

Source: Reports produced of various countries by Forest Trends, available at https://www.forest-trends.org/publications/tracking-redd-finance/, accessed 11 October 2019.

size of the country and area of forest cover. This is largely due to the fact that most funding is one-time readiness support and therefore not available for payment for services. This is reflected in the virtual drying-up of funds when they are supposed to reach the local project developer. Hence, the fund squeeze at the bottom of the ladder is a logical result of the REDD-Plus arrangements of performance-based payments which are rooted in the commodification of nature in a new form. Here, the production of nature is done through a conservation-based system, where the maintenance of natural forest is assessed only in terms of its output (that is, reduction of emissions) and the opportunity costs arising over non-use of forests. In other words, the labour that goes into the maintenance of the forest is not remunerated. This method is based on a very conventional view of conservation, where it is assumed the use of forests is against the interests of the planet as a whole. Such a conception has brought about enormous dispossession and deprivation, a discussion of which is beyond the scope of

Table 6 *Available REDD-Plus Finance in Ten REDDX Countries*

Country	Dollars per metric ton CO_2 emissions, 2009–14	Dollars per hectare of forest cover loss, 2009–14	Dollars per hectare of forest cover
Brazil	0.57	143	3.65
Colombia	0.67	212	3.00
Democratic Republic of Congo	0.31	114	2.58
Ethiopia	2.12	567	6.35
Ghana	1.70	376	11.15
Indonesia (excluding peat emissions)	0.53	178	10.73
Indonesia (including peat emissions)	0.26		
Liberia	1.25	420	21.01
Mexico	2.02	421	7.90
Peru	0.98	377	5.33
Tanzania	0.36	67	1.44
Median	*0.67*	*293.85*	*5.84*

Source: Wolosin *et al.* (2016): 12.

this paper. It will suffice to state here that the REDD-Plus design is meant to make conservation worthwhile for capitalists by altering the division of labour within the world capitalist system, even while it leads to greater dispossession and displacement of the forest-dependent people.

Conclusion

This essay traces the history of the REDD-Plus initiative within a broader understanding of the changes within the international division of labour in world capitalism. It shows that the reconfiguration of nature is an important feature of resolving the crisis of accumulation within capitalism. Seen from this perspective, it is not surprising that political and economic domination is a driver of uneven development in the reordering of world capitalism itself. This theme is often ignored in the work of eminent theoreticians like David Harvey and Jason Moore, who see accumulation as a process of capital circulation and adaptation, rather than a process that is nurtured simultaneously through expropriation by restructuring North–South relations through the multilateral REDD-Plus system. By ignoring this extractive capacity, they make the crucial mistake of treating 'nature' as an entity which becomes commodified into capital merely through its embeddedness in society. I demonstrate the problems with this perspective through an analysis of the REDD-Plus architecture and its embeddedness within the ascendency of finance capital. In this sense, REDD-Plus represents the highpoint of green capitalism, which has altered the forms of primitive accumulation after the REDD-Plus regime has been institutionalized. Through a reconfiguration of the relationship between the global North and the global South, contemporary capitalism has tried to resolve its own latest crisis.

Notes

[1] These figures are calculated from the data downloaded from the FAOSTAT (Food and Agriculture Organization Corporate Statistical Database) website accessed at different periods in time: http://www.fao.org/faostat/en/#data/FT.

[2] These data have been compiled for different years from the FAOSTAT database.

[3] Calculated from FAOSTAT Emissions Data.

References

Bond, I., M. Grieg-Gran, S. Wertz-Kanounnikoff, P. Hazlewood, S. Wunder and A. Angelsen (2009), *Incentives to Sustain Forest System Ecoservices: A Review and Lesson for REDD+*, London: International Institute for Environment and Development.

Engels, F. ([1876] 1950), *The Part Played by Labor in the Transition from Ape to Man*, New York: International Publishers.

Forest Carbon Partnership Facility (FCPF) (2011), *National Registries for REDD+: An Overview of Issues and Designs*, Washington DC: World Bank.

——— (2016), *Annual Report*, Washington DC: World Bank.

Foster, J.B. (1994), *The Vulnerable Planet: A Short Economic History of the Environment*, New York: Monthly Review Press.

Foster, J.B. and P. Burkett (2018), 'Value Isn't Everything', *International Socialism: A Quarterly Review of Socialist Theory*: 160.

Foster, J.B. and B. Clark (2018), 'The Expropriation of Nature', *Monthly Review*, 69 (10): 1–27.

Global Environmental Facility (GEF) (2014), *GEF Investments on Payment for Ecosystem Services Schemes*, Washington DC: World Bank.

Grove, R.H. (1995), *Green Imperialism: Colonial Expansion, Tropical Island Edens and Origins of Environmentalism, 1700–1860*, London: Cambridge University Press.

——— (1998), *Ecology, Climate and Empire: the Indian Legacy in Global Environmental History, 1400–1940*, Calcutta: Oxford University Press.

Hamrick, K. and M. Gallant (2017), 'Fertile Ground: State of forest finance', Washington DC: Forest Trends.

Harvey, D. (2006), *Spaces of Capital: A Theory of Uneven Geographical Development*, London: Verso.

——— (2011), *The Enigma of Capital and the Crises of Capitalism*, London: Oxford University Press.

Houghton, R.A. and A.A. Nassikas (2017), 'Global and Regional Fluxes in Carbon from Land Use and Land Cover Change, 1850–2015', *Global Biogeochemical Cycles*, 31: 456–72.

Moore, J.W. (2003), 'Capitalism as World Ecology: Braudel and Marx on environmental history', *Organization and Environment*, 16 (4): 514–17.

——— (2018), 'The Capitalocene Part II: Accumulation by Appropriation and the Centrality of Unpaid Work/Energy', *Journal of Peasant Studies*, 45 (2): 237–79.

O'Connor, J. (1991), 'On Two Contradictions of Capitalism', *Capitalism, Nature, Socialism*, 2 (3): 107–09.

Ramankutty, N. and J. Foley (1999), 'Estimating Historical Changes in Global Land Cover: Croplands from 1790 to 1992', *Global Biogeochemical Cycles*, 13 (4): 997–1027.

The Global Canopy Programme (2008), *The Little REDD Book*, United Kingdon: The Global Canopy Programme.

Thompson, E.P. (1978), *Whigs and Hunters: The Origins of the Black Act*, New York: Pantheon Books.

Tucker, R. (2000), *Insatiable Appetite: United States and the Degradation of the Tropical World*, Berkley: University of California Press.

United Nations Environment Programme (UNEP) (2013), *Towards a Green Economy*, Geneva: UNEP.

United Nations Framework Convention on Climate Change (UNFCCC) (1998), *Kyoto Protocol to the United Nations Framework Convention for Climate Change*, Geneva: United Nations.

——— (2005), 'Report of the Conference of Parties Serving as a Meeting of Parties to Kyoto Protocol in Montreal', Geneva: UNFCCC.

——— (2008), 'Report of the Conference of Parties to the Kyoto Protocol held in Bali', Geneva: UNFCCC.

——— (2013), 'Warsaw Framework for REDD plus', Geneva: UNFCCC.

United Nations (1992), *United Nations Framework Convention on Climate Change*, Geneva: United Nations.

Wolosin, M., J. Brietfeller and B. Schaap (2016), *The Geography of REDD+ Finance: Deforestation, Emissions and Targeting of Forest Conservation Finance*, Washington: Forest Trends.

World Commission of Environment and Development (1987), *Our Common Future*, Geneva: United Nations.

12

Subversion of Pro-Farmer Provisions in the New Land Acquisition Act in India

Smita Gupta

Eminent Domain is a Power of the State, not of the Executive

In India, the eminent domain of the state is embodied in the land acquisition acts and is a power of the state (judiciary, executive and legislature), not to be usurped by the government alone. Eminent domain of the state is subject to the 'rule of law', and there can be no arbitrary exercise of power, transcending judicial scrutiny and legislative intent, by the government to deprive land-dependants of their livelihood. Justice Gopala Gowda acknowledges this:

> When the brunt of . . . 'development' is borne by the weakest sections of the society . . . it is the onerous duty of the state Government to ensure that the mandatory procedure laid down under the L.A. Act and the Rules framed thereunder are followed scrupulously, otherwise the acquisition proceedings will be rendered void ab initio in law. *Compliance with the provisions of the L.A. Act cannot be treated as an empty formality by the State Government, as that would be akin to handing over the eminent domain power of State to the executive, which cannot be permitted in a democratic country which is required to be governed by the rule of law.*[1] (Emphasis added)

It is by now well known that the Indian colonial-era Land Acquisition Act of 1894 was draconian and anti-farmer. The land rights movements that demanded reform in the law were not contesting eminent domain per se, but the manner and purpose of its exercise. If it is used to end landlordism and exploitation through land reforms, or to provide public housing, schools and other such development infrastructure for the masses, it is acceptable. Increasingly, however, under neoliberal policies in the last quarter-century, the imperative to incentivize private investment in 'infrastructure, urbanization and industry' through the handing over of land and other natural resources to unleash 'animal spirits' has meant a far more ruthless exercise of the state's eminent domain to expropriate the lands and resource rights of small and marginal farmers, Adivasis, Dalits and women, among others. This happened, perversely, at a time when the agrarian distress peaked. Priority given to attracting foreign investment and the lifting of restrictions on private corporate investment generated an extraordinary 'race to the bottom' among the state governments, which competed to offer more and more attractive concessions to woo private capital. The land rights movements opposed this partisan and ruthless exercise of the state's eminent domain, appearing increasingly in the form of a 'land grab', transferring land resources of farmers and other land-dependent workers to big business in industry, infrastructure, mining and real estate.

As far as the corporate sector is concerned, they have had a very pragmatic approach towards eminent domain. Where they can simply grab land from the peasantry through the market or other means, they have only needed the state's ratification of changed land use. Where the peasantry has proven to be more recalcitrant, eminent domain has come to their rescue. State governments and industry bodies have demanded more investor-friendly provisions. Simultaneously, as the intensity of forcible acquisition has grown with worsening rural livelihoods and growing agrarian distress, there have been massive protest movements which have demanded a more accountable, just and stringent law.

The United Progressive Alliance (UPA) government negotiated what it considered a compromise between two contending demands – to give farmers and other land-dependants a voice and their due share, as well as meet the needs of industry. The fierce battle over its provisions are evident from the number of times the Act was drafted and redrafted, through UPA I and II; ultimately, the 2013 Act was passed with 154 official amendments. The Statement of Objects and Reasons is quite candid about this balancing act: 'Hence the proposed legislation proposes to address concerns of farmers and those whose livelihoods are dependent on the land being acquired, while at the same time facilitating land acquisition for industrialization, infrastructure and urbanization projects in a timely and transparent manner' (Government of India 2013). This is very different from the legislative position even in 1984: 'Promotion of public purpose has to be balanced with the rights of the individual whose land is acquired, thereby often depriving him of his means of livelihood' (Government of India 1984).

Unfortunately, even after the 1984 amendment, through which

acquisition for a public purpose for the 'State or an enterprise under it' was to be made under Part II and acquisition for a company under Part VII through separate processes, the 'colourable exercise of power'[2] by governments continued. The acquisition ostensibly for public purpose affords governments unfettered discretion and executive powers mostly beyond the courts' purview, and therefore avoids the more stringent and mandatory provisions, with greater scrutiny and monitoring, of Part VII and the rules governing it, all of which are justiciable. And so land grabs for private profit began to be routinely cloaked as public purpose acquisition. For example, according to Justice Gowda in one of the two judgements in the infamous Singur case of West Bengal, the acquisition

> for and at the instance of the company was sought to be disguised as acquisition of land for 'public purpose' in order to circumvent compliance with the mandatory provisions of the Land Acquisition Act. . . . This action of the State Government is grossly perverse and illegal and void *ab initio* in law and such an exercise of power by the State government for acquisition of lands cannot be allowed under any circumstance.[3]

Fast forward to the 2013 Act which replaces the colonial Act. There is often a presumption that the RTFCTLARRA (Right to Fair Compensation and Transparency in the Land Acquisition, Rehabilitation and Resettlement Act), 2013 would not allow such a 'colourable exercise' of power by the executive. The reality, however, is not so straightforward, as we shall see. It is true that there are three very important safeguards against mindless forcible land acquisition – social impact assessment (SIA) of proposed projects, prior informed consent from those whose farm land is being acquired and protection of irrigated multicrop land in the interest of food security. The catch is that these are not applicable to a burgeoning list of exempted projects in several states. The 2013 Act itself suffers from a fundamental flaw. It abandons the one very important aspect of the 1894 Act, that is, the distinction in procedures between acquisitions for the state and acquisition for private companies, a crucial element to restrain the colourable exercise of the state's power of eminent domain.

The very aim of the legislative exercise, ostensibly to protect farmers' livelihoods and national food security, may in fact be completely compromised when acquisition for profit and for public purpose are brought on the same footing. With a few clever tweaks to the new Act, it may have become far easier for private companies to acquire land than under the colonial dispensation. The landslide electoral victory in 2019 of the Bharatiya Janata Party (BJP) does not augur well for farmers, at least in this respect, given their interventions in the previous term. The BJP government's 2015 amendments (currently pending in Parliament) would make it even easier for a government to acquire land for private companies, openly and legally.

Acquisition for Companies before 2013

H.W. Bliss, who introduced the colonial 1892 Bill which continued to be operational (with a few changes) till 2013, stated that:

> Part VII of the Act lays down the procedure to be adopted when it is sought to acquire land for companies. . . . It is not intended . . . that the Act shall be used for the acquisition of land for any company in which the public has merely an indirect interest . . . the Act will not be used in furtherance of private speculations. (Gazette of India 1892: 26, quoted in Mandke 2004)

This would prevent the state from being reduced to a real estate agent for private companies, acquiring land on demand, since under Part VII the company is subject to greater scrutiny and monitoring.

Despite this clear-cut separation, governments have misused their powers and fraudulently done forced acquisition for private companies under Part II of the Act.[4] Taking advantage of the loophole that partial payment out of public revenue constitutes public purpose, the government would put in a 'part' of the cost of acquisition and compensation from public revenue. Courts have accepted even the minutest contribution out of public revenue to be adequate to qualify as acquisition for 'public purpose' of the state. The Supreme Court held as 'well established that if the cost of acquisition is borne either wholly or partly by the Government, the acquisition can be said to be for a public purpose within the meaning of the Act'.[5] There is an overwhelming case law reflecting the obfuscation between acquisition for public purpose and acquisition for private profit:

> One thing which deserves particular notice is the rider . . . by which the acquisition of land for Companies is excluded from the purview of the expression 'public purpose'. However, notwithstanding this dichotomy, speaking from the point of view of public purpose, *the provisions of Part II and Part VII are not mutually exclusive*.[6] (Emphasis added)

Thus, 'the distinction between public purpose acquisition and Part VII acquisition has got blurred under the impact of judicial interpretation of relevant provisions'.[7]

Of course, the judiciary has tried sometimes to restrain land grabs through the colonial Act, and in 1962, the Supreme Court stated that the government could only acquire land for a private company if the public has a direct right to access and participate in the work, and the products are 'directly' useful to the public.[8] To bypass this judgment which jeopardized most acquisitions for private companies, an ordinance was promulgated to retrospectively ratify acquisition of land for a company 'likely to promote economic development . . . notwithstanding any judgment, decree or order of any court'. Ironically, misuse of eminent domain to forcibly take over land for private profit increased after the judgment against such misuse (Government of India 1962)!

In fact, while moving the amendment in 1962, Minister of Agriculture S.K. Patil frankly admitted in Parliament:

> Part II puts no obligation on the Government of any type . . . they paid Rs 100 and acquired the land for themselves which they have a right to do. . . . Once the State Government, in its wisdom, acquires the land for a public purpose, its decision is final and unchallengeable. . . . They are competent and the compensation is also not justiciable. . . . *I am restricting the law in order to take away the liberty of the States to acquire lands under Part II in which the final decision is only what they decide.* Here I am making it under Part VII so that . . . it should not be very easy for the State Government to acquire it for anything and everything. This is the distinction that is sought to be made.[9] (*Lok Sabha Debates* 1962; Mandke 2004; emphasis added)

Shri Homi F. Daji (Member of Parliament) too expressed a similar anxiety: 'The Government by having this Bill amended has taken upon itself a very serious responsibility, a responsibility for acquiring land not for public purpose but for privately owned companies. It is a contradiction and it has to walk on a razor's edge' (Dasgupta 2005: 17–18).

Once again an amendment was brought in 1984, the Land Acquisition (Amendment) Act, so that the 'mischief, defect and lacuna' in the existing law was addressed, as 'acquisition of land for private enterprises ought not to be placed on the same footing as acquisition for the State or for an enterprise under it'.

Private Companies Enter the Definition of Public Purpose

Therefore, even as governments misused their power of eminent domain to forcibly acquire land for private profit, and the judiciary rarely intervened to stop this, until 2013, the legislature did try to maintain a distinction between public purpose and private profit by keeping them on a completely different footing to restrict the unbridled powers of the executive.

The separation was an excellent legal principle in the otherwise draconian Land Acquisition Act (LAA) 1894, because it recognized that eminent domain should not become a handmaiden of private profit, and the state should not become a real estate agent for private companies. In contrast, the 2013 Act undermines (and the 2015 amendments abandon) the legislature's valiant, though unsuccessful, attempts by bringing private companies into the very definition of public purpose, clearly in response to the growing role of the private sector.

True, the 2013 Act does place a higher burden by way of safeguards on acquisition for private companies and public–private partnership (PPP) projects. While bringing private companies into public purpose, it tries to create a measure of fairness and transparency through four measures: social impact assessment, prior informed consent, limitations on acquisition of irrigated multicrop agricultural land and return of unutilized land after a certain time period. When the government acquires land for itself for public purpose, consent is not required. When government acquires land for PPP projects for public purpose and the land continues to be owned by the government, the prior consent of at least 70 per cent of affected families is required. For private companies, for public purpose, the prior consent of at least 80 per cent of affected families is required at the time of SIA. Additionally, irrigated multicropped land may be acquired only as a 'demonstrable last resort' with limitations on extent acquired in a district.

The biggest problem is the limited and discretionary applicability of these provisions that unfortunately allows exemptions and continuing executive manoeuverability, through carefully crafted loopholes. The most sweeping exemption is that land acquisition under thirteen legislations mentioned in the Fourth Schedule is exempt from all its provisions except compensation or rehabilitation and resettlement, when notified.[9] The central government can add any other enactment to the list of exempted legislations. The much abused powers under 'urgency' provisions are retained for a wide range of situations left to the discretion of government, with only 75 per cent extra compensation. Projects acquired under urgency are exempt from SIA. The Act also retains the LAA 1894's provision for 'temporary occupation and use of any waste or arable land' (Section 81) at government-determined compensation. In addition, the appropriate government may direct that any or all of the provisions of Chapter II to Chapter VI (covering the safeguards against executive misuse) 'shall not apply' (Section 40[4]).

In any case, the provisions for SIA, consent and protection of food security are weak, narrow and often not enforceable. For instance, recommendations of the SIA are not binding, and the Act allows the government to proceed with the acquisition in spite of a negative SIA recommendation if 'it shall ensure that its reasons for doing so are recorded in writing' (Section 7[b]). Consent is only sought from a small section of landholding-affected families, 3(c)(i) – 'a family whose land or other immovable property has been acquired' – and 3(c)(v) – 'a member of the family who has been assigned land by the State Government or the Central Government under any of its schemes and such land is under acquisition' – excluding landless workers, artisans, forest rights holders and common property users, among others. Adivasis, Dalits and other marginalized sections will thus be left out of the decision-making process entirely, since several occupiers of land may not be able to provide proof of ownership. The Act has a whittled-down definition of affected family (Section 3), with the additional burden of having to provide documentary proof for 'three years' residence' and 'primary source of livelihood' on the land. The principle that anyone who is adversely affected should be recognized as an affected/interested person is not followed.

Land-use policies have far-reaching implications for food security, and the Act is very narrow while safeguarding food security (Section 10), providing for a maximum limit only for irrigated multicrop land that may be acquired. This ignores the fact that in India, over two-thirds of agriculture is rain-fed, contributing to two-fifths of food production. Even the so-called barren and wastelands can be reclaimed for dryland farming, and many poor communities depend on such marginal land through agro-silvi-pastoral systems, and need to be protected.

In any case, the distinction between acquisition with consent for private companies and acquisition without consent for the government is a chimera, since private use is built into the very definition of public purpose. The condition that land acquired without consent is only for the government or public sector undertakings (PSUs) to 'own, use, hold and control' is a trifle obscured by the Act allowing common facilities like 'zones' and 'corridors' to fall within the rubric of 'public purpose', where land transfer by lease or other mechanisms to private companies is inbuilt.

Outside such zones/corridors, the private companies did face the four safeguards (such as they were) of SIA, consent, land use and timely utilization, which gave peasant organizations space to fight for their land rights. Perhaps fearing this, the BJP-led NDA government promulgated two ordinances and passed amendments in the Lok Sabha in 2015 (pending in Parliament) (Gazette of India 2016a) exempting a long list of projects from these four provisions irrespective of which entity executes them. If passed, the Act for all practical purposes would put acquisition by the state and acquisition by companies on the same footing, undoing the separation. Nudged by the central government, many states are moving rapidly towards this.

Public Purpose: The Crux of the Matter

Public purpose is the sole justification for compulsory land acquisition and legitimizes the use of eminent domain of the state, lending it 'a touch of public morality' (Ramanathan 2011: 10). The most crucial requirement of a law giving expropriatory powers to the state, for it to be strictly construed, is that the definition, scrutiny and approval of public purpose be based on just and democratic principles and procedures. This is all the more so when these powers deprive the rural poor from their principal means of subsistence, affecting their right to life itself. The public purpose of redistribution of state-acquired land to the landless, for example, is different from the current tendency to hand over farmers' and community lands to large private corporations.

As Justice Krishna Iyer stated:

> The State may need . . . innumerable items to run a welfare-oriented administration or a public corporation or answer a community requirement. . . . *The nexus between the taking of property and the public purpose springs necessarily into existence if the former is capable of answering the latter.* On the other hand, if the purpose is a private or non-public one, the mere fact that the hand that acquires or requires is Government or a public corporation, does not make the purpose automatically a public purpose. . . . If a fleet of cars is desired for conveyance of public officers, the purpose is a public one. If the same fleet of cars is sought for fulfilling the tourist appetite of friends and relations of the same public officers, it is a private purpose. *If bread is 'seized' for feeding a starving section of the community, it is a public purpose that is met but, if the same bread is desired for the private dinner of a political maharajah who may pro tem fill a public office, it is a private purpose.*[10] (Emphasis added)

In keeping with the colonial agenda, the definition of public purpose in the 1894 Act was left open intentionally, with the government having the power to determine and declare with 'finality' that valid public purpose is involved. In 1984, Mohsina Kidwai, while moving the Bill in Parliament, said: 'The scope of the term "public purpose" has been revised so as to provide for acquisition of land for all socially important purposes, but at the same time to obviate the possibility of misuse of this provision' (*Rajya Sabha Debates* 1984).[11]

Courts have by and large refused to interpret and interrogate public purpose. They have tended to take the position that the government has 'sole and absolute' discretion in deciding public purpose, and has usually considered it beyond the jurisdiction of the judiciary.[13] This is in consonance with the view best summed up by the Law Commission of India (LCI):

> It is, in our view, neither possible nor expedient to attempt an exhaustive definition of public purposes. . . . All that can, therefore, be attempted in a legislation of this kind is to provide an inclusive definition, so as to endow it with sufficient elasticity to enable the courts to interpret the meaning of the expression 'public purpose' according to the needs of the situation. (LCI 1958: 17)

The acceptance of such a wide definition so as to include any and every infrastructure and production activity in the private sector not only makes a mockery of 'public purpose', but is disastrous in the context of eminent domain.

Apart from its elastic definition, there was an absence of democratic and judicial mechanisms to scrutinize the government's claim of public purpose. Who will examine and decide that public purpose is indeed being served? Until 1923, the Act did not follow this basic tenet of natural justice, the right to be heard by those adversely affected by the project at hand. In order to address this, an amendment was introduced on 11 July 1923 by the British rulers, to incorporate Section 5A. The Statement of Objects and Reasons declared:

> The Land Acquisition Act 1 of 1894 does not provide that persons having an interest in land which it is proposed to acquire, shall have the right of objecting to such acquisition; nor is Government bound to enquire into and consider any objections that may reach them. The object of this Bill is to provide that a Local Government shall not declare . . . that any land is needed for a public purpose unless time has been allowed . . . for persons interested in the land to put in objections and for such objections to be considered by the Local Government.[12]

This was the only opportunity for affected families to question public purpose and they held even under urgency powers that 'the right to file objections under Section 5-A is a substantial right when a person's property is being threatened with acquisition and we cannot accept that that right can be taken away as if by a side wind'.[13] In fact, the Supreme Court in the same judgment held that 'Section 5-A of the Act, 1894 confers a valuable important right and . . . has been held to be akin to a fundamental right'.[14] However, since the hearings of Objections were held by the Collector, who was also the acquirer, it had become a mere formality.

Given this 120-year-long background of misuse, when repealing the draconian colonial Act in 2013, it should have been evident to law makers that one of the fatal flaws – the crux of the matter really – that needs to be fixed is the malleability in the definition of public purpose. The new Act in 2013 should have moved far ahead of the colonial state to make public purpose more accountable, and subject to expert and public assessment. The definition should have been exhaustive and limited so that it can be strictly construed in courts, replacing the very wide amplitude in the previous elastic and illustrative definition.

However, the 2013 Act disappoints and, once again, defines public purpose in a very inclusive manner. Here, 'infrastructure' becomes the new 'code word' (Davis 2006) for displacement and dispossession, with an open-ended and inclusive definition of infrastructure under public purpose that covers practically anything and everything, relying on executive notifications and the manufacturing policy, including mining, real estate development, manufacturing zones and industrial corridors. And if this was not flexible enough, there is the residual provision (Section 2[1][b][vii]) which covers 'any infrastructure facility as may be notified in this regard by the central government and after tabling of the notification in Parliament'.

The Act in Section 15 retains the 1894 provision for objections by those adversely affected by the project, and outlines the grounds on which objections may be raised, including public purpose and the SIA report. However, it also retains the Collector's role to hear the objections and, worse, sanctifies the decision of the government on these objections as final, reducing it once again to a perfunctory and bogus exercise. The Act bars civil courts from any jurisdiction over land acquisition (Section 63) and people cannot approach local courts – they have to go only to a government-appointed state or central authority, thus undermining the separation of executive and judicial functions, a violation of the sanctity of the 'basic structure'. This authority can only award increased compensation and can be approached only through the Collector (Section 64); thereafter, any appeal to the High Court is permanently barred after 120 days (Section 74). Furthermore, even if the law is violated, the acquisition will always go ahead, as Section 63 bars any court from issuing a stay order. Even if R&R (rehabilitation and resettlement) is not provided, people will be displaced anyway, and they can spend the rest of their lives chasing their rights in the authority or higher courts (if they have the resources to do so). A fair and just definition and effective mechanism to scrutinize and ascertain public purpose remains elusive, with transparency provisions chiselled away by the many loopholes and exemptions in the Act.

Centre and State Governments Dilute Farmer-friendly Provisions

The NDA-sponsored 2015 amendments exempt industrial corridors, national security, rural infrastructure, housing and related infrastructure, and other infrastructure including projects under PPP, from the four safeguards of SIA, consent, food security and return of unutilized land. There are over a dozen laws under which land can be acquired and each state has its own adaptation of the Union laws, tweaked in accordance with their requirements. After the impasse over the dilutions of the RTFCTLARRA in Rajya Sabha, nudged on by the NDA government, many states took matters into their own hands and have even received presidential approval for these dilutions. Tamil Nadu was the first off the block. It amended the RTFCTLARRA and received the President's assent on 1 January 2015 to exempt acquisition under three Acts from the 'provisions of the Act . . . relating to land acquisition', a sweeping formulation that implies that SIA, consent, etc., will not apply; about two-thirds to four-fifths of land acquired in Tamil Nadu is under these three Acts (Gazette of India 2015).

Gujarat was not far behind in incorporating the most contentious aspects of the NDA's parliamentary amendments, exempting a long list of infrastructure and linear projects from consent, SIA and irrigated land limits. It moved far beyond the Lok Sabha's dilutions in the central Act, claiming that 'the new Act will help in attracting investments in industrial and infrastructure projects in the state'. For instance, it sidestepped enquiry for determination of compensation by empowering the Collector to make an award without enquiry through a non-registered agreement between interested persons (Section 23). It even short-circuited R&R in Section 31A 'whenever the land is to be acquired for its own use amounting to less than one hundred acres or whenever the land is to be acquired in case of projects which are linear in nature', by paying a lump-sum amount equal to 50 per cent of the amount of compensation. This reduced the list of twenty-five infrastructure amenities (Schedule 3) and eleven R&R elements (Schedule 2) to a cash transfer, which is completely against the very definition of R&R. Expanding the scope for misuse of the already abused urgency section (Section 40), Gujarat added the words 'or to comply with the directions given by the Central Government to the State Government'. Incidentally, it dropped some of the positive farmer-friendly amendments moved by the NDA, which included a wider definition of company and private entity, and compulsory provision of employment under R&R.

Rajasthan's erstwhile BJP government introduced the Rajasthan Land Acquisition Bill 2014, where 'resettlement and rehabilitation' is cashiered at 10–30 per cent of compensation (Section 22). Anyone who opposes the acquisition of land or 'wilfully obstructs any person in doing any of the acts authorized' by Section 4 or 8 will be punished with at least six months' imprisonment and a fine of anywhere between Rs 10,000 and Rs 3 lakh. With this hanging as a Damocles' sword, it is unlikely that farmers will object. In any case, landowners' consent is effectively required only for 'purely private projects'. It is not be required for any PPP core infrastructure projects, such as railways, ports, airports, bridges, pipelines, and other projects 'needed for the social and economic operation and development of the state'. There is no provision of SIA and the percentage of affected families from whom consent is required for PPP is lowered to 60 per cent (Rajasthan Land Acquisition Bill 2014). Some states have taken the Rules route to dilute the Act. Maharashtra, for instance, requires consent only for private land acquisition and not for PPP projects as per the state's rules.[15]

Most state governments are now choosing the route of market-based purchases by private companies by easing *post facto* land-use changes. Many states have used Entry 18 of the State List, Seventh Schedule to resort to market purchases through a land purchase policy. This falls foul of the central Act (Section 2[3][a] and Section 46), which has provisions to regulate land bought through private negotiations, and which requires prior application to the Collector by the buyer with a clear statement of the purpose and specification of land to be purchased (Section 46). Compliance with R&R is mandatory (2[3][a]), in the absence of which land-use changes will not be approved and the purchase will be considered void *ab initio*. There is a catch, though, since the states are allowed to set the limits of the land that has to be purchased for this provision to kick in. Any project can be broken into smaller blocks to get around this. Furthermore, with no comparable provisions, private companies no longer have to establish public purpose through SIA. On 9 February 2016, the central government notified 20 hectares in urban areas and 40 hectares in rural areas as the limit. Kerala has raised it to 101.17 hectares for rural areas and 40.47 hectares for urban areas (Gazette of India 2014). Telangana has diluted the protection to sellers in such market sales to 2,000 acres. This ridiculously high limit makes the provision meaningless (Telangana State Extraordinary Gazette 2014).

Madhya Pradesh has a 'comprehensive mutual consent land purchase policy' whereby farmers are paid 200 per cent of the land and asset market price as compensation and a rehabilitation grant. The catch is that when farmers do not give their consent for purchase of their land for government projects, the provisions of the Land Acquisition Act are invoked. Maharashtra, with pending mega projects worth Rs 50,000 crore in various stages of implementation, has proposed a policy allowing direct purchase of land by private entities from land owners without government regulation or R&R as mandated by Section 46 of RTFCTLARRA (Madhya Pradesh State Government Order 2014).

Madhya Pradesh and Gujarat have found expedient ways to remove the remaining impediment of approval for land-use change after purchase of agricultural land. The driving force is to ease land purchase and land transfer to industry and industrialists, and to have retrospective effect clauses to legalize past transgressions. There is no limit to the quantum of this land, and private players can easily purchase as much agricultural land as they want for non-agricultural activities – all this with retrospective effect. This opens the door to huge unregulated land-use changes, undermining food security. The power to decide the legality of dubious transactions rests with the Collector or other government officials who have been vested with immense authority.

The Madhya Pradesh Ceiling on Agricultural Holdings Act of 1960 mandated that the owner should get permission for diversion of agricultural land for non-agricultural purposes before its sale. This was amended in 2015 and it only requires the buyer 'to intimate in writing the competent authority within 90 days from the date of acquisition that he shall get his land diverted to non-agricultural purpose'. The Gujarat Assembly, too, has recently amended several critical laws to facilitate private land purchases and land-use changes, especially through changes to the Gujarat Agricultural Lands Ceiling Act of 1960. In complete disregard of justice and equity, in the case of Gujarat, pending legal cases are also to be deemed to have lapsed!

Gujarat's Agricultural Land Ceiling (Amendment) Bill of 2015, recently given presidential assent, permits transfer of unutilized ceiling surplus land (acquired during the land reforms in the 1960s) to industry for 'public purpose', instead of to the landless and marginal peasants for whom it was meant. The preamble lets the cat out of the bag: the Bill is meant to achieve 'rapid industrialization and urbanization', and use available surplus land for 'industrial purpose or for the development thereof or for any public purpose'. Paradoxically, the amendments will encourage 'speculative squatters' because there is no binding time limit for utilization, and transfer and resale is permitted (Gazette of India 2016b).

It is now clearly a ruthless race to the bottom to be high on the 'ease of doing business' index, a euphemism for corporate land grabs, amongst the states.

Towards Sustainable and Equitable Land Rights

What, then, is the way to protect livelihoods, land rights and food security? In a recent judgment, Justice Gopala Gowda (along with Justice Amitava Roy) equated property rights with human rights:

> The right to property though no longer a fundamental right is otherwise a zealous possession of which one cannot be divested save by the authority of law . . . even though the right to property is no longer a fundamental right and was never a natural right, it has to be accepted that without the right to property, other rights become illusory . . . the right to property having been elevated to the status of human rights . . . and thus has to be venerably acknowledged and can, by no means, be belittled or trivialized by adopting an unconcerned and nonchalant disposition by anyone, far less the State, after compulsorily acquiring his land by invoking an expropriatory legislative mechanism.[16]

The right to own property was a fundamental right and had a countervailing effect on the state's eminent domain. Since landlords took recourse to this to thwart land reforms in courts, it was scrapped. The 44th Amendment removed the right to property as a fundamental right under Article 19(1)(f) of the Constitution, as well as the constitutional obligation to pay compensation (except in some cases) under Article 31. This had the unfortunate consequence of reviving the 'problematic aspects of the 1894 Act . . . working against the small and middle peasants in their battle against the state' (Ananth 2016: 14). Even though 'land to the tiller' remained a far cry, paradoxically, it was now far easier to acquire the land of the tiller.

> The constitutional status of the doctrine of eminent domain and the unqualified removal of the right to property as a fundamental right without attention to existing social, political and economic inequalities resulted in making Dalits, Adivasis, poor peasants and the urban poor most vulnerable to the exercise of eminent domain under the LAA 1894. (Sampat 2013: 42).

It is sometimes argued that misuse of eminent domain can be addressed by restoration of the right to property, but this would undermine the state's ability to undertake redistributive land reforms, welfare and equitable development. There is an equally strong view that the power of eminent domain should be withdrawn from the state, since it has been mostly misused. This, too, is problematic in a society marked by class, caste, gender and ethnic inequalities. There is another view that the state should have nothing to do with forcible acquisition, especially for private companies, and should leave it to the market. This ignores the power wielded by corporate buyers and the unconscionable means adopted by them.

Instead, eminent domain has to be rooted in a system of property rights and land-use that goes beyond private property and expropriatory developmentalism, undertaken by a decentralized, democratic and accountable state. Land rights are much more than the ownership of privately held property. Land resources include soil, biomass and vegetative cover, and water in three types of property relations: common property resources, state-owned resources purportedly held in public trust, and private property. Viewed this way, the question is not of ownership or access alone, it is most crucially of land-use policies. The pillars of a democratic understanding of land rights are the protection of and access to commons, redistributive land reforms in urban and rural areas, environmental regeneration, and making area-specific land-use plans.

All land acquisition and land-use changes, including from private purchase and transfer of government land, should be in accordance with decentralized land-use plans, and fulfil redistributive and economic justice. As argued earlier, the public purpose itself should be restricted to tightly defined, objectively determined and collectively approved projects, and displacement should be minimized by choosing the least displacing options. Forcible land acquisition from those holding land within prescribed land ceilings should be done away with and replaced with the principle of prior informed consent. Compensation, resettlement and rehabilitation should become avenues to give affected families a share in the enhanced land value and a far better life than before. Mere restoration of the fundamental right to property will not do this, and may even be counter-productive.

The battle for fairness and justice in land acquisition will continue to be fought in the political space through movements of the displaced raising the same questions that have been around for over a century, until there is a law that minimizes displacement; adheres to equitable and sustainable land-use plans; defines public purpose tightly to be determined objectively and collectively; eliminates forcible land acquisition and institutionalizes the principle of prior informed consent; protects forest dwellers, Dalits, Adivasis; and treats compensation and resettlement and rehabilitation as an avenue to give those tilling and working the land a share in the enhanced land value and a far better life than before. This was the vision shared by Sam Moyo and all of us in the movement.

These ideas have developed through continuous and intense discussions over a decade with activists, notably Chittaroopa Palit, Prasenjit Bose, Shankar Gopalakrishnan, Vijoo Krishnan, Sudha Bharadwaj and Madhuri Krishnaswamy. I am extremely grateful to Jayati Ghosh for her comments that have greatly enriched the paper.

Notes

[1] *Kedar Nath Yadav vs State of West Bengal and others*, reported in AIR 2016 SC 4156.

[2] In *State of Punjab vs Gurdial Singh & Ors*, AIR 319, 1980 SCR (1)1071, Justice Krishna Iyer held: 'The power to select land for acquisition proceedings is left to the responsible discretion of Government under the Act. . . . Wisdom in administrative action is the property of the Executive and judicial circumspection keeps the court lock-jawed save where power has been polluted. . . . When the custodian of power is influenced in its exercise by considerations outside those for promotion of which the power is vested, the court calls it a colourable exercise and is undeceived by illusion.'

[3] *Kedar Nath Yadav vs State of West Bengal and others*: 92.

[4] For an excellent discussion, see Avinash Mandke (2004); Colin Gonsalves (2010) covers similar ground.

[5] *Pandit Jhandu Lal vs. the State of Punjab* (1961 (2) SCR 459); *Amarnath Ashram Trust Society and Anr vs the Governor of Uttar Pradesh & Ors* on 3 December 1997, available at https://indiankanoon.org/doc/291475/?type=print, accessed 7 January 2017.

[6] *Pratibha Nema and Ors vs State of M.P. & Ors*, AIR 2003 SC 3140, 30 July 2003, available at https://indiankanoon.org/doc/129701035/

[7] *Kedar Nath Yadav vs State of West Bengal and others*: 155.

[8] *R.L. Arora vs State of U.P.*, 1962, Supp (2) SCR 149: AIR 1962 SC 764: 'It . . . could not be the intention of the legislature that the Government should be made a general agent for companies to acquire lands for them . . . for private profit. . . . If we were to give the wide interpretation . . . it would amount to holding that the legislature intended the Government to be a sort of general agent for companies to acquire lands for them, so that their owners may make profits. . . . What these provisions require is that the work should be directly useful to public and the agreement shall contain a term how the public shall have the right to use the work directly themselves.'

[9] The original Bill exempted even the Cantonments Act, 2006, the SEZs Act, 2005, and the Work of Defence Act, 1903, but these three Acts were later removed due to public outcry.

[10] *State of Karnataka vs Ranganatha Reddy* (1977), 4 SCC 471 (SCC: 502, para 57).

[11] There are a few exceptions, like when th SCI said that 'the concept of public purpose in land acquisition has to be viewed from an angle which is consistent with the concept of a welfare State' (*Dev Sharan and Ors vs State of U.P. & Ors*, 4 SCC 7695, 7 March 2011, available at https://indiankanoon.org/doc/1992267), and that it must be of 'interest of the community as distinguished from the private interest of an individual' (*State of Bihar vs Maharajadhiraja Sir Kameshwar Singh Bahadur of Darbhanga*, 1 SCR 889, 2 May 1952, available at https://indiankanoon.org/doc/49043).

[12] In *Nandeshwar Prasad vs. U.P. Government*, AIR 1964 SC 1217, cited in *Union of India & Ors vs Shiv Raj &Ors*, 7 May 2014, available at https://indiankanoon.org/doc/90662043.

[13] Ibid.

[14] *Union of India & Ors vs Shiv Raj & Ors*, available at https://indiankanoon.org/doc/90662043, accessed 23 April 2017.

[15] Jairam Ramesh and Muhammad A. Khan (2016) have discussed this in an op-ed article.

[16] *Lalaram and Ors vs Jaipur Devt. Auth. & Anr* on 1 December 2015, available at http://indiankanoon.org/doc/168139441/

References

Ananth, V.K. (2016), 'Singur case and the idea of justice', *Economic and Political Weekly*, 51 (38): 14–17.

Davis, M. (2006), *Planet of Slums*, London and New York: Verso.

Dasgupta, R. (2005), *Changing face of the law: A global perspective*, New York: iUniverse, Inc.

Gonsalves, C. (2010), 'Judicial failure on land acquisition for corporations', *Economic and Political Weekly*, XLV (32), 37–42.

Gazette of India (1892), *Proceedings of the Council of the Governer General of India*, Part VI, 12 March: 25–32.

Gazette of India (2014), 'Right to Fair Compensation and Transparency in Land Acquisition, Rehabilitation and Resettlement Act, 2013, Kerala Rules', *Kerala Government Gazette Extraordinary*, Thiruvananthapuram.

Gazette of India (2015), 'Right to Fair Compensation and Transparency in Land Acquisition, Rehabilitation and Resettlement (Tamil Nadu Amendment) Act, 2014, Act 1 of 2015', *Tamil Nadu Government Gazette Extraordinary*, Chennai.

Gazette of India (2016a), 'Ministry of Rural Development', *Gazette of India Extraordinary, F. No. 13011/04/2015-LRD*, Tuesday, 9 February.

Gazette of India (2016b), 'Right to Fair Compensation and Transparency in Land Acquisition, Rehabilitation and Resettlement (Gujarat Amendment) Act', *Gujarat Government Gazette Extraordinary*, Ahmedabad.

Government of India (1962), *The Land Acquisition (Amendment) Act, 1962, Act No. 31 of 1962*, Government of India.

Government of India (1984), 'Statement of Objects and Reasons', *The Land Acquisition (Amendment Act) 1984 , Bill No. 63 of 1984*, Government of India.

Government of India (2013), *Right to Fair Compensation and Transparency in Land Acquisition, Rehabilitation and Resettlement Act, 2013; No. 30 of 2013*, Government of India.

Law Commission of India (1958), 'Tenth Report of the Law Commission of India on "The Law of Acquisition and Requisitioning of Land"', http://indiankanoon.org/doc/107173613/, accessed 21 October 2019.

Lok Sabha Debates (1962), 3rd Series, Vol. 7, 30 August, cols. 5129 and 5130 and cols. 5177 and 5178.

Madhya Pradesh State Government Order (2014), *Aapsi sahamati se bhumikreyneeti*, 12 November, Revenue Department, Madhya Pradesh Government.

Mandke, A. (2004), 'Land Acquisition for "Companies": Part II or Part VII?', *PL WebJour 15*, http://www.ebc-india.com/lawyer/articles/850.htm.

Sampat, P. (2013), 'The limits to absolute power', *Economic and Political Weekly*, XLVIII (19): 40–52.

Rajasthan Land Acquisition Bill (2014), available at http://www.rlarrdc.org.in/images/Rajasthan_Draft_Rules.pdf

Rajya Sabha Debates (1984), Vol. 131 (26), 28 August, col. 113.

Ramanathan, U. (2011), 'Land Acquisition, Eminent Domain and the 2011 Bill', *Economic and Political Weekly*, 46 (44–45): 10–14.

Ramesh, J. and M.A. Khan (2016), 'Winking at the states', 2 November, http://www.thehindu.com/opinion/lead/jairam-ramesh-muhammad-a-khan-on-land-acquisition-law-winking-at-the-states/article9292353.ece, accessed 21 October 2019.

Telangana State Extraordinary Gazette (2014), 'Telangana State Right to Fair Compensation and Transparency in Land Acquisition, Rehabilitation and Resettlement Rules, 2014', available at http://mdp.telangana.gov.in/pdfs/3.R&R%20GO.pdf

13

A Future of Urbanity

Cities and Countrysides for All

Sandeep Chachra

The twenty-first century is often projected as one of urbanity. Some say that if the hallmark of the twentieth century was the rise of nation-states and welfarism, the defining feature of the current century will be the rise of cities and global ecologies, played out by the struggles of millions to claim urban spaces, give new meaning to life in cities and assert collective responsibilities for ensuring control over human-made climate change, ecological destruction and its mitigation.

The primacy of cities in the twenty-first century is not hard to imagine, given what the world looks like in these early decades. The *World Migration Report 2015*, which focused on 'Migrants and Cities', reported that over 3 million people were arriving in cities every week (International Organization for Migration 2015). The *World Migration Report 2018* speaks of how, by 2018, cities, not countries, have become the dominant destination for migration (International Organization for Migration 2018). The United Nations Habitat Agency says that by 2030, there will be forty-three megacities across the globe, each with more than ten million inhabitants and most of which will be in developing regions. Judging on the basis of current trends, by the middle of this century, 68 per cent of our world will be living in cities. In some parts of the globe, this has already been the case for some decades now.

With population shifts economic activity is shifting to cities, and will continue to do so. Urban-biased policies, founded in the generalized imagery that cities are the engines of future economic growth, reinforce the urban over the rural and the countryside, leading to rural economic depression. An estimated 70 per cent of global gross domestic product (GDP) currently comes from cities (UN-Habitat 2016a). And as this happens and further concentrates, the contributions of the countryside to the national economy continue to shrivel, as does its voice in the national decision and policy-making. Some celebrate these tendencies as signs heralding the 'birthing of a new world', a planet of cities.

However, is a world of city-states, which many see as the imagery of this century, the future we wish to see? Is such a momentous transition possible, or even desirable?

Aided by the plunder of wealth and territorial control over centuries of colonial rule, several countries of the global North were able to generate significant productive employment opportunities, together with shifts in employment structure. In the colonial powers of the North, the share of agriculture in total economic output and labour force in agriculture declined dramatically in the late nineteenth and twentieth centuries. Accumulation based on colonial plunder provided ample capital in the hands of the state for investment in industrialization, while territorial control provided 'empty' lands afforded by settler colonialism for out-migration of European populations dependent on agriculture. It is estimated that in the nineteenth century alone, approximately 50 million people left from Europe to settler colonies in the Americas and Africa.

Additionally, developments in agriculture in the late nineteenth and twentieth centuries placed countries of the global North firmly on a trajectory of industrial agriculture, where agriculture became a hub of intensive mechanized production with minimal labour requirements, fuelling engines of growth of non-agriculture sectors, including a phenomenal growth of cities. Over these centuries, a large-scale exodus occurred from the countryside and from agriculture, in most countries of the North.

Although there are important variations in the South and these have their own lessons, it could be said that this 'particular' experience of economic transition in the North became a 'generalized' imagery for development thinking on economic transition possibilities in the South. Too often, it was hypothesized as the final destination of economic transformation in the South.

In the aftermath of liberation from colonial conditions, newly independent countries of the global South managed to create varying degrees of economic transformation. Hinging on public sector-driven industrialization, their economic transformation was predicated on growth in the economy through attempts to develop industry, create employment in the public sector and modernize peasant agriculture. Under the 'nation-building' challenges of the time, in the second half of the last century, while this transformation could be considered as fairly respectable and hopeful, it could not address the basic needs of the vast majorities.

In the East Asian countries, and among them, those considered as the East Asian miracles, emphasis on export-oriented industrialization (and, in some others, on import-substitution industrialization) created a variety of jobs in the non-farming sector. In countries where this was coupled with land reforms in the rural sector, such as South Korea and Taiwan, it led to significant growth and employment outcomes. In India, the seriousness of planned development led to a well-diversified industrial structure within a short period. Together with attempts to modernize agriculture, albeit without a serious basis in land reform, it did create a momentum and a base for economic revival. In China, quite differently from some others, strong land reforms served as the basis for economic transformation and led to significant growth and employment. These served as a fuel for massive economic growth in the last decades of the twentieth century. In several other countries of Asia, Africa and Latin America, economic transformation was attempted without basic land reforms or substantial industrialization.

The experience of most countries in the global South – in Asia, Africa and the Americas – has demonstrated that despite relatively respectable economic outcomes in the historical phase of planned economic development, a vast majority of the population continues to derive its livelihood from agriculture. Yet, the lack of agrarian reform has resulted in precarious living conditions, in what is now labelled as a generalized 'agrarian crisis'. Failure to address historic inequalities in land ownership – strongly premised on caste, race, gender, class and ethnic inequalities – and provide adequate investments and technology to the agriculture sector alongside population growth has meant that distress in agriculture has been exacerbated with every passing decade, creating an outflow from agriculture to a swelling reserve army of labour.

A study published by economists associated with the Food and Agriculture Organization (Lowder, Skoet and Raney 2016) examined agricultural census data from more than 200 countries and concluded that globally, about 84 per cent of farms are smaller than 2 hectares. A close examination of the data shows that the bulk of these farms are in countries at lower levels of income, and they operate on a far greater share of farmland than do smaller farms in higher-income countries. As such, replicating in the global South, whether fully or largely, a demographic transition in the image of the North – from agriculture to industry and from country to city – would simply spell disaster to the millions of people dependent on agriculture and living in rural areas. In several ways, this future is already unfolding in the face of the crisis that agriculture has been witnessing in the South over recent decades, unleashed by a variety of factors including a failure to carry out land reforms, gradual withdrawal of state support to peasant farming and agricultural development, and, of course, climate change. Given that cities are projected as economic possibilities of hope, millions variously 'pushed or starved out of agriculture' will continue to move to cities to look for possibilities for work there.

Development of services and economic growth make the cities of today the only hope for any employment for millions, and directs the physical movement of populations to look for work. But is there work to be found in cities? And what kind of work?

The recent *World Employment and Social Outlook* report of the International Labour Organization (ILO 2019) states that 2 billion people of our planet are already consigned to what is called 'informal work', or work in conditions of extreme precarity. This growing number includes people who straddle the worlds of the country and the city – as peasant-workers. In both the worlds they inhabit, theirs is a story of battle against conditions of present precariousness and a bleak future.

Their world of work is one full of fragility and vulnerability. Ever-increasing flexibilities in labour markets and lack of options push workers further into 'wage bargaining inabilities' and 'working condition vulnerabilities'. The ascendance of 'global value chains' exacerbates the conditions of wealth accumulation at higher ends, pushing for further appropriation of labour; contract-based outgrower schemes make matters worse for the labouring millions. Vast majorities of our workers in the global South fall in the category of those vulnerably employed – with no regularity of wages, measly, if any, forms of social security and protection, and, needless to say, human rights. Workers have little prospect of joining the ranks of regular wage work, which, in any case, is itself facing crisis. In fact, if anything, in this century we also face another spectre of further constriction in labour absorption, particularly at lower ends of the value chain, on account of industrial developments led by artificial intelligence and industry 4.0.

Any process that leads to further dispossession of workers and their release into an already large pool of labour means that opportunities for work and livelihood will either need to expand dramatically, or there will be further impoverishment and vulnerability. Expansion of labour requirements in industry and services depends on the level of aggregate demand in the economy. On its own, any dramatic rise in demand needed to gainfully employ existing informal workers appears to be impossible under the conditions witnessed in the early decades of this century. There simply are not enough jobs, and levels of unemployment climb with every passing year. ILO estimates suggest that to eliminate unemployment, counting those unemployed today, more than half a billion jobs will need to be created in the next decade.

There remains little doubt that the current squeeze on labour's share in growth and development will be hotly contested by social struggles of all kinds. Labour simply cannot be reduced to a commodity to be traded at the lowest price, or held up in the market as a placard of comparative advantage. Furthermore, the current path of development is an ecological dead-end. Industrial food production based on intensive use of inputs such as fertilizers and pesticides, as well as gene modifications, enhance production in the short run, but they eventually produce outcomes that erode the very basis of agriculture. The example of the 'green revolution' in northern India in the 1970s is one among several such unsustainable and soil-damaging experiences of agricultural development.

On the other hand, and by the same logic, it is also clear that the current development of cities is a resource-intensive process and is unsustainable, and in many cities the strain is showing. The 2016 report by UN-Habitat, *New Urban Agenda*, shows that cities consume 75 per cent of global primary energy and emit 50–60 per cent of the world's greenhouse gases (UN-Habitat 2016b). This figure rises to about 80 per cent if indirect emissions of urban inhabitants are considered.

The population influx into urban areas across the globe has resulted in a whopping billion-plus population living in squatter settlements without basic facilities and services, in a life of insecurity, fear and indignity. Urbanization of this kind poses severe sustainability challenges on all fronts, giving rise to deep speculations, contests and uncertainties about the fate of cities and urbanity. An urban future with the spectre of majorities of populations squeezed into neglected corners of what are called slums, and small populations occupying expansive greens, is already raising nightmares of inequity and injustice.

In the twenty-first century, cities represent the theatre of a contest of two interwoven struggles, spanning the countryside and cities. The outcome of these struggles will no doubt define the future of our planet across all spatial dimensions. The first is a struggle of billions for work and survival; the second is a struggle for space and decent conditions of living for the majorities of our world, in both rural and urban areas. The future of urbanism lies, therefore, not in conjuring up smart imageries of future cities alone; it lies in the conjoined development of the countryside and the city. It lies in choosing roads to social and economic justice, and moving away from pathways that lead to catastrophic destinations and dead-ends.

The rural economy accounts for more than 40 per cent of our planet's workers. The numbers are much higher in Asia and Africa. A large number of rural workers are not owners of land, but merely informal workers in the agriculture sector. For women and the landless, land rights constitute the first step in reviving a strangulated rural economy. The liberation promise that provided motive to the liberation struggles of the South cannot be abandoned. Whether in South Africa, where the black population, at 79 per cent of the total, owns only 4 per cent of agricultural land, while the white minority of 9 per cent owns 72 per cent (South Africa Department of Rural Development and Land Reforms 2018), or in India, where as much as 41.86 per cent of rural households are without agricultural land (compiled from NSSO 2013), something is fundamentally wrong and unfinished. The struggle for land constitutes not a memory of history, but a design for the future; one that can be silenced only at the cost of the future of our people and planet.

In addition, the billions living and working in the countrysides of the world must be supported by investments in the rural economy and agriculture, including establishing mechanisms for fair and stable crop prices for food security. Upgrading and modernizing peasant agriculture and removing drudgery in subsistence farming will provide headway into lifting people out of poverty and the countryside out of the distress that it faces. A further step across both cities and countryside is embracing the fundamental 'right to work', and to realize it by creating policies to instal universal labour guarantees. Experiences with limited employment guarantee schemes in rural contexts, such as in India, show their immense potential in reviving the rural economy and social welfare, and is surely an idea to further build on. It would need expansion not just in what are promised as wages, but should also see year-round coverage, and extension into urban areas and universal adoption. Welfare states stand at crossroads in this century and must face this fundamental challenge squarely, otherwise welfare and human rights will only be remembered as hollowed-out promises, vestiges of the past that were sacrificed at the altar of market-led economics. The right to work is a sure pathway that ensures dignity, security and equal opportunities, expanding human freedoms and creativity.

For the 4.2 billion who live in cities, urban centres of this century must also be inclusive and 'embracing'. Cities cannot continue to be 'enclaves' for a few, colonized as assets such as land and spaces. Land in the cities, as in the countryside, needs reforms for it to be reclaimed for public good, that is, public projects for housing and social infrastructure such as urban commons. Master plans and development plans for cities, therefore, would need to be based on reservation of land for the majorities of city makers – the workers – as well as regularization of land occupied by slums and squatter settlements, together with *in situ* redevelopment of existing settlements as far as possible. Only then will cities embrace their 'majorities', the 'city makers', the most vulnerable peoples – the destitute, the homeless, and those discriminated and exploited, such as migrants, refugees, Dalits, indigenous populations and minorities. Cities need to provide opportunities to all of them. Cities need to enable women and children with opportunities that their gender and social positioning did not allow in the past, whether in the city or the village.

Steps, therefore, need to be taken by governments to ensure that urbanization does not remain a market-led and directed path, and move away from the current urban development scenario. Interventions to ensure access to land, housing and civic amenities for all, as well as to protect, nurture and advance nature and public commons, will enable just and equitable urbanization. In this regard, the 'Right to the City' provides a paradigm for an alternative framework to design and rethink cities and urbanization on the promise of 'Cities for All', on the basis of equality and justice. This refers to a human right to sustainable urbanization, to a decent and full life for all urban people. It is a right which not only advances human dignity, but also opens doors for the right to housing and the rebuilding of commons, and affords protection against evictions and forcible displacements.

The *New Urban Agenda* outlines a vision of cities for all as:

> referring to the equal use and enjoyment of cities and human settlements, seeking to promote inclusivity and ensure that all inhabitants, of present and future generations, without discrimination of any kind, are able to inhabit and produce just, safe, healthy, accessible, affordable, resilient and sustainable cities and human settlements to foster prosperity and quality of life for all. (UN-Habitat 2016b: 5)

As outlined by the World Urban Campaign (of the UN-Habitat Agency) manifesto (2016c) on 'The City We Need', the following principles serve as touchstones for the new urban paradigm:

1. The City We Need is socially inclusive and engaging. It is people-centred, ethical, just and promotes a right to the city for all.
2. The City We Need is affordable, accessible and equitable – where resources are distributed equitably and opportunities are available for all.
3. The City We Need is economically vibrant and inclusive, and fosters local economic development.
4. The City We Need is collectively managed and democratically governed. It safeguards local democracy by encouraging participation, transparency and accountability. It places centrality on the role of women in its advance.

5. The City We Need fosters cohesive territorial development. It is a catalyst for sustainability planning.
6. The City We Need is regenerative and resilient, and improves quality of life.
7. The City We Need has shared identities and sense of place. It generates a sense of belonging for all. It fosters diversity.
8. The City We Need is well-planned, walkable and transit-friendly. It adopts integrated planning to meet present and future needs of land, housing, infrastructure and services.
9. The City We Need is safe, healthy and promotes the well-being of all. It is free from violence and fosters a culture of peace, and promotes the fundamentals of good health.
10. The City We Need learns and innovates. It creates opportunities for alternative scenarios for the future, and revisits urban paradigms for sustainable and inclusive futures.

Responsive and responsible action to these fundamental questions and ideas will define a future of urbanity in the twenty-first century. For, these are key struggles for the vast majorities of our planet, and they matter for the future of our planet.

References

International Labour Organization (ILO) (2019), *World Employment Social Outlook: Trends 2019*, Geneva: ILO, available at https://www.ilo.org/wcmsp5/groups/public/---dgreports/---dcomm/---publ/documents/publication/wcms_670542.pdf, accessed 19 August 2019.

International Organization for Migration (IOM) (2015), 'Migrants and Cities: New Partnerships to Manage Mobility', *World Migration Report 2015*, Geneva: IOM, available at http://publications.iom.int/system/files/wmr2015_en.pdf, accessed 19 August 2019.

——— (2018), *World Migration Report 2018*, Geneva: IOM, available at https://www.iom.int/sites/default/files/country/docs/china/r5_world_migration_report_2018_en.pdf, accessed 19 August 2019.

Lowder, S.K., J. Skoet and T. Raney (2016), 'The Number, Size and Distribution of Farms, Smallholder Farms, and Family Farms Worldwide', *World Development*, 87: 16–29, available at https://doi.org/10.1016/j.worlddev.2015.10.041, accessed 18 August 2019.

National Sample Survey Office (NSSO) (2013), *Land and Livestock Holding Survey: NSS 70th Round, Schedule 18.1*, January–December, National Sample Survey Office, Ministry of Statistics and Programme Implementation (MoSPI), Government of India, available at http://microdata.gov.in/nada43/index.php/catalog/LLS, accessed 19 August 2019.

South Africa Department of Rural Development and Land Reforms (2018), *Land Audit Report, Phase II: Private Land Ownership by Race, Gender and Nationality*, available at http://www.ruraldevelopment.gov.za/publications/land-audit-report/file/6126, accessed 19 August 2019.

UN-Habitat (2016a), *Urbanization and Development: Emerging Futures, World Cities Report 2016*, available at https://wcr.unhabitat.org/, accessed 19 August 2019.

UN-Habitat (2016b), *The New Urban Agenda*, available at http://habitat3.org/wp-content/uploads/NUA-English.pdf, accessed 23 October 2019.

UN-Habitat (2016c), *The City We Need (TCWN) 2.0: Towards a New Urban Paradigm*, World Urban Campaign, adopted on 16 March 2016 in Prague/Czech Republic, available at https://unhabitat.org/wp-content/uploads/2016/03/The%20City%20We%20Need%20TCWN_2.0.pdf, accessed 19 August 2019.

14

Employment Opportunities in India's Unregistered Manufacturing Sector

Anamitra Roychowdhury

One of the remarkable features of India's post-independence development experience is her continued heavy dependence on agriculture to provide livelihoods to millions, even when the sector's share in gross domestic product (GDP) has steadily declined over the years.[1] This inability of the Indian economy to undergo structural change – in terms of shifting people out of agriculture – is primarily due to its failure to build a vibrant manufacturing base, instead leapfrogging into services (Chandrasekhar 2018). However, since services typically have low employment elasticity, even with a rising share of services in GDP, India could not go through a Lewisian transformation.

Moreover, for the first time since independence, there is evidence of people continuously leaving agriculture since 2014 – leading to an absolute decline in agricultural employment (Mehrotra *et al.* 2014; Thomas 2014). Compounding the problem in recent years, this negative growth in employment has spread to wider sectors of the economy (Abraham 2017). In this context, it becomes important to explore the scope of employment creation outside of agriculture, and the interest in more employment-intensive unregistered manufacturing that arises due to this reason.

In this essay, we first elaborate the structural problem afflicting the Indian economy. Next, we delineate the structure of the unregistered manufacturing sector, drawing on data from the National Sample Survey (NSS) of 2015–16. Finally, the scope of gainful employment opportunity in an average firm in the sector is examined. The results allow us to reach some conclusions regarding the prospect of gainful and productive employment generation in the unregistered manufacturing sector.

Structural Rigidity and the Employment Debacle in India

The failure of the Indian economy to successfully bring about structural change can be traced from Table 1. As already mentioned, agriculture still remains home to a very substantial section of the Indian workforce; in fact, while a huge 72 per cent of working population depended on agriculture right after independence, even after 64 years, in 2015–16,[2] around 47 per cent of workers were still stuck in that sector.

The above-mentioned phenomenon is largely explained by India's failed efforts to industrialize – specifically, the remarkable stagnation that characterizes its manufacturing sector. Figure 1 shows that, in over six decades, the share of manufacturing value added in GDP failed to double. This is in sharp contrast to China: beginning from roughly the same level of industrialization as India in the 1950s (Nagaraj 2017; Chandrasekhar 2014), China's industrial sector, including construction, contributed around 40 per cent of the GDP in 2015, and the manufacturing sector alone formed 29 per cent of aggregate output.[3] Therefore, the benefits of a rapidly growing manufacturing sector on the larger economy (Kaldor 1960) were simply not realized in India.

However, more significant is the static share of manufacturing employment in India. Table 1 shows that the share of manufacturing employment in the total never reached 13 per cent over the 60-year period.

Table 1 *Sectoral Distribution of Workforce* (percentages)

Year	Agriculture	Industry	Manufacturing	Services
1951	72.4	10.6	9.0	17.0
1961	71.9	11.7	10.6	16.4
1971	72.0	11.5	9.5	16.5
1981	68.8	13.5	11.3	17.7
1983	68.0	15.2	11.5	16.8
1987–88	64.2	17.8	12.2	18.1
1993–94	63.3	16.7	11.6	20.1
1999–00	59.8	18.0	11.1	22.2
2004–05	56.4	18.8	12.2	24.8
2009–10	51.8	21.9	11.0	26.3
2011–12	48.9	24.3	12.6	26.8
2015–16	46.9	22.9	10.3	30.2

Source: Data up to 2009–10 from Nagaraj (2014): 279; 2011–12 data from Government of India (2014b); 2015–16 data from Government of India (2016) – for workers above 15 years.

Figure 1 *Share of Manufacturing Output in GDP*

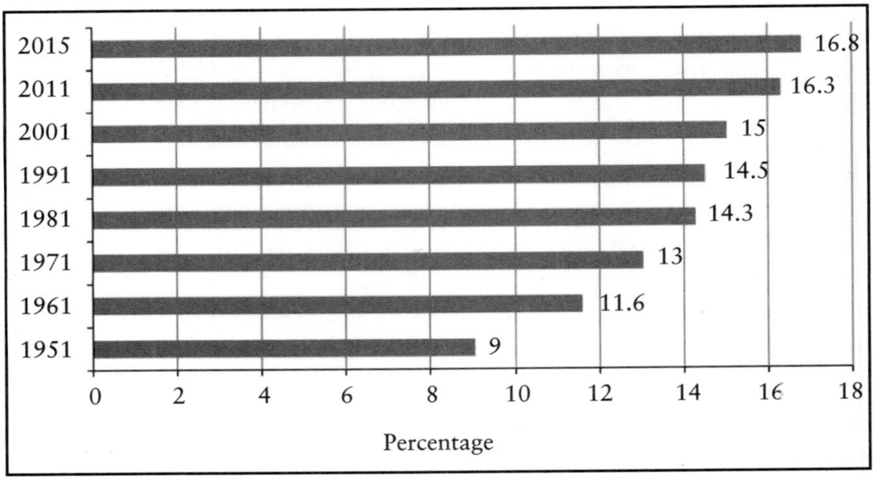

Note: 1951–2001 data at 2004–05 prices from NAS back series, 2011; 2011 data at 2004–05 prices from Government of India (2014a); 2015 data at current prices from Government of India (2018c), hence not directly comparable. At 2011–12 prices, manufacturing output to GDP ratio in 2015 turns out to be 18.1 per cent. However, 2011 figure at current prices is 17.4 per cent whereas at 2004–05 prices it is 16.3 per cent.
Source: National Accounts Statistics (NAS), various years.

The inability to draw out people from low-productivity agriculture is mainly due to the failure of manufacturing sector to generate adequate employment. This is because services typically have low employment-creating capacity, evident from the fact that with a share of over 50 per cent in output it barely employs 30 per cent of the workforce.

Aggravating the problem is the fact that people started leaving agriculture in large numbers since 2004 – in contrast to Lewisian transformation – due to push factors (Table 2). Continued withdrawal of the workforce from agriculture due to unremunerative returns has led to a complete disaster on the employment front.[4] This is simply because workers getting detached from agriculture were inadequately absorbed elsewhere.

Employment in rural agriculture and allied activities contracted sharply (32.3 million) between 2004–05 and 2011–12, as shown in Table 2. This collapse in primary sector employment was insufficiently compensated by rural non-agricultural employment (27.3 million) led by rural construction (20.5 million), possibly driven by asset creation under the Mahatma Gandhi National Rural Employment Guarantee Scheme (MGNREGS) – and it was only due to job creation in the urban non-agricultural sector (20.8 million) that the period saw modest employment growth.

The scenario, however, changed between 2013–14 and 2015–16.

Table 2 ***Change in Employment between 2004–05 and 2011–12, and between 2013–14 and 2015–16*** (millions)

Sector	Rural	Urban
Change between 2004–05 and 2011–12		
Agriculture and allied activities	–32.3	–1.0
Manufacturing	1.5	3.6
Construction	20.5	3.3
Non-agricultural employment	27.3	20.8
Change between 2013–14 and 2015–16		
Agriculture and allied activities	–7.79	–0.67
Manufacturing	0.16	–1.74
Construction	0.4	–1.32
Non-agricultural employment	5.99	–2.83

Note: Non-agricultural sectors other than manufacturing and construction are not reported here.
Source: Change between 2004–05 and 2011–12 adapted from Thomas (2014), Table 2, and change between 2013–14 and 2015–16 adapted from Abraham (2017), Table 2.

In this later period, exodus from agriculture continued in large numbers (7.79 million) and rural non-agriculture fell short (5.99 million) of absorbing those deserting the farm sector. Additionally, unlike in the previous period, employment in urban areas turned negative in both the primary sector (0.67 million) and non-agriculture sector (2.83 million, spread over manufacturing and even construction). Thus, for the first time since independence, aggregate employment growth in India turned negative.

Persistence of this grim employment scenario is likely to turn the much talked about demographic dividend in India into a demographic disaster. Thus, there is an urgent need to explore the scope of gainful employment creation outside agriculture (along with devising strategies to revive agricultural incomes, which is outside the scope of this essay). Interest in unregistered manufacturing arises from this concern.

Structure of Unregistered Manufacturing and Scope of Gainful Employment Creation

We now analyse the structure of the unregistered manufacturing sector. Before that, we must clearly distinguish it from the registered segment. Registered/organized manufacturing sector encompasses manufacturing units registered under Sections 2m(i) and 2m(ii) of the Factories Act, 1948. Statistical information on these firms is collected by the Annual

Survey of Industries (ASI).[5] The definition of unregistered/unorganized manufacturing used in this essay is the same as that employed by the NSS in its Enterprise surveys, conducted as follow-up surveys of the Economic Census (Government of India 2018a; for details, see pages 1 and 6). According to this definition, the unregistered/unorganized manufacturing sector comprises manufacturing units (i) *not* covered in ASI; (ii) registered under Section 85 of Factories Act, 1948; (iii) engaged in cotton ginning, cleaning and baling, other than firms already registered under Factories Act, 1948; and (iv) engaged in *beedi* and cigar production, excluding those registered under The Beedi and Cigar Workers (Conditions of Employment) Act, 1966. However, this division between the registered and unregistered sectors purely on the basis of factory legislation is arbitrary and more functional in nature; for example, it often does not take into account the ground realities prevailing in developing countries such as India (Chandrasekhar 2004).

The data-set used in this study is the NSS survey on unincorporated non-agricultural enterprises (excluding construction) conducted between July 2015 and June 2016 (73rd Round), covering the whole of the Indian Union. The 73rd Round covered the *entire* unincorporated non-agricultural sector (excluding construction)[6] as a follow-up survey of the Sixth Economic Census.

Let us now consider the division between registered and unregistered manufacturing. Table 3 shows that close to 83 per cent of manufacturing GDP in 2015–16 originated in the registered segment.[7] The picture, however, drastically changes if the focus shifts to employment. Th unregistered sector constituted nearly 72 per cent of manufacturing employment in 2015–16.[8] Thus, from the point of view of employment, exploration of unregistered manufacturing appears important. From the point of view of distribution of firms, the unregistered sector constituted around 99 per cent of the manufacturing units in 2015–16.

Shifting our attention entirely to the unregistered sector, we find

Table 3 *Registered–Unregistered Divide in Manufacturing, 2015–16* (percentages)

Variables	Registered	Unregistered
Gross value added (GVA)	82.6	17.4
Employment	28.4	71.6
Firms	1.2	98.8

Source: Registered sector from Annual Survey of Industries, and unregistered sector from Characteristics of Unincorporated Non-agricultural Enterprises (excluding Construction) in India, 2015–16.

Table 4 ***Relative Shares of OAE and Establishment by Sector*** (percentages)

Variables	OAE	Establishment
Rural		
Firms	92	8
Employment	76	24
Gross value added (GVA)	57	43
Urban		
Firms	77	23
Employment	49	51
Gross value added (GVA)	30	70
Rural + Urban		
Firms	86	14
Employment	63	37
Gross value added (GVA)	39	61

Source: Characteristics of Unincorporated Non-agricultural Enterprises (excluding Construction) in India, 2015–16.

that it comprises two kinds of firms: (i) own account enterprises (OAE), operating without any hired worker (these are primitive firms/enterprises functioning solely on the basis of unpaid family labour and owners); and (ii) establishments that employ at least one hired worker (relatively less primitive) (see, for details, Government of India 2017: 9).

Table 4 provides the OAE–establishment divide separately for rural and urban areas. Note that for the combined sector (rural and urban), more primitive OAE firms constitute the overwhelming majority of enterprises (86 per cent) employing the bulk of the workers dependent on the sector (63 per cent). However, relatively less primitive establishments dominate the scene when it comes to GVA, forming 61 per cent of the output originating from the sector. This mismatch in shares of output and employment (as well as firms) broadly indicates the problem of low productivity plaguing the OAE segment.

The dominance of the OAE segment is more prominently visible across *all* three categories in rural areas, whereas in urban areas, 70 per cent of output and 51 per cent employment were formed in less primitive establishments, comprising 23 per cent of firms. This domination of OAE firms in unregistered manufacturing can also be gauged from another indicator, namely, the location of enterprises.

To start with, focusing on the combined sector and abstracting

Table 5 ***Distribution of Manufacturing Enterprises by Location and Sector*** (percentages)

Location of enterprise	Rural			Urban			Rural + Urban		
	OAE	Est.	All	OAE	Est.	All	OAE	Est.	All
1. Within household premises	56.2	26.5	53.7	40.3	12.9	33.9	49.2	16.7	44.0
2. Outside household premises (with fixed location)	28.9	64.3	31.9	44.2	85.3	53.8	35.6	79.5	42.5
2.1 Permanent structure	24.0	59.2	27.0	39.1	83.9	49.6	30.7	77.0	38.0
2.2 Temporary structure	2.7	2.4	2.6	2.9	1.0	2.4	2.7	1.4	2.5
2.3 Without any structure	2.2	2.7	2.3	2.2	0.4	1.8	2.2	1.1	2.0
3. Outside household premises (without fixed location)	14.8	9.3	14.3	15.6	1.8	12.3	15.2	3.9	13.4
3.1 Mobile market	5.5	3.6	5.3	4.3	0.6	3.4	5.0	1.4	4.4
3.2 Street vendor	9.3	5.7	9.0	11.3	1.2	8.9	10.2	2.5	9.0
Total	100.0	100.0	100.0	100.0	100.0	100.0	100.0	100.0	100.0

Source: Same as Table 4.

from the underlying labour contract (i.e. the last column), one finds that the majority of the firms were either operating from within the household (44 per cent) or outside the household without fixed location (13.4 per cent). In so far as 'modern' firms are located outside the household and operate from a fixed location, 57.4 per cent of unregistered manufacturing firms did not meet this criterion. This phenomenon gets more pronounced in rural areas with 53.7 per cent of firms operating from household premises and a further 14.3 per cent without fixed location. The trend gets reversed in the case of urban enterprises, in which 53.8 per cent of firms function from a fixed location outside household premises. However, note that it is ultimately the dominance of OAE firms that is driving the result (remember 86 per cent of firms are OAE), for within the establishment category, firms outside household premises with fixed location dominate in both rural (64.3 per cent) and urban areas (85.3 per cent).

Next, we discuss the concentration of activities in unregistered manufacturing. Table 6 shows (highlighted) that 81 per cent of enterprises, 71 per cent of workers and 59 per cent of output were concentrated in just six two-digit industry groups. Such heavy concentration of activities implies failure of broad-based manufacturing development in the sector. Furthermore, these activities are relatively simple to carry out with the majority of industries typically producing traditional consumer non-durables. This abundance of simple activities is understandable given the predominance of OAE and the location of the majority of firms either within households or without fixed location.

Given this background, we examine the possibility of productive/gainful employment generation in the sector. It is an important question because, in 2015–16, the manufacturing sector constituted around 10 per cent of aggregate employment (see Table 1) and the unregistered segment's contribution in the former was around 72 per cent (see Table 3). As unregistered manufacturing formed the greater part of manufacturing employment, the question arises as to how much of this can be considered gainful employment.

Evidently, the next step is to define gainful employment properly. Perhaps it will be readily accepted that for a person to be considered gainfully employed in any activity, at the very least his/her subsistence needs must be met from this engagement. In this context, subsistence must be carefully defined, for this need not merely mean bare physical subsistence. It may also include commodities acquired through 'habit and custom [that are] were instrumental in determining what [is] was "necessary" in the workers' diet . . . [consequently] the subsistence level not only [includes] bare physical necessities, but also a modicum of comforts as well' (Dobb

Table 6 *Concentration of Manufacturing Activity: Enterprises, Workers, GVA*

Manufacturing of	Enterprise share (%)	Worker share (%)	GVA share (%)
Food products	11.57	13.23	13.73
Tobacco products	16.65	10.95	3.37
Textiles	13.24	13.81	11.13
Wood products	6.06	6.04	4.59
Other manufacturing	4.83	5.20	6.54
Wearing apparel	28.53	21.82	19.29
Wood + Other manufacturing + Food + Tobacco + Textile + Wearing apparel	81.00	71.00	59.00
Cotton ginning, cleaning and bailing	0.01	0.03	0.03
Beverages	0.94	0.95	0.71
Leather products	0.79	1.27	1.60
Paper and paper products	0.55	0.68	0.73
Printing and reproduction of recorded media	0.82	1.28	2.22
Coke and refined petroleum products	0.01	0.03	0.04
Chemicals and chemical products	0.88	1.03	0.87
Pharmaceuticals, medicinal chemicals and botanical products	0.03	0.06	0.10
Rubber and plastic products	0.63	1.16	2.36
Other non-metallic mineral products	3.12	7.79	6.60
Basic metals	0.26	0.49	0.80
Fabricated metal products, except machinery and equipment	4.01	5.61	9.20
Computer, electronic and optical products	0.07	0.10	0.24
Electrical equipment	0.19	0.50	1.11
Machinery and equipment N.E.C.	0.41	1.52	5.36
Motor vehicles, trailers and semi-trailers	0.11	0.27	0.56
Other transport equipment	0.03	0.06	0.16
Furniture	4.43	4.59	6.32
Repair and installation of machinery and equipment	1.83	1.55	2.33
Total	100.00	100.00	100.00

Source: Same as Table 4.

1941: 95). There is a long tradition in economics to define the subsistence wage in these broad terms, and the above idea was first conceived by one of the central figures of classical economics, David Ricardo.

However, for empirical purposes we need a concrete subsistence equivalent with which to work. In this essay, the national floor-level minimum wage (NFLMW) for unskilled workers proposed by the Government of India (GoI) in September 2016 is taken as the subsistence-level wage.[9] Is it justified to take the minimum wage as a proxy for subsistence-level wage? This depends on the norms broadly followed for setting minimum wages in India.

The International Labour Office describes the underlying philosophy succinctly: '[a] minimum wage [in India] [is] was defined as one necessary for sustenance of life and some measure of education, meeting medical requirements and for amenities for the preservation of the efficiency of the worker' (ILO 2018: 74). These determinants follow from the recommendations of the Committee on Fair Wages 1949, the 15th Indian Labour Conference in 1957 and a 1991 Supreme Court judgment, which considered food intake (with specific calorie norms), clothing, housing, energy requirements, along with 'children's education, medical requirement, minimum recreation, including festivals ceremonies, provision for old age and marriage [that] should further constitute 25 per cent and be used as a guide for fixing the minimum wage'.[10] Therefore, although there is evidence of low-level compliance with minimum wages in India (Rani and Belser 2012), the idea itself very closely encapsulates the concept of subsistence-level wage.

Now we ask the question: was a typical unregistered manufacturing unit in a position to offer gainful employment in 2015–16? The analysis is carried out separately for OAE and establishment firms due to their fundamental differences in terms of organization of production (labour contracts) and 'revealed' modernity (location of enterprise).

We first analyse OAE. Analysis is carried out at the level of an average firm,[11] and column D (Table 7) represents the surplus (output left after paying rent and interest) available to an average unit run solely on the basis of unpaid family labour and owner; thus, it can also be seen as the total product available for sharing among family members engaged in the unit. Column E shows the monthly NFLMW.[12] The annual subsistence wage bill per worker is given in column F. Comparing values in columns D and F reveals that an average OAE, irrespective of location, was unable to provide subsistence to even one worker. Thus, the whole OAE segment – constituting 86 per cent of firms in unregistered manufacturing – was unable to provide gainful employment, on average.

Table 7 ***Scope of Gainful Employment in a Typical OAE Manufacturing Unit: Rural and Urban***

Sector	GVA/ firm (A)	Interest/ firm (B)	Rent/firm (C)	(GVA–R–I)/ firm (D = A–B–C)	Subsistence wage/ month (E)	Annual wage bill/ worker (F = Ex12)
Rural	48,565	335	464	47,766	9,100	1,09,200
Urban	84,699	506	3,548	80,645	9,100	1,09,200

Note: All figures in rupees.
Source: Same as Table 4.

Table 8 ***Scope of Gainful Employment in a Typical Establishment Unit: Rural and Urban***

Sector	GVA/ firm (A)	Interest/ firm (B)	Rent/ firm (C)	(GVA–R–I)/ firm (D = A–B–C)	Workers/ firm (E)	Subsistence wage/ month (F)	Annual wage bill/firm (G = ExF)
Rural	4,23,610	9,422	5,781	4,08,407	4.91	9,100	5,36,172
Urban	6,44,964	16,538	27,869	6,00,557	4.59	9,100	5,01,228

Note: All figures in rupees, except column E in pure numbers.
Source: Same as Table 4.

Next we turn to establishments. As before, column D shows the excess output available in an average firm after paying rent and interest. Column E denotes average worker per firm and the next column (F) represents NFLMW per worker. Therefore, multiplying the two (columns E and F) gives the annual subsistence wage bill of an average establishment (column G). Note that the wage bill in column G for rural areas exceeds the output remaining after distribution of rent and interest (column D). Therefore, like OAE firms, rural establishments, on average, were incapable of providing gainful employment to their workers. However, for urban establishments, the subsistence wage bill (5,01,228) was less than the surplus (6,00,557) available for distribution between wages and profits. Thus, within the unregistered manufacturing sector, only the urban establishment segment could gainfully employ workers.[13]

What can we conclude about gainful employment in unregistered manufacturing from these results? Table 9 shows the simple point growth rate of firms and workers between 2010–11 and 2015–16 in unregistered manufacturing.[14] If past trends are to be relied upon, then rural establish-

Table 9 ***Point Growth Rate of Firms and Workers between 2010–11 and 2015–16*** (percentages)

	OAE		Establishments	
Growth of	Rural	Urban	Rural	Urban
Firms	14.9	19.3	–6.1	7.3
Workers	7.1	11.6	–15.0	1.4

Source: Same as Table 4.

ments are not in a position to absorb people, since this segment contracted as a whole. For the own-account segment firms expanded and recruited workers, but preceding results show that these cannot be considered as gainful employment (see Table 7). It is only the urban establishment section that is suited for gainful employment generation; however, note that among the segments registering positive growth, its magnitude is the least (for both workers and firms). Therefore, it requires focused policy intervention to improve chances of gainful employment creation in unregistered manufacturing; otherwise, given the current state of affairs, such a prospect appears considerably muted.

Interestingly, firms perceive the lack of dynamism in the sector. Table 10 reports the self-assessed growth status of firms. It is to be noted that the share of firms either stagnating or contracting beat the expansionary firms by a wide margin. This tendency is more pronounced in the OAE segment. However, in light of Tables 8 and 9, it is puzzling to note that a greater proportion of rural establishments (36.6 per cent) perceived an expansionary trend, whereas only 32.4 per cent of their urban counterparts reported such status. Further research is certainly needed at a disaggregated level to resolve this puzzle. But it is clear that if the majority of firms experience dull market conditions, this is bound to have a negative impact on their employment drive.

Furthermore, it is disturbing to note that the overwhelming proportion of firms in the sector, without much prospect for growth and irrespective of location, were still operating for the major part of the year. In fact, except rural establishments, more than 90 per cent of firms in every segment ran for more than nine months (Table 11). This probably matches up with the lack of employment opportunity available elsewhere in the economy, documented above. Moreover, acute crisis of employment is traced from the fact that demand for MGNREGS work was on the rise despite a meagre rise in wages.[15]

This hypothesis is confirmed by Table 12, in which a very high

Table 10 ***Distribution of Firms by Perceived Growth Status of Firms in Last Three Years*** (percentages)

Growth status of firms	OAE		Establishments	
	Rural	Urban	Rural	Urban
Expanding	22.5	24.7	36.6	32.4
Stagnant	49.7	44.9	34.3	39.8
Contracting	15.0	13.6	11.2	9.6

Note: Shares may not add up to 100 for there are firms operating for less than three years.
Source: Same as Table 4.

Table 11 ***Distribution of Manufacturing Firms by Number of Months in Operation*** (percentages)

Months of operation	OAE	Est.	All
Rural			
0–6	5.2	13.8	5.9
7–9	4.0	4.6	4.1
> 9	90.8	81.6	90.0
Total	100.0	100.0	100.0
Urban			
0–6	4.5	3.9	4.4
7–9	3.0	2.1	2.8
> 9	92.5	94.0	92.8
Total	100.0	100.0	100.0

Source: Same as Table 4.

proportion of firms reported not to have faced any kind of problem in operations. Strangely, this proportion was greater for OAE firms (60 per cent) as compared to establishments (52 per cent), although we found that the whole of the OAE segment would be in deficit if subsistence wages were paid. Clearly, the opportunity cost of continuing in business must be lower than existing returns from the segment.

Additionally, Table 12 arranges firms by the nature of problems faced. Note that the factors pulling back firms' growth affect both on the demand and supply sides. Although shortfall in demand is identified as the most important factor affecting both kinds of firms, supply-side factors such as financial dues (fin. dues) and lack of credit availability were dominant problems plaguing the OAE segment. Establishments reported

Table 12 *Distribution of Firms by Nature of Problems* (percentages)

Firm type	No problem faced	Demand shrinkage	Non-recovery of fin. dues	No/ high credit cost	Erratic power supply	Raw material shortage	Labour-related	Others
OAE	60.1	17.9	6.1	6.8	4.6	4.6	0.8	10.4
Establishments	51.6	16.1	9.1	7.7	11.5	3.2	13.9	6.8

Note: Shares may not add up to 100 for one firm can report under two categories.
Source: Same as Table 4.

Table 13 *Distribution of Firms Not Receiving Any Government Assistance* (percentages)

Sector	OAE	Establishment	All
Rural	99.2	96.1	99.0
Urban	99.1	98.2	98.9

Source: Same as Table 4.

other supply-side factors such as labour-related problems and unavailability of uninterrupted power supply as leading constraints.

Despite such specific problems identified by 40 per cent of OAE firms and 48 per cent of establishments (from Table 12), almost no firms (99 per cent) received any kind of government assistance for a turnaround (Table 13). It hardly requires mentioning that focused policies in these fronts are essential for productive employment generation in this sector.

Conclusion

The motivation of this study was to check the possibility of creation of productive/gainful employment in India's unregistered manufacturing sector, given the backdrop of a consistent decline in agricultural employment in absolute numbers since 2004. The situation has been aggravated as aggregate employment shrank in the most recent period, prompting one to look for alternative employment avenues to stem the impending crisis.

Analysis of the unregistered manufacturing sector using the NSS unincorporated sector survey 2015–16 revealed the heavy dominance of OAE firms. Furthermore, the simple character of the sector is mirrored in the majority of the firms being either located within households or without a fixed location. A defining feature of the sector is its highly concentrated nature of activities, mainly limited to the production of a few simple consumer non-durables.

Then, we defined gainful employment and tested the opportunity of such job creation in OAE firms and establishments separately, due to their fundamentally different character. The results show the inability of OAE firms, irrespective of their location, to generate such jobs. Even within establishments, rural firms were incapable of employing workers gainfully, and it was only the urban units which fulfilled this objective. However, analysis of actual growth experience of firms revealed the limited ability of the unregistered manufacturing sector to generate gainful employment. Moreover, these firms (and workers therein) seem to have been stuck in a low-level equilibrium trap, in the absence of more rewarding opportunities. Finally, the study reports various constraints on growth as identified by firms, spreading across specific supply- and demand-side factors; however, there is complete absence of any government initiative to alleviate these problems. In the absence of such intervention, the scope of gainful employment creation in the unregistered manufacturing sector remains bleak.

Non-incriminating thanks are due to Nivedita Sarkar, Sangeeta Ghosh and Bhagyashree Paul.

Notes

[1] For example, data from National Accounts Statistics (NAS) shows that the share of agriculture in GDP was 51.44 per cent in 1951–52, which came down to 14.4 per cent in 2011–12 (at 2004–05 prices). In 2016–17, its share was 15.3 per cent at 2011–12 prices. However, the broad trend is indicative.

[2] Most recent employment figures for the year 2017–18, although vetted by the Statistical Commission, have been withheld by the government, leading to the resignation of the Commission's chairman. It is widely speculated that the government is wilfully suppressing employment data, as a media leak exposed the employment figure to be at a forty-five-year high.

[3] Seehttps://data.worldbank.org/indicator/NV.IND.MANF.ZS?locations=CN,accessed 16 June 2019.

[4] On unremunerative returns in agriculture, see De Roy (2017).

[5] Firms covered by ASI either employ ten (or more) workers using power or employ twenty (or more) workers without using power.

[6] It covered trade and other services in the unorganized sector, along with manufacturing. This study, however, focuses only on unorganized manufacturing activity.

[7] However, the registered–unregistered divide in gross value added (GVA) obtained from National Accounts Statistics is substantially different from the ASI–NSSO figures; for example, in 2012–13 the share of the unregistered segment in manufacturing GDP was 28.9 per cent (NAS 2014; the division of output between the registered and unregistered segment was discontinued by NAS from 2015).

[8] This more or less matches the census estimate; for example, employment share of the factory sector (i.e. registered manufacturing) was 27.7 per cent in 2011.

[9] The unincorporated sector NSS survey was conducted between July 2015 and June 2016; therefore it is appropriate to take the September 2016 NFLMW proposal by GoI; see https://labour.gov.in/sites/default/files/MW_notification.pdf, accessed 16 June 2019.

[10] See http://labourbureau.gov.in/Mini%20Wages%202k5%20Intro.htm, accessed 16 June 2019.

[11] Figures (in columns A, B, C) at the average firm level are obtained by dividing the aggregate sector-wise values by the total number of firms, all through. Aggregate sector-wise values are available in the NSS report.

[12] This is obtained as follows: NFLMW/month = (NFLMW/day) x 26 days; the proposed NFLMW/day for unskilled work in September 2016 was Rs 350. See https://labour.gov.in/sites/default/files/MW_notification.pdf, p. 15, accessed 16 June 2019. Thus the subsistence wage per month, taken as the monthly NFLMW in this study, turns out to be Rs 9,100.

[13] If, however, the trade unions' demand for minimum wages of Rs 18,000/month is considered then, of course, even urban establishments were unable to provide subsistence; see Roychowdhury (2017), http://column.global-labour-university.org/2017/06/how-to-read-2-september-strike-in-india.html, accessed 16 June 2019.

[14] This does not refer to the annual compound growth.

[15] For example, in 2011–12, the first year of the decade, 218 crore person-days of work was sought under MGNREGS; by 2018–19 this went up to 257 crore (Government of India 2018b).

References

Abraham, V. (2017), 'Stagnant Employment Growth: Last Three Years May Have Been the Worst', *Economic and Political Weekly*, 52 (38): 13–17.

Chandrasekar, C.P. (2004), 'Forms of Dualism: An Analysis of the Structure of India's Unregistered Manufacturing Sector Based on the 56th Round Results', *Arthaniti*, 3 (1–2): 17–29.

Chandrasekhar, C.P. (2014), 'Promise Belied: India's Post-Independence Industrialization Experience', in C.P. Chandrasekhar, ed., *Indian Industrialization*, ICSSR, Research Surveys and Explorations: Economics, Volume 1, Oxford: Oxford University Press.

Chandrasekhar, C.P. (2018), 'Leapfrogging into Services', https://www.networkideas.org/news-analysis/2018/04/leapfrogging-into-services/, accessed 11 October 2019.

De Roy, S. (2017), 'Economic Reforms and Agricultural Growth in India', *Economic and Political Weekly*, 52 (4).

Dobb, M. (1941), *Wages*, Cambridge Economics Handbooks, Cambridge.

Government of India (2014a), *National Accounts Statistics 2014*, New Delhi: Central Statistics Office, Ministry of Labour and Programme Implementation.

——— (2014b), *Employment–Unemployment Situation in India 2011–12*, New Delhi: National Sample Survey, Ministry of Labour and Programme Implementation.

——— (2016), *Report on Employment–Unemployment Survey 2015–16,* Volume 1, New Delhi: Ministry of Labour and Employment, Labour Bureau, Chandigarh.

——— (2017), *Key Indicators of Unincorporated Non-Agricultural Enterprises (Excluding Construction) in India, 2015–16*, New Delhi: National Sample Survey Office, Ministry of Labour and Programme Implementation.

——— (2018a), *Economic Characteristics of Unincorporated Non-Agricultural Enterprises (Excluding Construction) in India, 2015–16*, New Delhi: National Sample Survey Office, Ministry of Labour and Programme Implementation.

——— (2018b), *Statistical Year Book India*, http://www.mospi.gov.in/statistical-year-book-india/2018, accessed 11 October 2019.

——— (2018c), *National Accounts Statistics*, New Delhi: Central Statistics Office Ministry of Labour and Programme Implementation.

International Labour Office (2018), *India Wage Report: Wage Policies for Decent Work and Inclusive Growth*, https://www.ilo.org/wcmsp5/groups/public/---asia/---ro-bangkok/---sro-new_delhi/documents/publication/wcms_638305.pdf, accessed 11 October 2019.

Kaldor, N. (1960), *Causes of Growth and Stagnation in the World Economy*, Cambridge: Cambridge University Press.

Mehrotra, S., J. Parida, S. Sinha and A. Gandhi (2014), 'Explaining Employment Trends in the Indian Economy: 1993–94 to 2011–12', *Economic and Political Weekly*, 49 (32).

Nagaraj, R. (2014), 'Trends and Patterns in Industrial Growth: A Review of Evidence and Explanations', in C.P. Chandrasekhar, ed., *Indian Industrialization*, ICSSR Research Surveys and Explorations: Economics, Volume 1, Oxford: Oxford University Press.

Nagaraj, R. (2017), 'Economic Reforms and Manufacturing Sector Growth: Need for Reconfiguring the Industrialization Model', *Economic and Political Weekly*, 52 (2).

Rani, U. and P. Belser (2012), 'The Effectiveness of Minimum Wages in Developing Countries: The Case of India', *International Journal of Labour Research*, 4 (1): 45–66.

Roychowdhury, A. (2017), 'How to Read the September 2 Strike?', *Global Labour Column*, http://column.global-labour-university.org/2017/06/how-to-read-2-september-strike-in-india.html, accessed 16 June 2019.

Thomas, J.J. (2014), 'The Demographic Challenge and Employment Growth in India', *Economic and Political Weekly*, 49 (6).

PART THREE

Unfinished Dialogues on Revolution and Liberation

15
In Memory of Sam Moyo

Samir Amin

The brutal disappearance of Sam Moyo has left us without a voice. Sam was a very dear personal friend. He was one of the key founders of the activities we developed within the Third World Forum (TWF) and the World Forum for Alternatives (WFA) over the past ten years. From our first meeting, it was clear that beyond his qualities as a cultivated and intelligent scientific researcher, he was also a courageous and determined activist who pursued the cause of peoples and nations – his own (Zimbabwe), of Africa and of the global South – with conviction. With every passing day, our collaboration brought us closer.

Sam's major works addressed the agrarian question. He had understood that the deployment of imperialist strategies could produce nothing other than the savage and tragic destruction of the rural sphere and the decimation of peasants in Africa and Asia.

Drawing on his own country's experiences, where millions of peasants were expropriated from the land of their ancestors to make way for a few thousand colonists, Sam had rigorously examined the systematic application of such criminal policies. He had grasped the dramatic realities of the situation and placed himself firmly in support of the agrarian reform programme undertaken by President Mugabe. In spite of its limitations – which Sam also measured – he denounced the hypocrisy displayed by the United Kingdom in its refusal to honour its engagements in this area.

Sam did not content himself with analysing reality and denouncing its tragic nature. He made major contributions to the formulation of humane alternatives to these challenges – elaborating options for sovereign, genuine, national and people-orientated development projects – which would have the capacity to promote real democracy within the context of reinvigorated peasant production and renewal in the countryside. He could locate the struggle for the pursuit of such alternatives in his own national political context, as well as in the broader international situation. He knew that this struggle was inseparable from popular struggles against contemporary forms of imperialism. He had the courage to analyse its manifestations and its outcomes and to use the conclusions he drew from this work to confront the tenuous debates advanced by the proponents of the so-called 'neoliberalism'.

Sam had become a pillar of our discussion circles dedicated to addressing the agrarian question in Africa and in the global South. In this respect, he was a central figure in organizing highly successful round table discussions – notably for our interventions at the African and World Social Forums. These enabled thousands of experts from the three continents in which popular and peasant social struggles were taking place to come together to examine the peculiarities and similarities of their experiences, and to gain a better understanding of their collective struggles for the social and political emancipation of each respective nation.

Sam was the vice president of the WFA (for the Southern African region). He was the executive director of the African Institute for Agrarian Studies, an important institution which was one of the most active members of the 'network of networks' which constitutes the TWF and the WFA.

The prolific works authored by Sam and his colleagues were featured in major publications. Two such collective works which appeared only months before Sam's tragic death – *The Struggle for Food Sovereignty: Alternative Development and the Renewal of Peasant Society Today* (2015) and *Réponses Radicales aux Crises Agraires et Rurales Africaines* (2015) – embody his powerful contribution to the debates. One of the authors of the latter title, our friend Issaka Bagayogo, also passed away in 2015. The texts produced by Sam are, and will remain, central to all those engaged in the struggles for Africa and its peasants.

Historically, the development of capitalism in Europe, the United States and in Japan reduced the active population engaged in agriculture to 5 per cent in each of its regions, without compromising the capacity of the new capitalist modernized agriculture to meet demands for expanded food production. Why then should it not be possible for the countries of the periphery to be set on an accelerated course down this same path – even if somewhat belatedly? This proposition is unsustainable because it ignores the specific conditions which allowed the west to prosper and which, in themselves, preclude their own reproduction elsewhere. Its success, for instance, was only made possible because the industries established at the time, during the nineteenth century, were able to absorb a large proportion of rural populations expelled from the countryside. In addition, surplus populations had the option of mass migration to the Americas (considering that the European population made up 15 per cent of the world's population in the 1500s and that combined with the European descendants in America, it made up 36 per cent of the population in 1900, emigration abroad allowed for the development of a 'second Europe'). In the contemporary situation, the demands that industries in the peripheries should be 'competitive' on world markets justify the use of modern technologies which reduce the level of labour-intensive work. At the same time, there are no new Americas to open for mass migrations from Asia or Africa. In such conditions, the pursuit of a model based on historical capitalism produces nothing other than migration from devastated countrysides to squalid urban slums.

The conclusion that emerges from these facts is that another trajectory of development is required for today's periphery. It is necessary to imagine and to articulate a new model of industrialization shaped by the renewal of non-capitalist forms of peasant agriculture, which in turn implies delinking from the imperatives of globalized capitalism.

Firmly anchored in this perspective, Sam Moyo's works provide us not only with the best analyses of rural disaster in Africa but also with the frameworks for an alternative. I need say no more – Sam's work speaks for itself and the analysis here converges with his contributions to the publications cited above.

In this context, I will elaborate on a few reflections concerning other dimensions of the challenges which have been at the centre of debates between myself, Sam and others, during our frequent meetings (Amin 2014a, 2014b, 2014c, 2015a).

What is the 'Emergence' of States and Nations?

The term 'emergence' is and has frequently been employed to characterize radically different contexts, often without specifying which particular meaning is implied or attributed to it. I take this opportunity to specify the meaning I would attribute to the collective processes of economic, social, political and cultural transformations which make it possible to speak of the 'emergence' of a state, a nation or a people which have been placed in a peripheral position (in the sense I have personally attributed to this term) at the heart of the globalized capitalist system.

Emergence is not measured by high levels of gross domestic product (GDP) growth rates (nor exports) over a long period (exceeding a decade), nor, in fact, by society having achieved a high level of GDP per capita, as the World Bank would have it. Rather, emergence implies sustained growth of industrial production in the country concerned and an increase in the capacity of local industry to be competitive on a global scale. It is, however, still necessary to specify the relevant industries and to define what is meant by competitiveness.

Extractive industries (minerals and fuels) must be excluded from the analysis, since they alone can generate accelerated growth without making any significant change to the overall productive capacity of the country in question. An extreme example of such 'non-emerging' countries is that of the Gulf States, Gabon and others. The competitiveness of productive activities must also be considered as part of the economy's production system as a whole and not by measuring the performance of a number of units of production on their own.

Through the relocation of production, or subcontracting, multinationals operating in countries of the South can establish local production units (either as branches of multinationals or as independent productive units) capable of exporting to external markets. In the language of conventional economics, this qualifies them as competitive. This truncated concept of competitiveness – which proceeds from an empiricist methodology of the first order – does not correspond to our way of seeing things.

Competitiveness relates to the productive system as a whole. A productive system should exist – which is to say that the economy under analysis should be made up of productive establishments and branches which are sufficiently interdependent to justify the term 'system'. The competitiveness of this system then depends on various economic and social factors, amongst them, the general level of education and of technical training of workers across sectors, as well as the efficiency of institutions responsible for executing national policies (fiscal, the regulatory environment for business, employment, credit, public services, etc.).

Nor is a country's productive system reducible to the industries dealing with transformative processes for manufactured goods destined to either production or consumption (although their absence makes it impossible to consider the existence of a productive system worthy of its name). Rather, it integrates food and agricultural production as essential services for the normal operation of the system.

The concept of emergence implies an approach which is both political and holistic. A country can be considered to be emergent only to the extent that the logic of those in power prioritizes the construction of a strong nationally focused economy (albeit open towards the exterior) and its national economic sovereignty. This complex objective implies the affirmation of sovereignty in all aspects of economic life. Notably, it implies policies that promote the consolidation of food sovereignty, and sovereignty in the control of its own natural resources, as well as access to these outside of its own territory. These multiple and complementary objectives stand in stark contrast to those of a comprador political authority which contents itself with subjugating the country's growth model to the demands of the dominant liberalized global system and to the possibilities it offers. The relationship between policies concerned with a country's emergence, on the one hand, and the social transformations which accompany them, on the other, does not depend exclusively on the internal coherence of such policies. Instead, they depend on the degree of complementarity to (or contradiction with) the social transformations they engender.

Social struggles – class struggles and political conflicts – do not 'adjust' themselves to the outcomes produced by the logic underlying the deployment of projects ostensibly aimed at a state's emergence. On the contrary, they are shaped by these outcomes. Experiences from such transformations currently under way illustrate the diversity and fluctuations in the relationships between policy logics, policy outcomes and social transformations: 'emergence' is often accompanied by increased inequality.

It is necessary to specify the exact nature of these inequalities, namely, inequalities which benefit a small minority or a strong minority (such as the middle classes) and which occur in a framework that brings about the pauperization of the working-class majorities; or, on the contrary, if it does bring about an improvement in the conditions of the working class, this framework nonetheless fails to bring about increases in rates of remuneration of labour which are commensurate with the level of increases in income accruing to the system's beneficiaries. In other words, the implementation of policies aimed at a state's emergence is capable of bringing about pauperization, with or without emergence. Emergence does not constitute a definitive or immovable condition for a state; it occurs in successive stages, the earlier stages successfully laying the groundwork for what follows, or conversely, moving towards deadlock.

Similarly, the relations between the emerging economy and the globalized economy are themselves in a state of continuous transformation and are influenced by changing rationales and perspectives. They may favour the consolidation of sovereignty, or promote its weakening, and they may support the consolidation of national social solidarity, or promote its weakening. Measured in this manner, we can see that emergence is neither synonymous with export growth nor with economic consolidation for the country concerned. Growth in exports occurs at the expense of domestic/internal markets (specifically, popular, middle class), and can, in fact, become an obstacle to national economic consolidation. Growth in exports can weaken or reinforce the relative autonomy of emerging economies in their relationships to the world system.

Thus, emergence is a political project, not simply an economic one. The measure of its success relates to its capacity to reduce the means through which the currently existing dominant capitalist centres reproduce their domination, despite the success achieved by emerging countries measured in conventional economic terms. I define these means in terms of the control exerted by the dominant powers over technological development, natural resources, the globalized financial and monetary system, information systems and arsenals of weapons of mass destruction. I subscribe to the thesis concerning the existence of a collective form of imperialism exercised by the Triad (United States, Europe and Japan) whose aim is to maintain, at all costs, its privileged position of domination over the entire planet and to preclude any questioning of this order by emerging countries. I have concluded from this that the ambitions of emerging countries are in conflict with the strategic objectives of this imperialist Triad. The levels of this conflict are themselves determined by the degree of radicalization with which attempts to question the dominant order are pursued by individual countries and by their place in the present ordering of the system, on the one hand, and the status of individual countries in the present economic order on the other hand, considering that the economy of emerging countries is inseparable from their foreign policies. Are they aligned to the North Atlantic Treaty Organization's (NATO) political and military complex? Do they accept NATO strategies? Or do they attempt to resist them?

There can be no emergence without the policy of a state, which derives its legitimacy from a progressive relationship with society. Such a state should possess the capacity to coherently construct and implement a project of production geared primarily to serve national requirements. Its effectiveness is also complemented by policies to ensure that the majority of popular classes are also able to benefit from growth.

At the opposite end of the scale from the positive evolution of a project geared towards genuine emergence of the type described above, there stand states which unilaterally submit to the imperatives of globalized capitalist deployment through generalized monopolies which produces 'lumpen development'. I borrow this term freely from Andre Gunder Frank who used it to analyse similar changes under other conditions. Today, lumpen development is produced by accelerated social disintegration associated with the model of 'development' (which is not in fact worthy of its name), imposed by monopolies in the imperialist centres on the societies of the periphery which they dominate. It manifests itself by the dizzying growth of survival strategies (the so-called informal sphere), or, in other words, pauperization, which is inherent in the unilateral logics of capital accumulation.

Amongst the experiences of emergence, certain instances appear fully to deserve the qualification because they are not associated with the process of lumpen development; there is no occurrence of pauperization of the popular classes, but on the contrary, there occurs progress in their conditions of life. Two of these experiences are visibly and entirely capitalist – those of Korea and Taiwan (I will not discuss here the particular historical conditions which enabled the deployment of this project to succeed in both countries). Two others inherited their aspirations to revolutions in the name of socialism – China and Vietnam. Cuba could join this group if it succeeds in managing the contradictions it is currently experiencing. But we know other cases of emergence associated with the deployment of a process of lumpen development on a massive scale. India is perhaps the best example in this category as its reality displays characteristics which correspond with the conditions for emergence. State policy promotes the consolidation of a strong system of industrial production associated with a significant expansion of the middle classes. There is also significant development of technological and educational capacities and an autonomous foreign policy approach capable of standing independently on the world stage. But there is simultaneously a great majority – two-thirds of society – trapped in accelerated pauperization. This is a hybrid system that simultaneously connects 'emergence' and lumpen development. It is even possible to highlight the complementarity of relations between these two faces of reality. I believe, without suggesting an abusive generalization, that all the other countries considered emergent actually belongs to this hybrid family, be they Brazil, South Africa or others.

But there are also many countries of the South in which elements of 'emergence' do not appear at all. In such countries, the processes of lumpen development, virtually on their own, characterize almost the entire developmental process. African countries, in a general manner, can be organized into this unfortunate category.

The Question of Emergence under Contemporary Conditions in Sub-Saharan Africa

Flattering accolades have been delivered by the World Bank over the past few years to African economies: 'Africa Emerging' and 'Africa: Continent of the Future'. The objective, however, has certainly not been to support the establishment of sovereign African projects. Quite the opposite: by purporting to set African countries on the path of emergence, the objective has been to lock the continent's economies into the dead-end path of neoliberalism, which is in fact likely to preclude any likelihood of emergence. The type of 'emergence' conceived by the World Bank and its cohorts (notably the European Union) never speaks of the continent's industrialization, which is considered to be contrary to 'Africa's vocation' (with all its racist implications). Papers published by US politicians and journalists on this point are highly instructive. The shining future of Africa rests on its abundant natural resources, oil, minerals, agricultural land, sun and water. Future advancement is simply a matter of paving the way for the entrance of western multinationals to pillage these resources, nothing more.

At a general level, independent Africa has not overcome the modes of its insertion into the world system shaped under colonization. The term 'neo-colonial', previously in vogue among left-wing national liberation movements, was entirely justified. I personally found such a qualification 'moderate'; in my estimation, the reality would be better described as 'paleo-colonial' in view of structural adjustment plans which were imposed from the 1980s. Since then, all governments on the continent have – in spite of themselves – accepted the dictates of this form of globalization. Worse still, popular resistance movements do not appear to be conscious of the fact that economic neoliberalization lies at the root of the problem.

Viewed from this perspective, the situation can be considered desperate. In my opinion, it is, in fact, less so than it appears. The history of the past fifty years shows that people, and to a certain degree even African states, have never considered their submission as necessarily being final. Attempts to exit the neo-colonial impasse through projects of national and popular sovereignty have been rapidly increasing throughout the continent; the substantive analysis of these is, in fact, the subject of my book entitled *L'Eveil du Sud* (Amin 2008).

I recently reread what I wrote at the end at the first decade of independence: *Trois expériences africaines: le Mali, le Ghana, Guinée* (1965), *Le développement du capitalisme en Côte d'Ivoire* (1967) and *L'Histoire économique du Congo* (1969). My conclusions could appear pessimistic, but history has – in the interim – confirmed my predictions, i.e. my thesis of 'miracles without a future', such as the one in the Ivory Coast (to which the World Bank saw fit to respond with a report 'proving' that Ivory Coast would have overtaken South Korea in 1985 – which is utterly laughable). My rigorous examination of attempts at emergence, highlighting their original conceptual and practical weaknesses, has also been confirmed by subsequent developments. Advances have always been followed by predictable regressions (Amir 2008). The general thesis that I formulated in *L'Afrique de l'Ouest bloquée* always appears to me as essential to understand Africa's history over the past 60 years. The potential of the colonial model of development was already redundant well before political independence had been achieved by the peoples of the African continent. Colonies that had been 'valorized' (the term 'valorized', which was utilized by the colonial powers themselves is, in fact, more accurate than the term 'developed') before others, such as Senegal, Gold Coast (now Ghana), Dahomey (now Benin) or Togo, became suffocated and trapped in an impasse. These offered an instructive picture of the fate awaiting the new arrivals to this model of 'development' (Ivory Coast, Kenya and Malawi), which in their turn were to become trapped in the same impasse.

The diagnosis I make today of the causes underlying the impasses to development in Africa would not be different from the assessment I made forty years ago in *L'Afrique de l'Ouest bloquée* (which is also why I also subtitled this book 'the political economy of colonization, 1880–1970'). Africa has persisted on this path beyond 1970 to this day, in spite of the somersaults associated with attempts to extricate itself from this rut. This discouraging observation is a sorry reminder that Africa has lost 60 years as a result of following the advice of the World Bank and Europe.

So is there no hope? Is Africa condemned forever? Such an idea is not only unthinkable to me, as it is to all Africans; it actually also appears quite baseless, both theoretically and empirically. Certainly, evidence abounds of the dramatic involutions and total disintegration of societies and states which have resulted from the crisis of the exhausted/redundant colonial and post-colonial model: the spread of criminal delusions carried by politically reactionary forms of Islam in the Sahel countries (Mali, Niger and Chad) – launching from new bases created by the planned disintegration of Libya (now bases for Qaïda and Daesh) – Boko Haram in Nigeria, the Shebabs in Somalia and others; ethnic wars without end (Congo, Rwanda and Central African Republic) and similar threats elsewhere. These involutions are not only the predictable outcomes of the senseless pursuit of neoliberal policies, often supported by the poison of 'aid' (see the analysis of Tandon [2008]). They are also openly or surreptitiously supported by political strategies deployed regionally by the United States and Europe. The Sahelistan project pursued by the Islamists from the area needs to be analysed from the perspective I have elaborated here. The realization of the Saharo-Sahelian project, similar to that of Daesh in the Middle East, would be extremely useful in the systematic pillaging of the region's natural resources for the greatest benefit of imperialist monopolies. This is a model inspired and embodied by Saudi Arabia, which, as we know, represents an endless source of unconditional supply of oil for the west to squander, and for this reason of course, it is also a favoured ally of the west. Predictably, terrorist abuses are of little consequence in the face of the benefits to be gained from the west from this system (Amin 2013b).

But this saddening image is only half the real story. The proliferation of organized and unorganized social movements engaged in social and political struggles which unequivocally formulate legitimate demands (sometimes fragmented and at other times coherent and lucid) bears testimony to a real potential or the radicalization of progressive visions of the future. New initiatives could equally be undertaken by governments on the continent – these should not be dismissed lightly because of their timid ambitions or the ambiguities of their initial formulations. Associated with this is the opening of new paths for international cooperation with China and other countries of the South, to the practice of a more democratic tolerance of popular movements. These initiatives must be supported. The African peoples concerned have the right and duty to discuss such initiatives freely with their governments. It is also incumbent on popular movements to propose alternatives to enable the effective participation of the popular classes in the formulation and implementation of projects aiming to contribute to their development.

I need say no more. The concrete formulation of sovereign projects and of the objectives driving their initial phases makes sense only if they are serious, realistic and adapted to local conditions and the actual options open to the states and peoples concerned. One can do little more here than formulate broad strokes of the objectives which would characterize desirable forms of emergence, standing on one's own two feet, in other words, engaging a process of industrialization, on the one hand, and promoting the renewal of family-based peasant agriculture on the other; opening up to new partners in the global South (China and others) and to the best options that regional cooperation can offer; connecting advances in national sovereignty to policies promoting genuine social progress for the popular classes; and opening new channels to the democratization of politics and society. 'Experts' from the World Bank and the European Union are poorly equipped to contribute to such formulations. In the first instance, the task of defining appropriate paths towards these objectives has to be taken up by the best intellectual minds and militants from the national sphere – and later extended to encompass voices from the global South whose knowledge and experiences can usefully contribute to the debates.

The End of the Debate About Emergence?

The term 'emergent' was put into common usage by the World Bank a few years ago. It has been used by the historical powers of imperialism (the United States and its junior allies in Europe and Japan) as their Ministry of Propaganda. Orchestrating successive campaigns of ideological intoxication to give an appearance of legitimacy to the deployment of their strategies for globalized and financialized monopolies (the 'great' multinationals), it has allowed the United States, Europe and Japan to assume the control over these processes. By imposing a 'fashion' of always using the same name to designate – and hide – the same thing, in successive discourses (which always fail to deliver on their promises), the term 'emergent' has become meaningless.

The World Bank's response has been to launch the idea of 'emerging markets', where the choice of the word 'markets' is far from neutral. For the past four decades (since 1975, to be precise), growth levels amongst the imperialist Triad have collapsed. In other words, the expansion of markets in these economies has only slowed down. To acknowledge this would be to accept that the long and profound crisis affecting these economies risks raising questions about the capitalist system's ability to meet the simple popular expectations for an improvement in the living conditions of the majority. The World Bank has drawn attention to the fact that outside of the Triad (the 'old countries'), growth rates have been acceptable and, in some cases, exceptionally high (as in China). The expansion of markets equals GDP growth – at least according to the simplistic economic dogmas which feed World Bank thinking (or rather, non-thinking). According to this logic, the world system is not in crisis, only the 'old countries' are momentarily affected. The presence of 'emerging markets' provides opportunities to extract profits, in the first place, for 'old country' multinationals.

'Stages of growth', 'emerging markets', all originate in the same overly simplistic economic para-theory, which neither can nor wants to distinguish between concepts synonymous with growth and market expansion, on the one hand, and the concept of progressive development of society, on the other. Thinking in terms of development of society necessarily implies the articulation of a holistic and coherent theory of growth (measured by GDP, for want of a better indicator), of social progress, of the affirmation of national autonomy in its relation with others and of the transformation of its modes of governance over political power. The commonly used term 'development' itself is only meaningful if it produces an improvement in the living conditions of all, irrespective of class or social strata, or other distinctions (i.e., between men and women, nationals and immigrants, youth and adults, etc.). Growth which benefits only a minority, or even a majority whilst still excluding a significant number of the underprivileged, is not development. One can even be more demanding and consider that the improvement in the general conditions affecting all people is only valid if it actually aspires to the reduction of inequalities.

The analysis must also go beyond the purely economic aspect of the problem. The world is made up of nations and states, and is likely to continue on this foundation for a long time to come. It is, therefore, essential for development to enable 'emergent' nations (and not markets) to establish themselves in a way which allows them to grow stronger within the world system of nations and states. This will permit them to take an active role in shaping the operation of globalization; putting an end to the differentiation which opposes active states and shapes the world in which condemned states are compelled to adjust unilaterally, asymmetrically and passively.

Going further still, one can demand that material development (of productive capacity) should constitute the foundation stone of political progress, defined as active and increasingly decisive participation of people, particularly the majoritarian popular classes, in the decision-making processes at every level of social and political life. A good definition of democracy suggests a continuous process, probably endless.

Defining the concept of development in this way clearly calls for intellectual, political and ideological debates of major proportions, which in any case move away from the false discourses of 'growth', as advanced by conventional economists. It is in this context too that Marxist thought and the historical writings which inspired its elaboration in the area of global transformation need to be relocated. This is equally true of other thoughts/actions which have animated the workers' struggles in the west (such as historical social democracy), or those which have provided the building blocks for national liberation struggles in countries of Asia, Africa, Latin America and the Caribbean. Sam's remarkable work inscribes itself firmly in this defence of an innovative vision of an alternative for the countries of the South.

The World Bank not only evades the questions of the emergence of nations and their ambitions to become active protagonists in the world but also considers the questions of social justice which are of concern to the popular classes but damaging to the project of 'growth'. The consolidation of political power and the achievement of social advancement and autonomy of emergent nations undoubtedly constitute obstacles to the dominance of the Triad's multinationals and would, in this sense, certainly be 'damaging' to the World Bank's real objectives.

The World Bank is only interested in the expansion of 'solvent' markets. Its concept of 'development' congratulates itself on the development of a class system and the accession of the middle classes in the contemporary South, even if this comes at the expense and pauperization of the majority of the popular classes. Compelled to acknowledge the pauperization which occurs, the Bank contents itself with proposing 'plans for poverty reduction' which disregard the actual causes of poverty in the neoliberal policies it imposes.

A good example illustrating this contradiction is found in the neoliberal support of policies aiming at the systematic destruction of peasant agriculture in the South. These policies work for the benefit of international agribusiness and result in the consolidation of a minority of rich farmers and large landowners. These policies indisputably lead to the accelerated pauperization of hundreds of millions of peasants. On this topic, I refer the reader back to what I have written on the subject, with a few others, first amongst whom was Sam Moyo.

The underlying objective of the neoliberal project is to exploit the opportunity inherent in the expansion of markets in the South to reengage the process of accumulation in the historical centres of imperialism—in other words, the emergence of markets through the submersion of peoples and nations.

The emergence of nations is another question altogether, which has little to do with the emergence of World Bank-style markets. The global expansion of capitalism has always been, and remains, polarizing and imperialist in nature. The peoples and nations compelled to submit to the demands of accelerated capital accumulation imposed by the centres of the system have been quick to react. They have attempted to participate as independent partners in shaping this part of modern history, through 'emergence' projects, in the serious sense of the word, of nations. Not all of them are 'new' – amongst them are some of the 'oldest', such as China, Egypt, Iran and others.

Egypt's 'emergence' project proceeded successfully in the first two-thirds of the nineteenth century, from Mohamed Ali (1805) until the middle of Khedive Ismaïl's reign (1875). The project was defeated by the financial and military interventions of Great Britain, the major imperialist power of the time. In China, transformations brought about through the Taiping revolution (1855–65) and the reforms implemented by the imperialist Tseu Hi, Sun Yat-sen and the Kuomintang and, later, the Chinese communists constitute important and successive stages in the struggle for re-emergence of modern China. Confrontations with western and Japanese imperialism continue today in different forms. Ataturk, Reza Shah and Arab nationalisms (Nasserism, the Ba'ath Party, the Algerian FLN [Front de libération nationale/National Liberation Front]) also embody projects of national reconstruction and emergence. The Russian socialist revolution must also be placed in the wider frame of liberation struggles of peoples and nations on the peripheries of the system of globalized capitalism. I analyse the period of Bandung (1955–85) precisely as an expression of a large alliance of peoples, nations and states in Asia and Africa, engaged in a struggle for liberation from the forms of globalization of their time – an alliance which quite naturally found the favourable ear and support of the Soviet Union; an alliance of East and South not against the North but against a globalization dominated by the forces of historical imperialism in the North. The analysis I have made of the global expansion of capitalism elevates the struggles of people and nations in the peripheries to the ranks of a major factor in the transformation of the modern world (Amin 2015b).

As always in the history of humanity, the successes – not the failures – were remarkable, even though they were limited and relative. But progress has always been uneven and followed by regression. Undermined by their internal contradictions which generally opposed popular and potentially socialist aspirations ('emerging by withdrawing from capitalism') to the ambitions of local existing or aspiring bourgeoisies ('to avoid socialism'), these successes were provisionally derailed, at the end of the twentieth century.

The successes of Bandung benefitted all the nations involved – sub-Saharan Africa would probably not have gained its independence so quickly without Bandung; Gabon could not have collected its own incomes from oil without Bandung. The proof of this is in the counter-scenario of Niger, third largest producer of uranium in the world, which is prevented from benefitting from a large part of its mining income due to the triumph of neoliberal imperialism.

Do these sad contemporary realities express an absolute and final impossibility of meeting the outrageous ambitions of the peoples of the three continents? I do not believe so, because new waves of struggle by the nations of the South and the former East against the forms of globalization now in place, which assume the form of sovereign projects of emergence, are already visible. The World Bank conceived its ideological campaign under the name of 'emerging markets' precisely to constrain the entrenchment or advancement of projects of national sovereignty. Intended to play on major internal contradictions which characterize the major emancipatory struggles of yesterday and today, it aims to counter these projects by stoking illusions about the possibility of emergence into contemporary global capitalism.

There is a need for an interim assessment of the advances (and regressions) of the first years since the deployment of the second wave of resistance. Along with others, I am associated with these movements. I draw the following initial conclusions. China is at the heart of these debates (Amin 2013a). This is no coincidence, since the options currently at its disposal have their roots in the establishment of a uniquely daring project of national sovereignty whilst simultaneously remaining anchored in a fundamental contradiction which can be expressed in two complementary ways.

One way of addressing this dichotomy is as follows: Is the project aimed at emergence into the world system as it is, using the traditional capitalist methods/paths (private property, free enterprise, etc.), with at best a few mitigations (close negotiations with the dominant powers, the United States in the first instance; social concessions to the popular classes)? Or is it rather a project of emergence progressing in spite of its conscious conflict with logics underpinning the deployment of contemporary imperialistic capitalism?

The second way of considering the issue is to question the underlying reasons driving the state's active intervention in this project: whether its objective is transformation into a bourgeois project. In other words, would this imply Communist Party evolution in the direction of a successful Kuomintang? Or, alternatively, a project based on genuine popular concerns? Policies that have been implemented to promote renewal of the peasant economy would point towards the latter hypothesis. The case of China provides perhaps the best illustration of the tensions between the project's social dimensions and the class struggles which inherently develop in its framework, on the one hand, and the international dimension, on the other. I will not develop this point further but would refer the reader back to the suggestions which I, along with Sam and some others, have put forward in debates we have had on China.

The BRICS countries – Brazil, Russia, India, China and South Africa make up another special group in contemporary debates. One could also add a few other countries which are examples of apparent economic success: Mexico, Turkey, Thailand and Malaysia. In these cases, success is primarily defined in terms of the neoliberal ideology, as an example of the success of 'happy globalization'. My analysis of the experiences currently underway in these countries offers more nuanced conclusions. Russia hesitates between (destructive) submission to the contemporary form of globalization (a perspective which is defended by the country's comprador oligarchies) and a project of national renewal through the reconstruction of sovereign state capitalism. India and Brazil's projects are truncated and devoid of substance. South Africa is not engaged in any ordinary project of emergence.

The crisis currently taking place in Brazil actually signals the unravelling of the World Bank discourse on 'emerging markets'. As usual, propositions orchestrated by the World Bank, and rapidly contradicted by reality, have been short-lived. They have necessitated constant reformulations of their actual objectives, without being able to elude what constitutes the Bank's exclusive and permanent objective: the protection of finance capital and the interests of imperialist powers.

Brazil's emergence was from the outset established on a fundamental contradiction. On the one hand, the PT (Partido dos Trabalhadores [Workers' Party]) governments have undertaken important progressive reforms which have enabled growth to take place by opening up new internal markets. But, on the other hand, these governments did not challenge the dominant positions occupied by private Brazilian capital, which is both monopolistic and comprador in character. The type of growth engaged by these capitalist forces was established primarily on the back of natural resource exports (oil, minerals and capitalist agribusiness production) and integration into financial globalization. This odd couple worked as long as circumstances allowed it. However, under conditions where the offensive launched by financialized global monopolies led to a collapse in raw material prices, the balance of payments deficit compounded by the Brazilian currency's devaluation put an end to the much vaunted Brazilian miracle. Growth rates have collapsed and the public purse is no longer able to finance social programmes. Under conditions which are undoubtedly different, though for the same reasons, India's emergence remains vulnerable.

A new financial crisis, more serious than that of 2008, is currently taking shape on the horizon. Even though financial monopolies have been able to extract considerable profits from the opening up of markets in the South, and the pillaging of their natural resources, these profits have not been reinvested in the expansion of productive systems in the North. On the contrary, they have been accumulated as income by highly financially solvent monopolies to feed an infinitely spiralling growth in speculation. The inevitable financial demise of this system will put a term to illusions of emergence.

China is in a better position than others to face up to these financial troubles, precisely because to date, its financial system remains outside the system of globalized finance, and the country continues to pursue a model of non-capitalist agricultural renewal, as I have discussed elsewhere. This specificity has allowed China to better resist a reversal of fortunes by investing directly in the development of domestic markets, with the result that its growth rate has only dropped from 10 to 7 per cent per annum. If China is still outside the globalized financial system when the crisis hits, it will be in a position to reinforce its position in the world – the yuan will represent an important refuge to capital fleeing the devaluation of both the US dollar and euro. But if, in the interim, China has entered into the system of globalized finance, it will pay the exorbitant price of this decision and suffer a similar fate to that of the countries of the South. The imperial powers will be placed in a position to threaten its detractors with their superior weapon: military intervention.

The discourse about 'emerging markets' is already in decline. In view of the approaching financial catastrophe, the World Bank considers it more important to redirect its propaganda efforts and to exercise all its pressures to ensure the entrance of countries which have to date been recalcitrant to do so, namely, China, Russia and, to a lesser extent, India. The argument presented to convince them of such a path is that their entrance would purportedly reduce the risks of catastrophe. This is untrue. It would only enable the costs of repairing and rebuilding the system to be more easily transferred to the South; this is, in fact, the real objective of new discourses. Brazil only provides a tragic illustration of what others can expect.

Sovereign Projects are Needed for African Countries to Restore Hope for Development

Engagement is necessary with what we call sovereign projects – in other words, projects which are conceived of by us, for us and which are to the greatest extent independent of the tendencies and pressures exerted by the global capitalist system. Industrialization must be the goal of sovereign projects. There can be no development without industrialization. Even agricultural development, through efficient modernization, is impossible without industries to support it. It is necessary to walk on one's own two feet.

What goes by the name 'international aid', notably in African countries – in other words, aid extended by the World Bank, or by development agencies from western imperialist countries, the United States or the European Union – is not genuine development aid. It is a financial support intended to maintain our position as subordinate countries, and thus to reproduce underdevelopment.

The only solution is to forget all this and think differently. We must start thinking in terms of sovereign projects. Is this possible? Yes. The African continent is often dismissed as 'handicapped' by virtue of having generally small countries. This is not true of all African countries: Egypt has a population of 92 million, Ethiopia of 90 million and Nigeria of 180 million – these are not small countries. Nonetheless, the main structures of Nigeria's economy are not significantly different from those of a small country like Benin. One could say that in spite of its population of 180 million, Nigeria is just like fifteen Benins, nothing more. The advantage of size is not put to good use, even by large African countries.

Becoming engaged on the path of autonomous development, based on sovereign projects, is not easy for anyone, even China. For smaller countries of average size, the challenges are obviously greater. But there is always a margin, even though this margin may be very limited at the outset. If certain countries were to initiate autonomous development, independently and on the basis of sovereign projects (even modest ones to start off with), this could quickly snowball into something much greater. It would create favourable conditions for closer links, political solidarity, and, no doubt, for economic and possibly financial cooperation between African countries and the global South more generally. We could, in this manner, become active in shaping the world and be in a position to impose ourselves as such. Even though this may not be easy, we can also approach China which has now become financially powerful. We have witnessed the articulation of various proposals for cooperation during the meetings between China and African states in Johannesburg. The ball is in our court. We now have the prerogative to seize it and to open negotiations. But one can only open negotiations if one knows what one wants.

The constraint lies with the ruling classes. The ruling classes in African countries, such as those in Asian and Latin American countries, have largely been produced and shaped by the integration of their own countries as subaltern and dominated partners into the system of globalized capitalism. To describe these, I use the term 'comprador bourgeoisie' – which was first coined by Chinese communists, a long time ago, in the 1920s. The word comes from Portuguese and means 'traders, buyers, intermediaries' between the dominant imperialist world and the local world of notably peasant producers.

Our dominant classes are comprador classes. I would even say that state bureaucracies, which are neither entrepreneurial classes nor property owners in the capitalist sense, also constitute largely 'comprador' bureaucratic classes. The challenge, then, effectively exists in our own environment, at home with us; it is to be found in the actual nature of the dominant and political classes. But the deployment of social movements can modify these givens and thus create the conditions for coming out of the impasse.

It is in this framework that the contribution made by Sam Moyo's work has been of the greatest significance.

This article was originally published in *Agrarian South: Journal of Political Economy*, Vol. 5, Nos. 2–3, 2016. Copyright 2016 © Centre for Agrarian Research and Education for South (CARES), New Delhi. All rights reserved. Reproduced with the permission of the copyright holders and the publishers, SAGE Publications India Pvt. Ltd, New Delhi.

References

Amin, Samir (2008), *L'Eveil du Sud* (Awakening of the South), Paris: Le Temps des Cerises.

——— (2013a), 'China 2013', *Monthly Review*, 64 (10), http://monthlyreview.org/2013/03/01/china-2013/, accessed 12 March 2016.

——— (2013b), 'Rescuing Mali from Islamist militants', *Pambazuka*, 616, http://www.pambazuka.org/governance/ rescuing-mali-islamist-militants, accessed 12 March 2016.
——— (2014a), *Implosion of Capitalism*, London: Pluto Press.
——— (2014b), 'Understanding the Political Economy of Contemporary Africa', *Africa Development*, 39 (1), 15–36.
——— (2014c), 'Popular Movements Toward Socialism', *Monthly Review*, 66 (2), http://monthlyreview.org/archives/2014/ volume-66-issue-02-june/, accessed 12 March 2016.
——— (2015a), 'Agriculture Paysanne, Agriculture Familiale Moderne', in Bernard Founou, ed., *Réponses Radicales aux Crises Agraires en Afrique*, Dakar: CODESRIA: 14–33.
——— (2015b), 'From Bandung (1955) to 2015', *International Critical Thought*, 5 (4): 518–28.
Tandon, Yash (2008), *Ending Aid Dependency*, Cape Town: Fahamu Books.

16
In Conversation with Sam

Issa G. Shivji

In this essay, I intend to raise some agrarian issues as debating points that were very close to Sam and for which he was passionate.[1] We often discussed these issues, but never exhaustively. I raise them, somewhat tentatively, to contribute to the ongoing debate. All are, in a sense, classical questions, very commonly debated among Marxists, but we have to address them in a new, concrete situation. First is the much discussed yet elusive category of 'the peasant', in both its dimensions, analytical and empirical. Is 'peasant' a useful category of analysis? Do peasants exist as a social group? Second, linked to the peasant question is the national question. The third, in my view a central question, is the form and character of accumulation in the agrarian sector. The fourth relates to social agency for transformation and forms of its organization. All these issues are evident in Sam's writings spread all over his numerous chapters in edited books.

The Peasant Question

For Sam, if I understood him correctly, the agrarian question in Africa was a combination of the peasant and land question. And, of course, for historical reasons, both of these issues manifested themselves vividly in Zimbabwe, the terrain of his work and study. He had no doubt in his mind of the need and the necessity for land reform in the classical sense of confiscating land from the landlord and redistributing it to the peasant, whether through state policies from the top or grassroots struggles from the bottom. In real life, there is no Chinese wall between the two. Top–down and bottom–up may be interlinked, as indeed it happened in Zimbabwe. In Zimbabwe, it was the struggle of the war veterans from below which forced Mugabe to accelerate land reform from above (Moyo 2001; Moyo and Yeros 2005). While Sam thought redistribution would be the correct approach to a resolution of the land question, at least in the former settler colonies, it could not be generalized to other situations. In Tanzania, for example, where you have a small peasantry, I argue that land reform really means land tenure reform, which would address the question of insecurity of tenure of the small producer, both peasant and pastoralist. Sam probably agreed with me on this, but we never managed to tease out all the nuances of land reform in Africa and much less theorize it.

In regard to the peasant question, the debate that exercised Sam's mind a lot was the position taken by some agrarian experts from the North arguing that both the peasant and the land question are passé, and that what really exists is the labour question (Bernstein 2002; Bryceson 2000). First, they argued that the peasant no longer exists; rather, the rural sector has been de-peasantized and diversified, whereby livelihoods depend on multiple sources and not only on land. Hence the second point followed, which was that the issue of the producer in a rural setting could be best conceptualized as the labour question rather than the land/peasant question. I may have slightly oversimplified this position, but I think it does capture the essentials of the argument of the 'labour question' theorists. Sam felt that this position, which in his view was erroneous, was gaining currency because it had access to international mainstream journals like the *Journal of Peasant Studies*, where African writers did not have the same access. This is what led Sam and other like-minded scholars from the South to found the journal *Agrarian South*.

Sam worked on land reform in Zimbabwe where he advocated land redistribution, which would in fact lead to re-peasantization or re-constitution of the peasantry, rather than de-peasantization. Understandably, therefore, Sam could not accept the argument of de-peasantization. The question, however, still remains as to what would be the future trajectory of the re-constituted peasantry. This is precisely the issue that we have been discussing in our summer schools. I think he, together with some of us, believed that there are two possible paths which the peasantry could take: either in the direction of coming together in some kind of co-operative structures – the desirable path; or it would fall under imperialism and be subjected to exploitation through various forms of primitive accumulation, which characterizes the current fate of the peasantry in much of Africa – obviously an undesirable path. Sometimes, Sam and Paris used the term 'semi-proletarian' to describe the later type of peasantry. I think the concept of semi-proletarian in this context is not sufficiently theorized. We need to discuss it further. As I said, I am only flagging the issue which we need to discuss and debate in greater depth.

The National Question

The second question that was very close to Sam is the national question, which obviously is linked to the agrarian question. For him, the core of the national question, the core of the anti-imperialist question if you like, lay in the agrarian question, and unless you confront the agrarian question, you cannot confront the national question. Maybe they do not both stand and fall together, maybe equating them was somewhat stretching the truth, but occasionally, it is permissible to exaggerate the truth to drive home the point. And I believe that if you read Sam carefully, this is the message you get, the way he links the national question and the agrarian question. Once we talk of the national question, inevitably we have to deal with the issue of who would be its carrier in the actually existing conditions of Africa today. In the 1980s, we had intense debates on both the existence of the national bourgeoisie in Africa and, if it did exist, its capacity to address and resolve the national question, which per force is an anti-imperialist question. Admittedly, we were wedded to the Fanonist idea of the bankruptcy of the 'national bourgeoisie'.

Developments since, at least in Africa, have proved him right. In a capitalist-commodity economy, to be sure, bourgeois elements are born all the time, but get quickly compradorized under imperialist globality, as I argued in my 1987 article (Shivji 1987). On this, I think Sam and I did not quite see eye to eye. I felt that Sam and Paris exaggerated the national bourgeois character of the Mugabe regime. They described the Zimbabwean state as a 'radicalized state', which itself I found problematic as an analytical category. They identified the whole of the black bourgeoisie as part of the pro-land reform 'nationalist block'. In my view, this was too sweeping a statement and arose from a failure to make a clear distinction between a national and a comprador bourgeoisie. There was perhaps also a conflating of the historical moment with a longer-term tendency. Sam rightly felt that we need to debate this question concretely in the context of a particular historical conjuncture, as we cannot simply generalize it.

There is also the more fundamental question of imperialism. At particular historical moments, some elements of the bourgeoisie may exhibit nationalist tendencies, but these usually do not congeal into a national bourgeoisie because they do not have a consistent anti-imperialist position. I know that the issue of imperialism does not feature these days in the dominant left discourse, yet for some of us from Africa, imperialism remains at the centre of understanding our conditions.

The Question of Accumulation

The third question around which our debates were centred was that of accumulation. I think this is one issue that we need to investigate and theorize. The character and form of accumulation under neoliberalism in the agrarian South would help us to understand better the agrarian question. I have been arguing for some time now that the dominant tendency of accumulation is primitive accumulation, as opposed to accumulation by expanded production. Both tendencies exist side by side, and the tension between the two helps us to historicize the development and trajectory of social struggles. I submit that the *differentia specifica* of primitive accumulation is that accumulation or exploitation cuts into the necessary consumption of the producer. This is another debate that we need to take further.

In my talks, lectures and writings, I found David Harvey's analysis quite handy, and I often quoted it. I think Sam was not always comfortable with this. He believed that Harvey was too Eurocentric and failed to integrate centre–periphery relations into his analysis. I think Sam was probably right. David Harvey has no doubt revisited Rosa Luxemburg's thesis in a refreshing way, and I think that is useful. But his writings do not fully take account of imperialism in the South, in particular in Africa. We need to debate very specifically forms of accumulation at particular historical moments and tease out all the nuances. Nonetheless, in my view, we have not done enough work to theorize sufficiently the question of accumulation. Unless we do that, we cannot really get to the heart of the agrarian question.

The Question of Social Agency and Organization

Finally, we debated the question of agency and organization. Of course, Sam was no armchair intellectual; he saw his work as a theoretical praxis. Therefore, for him, issues of social struggles and organization became predominant. I know he did not theorize a lot on this issue in his writings. However, in his talks and conversations he was extremely sympathetic and was attracted by the landless movement and social movements that deal with land and peasants. You can notice this in some of his writings, in his visits particularly to Brazil, and his great solidarity with the movements of the landless of Brazil and South Africa. Some of the first people to express their great shock, sorrow and sadness when Sam passed on were the activists of the landless movement in South Africa.

On the question of social agency, I have been suggesting for a while that the category of 'working people', rather than working class, as a harbinger of fundamental transformation would serve us well – working people assimilating the peasantry, the proletariat, however small, and the precariat of various kinds which exist in our countries in the so-called 'informal sector'. In our discussions we touched on this, but there were doubts. Again, that is something that we need to theorize vigorously, the question of social agency and organization.

As I said in the beginning, I am only flagging these issues. I hope we can have more discussions in the summer schools and in the pages of this journal [*Agrarian South*], as we pay tribute to Sam for his great scholarship and social commitment to the liberation of the African peoples.

This article was originally published in *Agrarian South: Journal of Political Economy*, Vol. 5, Nos. 2–3, 2016. Copyright 2016 © Centre for Agrarian Research and Education for South (CARES), New Delhi. All rights reserved. Reproduced with the permission of the copyright holders and the publishers, SAGE Publications India Pvt. Ltd, New Delhi.

Note

[1] This is a reconstruction from the transcription of my speech given at the Colloquium in Memory of Professor Sam Moyo, held in Harare, Zimbabwe, on 18 January 2016.

References

Bernstein, Henry (2002), 'Land Reform: Taking a Long(er) View', *Journal of Agrarian Change*, 2 (1): 433–63.

Bryceson, Deborah (2000), 'African Peasants' Centrality and Marginality: Rural Labour Transformations', in Deborah Bryceson, Cristóbal Kay and Jos Mooij, eds, *Disappearing Peasantries? Rural Labour in Africa, Asia and Latin America*, London: ITDG Publishing: 37–63.

Moyo, Sam (2001), 'The Land Occupation Movement and Democratization in Zimbabwe: Contradictions of Neoliberalism', *Millennium: Journal of International Studies*, 30 (2): 311–30.

Moyo, Sam and Paris Yeros (2005), 'Land Occupations and Land Reform in Zimbabwe: Towards the National Democratic Revolution', in Sam Moyo and Paris Yeros, eds, *Reclaiming the Land: The Resurgence of Rural Movements in Africa, Asia and Latin America*, London: Zed Books: 165–208.

Shivji, Issa G. (1987), 'The Roots of Agrarian Crisis in Tanzania: A Theoretical Perspective', *Eastern African Social Science Research Review*, 3 (1): 111–34.

17

Looking Back at Karl Marx's Analysis of Capitalism in the Context of Colonialism

Utsa Patnaik

I

Many millions of words were written on the occasion of the 150th anniversary of the publication of the first volume of *Capital* in 1867 and the bicentenary of Karl Marx's birth on 5 May 1818. The historic contribution made by 'the greatest living thinker' (in the words of Engels at Marx's grave) opened up an entire new intellectual continent of history (to paraphrase Louis Althusser 1971: 13–14) and inspired a new era of revolutionary praxis. This brief essay will be limited to discussing critically a particular aspect of Marx's vast *opus*, namely the relation that his work bears to an analysis of the contribution of colonialism and imperialism to the rise of capitalism as a global system. In the process we will necessarily critique the particular variant of 'Marxism' propagated in the North which entirely ignores colonialism and imperialism, and seeks to project a purely internal dynamic for the rise of capitalist industrialization in the core countries.

Marx spent the first thirty-one years of his life, up to 1849, in various European cities, engaged in developing his critique of idealist philosophy and writing for short-lived socialist journals. Hounded by censorship and state persecution, he moved along with Engels to London in the summer of 1849, and lived there for the rest of his life, passing away in 1883, a few weeks before his 65th birthday. Thus, during the period that Marx and Engels were formulating their path-breaking analysis of class exploitation and accumulation as the core reality of capitalism, they lived in Britain, the first country in the world to undergo capitalist industrialization and the centre of the largest colonial empire of the time, completely dwarfing the possessions of rival European nations. Yet, the other reality of the impact of the possession of colonies on metropolitan accumulation and industrial development was not addressed in his writings on political economy, neither in *A Contribution to the Critique of Political Economy*, published in 1859, nor in Volume I of *Capital*, published in 1867. As we know, the second and third volumes of *Capital* were edited by Engels from manuscripts and published long after the first volume – Volume II in 1885 and Volume III in 1894, over a decade after Marx's death. The rigorous, formal model of capitalist accumulation that Marx developed in the three volumes of *Capital* deals entirely with a *closed economy*, and international trade does not figure in it, and nor does colonialism, other than descriptive passages on slavery and many references to colonial loot and plunder. It is this fact that has given rise to the almost complete ignoring of colonialism and imperialism in the present-day Northern tradition of Marxist writings, most of which engages in a mechanical and purely textual interpretation of Marx's main works.

But two facts make it clear that Marx was well aware of colonial exploitation, and even, towards the end of his life, of the drain of wealth from India. First, in his articles contributed to the *New York Daily Tribune* that commented on and analysed current events, Marx frequently referred to Britain's exploitation of India, and he also referred clearly to the drain of wealth in a letter written a mere two years before his death. His extremely insightful writings on India in his contributions to the *New York Daily Tribune* have been available in *On Colonialism* from Progress Publishers, Moscow, and a recent collection has been put together under the title *Marx on India*, edited by Iqbal Husain, with an introduction by Irfan Habib.

Second, if we study Marx's intellectual project as he himself summarized it in his *Preface* to the 1859 book, *A Contribution to the Critique of Political Economy*, it becomes very clear that Marx never meant his analysis to remain confined to a closed economy, and fully intended to study the global working of capitalism under the topics of 'the State, foreign trade, world market'. He writes the following:

> I examine the system of bourgeois economy in the following order: *capital, landed property, wage-labour; the State, foreign trade, world market.* The economic conditions of existence of the three great classes into which modern bourgeois society is divided are analysed under the first three headings; the interconnection of the other three headings is self-evident. (Marx 1977)

In practice, however, Marx could not complete his stated intellectual project. The first three topics, namely the analysis of 'capital, landed property and wage labour', took up the remainder of his entire working life, and this was carried out within a formally closed capitalist system without external trade. Marx's seminal contribution as regards understanding the meaning of *exploitation* under capitalism was to demonstrate that although the worker *appeared* to get the full reward for his labour in the form of a market wage for a day worked, this wage embodied only the *necessary labour* required to reproduce his life for a day and this was only part of the working day, the remaining part being *surplus labour* whose product was appropriated as surplus value by the capitalist. The market transaction of wage payment for labour which *appeared* to be an exchange of equivalents thus masked the reality of the appropriation of surplus labour by the capitalist in the form of surplus value.

There was, however, another form of exploitation which was extremely important for capitalist accumulation from the beginning in today's advanced countries, but whose nature and underlying mechanism was never clearly explicated – and this remains the case to this day – and that was the exploitation of the subjugated peasants and workers in the colonies. The crucial point here is that the colonizing power obtained the right of extracting economic surplus – in India, for example, it was Britain's right of collecting taxes, with the taxes on land being the most important. The peasant either paid tax directly or paid rent to the landlord who in turn paid tax to the state. A large part of these taxes making up the budgetary revenues was set aside as 'expenditure abroad' (the items under this included Home Charges, dividends and interest on debt incurred in wars outside India, all payable in sterling). This part of the revenues was used by the government for 'buying' export goods, from the very same peasants and workers who had paid the taxes in the first place. Although the peasants *appeared* to be paid for their products since cash was exchanged for their output at the market price, they were not actually paid because this cash came out of their own tax contribution. All that happened was that a large part of their own tax contribution was made to change its form from cash to goods for export to the world, whose international earnings were taken by Britain.

This abnormal use of internal taxes converted to international purchasing power and taken by the ruling country was the essence of the 'drain of wealth' from Britain's most lucrative colony, India. It was first pointed out by those brilliant Indian pioneers, Dadabhai Naoroji and R.C. Dutt, but the mechanism of the drain has not been understood, nor was the drain ever mentioned by modern Marxists from Northern academia, with a very few honourable exceptions.

If we assume that all imports from Britain into India were actually necessary, then the drain of wealth can be measured by the global export surplus of commodities from India, which was 'unrequited' as per the classic and correct term used by the pioneers. It was 'unrequited' because the entire gold and foreign exchange earned from the world by Indian peasants and workers through their commodity export surplus were kept by Britain for its own use. Even the rupee equivalent of their international earnings was never paid out in India as an addition to the money supply (as it happens in a sovereign country like independent India today). The rupee equivalent was paid out to producers out of their own taxes, hence they were not actually paid although they *appeared* to be paid. The producers – peasants and artisans – did not themselves understand the trickery involved because the agent who collected the rent or tax from them and the agent who bought their produce out of the tax were different, and the two acts – collecting taxes and buying produce – took place at different times, so the actual connection between them was not obvious.

We must remember that all imports from Britain were not actually necessary for India since manufactured yarn and cloth imports were dumped on the deliberately unprotected Indian market, inducing very harmful decline of her own manufactures and creating massive unemployment. Provided we remember that export surplus as a measure of 'drain' does not capture the actual harm to the Indian economy, we can still use it to measure the transfer of international purchasing power to itself that Britain managed to accomplish by defrauding Indian producers of their earnings. This author has estimated the drain of wealth from India, on a highly underestimated basis, over the period from 1765 to 1938 as totalling £9.2 trillion. This comes to more than ten times the current value gross national product of Britain in 2015 (U. Patnaik 2017).

In Marx's writings on India contributed to the *New York Daily Tribune*, we find a very clear discussion in many places of the deindustrializing effects on India of the imports of cotton yarn and cloth from England. Marx wrote in detail on the discriminating policy England followed by banning, from 1700, the consumption of Asian textiles within the country (profitable re-exports of Indian textiles mainly to Europe were carried out by the Company), while the Indian market was kept completely open to imports. Marx gives valuable statistics from official sources which indicate that, by the late 1840s, India's export surplus with Britain disappeared as imports poured into the deliberately unprotected Indian market. Of course, India's export surplus with the rest of the world was rising fast, and it was the earnings from this global export surplus that Britain appropriated for itself. The period 1860 to 1880, in particular, saw an enormous rise in India's global export surplus, as well as a rise in expenditure by Britain using these earnings. But there is little indication of awareness of the mechanism of the drain of wealth even by the end of the 1870s in Marx's writings, although references abound to the English taking 'loot' and 'tribute' from India.

It is all the more interesting and intriguing that we suddenly find, in his letter to Danielson written on 19 February 1881, Marx giving a remarkably precise and detailed description of the drain from India to Britain. The well-known passage is reproduced below:

> In India serious complications, if not a general outbreak, is in store for the British government. What the English take from them annually in the form of rent, dividends for *railways useless to the Hindus*, pensions for military and civil servicemen, for Afghanistan and other wars etc. etc. – what they take from them *without any equivalent* and quite apart from what they appropriate to themselves annually within India, speaking only of the *value of the commodities* the Indians have *gratuitously and annually to send over to England* – it amounts to more than the total sum of incomes of the sixty millions of agricultural and industrial labourers of India! This is a bleeding process, with a vengeance. (Marx 1968; first emphasis added, remaining emphases in the original)

If the source of the above passage was not known to the reader, it would be reasonable for her to think that Dadabhai Naoroji himself was the author, given the use of the term 'without any equivalent', the use of the telling phrase 'the *value of the commodities* the Indians have gratuitously and annually to *send over* to England', and the precise reference to the incomes of Indian workers – at that time the only rough estimate of India's national income available was that made by Naoroji. We do not find any such clear formulation in Marx's earlier writings. It is well within the bounds of probability that Marx actually met Dadabhai Naoroji who had been resident in London for many years, perhaps through Henry Hyndman who was closely associated with Naoroji from the 1870s onwards. Naoroji had helped Hyndman with information and arguments for the latter's book on famine in India. Hyndman became a socialist, however, only after reading Marx's work rather late, around 1880, and is known to have invited Marx and his daughter to his house in early 1881. If Marx had known of the mechanism of the drain of wealth from India earlier, surely he would not have waited until 1881 to mention it, a mere two years before his death.

II

Some of the most powerful passages on the transformative role of capitalism in raising the level of productive forces are to be found, paradoxically, not in the writings of the votaries of capitalism but in Marx's *Capital*, presaged by the passages describing capital's destructive role in the *Communist Manifesto*. While capital 'tears asunder' all production relations based on direct patriarchal personal relations of servitude and destroys traditional society, this is seen as clearing the way for an immense upsurge of productive forces, as the extraction of surplus value from employing free wage-paid labour becomes the dominant production mode. Marx was insistent that the capitalist growth path, however productive in the technological sense, always leads to the creation of unemployment, to a deliberately maintained 'reserve army of labour', and it leads, therefore, to absolute poverty of the exploited majority, the working class at one pole of the social structure and to the accumulation of riches at the other. Capital itself eventually creates the social conditions for its own overthrow and the advance to an egalitarian socialist society.

Critics have said that Karl Marx was wrong; his predictions, in particular on the absolute immiserization of the working class, were not borne out by developments in Europe since there was substantial improvement in the living standard of the masses, nor did the insurrectionary phase of early industrial society in the 1840s ever develop later into a revolutionary upsurge of the working class. If we view capital as working within the narrow confines of national economies alone, then this criticism would be correct. But there is no reason to view capital as operating within national economies alone. From the very inception of the capitalist mode of production, capitalist accumulation has arisen not merely from domestic but from global trade and investment flows, and has involved the subjugation and enslavement of peoples of non-European origin. Marx's prediction of the accumulation of wealth at one pole and of misery and impoverishment at the other turns out to have been entirely correct, provided we look at the dynamics of capitalist accumulation in the global context.

As we have seen, Marx himself fully intended to analyse the global working of capitalism but his intellectual project was cut short by premature death. Indeed, how much can we expect of one individual, battling financial problems, his own ill-health and the early death of four of his seven children? The fact that Marx could not complete his own project does not mean that we should read his existing works in a scholastic manner, treating them as so many scriptures, but some intellectually lazy Northern 'Marxists' today are prone to do precisely that. Any discussion of colonialism and imperialism is anathema to them, because Marx himself did not *formally* analyse these phenomena. The subsequent brilliant analyses by Rosa Luxemburg of colonialism and by Lenin of imperialism, and his conceptual integration of the peasantry as a revolutionary force along with wage workers, were vital steps in the direction of a completion of Marx's unfinished project.

The actual history of capitalism raises important theoretical issues regarding the validity of associating capitalism with 'free' wage labour as contrasted with serfdom and slavery under pre-capitalist modes of production. In reality, the revival of modern slavery over a millennium after the slavery of the ancient world was the dubious gift of the rise of the capitalist mode of production. The same eighteenth- and nineteenth-century French and English landlords who leased out their land by contract to capitalist tenant farmers at home and obtained capitalist rent also operated plantations based on slave labour in the Caribbean to extract slave rent. Does it follow that it is incorrect to associate the rise of capitalism with the 'freedom' of the worker? No, for free wage labour is an indisputable fact in the core countries, but so is lack of freedom imposed on peripheral populations.

The Marxist analysis of the relation between the growth of free wage labour at one pole of capitalist accumulation and of chattel slavery at the other pole, an analysis which is yet to be undertaken, must take into account the dialectical interaction of these two antithetical forms of exploitation. The freedom of workers in the core countries was historically conditional on the imposition of unfreedom on non-European peoples. The capitalist ruling classes imposed servitude on many non-European peoples, forcibly removed them from their communities, enslaved and transported millions of persons to the other side of the globe to work plantations for their own benefit, treating slave rent as profit. After the formal abolition of slavery, another form of unfreedom continued under the indentured labour system. At the same time, the capitalist ruling classes bowed in their home countries to the pressure of struggles by wage labour for political representation and economic improvement through collective bargaining. The bargaining power of wage labour in the core countries necessarily improved through the dual route of out-migration of the unemployed which reduced the reserve army of labour, and the massive inflow of colonial transfers which boosted domestically generated profits substantially, serving to raise mass living standards.

A few words are in order regarding the unfettered out-migration of Europeans on a large scale to the lands they had seized from indigenous peoples in the Americas and elsewhere. Its complement was the creation of a bloated reserve army of labour in the subjugated, colonially exploited countries, as a consequence of resource transfers through colonial exploitation. It is these features that allowed the industrializing nations to *externalize the acute internal contradictions* which would otherwise have torn their societies apart, and served to undermine the potential for revolution at the core, while at the same time the conditions were generated for a shifting of the locus of struggles to the global South. Historically in the core capitalist countries, many millions more were displaced than were ever absorbed in non-agricultural activities within the boundaries of these countries. The nature of capitalist growth has always been, and continues to be, such that it engenders unemployment daily, hourly and on a mass scale. The objective of capitalist production is to maximize profits for capitalists, not to provide employment to the existing unemployed, nor are capitalists or the state they control usually concerned with ensuring minimum livelihoods for the labouring poor.

To illustrate the effects of permanent out-migration as a solution to labour displacement from agriculture, let us consider Britain, the first industrial nation. Small farmers evicted in the course of enclosures and the artisans thrown out of jobs as machinery was first introduced became vagrants of whom only a fraction found employment in the growing factory sector. Even though the early machines two centuries ago were very simple, they displaced labour on a massive scale – a single spinning 'jenny' had 80 spindles, needed only one to two workers to operate and threw 78 traditional spinners in Europe out of work (jennies with up to 800 spindles each were known to be used before being replaced by mule spindles). The effect of the much higher level of labour-displacing technology and of automation today in developing countries is to produce jobless growth; indeed, many sectors in India are seeing job-loss growth.

In Britain, the unemployed and the poorly paid workers alike rose in insurrection against the state under the banner of Chartism in the 1840s – only the safety valve of emigration prevented revolution. Britain's population was small, only 12 million in 1821, but 16 million Britons emigrated between 1821 and 1915, making up nearly two-fifths of all Europeans who emigrated to the lands they had seized from indigenous peoples mainly in the Americas. On average, half of the entire annual increment to its population left Britain every year for a century. For India to be able to export its displaced peasants and unemployed on a similar scale in the six decades from independence up to the present, at least 400 million persons should have emigrated and 10 million unskilled persons should continue to emigrate permanently each year. The actual total size of the Indian diaspora is 17 million.

Unlike the populations of European colonizing countries that seized global land resources on an unprecedented scale, the displaced peasants and workers in developing countries like India and China today have nowhere to go. The solution to their unemployment and livelihood problems, therefore, has to be sought in a thought-out alternative to following the anarchic, mindless path of capitalism.

In the present era of globalization, since the route of massive out-migration to new economic frontiers is closed for advanced country populations as well, the unemployment-generating effects of the capitalist trajectory manifest themselves much more clearly and to devastating effect. The employment crises produced by the capitalist system can no longer be camouflaged to anything like the same extent as in the past. True, the burden of unemployment is still sought to be externalized through policies pushed by the global financial institutions, but their success is more limited and these policies are constantly contested.

The capitalist system of production rules virtually the entire world today after the break-up of socialist Soviet Union in the early 1990s, and the increasing market and profit orientation of economic policies in China since the 1980s, where private property has been re-introduced over significant areas of activity. Despite the deep financial and employment crises which have engulfed the advanced capitalist nations, we see therefore a certain arrogance, a *hubris*, which marks the class of finance capitalists that continues to rampage over the world seeking to remake it after its own image, against a backdrop where alternative models of socialism have either collapsed or exist only in a formal sense. It is only a matter of time, however, before there is a resurgence of progressive movements combating these developments, for the present situation is not a viable one in any long-term sense, whether in the industrially advanced world or in our own countries.

An earlier version of this essay in the Bengali language, 'Upanibeshbader Poriprekhitey Punjibad Samparkey Karl Marx-er Bisleshankey Phirey Dekha', was carried by the journal *Deshkal Bhabna* (Kolkata), Special Number (Bicentenary), Vol. 9 (4), 2017: 5–9.

References

Althusser, L. (1971), *For Marx*, translated by Ben Brewster, London: Allen Lane.

Marx, K. ([1881] 1968), 'Letter to Danielson, 19 February 1881', in *Marx–Engels Correspondence*, translated by Donna Torr, International Publishers (first published by Gestamtausgaben in 1968), https://www.marxists.org/archive/marx/works/1881/letters/81_02_19.htm, accessed 17 October 2019.

Marx, K. ([1859] 1977), 'Preface' to *A Contribution to A Critique of Political Economy*, Moscow: Progress Publishers.

Patnaik, U. (2017), 'Revisiting the Drain or Transfers from India to Britain in the Context of Global Diffusion of Capitalism', in Shubhra Chakrabarti and Utsa Patnaik, eds, *Agrarian and Other Histories: Essays for Binay Bhushan Chaudhuri*, New Delhi: Tulika Books.

18

Making Sense of Global Capitalism in the Twenty-first Century

C.P. Chandrasekhar and Jayati Ghosh

Sam Moyo was one of the most remarkable development thinkers of his generation, someone who combined a sharp analytical approach and a wide political economy sweep with serious and painstaking empirical work. His untimely passing has left a void that is impossible to fill, not only because of his extraordinary intellectual generosity, deep political commitment and the humanism (and sense of fun) that he brought to all his interactions. We miss him greatly also because Sam still had so much to contribute in terms of providing insights into how capitalism and imperialism work, how they express themselves within economies by entangling with domestic class relations, and how such forces can be meaningfully opposed. We have learned so much from Sam over the years and continue to rely on his important insights in so many ways. In this small tribute to him, we draw on the strand of his work that considered the unfolding of imperialism and its impact, to examine the issues of changing structures and distribution in the global economy and responses to neoliberal capitalism in this century.

We argue that, despite recent changes in the geographical distribution of economic growth (and in particular, the rise of China and other economies in East Asia), the fundamental forces that made for the uneven development of global capitalism have not changed, and, if anything, have been accentuated by changes in the international economic architecture. Furthermore, global capitalism – while superficially successful because it appears to have vanquished alternative economic systems – is in effect disintegrating. This disintegration is coming about not because of any external threat or combined socio-political opposition to it, but because it has been too successful for its own good and so has to confront the contradictions generated by its success. It has managed to outmanoeuvre opponents and elements that could check its excesses, such as associations of workers that could reduce capital's bargaining power, democratic accountability that might give rise to regulatory structures that limit or constrain its activities and its profits, collective action that reflects the requirements of the larger social good, and so on. So there are no checks and balances of the kind that in various periods in the past have generated both less economic volatility and more social stability. In an almost textbook extension of the biological argument of the prey–predator relationship, capitalism has killed off all its prey, to the point that its own very existence is now threatened. Indeed, as an economic regime it is increasingly unable to deliver on its own promise of continuous expansion within a largely stable society.

The Global Economy Since the 2008 Crisis

This is reflected most strongly at present in the overall deficiency of demand that characterizes the world economy, despite a few pockets of relatively faster expansion. And this demand deficiency is itself the result of the growing inequalities in income and asset distribution that have marked this phase of global capitalism. The underlying causes of this aggregate demand deficiency have existed for some time, but they were disguised by credit-driven expansions that were inherently unsustainable. The boom that preceded the crash of 2008 could occur – particularly in the United States, but also in parts of Europe and some emerging markets – because wage stagnation that would have led to stagnant demand was countered by financialization that enabled consumption to increase faster than the real incomes of the majority of workers. As has been widely argued (UN 2006; UNCTAD 2008; Ghosh 2010), the pattern of pre-global crisis economic growth in both developed and developing countries suffered from several limitations, paradoxes and inherent fragilities. These ranged from economic imbalances to environmental constraints, to social and political tensions and volatility emanating from increased inequalities. It is well known that in the United States and other advanced economies, the boom was based on speculative practices enabled and encouraged by financial deregulation. It also drew recklessly on natural resources in a manner that has created a host of ecological and environmental problems, especially in the developing world. Even during the boom, despite aggregate employment increases, most paid work became more fragile and less secure in both developed and developing countries. Furthermore, because its benefits were spread so unequally, most people in the developing world – even many in the most dynamic economic region of Asia – did not really gain from the boom.

Nevertheless, the crisis first erupted within the core of global capitalism, through the collapse of the sub-prime debt in the US housing market, which then rapidly spread to the banks and other financial agents that had been involved in the inherently unstable pyramiding of financial assets. That then heralded a crisis in the US economy, which has had massive external effects and in various forms still persists.

The combination of an excessive overhang of debt in corporate and household balance sheets, and unsustainable asset price inflation in equity and housing and real estate markets, were proximate determinants of both the intensity of the crisis and the manner in which it unfolded in the US economy. The main way this was dealt with was through large bailouts of financial institutions, which were seen as unavoidable because of the domino effects that the collapse of such institutions would have, especially since many financial firms were systemically important and 'too big to fail'.

The rescue effort launched after the crisis thus went through two phases. In the first phase, in order to prevent the recession from becoming a modern-day repeat of the 1930s' Depression, governments opted for debt-financed spending in the form of a fiscal stimulus to revive demand as well as to provide funds for financial sector recapitalization. This did manage to bring the major advanced economies back relatively quickly from the depths of the recession. But once this was done, governments succumbed to the pressure to avoid using debt-financed public spending as a means of stimulating a recovery. Instead, they focused on monetary policy measures such as liquidity infusion and interest-rate reduction. Since then, because of the domination of the ideology of fiscal prudence at all costs, governments in advanced countries and most emerging markets have in general resolutely abided by a conservative fiscal agenda and refused to return to the proactive fiscal policies adopted in the immediate aftermath of the crisis. In addition, policies in the core advanced economies moved away from the initial focus on tighter regulation of financial activities that would prevent such damaging consequences in future. Instead, in the name of addressing the Great Recession, policies designed for 'recovery' have increasingly contributed to re-creating the conditions that had preceded the crisis, albeit in slightly modified form, by allowing very loose monetary policy in a context of inadequate regulation (Chandrasekhar and Ghosh 2019).

A further result of this shift from dependence on fiscal policy to reliance on the monetary lever was that some of the buoyancy induced by the initial fiscal stimulus was lost. Output growth fell from its peak and settled at a 'new normal' that, though not a recession, was too weak to be a robust recovery. Monetary policy proved to be less effective in reviving growth, and so the recovery was weak and halting and the road to recovery became prolonged. It took a whole decade after the global financial crisis (GFC) before it could even be plausibly argued that the worst was over and the recovery had finally arrived. But even such assessments have proved to be premature. The recovery has not been particularly robust, nor is it likely to restore pre-crisis growth levels and resolve the problems inherited from the crisis. Indeed, as noted above, the very strategy for inducing recovery, by relying so heavily on loose monetary policy alone, has operated to increase the fragilities that could generate another similar crisis in future. These fragilities mostly relate to debt bubbles and asset price inflation.

The primary policy response to the 2008 financial crisis in the advanced economies was the adoption and prolonged use of 'unconventional' monetary policies, which have involved keeping interest rates near zero and infusing large amounts of liquidity into the system, with the expectation that this would spur investment and consumption demand and thereby ensure robust recovery from the recession. This strategy of massive liquidity creation – combined with the reluctance to impose regulations that would restrict financial activity – led to significant increases in debt-financed private expenditure. Therefore, even the modest and hesitant recovery relied on creating a credit bubble similar to the one that led up to the crisis of 2008–09. This was driven by the cheap liquidity infused into the system by the quantitative easing and low interest rate policies adopted by developed country central banks to deal with the crisis. Financial institutions with lots of liquidity were willing to lend, to avoid being penalized with low interest rates on deposits with the central bank, and borrowers encouraged by the boom in equity and real estate markets returned to the debt market.

This has led to a revival of debt ratios across the advanced economies (other than those such as in the European periphery, still struggling with adjustment). The stockmarket boom in the United States once again raised household wealth levels, triggering once again a 'wealth effect' that encouraged debt-financed spending by the private sector, which drove the growth underpinning the still weak recovery. This then fed back into stockmarket behaviour, especially in the United States. What is significant is that this problem is no longer restricted to the US economy, as it largely was in the run-up to the GFC of 2008. Rather, such bubbles are evident in a number of systemically important economies, in Europe and among emerging markets.

It should have been obvious because of both theory and bitter experience that growth of this kind is unsustainable. And while many different factors can lead to the end of such a speculative bubble, the phasing out of the era of cheap and abundant liquidity that could be leveraged for investments in capital markets could certainly become a proximate cause for such a denouement. That is, the emergence of such bubbles and the attendant fragility have created dilemmas for monetary policy in the advanced world. Central banks admit that they cannot stay with their 'accommodative' monetary policies and must trim their bloated balance sheets – but they cannot do so quickly or sharply without reversing whatever recovery is under way. Any sharp shifts in policy could shock and trigger a sell-off in equity and bond markets, and spur defaults on debt accumulated by households and firms in the era of cheap and plentiful money. That, in turn, could precipitate a financial downturn, which could lead to a crisis and have substantial external effects on real economies still struggling to recover.

Meanwhile speculative investments continue, as market participants take account of the gradual central bank retreat in their calculations. Since the resulting gradualism tends to dampen risk perceptions and reduce risk premia, it has the perverse result of encouraging further borrowing and even more risk-taking by effectively reducing uncertainty about the future, or at least the important element of policy uncertainty. So, the careful and gradual policy of central banks has effectively continued to encourage investors to borrow cheap and invest in risky assets. In this context, it is a valid question whether even a mild reversal of monetary policy stance would lead to a hard landing in asset markets, and the implications that would have for the rest of the economy. Thus, monetary policies in the advanced economies are caught in a cleft stick, made worse by the absence of supporting efforts by fiscal policy.

Meanwhile, the essential causes that led to the crisis – distributional inequalities and falling shares of wages in national income that contribute to suppressed demand – persist (Chancel *et al.* 2018). Despite widespread disaffection and even political instability because of such inequality, the current political economy of most advanced nations currently precludes serious policy measures designed to reduce such inequality of incomes and assets.

Emerging and Developing Economies

It is well known that capitalism is characterized by uneven development, and the evolution of the global economy provides strong evidence of this. As Reinert (2007) pointed out, a significant lesson of the past five centuries of economic history is that there are varying trajectories created by increasing returns and a large division of labour (the more dynamic path), and diminishing returns and monoculture (the path of stagnation or even regression). These are further complicated and often intensified by the interaction of trade and power, since economic environments that are more open to trade and capital flows tend to privilege locations with larger increasing returns industries, and thereby generate more differentiation over time. Patnaik (1997) made the even stronger point that such differences across regions – and in particular, the possibility of pushing adjustments on to some regions and countries – enable the stability of the more advanced economies and thereby create the illusion of stability in global capitalism as a whole.

Since neoliberalism has taken root across the world and (with very few exceptions) is now expressed strongly in the economic policies of most developing countries, the same forces that have created economic stagnation, inequality and alienation in the advanced economies also exist and have been getting stronger in the developing world. Therefore, even though some developing countries benefited from high growth because of their ability to take advantage of the new opportunities opened up by liberalized global trade and to attract relocative foreign direct investment (FDI), this process has been geographically quite restricted. Since the late 1960s, only the East Asian region has shown notable increases in share of global GDP (Ghosh 2019), and for the last two decades this has been dominated by the rise of China. And these successful economies were successful *not* because of neoliberalism but precisely because they did not follow completely neoliberal 'Washington Consensus' policies but rather a more heterodox mix, in which state intervention in different forms was absolutely crucial in enabling both external competitiveness and the expansion of domestic markets.

The spectacular recent economic expansion of China has been directly related to the ability of the Chinese state to control the economy (beginning on a base of relatively egalitarian income and asset distribution that enabled a large mass market) and implement heterodox policies with very high investment rates. These also provided for a mix of market-driven private economic activities along with substantial public investment and state control over finance. This enabled very noticeable structural change in the Chinese economy, with growing shares of manufacturing in both output and employment. This also powered the export-driven expansion that relied on manufactured goods produced cheaply because of labour surpluses combined with large infrastructure investments. More recently, active state involvement in promoting innovation has enabled China's manufacturing production to move rapidly up the value chain towards higher quality and more sophisticated products (UNCTAD 2018). Indeed, it is precisely these policies that are now the target of ire in advanced countries like the United States, where the Trump administration is effectively demanding an end to industrial policies that promote domestic investment and innovation.

But cases like those in East Asia are exceptional: few other developing countries have anything like that trajectory. In particular, the country that is most often compared to China, which is India, does not show anything like this pattern despite high rates of aggregate GDP growth over the past few decades. To begin with, there has been negligible increase in India's share of global GDP as compared with China, when measured at current market exchange rates (which is the true indicator of global economic power, unlike the misleading but widely used purchasing power parity exchange rates). China's share went up from less than 3 per cent in the late 1960s to more than 14 per cent by 2016. The increase in India's share over the same period was only from 2 to 3 per cent (World Bank 2018). Second, unlike Asian success stories like South Korea, Malaysia and now China, this rapid growth over three decades in India has *not* resulted in significant structural transformation: the share of manufacturing in both output and employment has remained stubbornly low, and while the share of the primary sector in GDP has fallen from nearly two-thirds to less than 15 per cent over the past forty years, its share of employment has declined much less, still accounting for more than half of the workforce (Ghosh 2015a). Third, recent economic growth in India has essentially resulted from credit-driven bubbles enabled by greater access to global liquidity within a neoliberal economic policy framework. So, this is more squarely within the basic neoliberal model than the Asian success stories. It has been associated with greater inequality, very poor employment performance with no increases in formal employment and declining women's recognized work participation.

Therefore, while the fulcrum of global growth is shifting to Asia, and to certain countries within Asia, it is still too early to assume that this will be as widespread as many imagine. Certainly, the recent travails of emerging markets in Asia and across the world suggest that notions of 'decoupling' are too optimistic, and that many such economies remain vulnerable to vicissitudes resulting from economic shifts in the advanced economies.

It is important to remember that the 'success stories' of industrialization in the late twentieth and early twenty-first centuries are precisely those countries that have managed external trade and domestic policies to enable late industrialization. The East Asian economies of South Korea, Taiwan and Singapore that emerged in the late twentieth century, as well as more recently China, share one crucial feature: they grew on the basis of significantly heterodox economic policies that involved substantial government intervention in trade, extensive management of capital flows and significant domestic regulation. Furthermore, in their phases of rapid growth and structural transformation, they all exercised significant control over finance and employed directed credit to chosen sectors and activities. In other words, they were able to utilize the opportunities provided by geopolitical contexts and conjunctures that allowed for a substantial degree of autonomy in policy space, because of their internal political economy processes.

Most other developing countries did not have the political economy configurations (either internal or external) that enabled such policies and made them effective. Their pattern of global economic integration, therefore, was associated with more predictable results in terms of the relative stagnation (or even decline) of income shares in the world economy and arrested or reversed structural transformation.

All this is made worse for most developing countries by the new forms that imperialism is taking in the twenty-first century. Changes in the position of certain countries in the economic and geopolitical ladder do not mean that the basic undercurrent of imperialistic tendencies that drive the global system have disappeared – indeed, they may even become more intense as the struggle for economic territory becomes more competitive.

Following Lenin and Patnaik, imperialism can be conceptualized as the complex intermingling of economic and political interests in relation to the struggle of large capital over economic territory. Such economic territory obviously includes land and natural resources, as well as labour. These are all still hugely contested, as testified by the open and latent struggles over control of land (especially in periods of rapid urbanization), forests, oil and other mineral resources, the wealth of oceans and rivers, and so on. And they are necessarily geographically determined, because of their location. But economic territory is also much broader, and also encompasses the search for and ability to control new markets. Such markets can be both defined in physical location as well as constructed out of economic processes.

One of the more intriguing aspects of recent capitalist dynamism has been its ability to create new forms of economic territory, and to bring them within the ambit of capitalist economic relations and therefore also subject to imperialist contestation. Two of the more prominent new forms of economic territory that are increasingly significant as arenas for imperialist penetration and competition today are: first, the privatization of basic amenities and social services that were earlier seen to be the sole preserve of public provision; and second, the commercialization and privatization of the generation and distribution of knowledge (Ghosh 2015b).

A major feature of our times is the privatization of much of what was earlier generally accepted as the basic responsibility of public provision, such as amenities like electricity, water and essential transport infrastructure, and social services such as health, sanitation and education. Of course, the fact that these were seen as public duties does not mean that they were fulfilled. Indeed, expanding public provision and enabling wider (and ideally universal) access to good-quality amenities and infrastructure has only come about historically as the result of prolonged mass struggles, and social and political mobilization to demand these. And issues of inequality in such provision have always existed. Nevertheless, the fact that provision is no longer necessarily in the public domain, and that private providers are increasingly seen as the norm, has opened up huge new markets for potentially profit-making activity. This may have been a crucial means of maintaining markets and effective demand given the saturation of markets in many mature economies and the inadequate growth of markets in poorer societies. The prising open of such markets has occurred through a combination of inadequate and reduced public delivery (for example, the expansion of the global bottled water industry is a result of the failure of public delivery of potable water), and changes in economic policies and regulatory structures that not only enable but actively encourage private investment in these areas. These changes, in turn, have been pushed by global institutions – formal organizations such as the Bretton Woods institutions and the WTO through its various agreements, as well as less formal but increasingly influential bodies such as the World Economic Forum. This is a more complicated playing out of the imperialistic drive for control over economic territory than can be expressed through purely national mechanisms, but that does not make it any less consequential.

Another new form of economic territory that is increasingly subject to imperialist struggle relates to the control of knowledge generation and dissemination. The privatization of knowledge and its growing concentration, through the proliferation and enforcement of intellectual property rights, have become significant barriers to technology transfer and social recognition of traditional knowledge that would be necessary for any kind of economic diversification as well as greater economic justice. They also matter greatly in determining the relative power of profits over people within countries as well as between countries. This is clearly evident in terms of access to medicines – even essential and life-saving drugs – and crucial technologies for food cultivation. But it is also very much the case with respect to industrial technologies as well as the transfer of critical knowledge required for mitigating and coping with adverse environmental changes that themselves result from the production systems created by global capitalism. The national and international institutional structures that should provide checks and balances to the privatization of knowledge, and ensure that knowledge production and dissemination are not subservient to a small elite but directed towards social goals, are not just more fragile and less effective in recent times but, in effect, work in the opposite direction.

Indeed, that is the basic import of the numerous 'trade agreements' that have been signed across the world, which have in recent years been much less about trade liberalization – which has already been so extensive that there is little scope for further opening up in many sectors – and much more about protecting investment and strengthening monopolies generated by intellectual property rights. The past two decades have witnessed an explosion in the treaties, agreements and other mechanisms whereby global capital imposes rules, regulations and modes of behaviour upon governments and their citizenry. Unlike the conditionalities imposed on developing countries by the IMF and the World Bank, these rules operate even for countries that are not in the positions of debtor-supplicants to international financial institutions, and so they require all countries to restrict their policies in ways that are directly related to the possibilities of generating autonomous development in periphery countries.

Similarly, the rules governing international finance and debt are generally recognized to work in ways that reinforce the unequal global power relations between large capital and people across the world. Nowhere is this more evident than in the rules and legal structures governing sovereign debt. The lack of any coherent system to deal with debt default and to enable the viable restructuring of sovereign debt has led to situations in which countries and their populations are bled over years and even decades, merely to service debt generated in the past and through the piling up of earlier loans at ever-higher interest rates. 'Austerity' measures that reduce public spending on social essentials are forced upon unwilling societies on the basis of supposedly 'technocratic' notions that are, in fact, deeply ideological and elite-serving. Developing countries have known this for some time, but this is now also being experienced by some developed countries such as the crisis-ridden economies of the European periphery. Countries that somehow manage to restructure some of their debt, or that unilaterally decide to renege on some patently unfair debt taken on in the past, are punished through complex and unbalanced legal systems that do not even accord to entire populations the minimum conditions of debt workout that are routinely accorded to private and corporate debtors within national systems. The fact that legal systems and other institutional structures in the core countries tend to support such biases and investors in general reinforces the point that this is another way in which contemporary imperialism is expressed.

This is particularly evident in the global spread of multinational corporations and their changed methods of functioning, particularly with respect to the geographic disintegration of production. Technological changes, particularly the advances in shipping and container technology that dramatically reduced transport costs and the time involved, as well as the information technology revolution that enabled a much more detailed breakdown of production into specific tasks that could easily be physically separated, have both been critical to this process. Together, they enabled the emergence of global value chains, which are typically led by large multinational corporations, but also involve regional and global networks of both competing and cooperating firms. The large corporation at the apex of the chain is not necessarily in direct control of all operations. Indeed, the ability to transfer control over production as well as the risks associated with production to lower ends of the value chain is an important element in increasing the profitability of such activities for the apex firm. This adds a greater intensity to the exploitation that can be unleashed by such global firms because they are less dependent upon workers and resources in any one location, can use competition across suppliers to push down their prices and conditions of production, and are less burdened by regulatory processes in any one location that would seek to reduce some of their market power.

These processes have resulted in an increase in the supply of the 'global' labour force, that is, workers and other small producers who are engaged in production activities of both goods and services. At the same time, the power of corporations to keep the benefits of rents arising from control over knowledge or from oligopolistic/monopolistic market structures or from the sheer power of finance capital to bend state policies in favourable directions, has greatly increased. Overall, this has meant a dramatic increase in the bargaining power of capital relative to labour, which, in turn, has been reflected in declining shares of wages to national income across the world, in both developed and developing countries (Stockhammer 2013). The associated erosion of the privileges that were earlier granted to the 'labour aristocracy' in the North is increasingly sowing the seeds of the political delegitimization of this economic system in the core of the global economy, since global capitalism is no longer perceived as a win-win economic system at least within rich economies. But growing material insecurity and fragility, as well as inadequate improvements in living standards also dominate mass conditions in much of the developing world.

The Current Conjuncture

The contemporary global economy is fragile and vulnerable in ways that reflect deep structural and systemic issues as well as the outcome of recent political, policy and regulatory changes. To the various concerns outlined above, we must add the crisis of legitimacy faced by a system that can no longer deliver on the promises of continuous and stable growth, and that generates more and more inequality. These deliver foci of friction and instability that need not be in places where people are the worst affected but simply where these forces have generated the greatest resentment, and such resentments have been most utilized politically. For example, the current 'trade war' between the United States and China is as much about technology (especially the control of frontline technology such as artificial intelligence) and other forms of economic territory as it is about trade *per se*. Yet the fall-out on trade may be the way in which the impact is felt most immediately in other parts of the world, especially the developing world. The potential for economic conflicts to spill over into geopolitical or military escalation, and vice versa, also cannot be underestimated. Possibilities of international cooperation on any of these issues seem more remote than they have been for some decades. All of these make the problems created and faced by global capitalism even more intense.

That does not mean that the system will collapse under the weight of its own contradictions – rather, it will remain as an underperforming, unequal and oppressive system that generates dysfunctional and potentially violent societies. Changing this requires both the development of theoretical and practical alternatives, and social and political mobilization in favour of such alternatives. This is precisely what Sam Moyo was so good at – and for this and for so many reasons, we need to take inspiration from his life and work.

References

Chancel, L., F. Alvaredo, T. Piketty, E. Saez and G. Zucman (2018), *World Inequality Report 2018*, Paris: World Inequality Lab.

Chandrasekhar, C.P. and J. Ghosh (2019), 'A Decade of Speculation', *Economic and Labour Relations Review*, 29 (4): 410–27.

Ghosh, J. (2010), 'Global Crisis and Beyond: Sustainable Growth Trajectories for the Developing World', *International Labour Review*, https://doi.org/10.1111/j.1564-913X.2010.00084.x.

——— (2015a), 'Growth, Industrialization and Inequality in India', *Journal of Asia Pacific Economy*, 20 (1): 42–56.

——— (2015b), 'The Creation of the Next Imperialism: The Institutional Architecture', *Monthly Review*, 67 (3), July–August.

——— (2019), 'A Brave New World, or the Same Old Story with New Characters? Forum Debate on Geographies of Development', *Development and Change*, 50 (2): 379–93.

Patnaik, P. (1997), *Accumulation and Stability under Capitalism*, Oxford: Clarendon Press.

Reinert, E. (2007), *How Rich Countries Got Rich, and Why Poor Countries Stay Poor*, London: Constable.

Stockhammer, E. (2013), 'Why Have Wage Shares Fallen? A Panel Analysis of the Determinants of Functional Income Distribution', ILO Working Paper, Geneva: International Labour Organization.

UN (2006), *World Economic and Social Survey: Diverging Growth and Development*, New York: United Nations.

UNCTAD (2008), *Trade and Development Report 2008: Commodity Prices, Capital Flows and the Financing of Investment*, Geneva: United Nations.

UNCTAD (2018), *Trade and Development Report 2018: Power, Platforms and the Free Trade Delusion*, Geneva: United Nations.

World Bank (2018), *World Development Indicators*, http:datatppics.worldbank.org/wprld-development-indicators/, accessed 16 October 2019.

19

Legacy of China's Land Revolution of 1949

An Unfinished Dialogue with Sam Moyo

Erebus Wong, Wen Tiejun, Sit Tsui, Lau Kin Chi

We had several discussions with Sam Moyo on issues of land reform and alternatives for rural regeneration in Africa and Asia, among which was the legacy of China's land revolution of 1949. In October 2008, in Caracas, Venezuela, Moyo attended the International Conference of Intellectuals and Artists for the Defence of Humanity and the General Assembly of the World Forum for Alternatives (WFA), which was founded by Samir Amin and François Houtart. There was a debate on how leftist governments could challenge the big landlord system and secure access to land by peasants. In 2011, in Beijing, at Renmin University of China, Moyo and Sandeep Chachra were invited to deliver lectures on land issues in Zimbabwe and India. The focus was on comparing land reforms in the global South. Moyo had further introduced the project of the Agrarian South Network, and invited us to contribute articles to the journal on the legacy of China's land revolution and rural reconstruction movement in contemporary China. In December 2011, Moyo attended the First South–South Forum on Sustainability, held at Lingnan University in Hong Kong, China, then joined the post-Forum tour to Chongqing. During a six-day trip, we visited the city and countryside of Chongqing and Chengdu, and talked to peasants, migrants, earthquake victims, cooperative members, social workers, officials and others. Along the way, we discussed the contributions of the small peasantry to China's economic growth as well as its challenges.

In the book project *The Struggle for Food Sovereignty: Alternative Development and the Renewal of Peasant Societies Today*, edited by Remy Herrera and Kin Chi Lau (2015), Moyo contributed a paper entitled 'Rebuilding African Peasantries: Inalienability of Land Rights and Collective Food Sovereignty in Southern Africa'. He argued that '"peasant-friendly" market-based green revolution deepened the peasantries' subordination to the global agribusiness oligopolies', and the dominant responses to the food crises 'tended to reinforce the incorporation of the peasantry into volatile global markets, extending land alienation and increasing import dependence' (Moyo 2015: 78). He urged for the realization of national food self-sufficiency that defends 'the inalienable land rights of small producers . . . [and is] built upon a socially and economically progressive development of the peasant, with substantive democracy and social progress' (ibid.: 82).

Against the background of the failures of current land reforms in developing countries such as Nepal and South Africa, it is necessary to revisit the land struggles for self-sufficiency in the twentieth century. The following is a tribute to Sam Moyo, an unfinished dialogue about the importance of defending the legacy of China's land revolution of 1949. The experience of how new China encountered economic crisis is not only a lesson to China itself in the era of speedy financialization, but also to developing countries after becoming independent and sovereign.

Old and New Economic Crises

The economic fluctuation in the early years (1949–52) of the People's Republic of China (PRC) led to new problems on top of old ones. On the one hand, China had had to deal with persistent hyperinflation since the old republic; on the other, a new crisis had to be tackled, namely, the contradictions innate to primitive capital accumulation for the development of 'national capitalism'.

The enormous institutional cost of modernization and its derivative, the urban crisis unfolding as hyperinflation in the era of the Republic of China could not be resolved by adopting the same old economic means by the new regime, whose success of revolution was marked by the occupation of cities. The new People's Republic resolved this chronic crisis (because of a half-century pursuit of modernization, since the late Qing dynasty) by a full restoration of the traditional peasant economy through agrarian reform, thus gaining the 'land reform dividend'. The policy of redistributing agrarian land to rural households has long been an effective measure in resolving urban crises. It was implemented not only in 1950 by Mao Zedong, but also thirty years later by Deng Xiaoping.

Colloquially, this was expressed in the saying, 'nine peasants are capable of supporting one urban citizen'. This expression inspired the late Du Runsheng, who as a leader of agrarian policy in the early 1980s (being Deputy Director of the National Agriculture Committee) had not only interpreted the distribution of land to households practised by the rural grassroots as a 'household joint production contract responsibility system', but also as a realization of the rural collective economy characterized by double-layer management and a combination of unity and division. In persuading the central leadership, he expressed it in a way that those leaders who were under a serious deficit crisis could understand: 'eight peasants are capable of supporting two urban citizens'.

Put into theory, it is not only about relieving the crisis of modernization through the restoration of a traditional institution, but also the expansion of the revolutionary experience to the surrounding cities from villages in peaceful times. Moreover, it lays the foundation of the three agrarian sectors – villages, peasantry and agriculture – to resolve the urban industrial capital crisis under a persistent dual urban–rural structure.

The substance of the land revolution in China is even distribution of land and tax exemption, which had been a practice of all the founding emperors during dynastic changes in the thousands of years of China's history. If the rulers maintained the basic economic institution of land to the tiller, the rural society, characterized as a 'sponge society', could secure about 200 years of stability in a dynasty cycle. It is a historical experience that has been inherited in Asian agrarian societies composed mainly of aboriginal populations. Borrowing from Marx's 'Asiatic mode of production' hypothesis, we propose the concept of 'East Asian stable society'. China, Japan, North Korea and South Korea, and Vietnam, all belong to the East Asian cultural sphere. No matter what kind of political and ideological system they claim to adopt, they all strive to build a 'sponge society' by the even distribution of agrarian land among peasants, and are, therefore, more stable than their counterparts in, for example, Latin America and Africa.

This historical experience was once again embodied in mainland China in the twentieth century. The land revolution, which had been interrupted by World War II and then resumed during 1946–49, can therefore be called the third revolutionary war for land. On 4 May 1946, the Communist Party of China (CPC) issued a document known as *The May Fourth Instruction*, which proposed to change the policy of tax and interest alleviation to the policy of 'land to the tiller'. Later, Outlines of Land Law was formulated. Land Reform Task Forces consisting of tens of thousands of cadres were sent to rural regions to mobilize peasants to struggle against landlords. As China regained sovereignty after partition by imperialist powers at the same time, it is also known as the independence war (against the semi-colonial situation).

The new government that was born out of the revolutionary war implemented agrarian reform in the entire country. Even distribution of land was achieved for nearly 90 per cent of the population. Nevertheless, to extract agricultural surplus for industrialization, the central government deliberately delayed tax exemption, which most new dynasties would immediately implement.

Consequently, this fundamental institutional transition in property relations by means of revolutionary war achieved three results. First, a vast and diversified physical economy was created by letting about 100 million rural households return to tradition and delink from modernization, so that the subsistence of urban residents – about 10 per cent of the total population – could be secured. The hyperinflation in cities since the last years of the old republic was then greatly ameliorated. Second, when peasants were mobilized by the idea of land reform, and committed to selling their products in exchange for money to secure their land, sufficient amounts of material products could be collected and transported to the cities. This represented the first triumph of state capital over private capital through revolutionary mobilization. Third, the state established its fiscal and financial system, which was necessary for economic regulation of the real economy. The experiences gained from the process became the foundation on which the state constructed its basic economic institutions. Achieving these three results by a single policy obtained the economic diversification of the Chinese revolution, from villages to the surrounding cities. It was the institutional heritage of so-called 'rural socialism with Chinese characteristics', which took shape through developing the real economy by self-reliance in the 'liberated' regions long before the final victory.

Then China faced a new crisis. The old crisis of developing national capitalism as led by the Nationalist Party (Kuomintang [KMT]) was yet to be overcome when the new Communist Party government faced an internal crisis in its effort to develop national capitalism. It was old wine in a new bottle with the same problems. Under the pressure of imperialist invasion, any modern Chinese government would unswervingly pursue modernization, no matter what ideology it adopted. Nevertheless, as long as the institutional cost incurred by primitive accumulation of capital necessary for industrialization could not be transferred outwards, internal crisis would occur.

The social structure of New Democracy as promulgated by the new government was represented by the national flag of the PRC. The large star represented the leadership of the CPC, including state capitalism controlled by the Party. The other four stars represented the working class (less than 5 per cent of the population), the peasant class (petit landowners or rural petit property owners, 88 per cent), the urban petit bourgeoisie and national capitalists. State capital, private capital and petit property owners constituted the major political sectors of the country. Workers and the urban poor, who, according to classical Marxism, should have the consciousness of a class revolution, were less than 7 per cent of the total population.

In short, China had long been an agricultural country composed mainly of peasants scattered geographically. What took place in 1949 was a pre-capitalist peasant revolution, asserted both by the Communist International headed by the Soviet Union and the CPC. Both agreed that China should develop national capitalism (which meant capitalism of and for the nation, as opposed to domination by foreign capital). Only after establishing social mass industrial production could China be transformed into a socialist country.

Accordingly, the new government, which was midwifed by a violent revolution to overthrow the oppressive old system in 1949, not only openly advocated market capitalism – 'The Common Programme of the Chinese People's Political Consultative Conference' adopted on 29 September 1949 stated that New Democracy is state capitalism under the leadership of the Communist Party[1] – it also took accelerating industrialization for granted, just like how regimes since the late Qing dynasty might have pursued modernization. As a consequence, China inevitably had to face the internal contradiction of a peasant country striving for primitive capital accumulation with a scarcity of resources, no matter how the predicament resulting from this contradiction was presented ideologically.

To summarize, right after the success of the revolution, China faced severe crises in cities where capital was concentrated. It was a great challenge to the new regime whose political subjects comprised peasants moving into cities. Meanwhile the government had political problems such as bureaucratization and cadre corruption, which could be viewed as the internal crisis of peasant politics.

The subsequent political campaigns were derived from this. The hyperinflation as a result of budget deficits and money oversupply was quickly suppressed, partly due to the fact that about one-third of the oversupplied money was absorbed by the sponge of the peasant household economy. However, as a result, the rural economy was monetized and polarized, which led to problems within the cooperative movement.

Anchoring Value in Staple Grains

As a newly independent nation, the measures taken to curb hyperinflation in a short time period, and to set up the fiscal and financial system by value-anchoring, could not be implemented in isolation. In fact, the strategy was an extension of Mao's revolutionary strategy of encircling cities from villages, now being implemented in the economy during peaceful times.

First, peasants who had land distributed to them returned to work in the traditional self-sufficient economy. That meant that 88 per cent of the population was immune to modern economic crises in cities, and that the government could focus its attention on the cities to deal with them. The case of the previous republic was different. The major agents of industrial capital were absentee landlords controlling commerce and industry, who had a high demand for agricultural raw materials. Cash-cropping, therefore, became a big part of peasant production. The result was greater commercialization of peasant livelihoods and monetization of peasant incomes. Peasant livelihoods were in turn hit hard by the devaluation of the legal tender (Wen and Feng 1999). Second, due to the accomplishment of the land revolution, the state succeeded in politically mobilizing almost all the peasants, which supported the policy of supply-based value-anchoring of the fiscal and financial system. That is to say, a historically unprecedented yet rigorous rural organizational system comprising 88 per cent of the total population became the means by which inflation in cities was stabilized.

During 1949–50, the government focused on dealing with hyperinflation. Even though the state had yet to announce the land reform law, the reform had been implemented in the liberated regions of Northeast China and North China since 1947. The combination of land reform and peasant mobilization was a basic principle formulated by the CPC during revolutionary struggle. Total mobilization of the population enabled the middle class and poor peasants, which comprised a majority of the peasant population, to sunder their dependence on the landlord class. For the first time in history, peasants gained the consciousness of political subjects playing an active part in the nation's polity, and new forms of rural political practice began to take shape.

Yet, how was the political subjectivity of peasants being expressed? This was determined by whether it was necessary to mobilize peasants in the state's strategies, and, accordingly, which group of peasants – rich, middle income, poor or tenant – needed to be mobilized. In Chinese history, state power was rarely imposed at the village level. Villages usually maintained a sort of autonomy regulated by the local gentry. Through selective mobilization, the new regime extended state power into natural villages for the first time in Chinese history. Properties inside villages, such as land, houses and livestock, were redistributed by way of revolutionary politics. A form of incomplete property rights as compared to individualized private property rights took shape. Thereby the state later found an institutional breach to intervene to reshape the property relationship.

Thereafter, the state faced little resistance from local interest blocs in implementing its will in villages, such as when it established a statemonopolized purchasing and selling system in the name of state-owned units or cooperatives, as well as the cooperative movement in the 1950s. It was a sort of 'revolution dividend'. The state's supreme political power was based on its right to regulate the collective interests of all social groups.

The most important function of land reform lay in the reduction of transaction costs when collecting surplus staple grains from self-sufficient and geographically scattered peasants. In the name of revolution, it became relatively easy for the state to tax and purchase supplies from villages.

Whether the state managed to collect enough staple grains and supplies was vital to its success in curbing speculation and hyperinflation. After speculation and hyperinflation were stamped out, the staples and supplies stocked by the state were redistributed to peasants through wage payment as a form of aid and investment into irrigation infrastructure, among others. On the one hand, agricultural production could be greatly improved; on the other, the surplus workforce could be prevented from flowing out of the villages during famines. In this way, a crisis could be quickly resolved before it resulted in social turmoil.

The next question then is: can the countryside continue to bear the costs of urban crises? This depends on whether the property relationship in villages is equitable and to what extent the peasants can organize themselves. With these two factors realized, the vast rural areas can be insulated against the crisis of inflation by providing basic supplies to cities.

Redistribution of Property Relationship and Organization of Peasants

After land reform, poor peasants (52.2 per cent of the total population) owned 47.1 per cent of arable land, 2.93 *mu* per capita on average;[2] middle-income peasants (39.9 per cent) owned 44.3 per cent, 3.67 *mu* per capita; rich peasants (5.3 per cent) owned 6.4 per cent, 3.8 *mu* per capita; and landlords (2.6 per cent) owned 2.2 per cent, 2.52 *mu* per capita (Xu 2007: 10). According to some studies, the level of unevenness was not as serious as expected (Wen and Feng 1998).[3] Nevertheless, after land reform, the fairness of land ownership had indeed improved. The institutional cost of land reform was a certain loss in terms of economies of scale, but the institutional benefit was the state's capacity for political mobilization of over half of the rural population.

Regarding support by rural areas, after land reform, peasants in the liberated regions still had a relatively heavy tax and levy burden of about 20 per cent. During the Sino–Japanese War, the average grain levy per capita was about 32 catty of rice.[4] In some areas it was as low as 18–19 catty per capita. In 1948, the average grain levy was 40 catty per capita. In 1949 it became 56 catty, about 18.2 per cent of total agricultural production. During the Sino–Japanese War, besides the grain levy, peasants had to pay some money without other additional charges. In 1949, the burden on the peasants increased. In some provinces, it was 5–15 per cent higher. Then the average total tax per capita was 58–64 catty of fine grains, about 20.6–22.7 per cent of total agricultural production in that year. Additionally, peasants had to bear a salt tax, a custom tax, civilian war service, and the invisible loss of currency depreciation.

The burden imposed on peasants after liberation was due to the pressure of the fiscal budget. In November 1949, non-productive personnel paid by fiscal revenues numbered more than 9 million. As the war raged on, fiscal expenditure increased (PRC 1995b: 186, quoted in Wu and Dong, eds 2010: 327). China's participation in the Korean War in October 1950 only made the economic situation more difficult.

As industry and commerce were just recovering from war, revenues from these sectors were not substantial. In consideration of the nation as a whole, the new government had to continue burdening peasants (Tables 1 and 2).

Although the CPC decided to reduce the tax burden on peasants in 1950, the policy was not implemented because of the Korean War. In general, due to the need for fiscal revenues, the tax burden on peasants became relatively heavy in the liberated regions until the restoration of the national economy.

On the other hand, a major function of the rural cooperative at the beginning of the PRC was to purchase supplies on behalf of the state. It

Table 1 ***Agricultural Taxes and Other Levies (RMB [renminbi] 10,000), 1950–52***

	*	Agricultural taxes	Other levies	Sub-total	** (per cent)	*** (per cent)
1950	2,431,212	229,277	56,093	285,370	9.43	11.74
1951	2,660,171	307,312	95,728	403,040	11.55	15.15
1952	3,227,600	329,853	47,819	377,672	10.22	11.70
Total	8,318,983	866,442	199,640	1066082	10.42	12.82

Note 1: * Net value of agricultural and side-line production.
** Agricultural taxes as percentage of total net value of agricultural and side-line production.
*** Agricultural taxes and other levies as percentage of total net value.
Note 2: (a) Net value of agricultural and side-line production was calculated according to the net value given by the National Bureau of Statistics minus the value of preliminary processing and handicraft for self-subsistence. The reduction of material consumption was 21.32 per cent. (b) Other agricultural taxes included animal husbandry tax, rural industry and commerce tax, land certificate fee, and various other levies. The last item might not be precise.
Source: Li (1962): 153.

Table 2 *Agricultural Taxes, 1949–52*

	1949	1950	1951	1952
Agricultural population (10,000)	44,726	46,059	47,626	49,191
Farmland area (10,000 *mu*)	146,822	150,534	155,507	161,878
Real agricultural production (fine grains 100 million catty)	1,847.1	2,195.4	2,493.2	2,924.2
Taxable production (fine grains 100 million catty)	1,809.6	1,860.0	2,090.4	2,374.2
Per cent of production	97.97	84.72	83.84	81.19
Real levy (fine grains 10,000 catty)	248.8	269.7	361.5	357.8
Per cent of taxable production	13.8	14.5	17.3	15.1
Per cent of agricultural production	13.5	12.3	14.5	12.2
Average per capita (catty)	56	59	76	73
Average per *mu* (catty)	17	18	23	22

Source: Ministry of Finance of the People's Republic of China (1994): 119.

Table 3 *Rural Cooperatives Purchase Products for the State as Ratio of Total State Purchasing*

Year	Purchasing	Staple food	Ginned cotton	Linen for gunny bag	Tobacco	Tea
1951	Purchase for the state (10,000 catty)	559,854	70,292	13,695	6,918	1,176
	As per cent of total cooperative purchasing	71.7	84.8	65.2	79.6	71.5
	As per cent of state purchasing	31.0	45.8	43.7	52.9	14.5
1952	Purchase for the state (10,000 catty)	1,502,100	158,982	32,075	18,408	6,168
	As per cent of total cooperative purchasing	82.0	95.0	80.8	88.9	85.4
	As per cent of state purchasing	49.7	79.9	72.6	51.8	56.1

Source: PRC (1993): 422, quoted in Wu and Dong, eds (2010): 189.

showed that a cooperative could cut transaction costs of collecting supplies from peasants (see Table 3). It is clear that in regions that were liberated earlier and where land reform was implemented, cooperatives developed better, which may be regarded as an institutional benefit.

In summary, the central government collected staple grains from the whole nation in order to suppress inflation in cities. The state regime that was based in cities, therefore, enjoyed the institutional benefit of social stability. However, in rural areas which were yet to be organized, the institutional cost in terms of social instability increased. The above analysis demonstrates that fair distribution of property and grassroots organizing were pivotal to the villages' capacity to bear institutional costs.

Irrigation Infrastructure Construction through State-mobilized Labour to Secure Food Production

The building of irrigation infrastructure proved remarkably effective in increasing food production. This was closely related to the organization and mobilization of peasants during land reform.

In the early years of the republic, under conditions of material scarcity, the most effective way to increase food production in a short period of time was through mobilization of the workforce, which was a way to earn labour rent at a relatively low cost. During the restoration of the national economy, irrigation was a crucial component of infrastructural investment, second only to transportation and communication (Table 4).

During 1949–52, the total investment in agriculture, forestry and irrigation was RMB 1.03 billion, 13.14 per cent of the total infrastructure investment, most of which was used in irrigation construction. In 1950, the value of loans for irrigation investment was equivalent to 500 million catty of rice, which was allocated to 21 million *mu* of arable land; and 320,000 soldiers were organized by the state to participate in irrigation construction.

During 1950–52, 420,000 km of embankments along rivers were repaired and reinforced across China. In the three years, 20 million people directly took part in irrigation infrastructural construction. The earthwork was estimated to be over 1.7 billion m^3, equivalent to the construction of ten Panama Canals or twenty-three Suez Canals. Up to 107 projects

Table 4 *Irrigation Infrastructure in China, 1949–52*

	Unit	1950	1951	1952
Infrastructure investment	RMB 10,000	9,206	19,508	32,799
Large lock gates built	Number	–	–	3
Enlarged irrigated areas	10,000 *mu*	1,204	2,796	4,017
Irrigation canals over 10,000 *mu*	Place	1,254	1,279	1,346

Source: PRC (1989): 942.

involved land over 10,000 *mu*. Collective construction work was being undertaken in 2.08 million places. Irrigation areas were extended by 32.4 million *mu*, 24 million of which reaped the benefits in the same year.

Flood-stricken areas rapidly decreased in the country. In 1949 there were over 100 million *mu* of them, declining to 60 million in 1950, 21 million in 1952 and down to 16 million in 1952. Meanwhile, extended irrigated areas were 49.5 million *mu*. A rough estimate had it that food production increased by a few million tonnes due to flood prevention and increased irrigation facilities (Wu and Dong, eds 2010: 479–83).

Irrigation infrastructural construction became another tool for extensive mobilization in rural regions after land reform. The experience of low-cost mobilization of the labour force was gained by having soldiers build the railway – which was Sun Yat-sen's idea, though not realized during his time. On the eve of the new republic, the task of railway restoration was heavy. CPC leader Peng Dehuai suggested having sappers do earthwork and cave-digging to build the Tianshui–Lanzhou railway line. The Central Committee of Finance and Economy also suggested using surplus troops for roadbed work and cave-digging. Earlier, the CPC had mobilized people in the liberated regions to build railway lines. Before leaving for Moscow in December 1949, Mao Zedong called military leaders Chen Yun and Bo Yibo to say: '[i]t is imperative to deploy troops to build Tianshui–Lanzhou, Tianshui–Chengdu, Chengdu–Chongqing, Yibin–Kunming, Yunnan–Guizhou, Guizhou–Guangxi, Hunan–Guangxi railway connections. Please work on it immediately' (PRC 1996: 169–70, quoted in Wu and Dong, eds 2010: 450–51). Consequently, despite a very tight fiscal budget, the state invested as much as possible in building railway lines in the early years of new China. With limited funds and heavy tasks, sappers were irreplaceable in this undertaking. For the construction of the Baoji–Tianshui, Tianshui–Lanzhou, Tianshui–Chengdu, Chengdu–Chongqing lines, 286,546 people were mobilized in 1950. The fund was equivalent to 997,475,095 catty of millet and the cost of dynamite equivalent to 27,725,000 catty of millet, most of which was taken from captured ammunition. The original salary budget was 379,147,426 catty of millet. It was later cut substantially. The total cost was reduced almost by half because of the participation of sappers.

Labour force mobilization was also applied in other domains, for example, 'disaster relief through work', which helped to achieve part of the government's relief tasks and also prevented famine-stricken people from flocking towards cities. In 1950, for refugee relief, 1,532 million catty of staple grains were used. Out of this, 545.64 million catty was relief in the form of remuneration to pay peasants working in irrigation construction and other projects, 37 per cent of total aid (Jin and Chen, eds 2005:

672). According to incomplete statistics, 123,854 people worked for relief allowance in 1950, 59,639 in 1951 and 85,128 in September 1952 (Wu and Dong, eds 2010: 873).

The rural economy in China has always been diversified. The peasant household economy has long comprised different businesses besides farming. After land reform, side-line production in the rural sector developed, which became an effective way to absorb surplus labour force in disaster-stricken times. This has been a feature of the village as a 'sponge society' capable of resolving disasters and crises.

In order to relieve the impact of extensive natural disasters, the government implemented a series of supportive policies and measures to revitalize and develop side-line production and the handicrafts industry in rural regions. In the winter of 1949 and spring of 1950, a great part of the 766 million catty of relief grains were used to support peasants in developing side-line production and the handicrafts industry. Rural side-line production rose from RMB 1.16 billion in 1949 to RMB 1.83 in 1952, an increase of 57.8 per cent, or annual growth of 16.4 per cent on average, which was slightly higher than the average growth of gross agricultural production (PRC 1991: 982, quoted in Wu and Dong, eds 2010: 531).

Preliminary Completion of State Regime Building

The central government's strong capacity for supplies allocation, on the one hand, profited from its experience in mobilizing people in the base areas – grassroots organizations that came into existence during land reform became the pillar of mobilization. On the other hand, it was the consequence of a highly centralized system, built by the CPC during the war for military command and unified local construction of base areas. Confronting the pervasive challenge of inflation, the Central Committee of Finance and Economy was sanctioned by the top military authority to work across regions and departments. It was therefore capable of collecting incredible amounts of supplies from different parts of the country.

The political and economic authority of the central government was rebuilt in a short time, which was an anomaly in the history of the centre–local relationship, particularly the lack of control of the central government over local regions since the late Qing dynasty.

The Central Committee of Finance and Economy was set up just before the establishment of the PRC, led by the Central Military Committee. Under this Committee, in each local region, a Committee of Finance was set up. In this way, the institutional structure of focusing power on large-scale tasks was formed.

This institutional advantage of centralization with Chinese characteristics facilitated the enormous allocation and mobilization of supplies in the whole nation. In a work meeting in Shanghai, Chen Yun emphasized the coordination within and among regions:

> On the matter of finance and economy, local governments would have their own agendas. However, if each local government has its own plan, our force will be too diffused to deal with the present situation. It is now impossible to concentrate all the reserve power. However, major reserve power must be used in a unified and systematic way. (Jin and Chen, eds 2005: 624)

In the meeting, a decision was made to form unified enterprises for purchasing. The allocation of supplies in different regions, which used to be under the command of the field army, was now centralized. Large amounts of supplies allocation were to be made through the Central Committee of Finance and Economy (ibid.: 625–26).

In order to make up for the shortage of 2.9 billion catty of staple grains due to natural disaster at the end of 1949, the Central Committee of Finance and Economy decided to allocate grains from Central, Northeast and Southwest China to East and North China. Out of this, 1.5 billion catty was from Northeast China and 1.1 billion catty from Central China. To secure the supply of food and cotton in major cities, grains were transferred from Sichuan regardless of cost. At that time, the grains reserve in Shanghai was less than 100 million catty. In order to prevent speculative merchants from making trouble, a stock of 400 million catty was needed. Grains were transported to Shanghai from different regions. Furthermore, 600–800 million catty of reserve was ready between Suzhou and Nanjing. After liberation, Shanghai had merely 20 million catty of staple grains. In the first half of 1950, the state managed to mobilize 1.7 billion catty of grains, enough for one-and-a-half years (ibid.: 669–73). The scale of supplies allocation for this purpose was enormous. Until the end of July 1950, 6 billion catty of staple grains were allocated in the whole nation (PRC 1995a: 24).

Furthermore, through land reform with extensive rural grassroots mobilization, the CPC managed a feat unparalleled in Chinese history – a complete arable land survey. Land was the foundation of tax for every dynasty throughout China's history. However, the total area of arable land was unknown to the rulers. The measurement of land was always a difficult task for politicians and reformers who hoped to suppress ownership concentration by landlords and land appropriation by powerful families. In history, only the founding emperor could have successfully implemented even distribution of land and tax exemption based on relatively transparent information. In comparison, the poll tax was much easier to operate. For example, Zhang Juzheng, the chancellor of the Ming emperor Wanli, took on the task of putting the tax problem in order. In 1580, measurement of land in the whole country was promulgated in the name of the emperor. The goal was to survey the total amount of farmland. However, the task had not even started when Zhang passed away in 1582. In some counties and districts, no land survey had ever been done for centuries (Huang 1981).

In the new republic, land reform through total mobilization achieved an outcome that exceeded expectations. Statistics show that the ratio of agricultural tax on real production decreased in 1950, increased in 1951 and then declined substantially in 1952. In 1951, the real agricultural tax, including formal tax and additions by local governments, was more than 36 billion catty, an increase of 34 per cent as compared to 1950. Besides the additional tax prepared for the Korean War, one of the reasons was an addition of 60 million *mu* of 'invisible' farmland found in the survey. The taxable production was therefore increased by more than 20 billion catty (Wu and Dong, eds 2010: 752). In 1951, an extra several billion catty of real agricultural tax was gained on top of the expected budget.

These were the mechanisms by which the state, based on the urban–rural dual structure, made use of internal power to resolve urban crises via agricultural policy and investment, making villages the institutional facilitators and bearers of soft-landing. Obviously, with a very tight fiscal budget, the key to the effectiveness of the various policies – whether concerning grassroots mobilization by land reform, irrigation infrastructure-building or side-line agricultural production – was mobilization of the labour force, a very rich resource in China. The reason the state benefited from it was that this labour force that answered the state's call to take part in building national infrastructure was paid according to the cost of rural labour reproduction under an urban–rural dual structure, which was obviously lower than the cost of urban labour. Therefore, China became a developing country which was able to rely on a low-cost labour force for a long period of time.

Conclusion

China's land revolution has enabled the new republic to resolve the economic crisis through three institutional arrangements, along with the interaction of three sectors: politics, economy and society. First, the overall land reform allowed the peasants, the majority of the population, to delink from the urban crisis of modernization and return to the traditional peasant economy. An extensive and vastly diversified physical economy took shape in rural regions. China thereby managed to resolve the hyperinflation crisis. From then on, rural regions became a vehicle for soft-landing in crisis. Second, a national fiscal-financial system was built upon the rural real economy. This system was connected directly with the policy of physical goods and supplies distribution, enabling the government to perform counter-cyclical economic regulation. Third, the government used military means of the lowest direct cost, with the aid of a political campaign, to forcibly put down the speculative behaviour of urban private capital. It successfully suppressed the exacerbation of the economic crisis by private enterprises, which would have followed the economic cycle out of economic rationality. This experience is relevant to the present-day situation in which money supply expansion leads to speculation while very little money created by quantitative easing is eventually channelled into the physical economy. As such, the same exogenous crisis appears again in China in the twenty-first century. The real estate bubble and financial speculation since 2008 marked the beginning of the new crisis.

Mao Zedong said that we should take heed of historical experiences. The thirteen-year hyperinflation in China before 1950 was exogenous and derivative of the economic depression in the west, which attempted to transfer the cost of crisis to other parts of the world. Under the pressure of war and inflation, the KMT government had to increase its dependency on the US dollar. The new regime born with the land revolution received no foreign aid and cut the nation's dependency on the US dollar. However, it succeeded in controlling inflation by the power of the rural real economy. This can be seen as a significant victory for a sovereign nation in the long struggle of delinking from dependency.

Under long-term inflation, capital tends to leave the real economy and rush into the speculative sector, which is the invariable behaviour of private capital under a free market economy. The new regime advocated the development of a system of national capitalism with private capital as the major agent. It promoted the development strategy of New Democracy after crushing speculation as a way to curb hyperinflation. As a result, recession in the real economy became inevitable.

At that time, the state was still not in the shackles of the interest bloc and could choose to 'go long' as a form of counter-cyclical regulation to tackle recession. The foundation of regulation was a combination of two apparently opposite elements – a dispersive peasant economy and centralized state capital. The relevance of this experience of curbing the crisis of urban capitalism for other developing countries should be heeded.

Furthermore, the historical significance of China's victory over hyperinflation lay in the establishment of a sovereign currency system, a success finally achieved after the efforts of two regimes over decades.

The United Kingdom, the United States and Japan had given up the gold standard in a short period of time. On the other hand, China, under the double pressure of an exogenous crisis originating from the west and war, eventually succeeded in paper money reform.

China in 1949 actually resolved the crisis of modernization by de-modernization, and cured the plague of hyperinflation by a high degree of organization in villages. Accordingly, we might generalize two important points. First, the real economy with independent sovereignty is the foundation of currency sovereignty. For a sovereign nation facing sanctions and a blockade but with a traditional peasant economy as its major mode of production, the key to securing the fruit of the revolution lies in the state taking staple grains (the most important factor for livelihood) as the major standard of currency value. Sovereign currency is correlated with staple grains. Thus, a stable expectation of floating interest rate is also formed. From there, a steady growth in the rural real economy and value anchored to basic agricultural products can prevent hyperinflation. Fiscal budget and finance are closely related to the distribution of supplies for livelihood. Given these factors, RMB became a widely accepted state credit tool both in cities and villages. All of these consolidated new China as an independent nation with its sovereignty fully intact.

Second, only by changing the mono-economic structure can developing countries get out of the colonial development trap. Many developing countries in the world are confined to being export zones of primary products. They lose the power of pricing, as logistics, trading and financial clearing are controlled by transnational corporations from former suzerains or master-states. As a result, they do not have the foundation to correlate agricultural products with currency. Many developing countries born during the decolonization movement after World War II have failed to achieve self-sufficiency in basic consumer goods (including industrial and traditional products) because of the mono-economic structure of agriculture. If they want to import these goods regardless of factors like trade sanctions or blockades, market prices at the destination are necessarily higher than in the place of origin. What is more, the goods have to be paid for with hard currency, which is generally scarce in developing countries. These countries might, on occasion, ride on booming international trade to enjoy handsome short-term benefits. However, the boom is often ephemeral. If the countries fail to mobilize domestic production and initiate import substitution, they will repeatedly face a scarcity of staple grains and hard currency under the convention of the market economy.

Notes

[1] 'The Common Programme of the Chinese People's Political Consultative Conference', in *The Common Programme and Other Documents of the First Plenary Session of the Chinese People's Political Consultative Conference*, Peking: Foreign Language Press, 1950: 1–20.

[2] 1 hectare = about 15 *mu*.

[3] In a letter to Mao Zedong, Dong Shijin mentioned that according to a survey by the Land Committee of the Republic of China, out of 1.75 million peasant households in 163 counties of 16 provinces, 35.6 per cent of peasant households owned arable land under 5 *mu*, 24 per cent owned 5–10 *mu*, and 13 per cent owned 10–15 *mu*. Big landlords owning land over 1,000 *mu* accounted for only 0.02 per cent of the rural population. See Dong (1951), quoted in Xiong (2010).

[4] The catty, kati or jin, a traditional Chinese unit of mass, is about 500–600 grams.

References

Dong, S.J. (1951), *On CPC's Land Reform*, Hong Kong: Freedom Press.

Huang, P.C.C. (2011), 'Chongqing: Equitable Development Driven by a Third Hand?', *Modern China*, 37 (6): 569–622.

Huang, R. (1981), *1587, A Year of No Significance: the Ming Dynasty in Decline*, New Haven: Yale University Press.

Jin, C.J. and Q. Chen, eds (2005), *Biography of Chen Yun*, Volume 1, Beijing: Central Literature Press.

Li, C.R. (1962), *PRC Agricultural Tax: A Preliminary History*, Beijing: China Fiscal and Economic Press.

Ministry of Finance of the People's Republic of China (1994), *A History of Burdens on Peasants*, Beijing: China Fiscal and Economic Press.

Moyo, S. (2015), 'Rebuilding African peasantries: Inalienability of Land Rights and Collective Food Sovereignty in Southern Africa?', in R. Herrera and K.C. Lau, eds, *The Struggle for Food Sovereignty: Alternative Development and the Renewal of Peasant Societies Today*, London: Pluto Press: 56–82.

People's Republic of China (PRC) (1989), *Selection of People's Republic of China Economic Archives 1949–1952: Infrastructure and Construction*, Beijing: China Social Sciences Press.

——— (1991), *Selection of People's Republic of China Economic Archives 1949–1952: Agriculture*, Beijing: Social Sciences Literature Press.

——— (1993), *Selection of People's Republic of China Economic Archives 1949–1952: Industrial and Commercial Institutions*, Beijing: China Social Sciences Press.

——— (1995a), *Selection of People's Republic of China Economic Archives 1949–1952: Commerce*, Beijing: China Supplies Publishing House.

——— (1995b), *Selection of People's Republic of China Economic Archives 1949–1952: Fiscal*, Beijing: Economic Management Press.

——— (1996), *Selection of People's Republic of China Economic Archives 1949–1952: Transportation and Communication*, Beijing: China Supplies Publishing House.

Wen, T.J. and K.W. Feng (1999), 'Be Mindful of the Danger of Rural Bankruptcy: The Overexploitation of Villages by Industrial, Commercial and Financial Capitals', *Strategy and Management*, 1.

Wu, C. and Z. Dong, eds (2010), *Economic History of the People's Republic of China 1949–1952*, Beijing: Social Science Academic Press.

Xiong, J.M. (2010), 'The Sorrow of the Prophet', *Twenty-first Century*, June.

Xu, J.W. (2007), *A History of Contemporary Agricultural Policy*, Beijing: China Agriculture Press.

20

The Agrarian Question, Rising Indian Right-wing Populism and Worker–Peasant Alliance Building

Dinesh Abrol

In the writings of Marxist scholars (U. Patnaik 2012; P. Patnaik 2014; Moyo, Jha and Yeros 2013), the agrarian question and formation of worker–peasant alliance have been discussed in the overall context of the global South. They have considered the formation of worker–peasant alliance in the context of the classical formulation of the agrarian question, namely: (i) breaking land concentration; (ii) establishing an alternative path of peasant capitalism that allows broad-based capitalist development and a more democratic polity; and (iii) formation of collective property on the basis of egalitarian land ownership in the countryside that can enable the proletariat to advance beyond the bourgeois democratic revolution towards people's democracy and socialism. Furthermore, due to the new developments in imperialism, the agenda of worker–peasant alliance formation has been considered in the context of the emergence of corporate capital, a new player integrated into the system of globalized finance, penetrating into agriculture in a major way.

In the Indian context, Prabhat Patnaik (2014) suggests five new areas of transitional demands: (i) resisting withdrawal of the state from the role of supporting the peasantry and petty producers; (ii) struggle against primitive accumulation of capital leading to dispossession of the peasantry and ensuring that land acquisition takes place in conformity with social rationality; (iii) struggle against corporate and contract farming practices; (iv) preventing the peasantry from making a shift to socially irrational technological and organizational changes; and (v) promoting the implementation of the Mahatma Gandhi National Rural Employment Guarantee Scheme (MGNREGS) by forming trade unions and uniting people against the privatization of education and health.

The left and democratic movement has continued to pursue the agenda of transitional demands, and during the last five years, the farmers' movement has focused on mobilizations against the neoliberal policies of the Modi government. These mobilizations allowed the left and democratic movement to bring together a large number of farmers' movements on one common platform and obtained success at the level of getting the twenty-two opposition parties to agree to pass two new central pieces of legislation, namely the Farmers' Freedom from Indebtedness Bill (2018) and the Farmers' Right to Guaranteed Remunerative Support Prices for Agricultural Commodities Bill (2018). These efforts could not bring to the fore the demands specific to and directly relevant to the protection of the interests of petty producers and labourers in the rural economy.

Although the twenty-two political parties opposed to the Bharatiya Janata Party (BJP) government supported this agenda during their election campaign among the electorate, they performed poorly in the 2019 elections and the Modi government received a massive mandate. The National Democratic Alliance (NDA) led by the BJP obtained 352 seats out of 542. Political formations backed by the left and democratic movement are now discussing the question of how to remain relevant in parliamentary and extra-parliamentary politics in the near future. The central government led by Modi is actively supported by the mobilization of cadres of the right-wing ruling party (BJP) and Sangh Parivar-affiliated organizations, and the left and democratic movement will need to discuss how a robust political alternative to the majoritarian politics under way on the ground can be pursued.

This essay focuses on the challenges arising from the ascent of right-wing authoritarian populism in India, reflects on the emerging response of the peasantry and rural labour, and discusses the agrarian question and worker–peasant alliance formation under these new circumstances. It suggests that there is a new mode of regulation of social norms, economy, ecology and culture based on the external intervention of right-wing authoritarian populist politics. It is further suggested that there is a challenge posed by new sources of primitive capitalist accumulation on the material front, aimed at the forcible separation of petty producers from the means of production. The left movement needs to consider how to build the agenda on the agrarian question and worker–peasant alliance formation. There is need for a new approach to struggle and organization-building.

Emerging New Political Order

Cow, land, wages, Hindu women and the Hindus' Ram temple, all these issues are the new means of ruling-class supremacy. India is now witness to the politics of the far right in full strength, with far-reaching consequences for the economy, polity and society, and to the weakening of the Congress party and the rise of Rashtriya Swayamsevak Sangh (RSS)-backed, BJP-affiliated organizations such as the Vishwa Hindu Parishad, Bajrang Dal, Hindu Yuva Vahini and other similar outfits (Harriss, Jeffery and Corbridge 2017). Between 2014 and 2019, the politics of the far right received a big boost from the effective leadership of Narendra Modi, an RSS *pracharak* (organizer) promising the dream of *acche din* (good days) for India. Using modern communication technology, the RSS has deepened the roots of Hindutva in Indian society, polity and culture, exerting a hegemony over public discourse via the idea of glorious Hindu culture. It is for the second time that the BJP government has been able to obtain a brute majority in Parliament (NDTV 2017; Prasad 2017a, 2017b).

Until the 1990s, the politics of the ruling classes was conducted with the Congress party in government at the centre. This kept the ideology of Hindutva in check on the ground, to some extent. The post-reform period's failure with regard to meeting the social demand for jobs and the frustration with corruption explain the rise of the BJP. The political strategy of the ruling classes has changed. The Congress party, which was so far the main national party, has been replaced by the BJP (Siddiqui 2017). The legitimacy of Modi came from the post-2008 crisis-induced approach to policy-making during the second United Progressive Alliance (UPA) government, with Manmohan Singh as prime minister for the second time, between 2009 and 2014. During the campaign for the 2014 elections, Modi successfully promised a depoliticized 'Gujarat model of development', of roads and electricity to the people of India across classes – the appeal of which continues even today.[1]

With the help of the corporate media, Modi was able to sell the non-class discourse of a 'corruption-free', Congress-*mukt* Bharat (Congress-free India). With the defeat of the Left Front in Tripura in a direct fight with the RSS-backed BJP, Modi as prime minister was also promising a Communist-free political system. The Modi government has been skilfully pandering to the communal sentiment among Hindus. Even when he talks of 'support from everyone and development for all' (*sab ka saath, sab ka vikas*), it cannot be overlooked that the social base of his party is now targeting Dalits, Muslims, liberals and the left through street mobs on the ground to create fear among the socially deprived. It is able to work openly in the name of the cow and majoritarian Hindu nationalism. The aim of authoritarian populist politics of the far right is to organize the country around a new non-secular, Hindu majoritarian political order. The BJP is undertaking micro-social engineering through the formation of 'social harmony' committees, with sections of socially backward classes on board. Although they are peasants and workers, they are getting swayed by the appeal of how the Hindu majority is necessary, and the enemies are Muslims, secularists and leftists.

A new political conservative order is in the making by which the emerging combined block of upper castes and upper middle classes are seeking to re-establish once again their hegemony and domination in the rural world. This also includes the efforts of RSS cadres to fracture the coalition built around the unity of the Other Backward Classes (OBCs) by mobilizing the social divides that exist at the level of caste and ethnicity. At least, this is very much the situation in the most populous states of northern and western India. RSS cadres are working towards the domination of school education, and now university life, in a variety of ways. This political project is in the process of being finetuned and expanded to the eastern, northeastern and southern states of India.

In some regions, new possible sources of state power have emerged through the National Register of Citizens (NRC). At the national level, the BJP has undertaken steps to implement the elements of a right-wing understanding of a civil code on marriage and love, with the help of the police and courts that they can use by virtue of being in power at the centre. This political order is aided by the RSS cadres on the ground in almost all the states. This kind of politics in which market authoritarianism will coexist with a conservative political order is now feasible due to the interventions of RSS-affiliated organizations and the growing influence of Hindu majoritarian politics on the everyday life and politics of the country.

Emerging Sources of Primitive Accumulation

The consequences of right-wing populist politics are visible on the ground in the form of a new political and economic order accelerating a new type of external intervention of the state apparatus in the process of capital accumulation. The core effect of external interventions of the state is about strengthening the processes of primitive accumulation in the rural economy. External intervention is aimed at forcible separation of petty producers from the means of production (Prasad 2017b, 2017c). It is being made possible through the perusal of legal, political, social and cultural means. Political governance of this process of primitive accumulation is being undertaken using judicial and extra-judicial enforcement of laws in-the-making.

The petty producers are being forced to abandon their traditional livelihoods linked to the crop and cattle economy, artisanal production and food processing. They are experiencing the loss of livelihoods more rapidly, such that we can expect further strengthening of a process of semi-proletarianization. It will not allow the rural world to settle in the process of complete separation from the means of production and livelihood because of lack of opportunities for their absorption. Right-wing politics can be expected to strengthen the process of enlargement of labour reserves in rural India. More will migrate to towns for employment and return when they are not able to make a living in urban India.

Most of these petty producers come from the strata of Scheduled Castes (SCs) and Scheduled Tribes (STs), Other Backward Classes (OBCs), and Muslims. The agrarian, merchant and industrial capital belonging to upper-caste Hindus is the main beneficiary of the process of primitive accumulation. The politics of the BJP and the RSS is clearly accelerating the process of creation of a larger semi-proletariat, and this will affect in a major way the social fabric of the rural world in India. Actions of the political-bureaucratic apparatus should be seen as the latest assault by the ruling classes in the series of attacks on the life and livelihoods of petty producers and workers since the introduction of neoliberal economic reforms.

It is an assault of a new kind, requiring a new approach to the formation of a worker–peasant alliance. Populist politics has been framed by the right-wing government in terms of the need to fight against black money; clean, formalize and broaden the fiscal base; and eliminate '*jihadi* Islamic' and 'Maoist' terror from Indian society. Right-wing authoritarian populist politics is consolidating the market authoritarianism-based political and social order in India. The challenge does not come from only the administration, the police and the courts. For example, the BJP governments in Rajasthan and Haryana had chosen to amend even the Panchayati Raj laws to expand the list of disqualifications with regard to who can stand for panchayat elections. These laws lay down basic minimum educational criteria, a two-child norm and several other bizarre eligibility conditions for standing for elections. The argument for 'minimum qualifications' is part of a larger right-wing project.

Attempts to restrict the space and scope for democracy have now an even wider political, ideological and popular support. The regressive agenda is also under perusal on the ground in the form of the politics of protection of the cow, implementation of a less-cash economy, a goods and services tax (GST)-based formal economy, Aadhaar-based identity linkage (use of unique identity number for the delivery of essential services), transfer of available state support (subsidies for food and nutrition, agricultural input and banking services, and social security), all of which mostly hurt petty producers and workers. The Gujarat, Chhattisgarh and Madhya Pradesh governments are leaders in corporate farming which requires real-time data for forecasting production and price estimates. They also have an unusually high growth of landlessness and are models for the ways in which farmers and agricultural workers have been displaced and exploited by companies.

The state-level BJP governments are known to be leaders in the sale of forest lands and their diversion to big companies in the name of projects. Following demonetization, the GST system is changing the commodity and labour markets in favour of big business. Given the structural inequities and power relations within these markets, GST is unlikely to benefit small and micro enterprises at the lower end of the market. It is thus necessary to do cost–benefit audits of GST through a transparent and participatory process, so that democratic mass organizations can raise the issues and concerns voiced by the working people within this pro-big business system (Prasad 2017c, 2017d). The BJP is pursuing systematically the politics of establishment of a new growth path to favour the consolidation of big capital over the economy.

Indian big capital is also open to alignment with transnational capital. Pathways establishing new sources of primitive accumulation are forming to accelerate capital accumulation under conditions of deceleration in the global economy. Encroachment and dispossession are the new sources of capitalist accumulation. Agricultural imports from the advanced capitalist countries to India are rising. Speculation and price volatility are currently integral features of the agricultural markets. The agrarian economy is today also subject to futures trade in India. Indian farmers are in acute distress due to the open-door neoliberal policies. The crisis was aggravated by policies aimed at dispossessing small and marginal farmers by a number of interrelated policy measures. With the new sources of primitive accumulation in the rural world, the production dimension is facing challenges on the ecological front as well.

The ruling-class parties have been reluctant to admit that the neoliberal policies have made agriculture unremunerative. Agriculture is deliberately being made unviable for the bulk of the peasantry. Only a small number of farmers are earning; the rest are in distress. Continuing suicides by thousands of peasants is a result of agrarian distress caused systematically by untenable policies. Spiralling input prices on the one hand and highly volatile output prices on the other, influenced by international trends rather than domestic output, explain the problem of unviability of cultivation of a large number of crops in several regions. The problem is severe for those cash crops where public procurement operations, such as intervention in the market by the government, are weak or non-existent. With the terms of trade also turning against agriculture during this period, peasants have been finding it difficult to continue in agriculture. The impact is also visible in the sharp drop in farming and the growing size of the rural landless population. Landless people were 23 per cent of the rural population in 1981, and rose to 55 per cent in the 2011 Census.

Effects of the Process of Primitive Accumulation

Information on the material effects of new sources of primitive accumulation on social and occupational life in the rural world has been emerging, including from the statistical agencies of the Indian state, which the BJP government tried quite desperately to suppress before the 2019 elections. During the polls, the statistics of rising debt and farmers' suicides since the 2000s were brought up, but with no data for 2016 and 2017. There was no government report on farmer suicides published for 2016–17. In the budget session, the Union Home Ministry told Parliament that it was yet to compile data on farmers' suicides for 2016. But a few days later the Home Ministry, to which the National Crime Records Bureau reports, tabled a provisional report for farmers' suicides in 2016, pegging the numbers at 6,351 farmers and 5,019 agricultural labourers. The provisional report did not have a chapter on the causes of those suicides.

There is evidence from the Periodic Labour Force Survey (PLFS) of the National Sample Survey Office (NSSO) that unemployment has risen mainly because of a collapse in agricultural jobs (NSSO 2019). The percentage of working-age women engaged in agricultural activities in rural areas shrank from 26.7 per cent in 2011–12 to 17.4 per cent in 2017–18, while for rural men in the same period the ratio dropped from 47.7 per cent to 39.7 per cent. In the manufacturing sector, the employment share of women in the total working-age population in rural areas dropped from 3.5 per cent in 2011–12 to 1.9 per cent in 2017–18. In the case of rural men the decline was lower, from 6.5 to 5.6 per cent. Overall employment in rural India dropped sharply. Rural women in the working-age population who are not employed increased from 64.3 per cent in 2011–12 to 76.3 per cent in 2017–18; for men, the share increased from 19.8 per cent to 27.6 per cent. Similar trends were observed in urban India too, but of a much lower magnitude.

A review of the PLFS report for 2017–18, which the government has withheld, shows that only 28.6 crore men were employed during 2017–18 as against 30.4 crore men employed five years earlier, in 2011–12. This means that nearly 2 crore men lost their jobs between FY 2012 and FY 2018 (ibid.). The decline in India's male workforce has occurred for the first time since 1993–94, when 21.9 crore men were employed. This had grown to 30.4 crore in 2011–12, before falling to 28.6 crore in 2017–18, as per the PLFS conducted between July 2017 and June 2018. For the first time in twenty-five years there has been a marked drop in male workforce in both rural and urban areas. The unemployment rates for males in urban and rural areas stood at 7.1 per cent and 5.8 per cent, respectively.

The PLFS report also shows a major decline in casual farm labour. More than 3 crore casual labourers in rural India lost their jobs between 2011–12 and 2017–18. Most of them worked on farms. The report states that the number of rural casual labourers declined from 10.9 crore in 2011–12 to 7.7 crore in 2017–18, a fall of 3.2 crore or nearly 30 per cent. Also, the share of rural households with major income from casual labour in farming declined from 3.6 crore families to 2.1 crore families during the five-year period. The shrinkage in casual farm labour workforce since 2011–12 was more than 40 per cent. The rural casual labour category comprising both farm and non-farm segments registered an overall slide of 7.3 per cent in male employment and 3.3 per cent in female employment. The labour participation rate among rural women fell by half over the past fifteen years, from 49.4 per cent in 2004–05 to 24.6 per cent in 2017–18.

According to the NSSO report, the decline is more acute in the working-age group of 15–59 years. Over 5 crore rural women have left the national job market since 2004–05, according to the report, adding that female participation has fallen overall by 7 percentage points since 2011–12, which means that there are roughly 2.8 crore fewer women looking for jobs. The share of rural female workers in the non-agricultural informal sector also slipped by 13.4 per cent. Irrespective of employment category (casual or regular/salaried), sector (organized or unorganized) and location (urban and rural), women workers in India are paid a lower wage rate, according to an Oxfam report.[2] Among urban female workers, the share of employment in the non-agricultural informal sector – unincorporated proprietary and partnership enterprises in areas such as manufacturing garments, paper, and wood and straw products – dropped sharply by 13.6 percentage points. The gender pay gap was 34 per cent in India; that is, women get 34 per cent less compared to men for performing the same job with the same qualifications, according to the same report.[3]

A report by the Centre for the Study of Developing Societies (CSDS) entitled *State of Indian Farmers* was released in March 2018 in New Delhi (CSDS 2014). The report states that the benefits of government schemes and policies are being mostly given to big farmers with landholdings of 10 acres (4.05 hectares) and above. Only 10 per cent of poor and small farmers with average landholdings of 1–4 acres (0.4 to 1.6 hectares) have benefited from government schemes and subsidies. The farmers blamed the state and central governments for their present condition, as 74 per cent of those interviewed alleged that they do not get any farming-related information from officials of the agriculture department. The survey shows that 62 per cent of interviewed farmers were not aware about the minimum support price (MSP), and among those who had heard of MSP, 64 per cent were not satisfied with the price that the government offered. The survey of 5,000 farm households across eighteen states says that 76 per cent of farmers would prefer to do work other than farming, and 61 per cent of these farmers would prefer to be employed in cities because of better education, health and employment avenues there. A high percentage of farmers complained of repeated losses; 70 per cent of the respondents said their crops were destroyed because of unseasonal rains, drought, floods and pests.

Yogendra Yadav reports:

> In its first four years in power, the government kept MSPs [minimum support prices] so low that for seven major crops they did not even cover production costs. . . . MSPs offered lower net returns on almost all crops than they had under the previous government. . . . Demonetization, of course, was a catastrophe made by Modi. (Yadav 2019)

He adds that 'the farming sector has been in a structural crisis' for some time now, but Modi was fortunate to inherit 'the most positive agricultural scenario there had been in a long time. From that relative high, Indian farming has plunged to a new low' (ibid.).

This kind of evidence needs to be analysed keeping in mind the understanding that agriculture has been left to fend for itself from 1991–92 onwards by the ruling classes. With the onset of neoliberal economic reforms, the agricultural sector was starved of funds and public policy support, leading to increased rural distress. To add insult to injury, most governments at the centre and in the states tried reversing land-ceiling laws, leading to dispossession of lands farmed by Adivasis and traditional forest dwellers. Land handed over for non-agricultural uses has increased from 3.3 per cent to 8.3 per cent. A significant shift has been building up on India's agrarian landscape. The core ideological belief that small and marginal farmers are unviable has been explicitly guiding the policies on the agrarian front. The belief of the dominant political, bureaucratic, scientific and technological elites is being actively nurtured by agribusiness and its supporters working in the World Bank and other such multilateral agencies.

Emerging Antagonisms

The majority of small and marginal farmers have access only to marginal lands which are their only means of survival. With extreme hard labour by this class of semi-proletarians, working on the farms of others and on their own farms, these families are producing grains and reproducing themselves with the unpaid labour of women farmers at home and in the fields. If India is self-reliant in food production, it is largely due to the hard labour of the peasantry. Agrarian depression and acute crisis are characteristically more visible in some regions where non-food crops are grown. There is a collapse of procurement of non-food cash crops by the commodity boards and procurement agencies involved in the purchase of food grains. The macroeconomic trends and the broad picture of depression region-wise due to the sharp cutback in rural development expenditure by the government are quite clear. Decline in public investment and open markets are also important causes of the aggravation of the agrarian crisis. When one compares the decline in public investment and market support being provided in India in the background of the World Trade Organization (WTO) Agreement on Agriculture, the answer becomes even clearer: the Indian government has been taxing, rather than subsidizing, the farmers. Advanced capitalist countries provide huge subsidies for farm producers. It was on the advice of the governments of these countries that successive Indian governments chose to withdraw the input and output price support available to farmers.

The rural economy is still on the precipice of a crisis. The resistance of the farmers can be rebuilt and sustained by farmers' movements with an upgraded agenda on the agrarian question and for the formation of a worker–peasant alliance. The situation can also change rapidly, even in the near future, in the Hindi heartland. In the case of small and marginal farmers, there are significant problems related to getting agricultural produce from the farm to its final point of sale. The rural economy needs support with respect to investment in irrigation and water management. As far as the ruling class is concerned, the solution to monsoon-dependence is crop insurance. But the state of crop insurance is dismal, with over 80 per cent of claims remaining unpaid. Desertification of farmland has increased in 90 per cent of the states, with 30 per cent of India being degraded or facing desertification. This affects the primary productivity of agricultural land, reducing returns from the use of secondary inputs in farming. In addition, there are structural issues related to the landholding pattern (land concentration is growing), lack of clearly defined property rights and lack of quick redress to disputes which require fundamental institutional changes. These changes are not on the agenda of the BJP, which has the backing of capitalist landlords and traditional rural elites of northern and western India.

Emancipatory politics needs to take into account the antagonisms that are likely to emerge on account of these very programmes. These new sources of primitive accumulation cannot remain unchecked. The difficulties of this project are going to continue to grow in both rural and urban India. The new conjuncture in-the-making at the level of the global economy is full of uncertainties. Therefore, even the core element of the authoritarian populist politics is not above the aspect of class. The significance of authoritarian right-wing populist politics for the rapidly evolving phase of primitive capital accumulation in the rural world requires actually more exposition on the material front, which includes ecological, social, technological and institutional questions. Furthermore, since the class aspect of the current version of right-wing politics is reflected in its support for the ideology of a new conservative market economy wherein Indian big business and finance capital are set to gain (Naseemullah 2017; Ahmad 2016; P. Patnaik 2014; U. Patnaik 2012), left politics should be far more complete in the approach to tackling the three new developments, namely, the emerging new political order, new sources of primitive accumulation on the material and ideological fronts to guide the vision of alliance formation, struggle and organization.

Left Politics and the Agrarian Front

The argument on strategy and tactics is that left politics should be dealing not only with the challenges arising out of class politics, but also with the challenges arising out of social mediation of right-wing populism. The politics of resistance to populism requires the left now to weave into the class politics of engagement, new forms of social mediation in-the-making. The politics of democratization of primordial identities based on caste, ethnicity, religion and gender needs special attention from the left on the material front as well. Organizing the unorganized in cooperation for production is itself becoming a priority of the left in rural and urban India. The politics of the left, with and without state governments, will have to equally focus on becoming a force for social transformation.

Of course, it is also necessary to reiterate that the interests of the Indian peasantry would be protected only by comprehensively reversing the neoliberal economic policies. It is these policies that are currently the cause of widespread peasant suicides, indebtedness and large-scale migration. Presently, the protest from the peasantry is essentially against neoliberal capitalism, and the perspective of having no peasantry is not really applicable to the agrarian situation in India. However, in the context of a lack of political consciousness and organized strength among farmers to influence the political process, the challenges of mobilization against neoliberal capitalism come for progressive left and democratic politics from the standpoint of how to gather support from all sections of the peasantry and the landless, and how to prevent the right-wing populist agenda from taking advantage of the social divides that exist in the Indian society. Dalits in the country live in constant fear. The suffering that needs to be addressed demands struggles for the right to land for social security, access to credit and a life of dignity.

The right to land and livelihood is a fundamental issue of the Dalit population to overcome social oppression, which can only be resolved by undertaking the task of the agrarian revolution. There is surplus land available for distribution to Dalits and other landless sections, for social security, a life of dignity and access to credit. Land, water and biomass are available for redistribution, from the government in some cases and from the landlords in others. Wastelands and disputed areas have been captured by powerful landed interests. In some cases, corporates and real estate interests are occupying these lands. The loss of commons is working to the detriment of sustainable agriculture. For the poor, who come mainly from populations of Dalits and Muslims and other socially backward classes, the commons have played and can play a critical role in the security of their livelihoods.

Storage and processing of infrastructure need to become the responsibility of the local, state and central governments. Drought-proofing and flood relief need a massive dose of public investment. The government needs to be pressured into assuring timely farm credit to get the farmers out of the grip of moneylenders and non-banking financial companies. The Indian farming population deserves not only relief in the form of immediate one-time debt waivers and guaranteed minimum support prices, but also public investment for the development of infrastructure for the supply of assured irrigation and power to farmers. The latest wave of consolidation in the agricultural input industry is having a pronounced effect on agriculture with regard to input supply. The import of raw materials and technologies related to agricultural input supply are rising. Agricultural input markets have come under the control of Monsanto-Bayer, Dow-Dupont and Syngenta-Chem China. There is no public or local private sector to challenge the technological monopoly of these companies with respect to agricultural input supply. Supply of agricultural inputs at reasonable prices can go far in alleviating the immediate suffering of farmers.

The ongoing process of differentiation among the peasantry is also critical to the shaping of the processes of strengthening alliances on the ground for the initiation of joint movements against neoliberal policies. Even if the impacts are not the same or of equal level on different strata of the peasantry in India, the neoliberal policies are adversely affecting the peasantry as a whole. Furthermore, opposition by the peasantry to neoliberal policies is acquiring a wider dimension. Today, the social demands of the semi-proletarian sections of petty producers (poor peasants, landless peasants, rural labour and artisans) include the demand of 'decommodification of essential public services', and support for the 'organization of women' around demands that can assist in reducing their burden and unpaid component of labour, because of the rise in cost of the social reproduction of labour. Although the income from farming has been on the decline, women are willing to form labour collectives and undertake leasing of land for cultivation to secure livelihoods.

The agrarian question is also acquiring the dimension of a larger question of land and labour for the semi-proletariat. The rural link of semi-proletarians is alive. In the states of northern and western India, where the BJP is a stronger force, because of semi-proletarianization and the inability of industry to absorb the surplus population of the rural world as a proletariat, the movements of Dalits and Muslims are far more ready and organized around the question of land and labour rights. It is now acknowledged far more universally that the Dalit leadership and the movements are viewing in all regions the right to land as a question of social security in India. While the break-up of land monopolies through a larger programme of land redistribution is not feasible everywhere, the agrarian question is a gender question as well as a social and ecological question, on the basis of which innovative experiments are generating new ideas for wider implementation in several states where the left has some presence.

Since agribusiness offers only the path of agro-industrialization, which is more of a path of rural and agrarian extractivism, it is clear that such a path cannot absorb the teeming millions of underemployed youth. Today, the struggles emerging for the realization of ecological justice within the Indian agrarian scene provide a significantly new opportunity for the organization of the unorganized. Realization of the potential of semi-proletarian power needs the construction of a strategy of mobilization of the peasantry, artisans and rural labourers, for the systemic transformation of productive forces. Spaces for the construction of all-in peasant unity, unity of petty commodity producers from both the farm and non-farm sectors, and leadership of the working class including rural labourers, all are rapidly growing, due to problems arising from the environmental impacts of the mainstream pathways of agricultural development. Socio-ecological problems present these new opportunities more than ever before to the left and democratic movement, to get the peasantry, petty producers and rural labourers as a whole to move away from the grip of capitalist landlords and big business over Indian agriculture in India.

Our future thinking on industrialization needs to entertain the ideas of a circular economy in an immediate sense. Experiments being undertaken by the people's science movements (PSMs) for agro-ecology and rural industrialization are making much more sense to the larger kisan and labour movement. There are positive lessons from the ongoing niche experiments of rural industrialization in the states of Uttarakhand, Himachal Pradesh and Kerala. The Communist Party of India (Marxist) (CPI[M]) in Kerala is taking up this challenge and is ready to multiply this effort on the ground. The BJP is calling this programme of the CPI(M) in Kerala an example of the Party turning into an NGO. It seems that the CPI(M) is finally learning from the failures of the Party in West Bengal. Experience tells us that dispossession can continue even after the redistribution of land rights to tenants and landless. This is the experience of the West Bengal peasant movement, which secured tenurial rights for *bargardar*s on a large scale under the left rule.

Opportunities need to be recognized and pursued on a large scale. Peasants and rural labourers need to be mobilized on the ground to resist the ruling classes, by supporting the diffusion of socio-technical changes that pass the test of social rationality in agro-ecological approaches to the development of agriculture and rural industries. Peasant rationality will change if the impact of the consequences emerging for the state of health of the soil and water, incidence of pest and disease, and climate change are recognized as direct outcomes of the neoliberal capitalist path of agricultural development adopted by India's ruling classes. Currently, the peasantry and rural labour do not have support from the formal systems of research for the development of technologies for agriculture and allied sectors and rural industrialization. Innovation systems that the left and democratic movement need to help build must encompass complexity of resource and capability use by addressing not only the biophysical, but also the social dimensions of agriculture, including equity of distribution of benefits.

There is a need to focus on broader processes emerging with respect to the influences on agri-food systems, including processes concerning the conservation and conversion of natural resources, efficiency of production, processing of food, marketing and consumption issues. There is a need to look at how the national and global food chains are interacting with, and impinging on, local food systems. The question of how to tap into the knowledge and skills of peasants and rural labour involves gaining an understanding of the changes taking place in the environment and local agri-food systems. It needs to be kept in view that agro-ecosystems are also a part of wider socio-ecological (climate change) and socio-technical (class and gender) relations, that they embody inequalities and differentials in terms of access to resources, capabilities and markets.

Just as the *kisan* (farmers') organizations need to go beyond the redistribution of land as private property, they also need to facilitate the pathway of promotion of cooperation between small and marginal farmers and rural labour. The organization of cooperative farming and its intimate links with non-farm activities is essential to building class alliances between agricultural workers and peasants. Access to water, forests, grasslands and wetlands is essential for the survival of the agrarian system. Fifty per cent of the Indian population will still be living – in the near future, if not forever – in areas dependent on the rural world involving an agriculture-based production economy. Agriculture and rural industries need simultaneous upgrading for reasons of limitations of both infrastructure and employability of rural migrants in the metropolises and cities. In order to realize the true potential of agriculture as a driver of rural industrialization, the strategy of development of agriculture itself must be changed. In the long run, the framework of rural industrialization needs to be realigned with the proposed strategy of agricultural development wherein the use of resource-conserving technologies and integrated bio-farming systems involving multi-storied agriculture provide opportunity for rural industrialization.

Concluding Remarks

The path to structural transformation cannot be obtained by linear thinking. Rural poverty exists but it cannot be resolved with a linear view of structural transformation. Primary productivity is dependent on soil, water and biodiversity, while secondary productivity is dependent on costly agricultural inputs, such that the search for alternatives is also leading to the challenge of sustainable agriculture. Furthermore, the left should be making efforts to unite the basic classes and socially marginalized and discriminated people by mediating through social reform within the rural areas. Reversal of the extreme character of agrarian distress can only be envisaged with an alternative paradigm that entails a total repudiation of the politics of right-wing authoritarianism, and the policies of neoliberal economics promoting ecologically and economically unsustainable agriculture. There is an urgent need for integrating the fight against majoritarian politics into the structure of transitional demands and organization-building. The *kisan* organizations will have to strategize and organize their own resistance to the current policy framework by incorporating the new challenges. The left must articulate a vision of agrarian and industrial development, as well as its own updated idea of secular, democratic and socialist India.

Notes

[1] See the contributions of Prasad (2014), R. Desai (2014), M. Desai and Roy (2016), Ahmad (2016) and Vanaik (2017) for much more on how the RSS-backed BJP has secured the support of the provincial propertied classes and India's capitalist classes.

[2] http://www.indiaenvironmentportal.org.in/content/462432/mind-the-gap-state-of-employment-in-india, https://www.downtoearth.org.in/news/india/women-s-labour-force-participation-in-india-among-the-world-s-lowest-oxfam-63743, accessed 13 October 2019.

[3] The report based its estimates on the Employment and Unemployment Survey (EUS) of 2011–12, produced by the NSSO, and International Labour Organization (ILO) studies, and also builds on the first inequality report launched by Oxfam in 2018.

References

Abrol, Dinesh (2015), 'Agrarian Transition, Transformative Change and Systems of Innovation: Lessons for SDGs Implementation', paper presented at Anveshan Conference, Jawaharlal Nehru University, New Delhi.

Ahmad, Aijaz (2016), *On Communalism and Globalization: Offensives of the Far Right*, Delhi: Three Essays Collective.

Centre for the Study of Developing Societies (CSDS) (2014), *State of Indian Farmers: A Report*, https://www.lokniti.org/pdf/FarmersReportfinal.pdf, accessed 3 November 2019.

Desai, Manali and Indrajit Roy (2016), 'Development Discourse and Popular Articulations in Urban Gujarat', *Critical Asian Studies*, 48 (1): 1–26.

Desai, Radhika (2014), 'A latter-day fascism?' *Economic and Political Weekly*, 49 (35).

Harris, J., C. Jeffrey and S. Corbridge (2017), 'Is India Becoming the "Hindu Rashtra" Sought by Hindu Nationalists?' *Simons Working Papers in Security and Development*, 60, Canada: School for International Studies, Simon Fraser University.

Moyo, Sam, P. Jha and P. Yeros (2013), 'The Classical Agrarian Question: Myth, Reality and Relevance Today', *Agrarian South: Journal of Political Economy*, 2 (1): 93–119.

Naseemullah, Adnan (2017), 'The Political Economy of Economic Conservatism in India: From Moral Economy to Pro-business Nationalism', *Studies in Indian Politics*, 8 (2): 233–47.

NDTV (2017), 'All India Modi Government spent Rs 3,755 Crore on advertisements: RTI: The expenditure on advertisements from April 2014 to October 2017 through electronic, print media and outdoor publicity is Rs 37,54,06,23,616, according to the RTI reply', All India Indo-Asian News Service IST, 9 December, https://www.ndtv.com, accessed 25 May 2019.

National Sample Survey Office (NSSO) (2019), *Annual Report of Periodic Labour Force Survey, June 2017–July 2018*, Delhi: NSSO.

Patnaik, P. (2014), 'Imperialism and the Agrarian Question', *Agrarian South: Journal of Political Economy*, 3 (1): 1–15.

Patnaik, U. (2012), 'Some Aspects of the Contemporary Agrarian Question', *Agrarian South: Journal of Political Economy*, 1 (3): 233–54.

Prasad, Archana (2014), 'BJP, Modi and the Idea of India', *People's Democracy*, 18 May, available at https://peoplesdemocracy.in/2014/0518_pd/bjp-modi-and-idea-india, accessed 25 May 2019.

——— (2017a), 'Cover-up and Coercion in the Name of the "Holy Cow"', *People's Democracy*, XLI (47), 19 November, available at http://peoplesdemocracy.in/2017/1119_pd/cover-and-coercion-name-%E2%80%9Choly-cow%E2%80%9D, accessed 25 May 2019.

——— (2017b), 'Slaughter House Ban: Gainers and Losers', *People's Democracy*, XLI (16), 16 April, available at https://peoplesdemocracy.in/2017/0416_pd/slaughter-house-ban-gainers-and-losers, accessed 25 May 2019.

——— (2017c), 'Fifty Days of Demonetization and the Unorganized Sector', *People's Democracy*, XLI (1), 1 January, available at https://peoplesdemocracy.in/2017/0101_pd/fifty-days-demonetisation-and-unorganised-sector, accessed 25 May 2019.

——— (2017d), '"One Tax, One India": The Gainers and Losers', *People's Democracy*, XLI (29), 16 July, available at https://peoplesdemocracy.in/2017/0716_pd/%E2%80%9Cone-tax-one-india%E2%80%9D-gainers-and-losers, accessed 25 May 2019.

Siddiqui, Kalim (2017), 'Hindutva, Neoliberalism and the Reinventing of India', *Journal of Economic and Social Thought*, 4 (2), 142–86.

Vanaik, Achin (2017), *Hindutva Rising: Secular Claims, Communal Realities*, New Dehli: Tulika Books.

Yadav, Yogendra (2019), 'A Plaque of Promises: What the Modi Economy Has Done to Farmers', *Caravan*, 1 January, available at https://caravanmagazine.in/agriculture/what-modi-economy-done-farmers, accessed 3 November 2019.

21

Ways of Returning to the Source

Emancipatory Discourses in Japan and South Africa in the 1970s

Yoichi Mine

In March 2015, Professor Sam Moyo stayed in Japan as a visiting professor at the Centre for African Studies, Kyoto University. During the sojourn, he was greeted by a wide variety of local scholars and activists who admired his empathy, perceptiveness and integrity. As a response to his questions about social movements in Japan, I began to write an essay that eventually became a core part of this essay, though the chance of obtaining critical comments from him was lost.

This essay aims to compare radical activist narratives of Japanese social movements and South Africa's Black Consciousness Movement that were printed and circulated in the 1970s.[1] It may appear impracticable to compare the nature of radical movements in an Asian and an African country, given their historical, cultural, socio-economic and geographic distance. However, I believe that such a comparison is worth trying, not least because concerned activists at the time used to think and act in a universal reference frame at a certain theoretical level. In many quarters of the world, people read writings by Karl Marx and Frantz Fanon, for example, often in their local languages, and tried hard to apply what they hypothesized in practice, in villages, workshops, schools and streets. Even though the activists believed in secular values and creeds, their conscience and intellectual dynamics were analogous to those of the best practice of world religions based on the holy books and texts. They were aware that their movements were distinctive parts of a bigger collective endeavour. Here lies a commensurability in comparing discourses of progressive social movements across the world in the twentieth century.

For the sake of heuristic comparison, it is better not to think of an ideal model against which deviations of social realities are measured. Marxists have long been placed in a straitjacket of 'British capitalism' as an ideal, purified state of economy. Rather, it will be more fruitful to attempt to discover patterns of development and interactions between national economies by means of 'reciprocal comparison' of equally important geographic units, such as China and Western Europe, as undertaken by the economic historian Kenneth Pomeranz in his *Great Divergence* (Pomeranz 2000). In political science, Barrington Moore once tried to compare patterns of bourgeois revolutions and dictatorships in groups of nations by setting the positions of agricultural classes as explanatory variables (Moore 1966). In sociology, Ronald Dore compared British and Japanese work ethics, and attributed the collectivism of Japanese factory workers to the fact that Japan was a late starter of industrialization. Provided that all nations other than Britain were late developers, comparing a Japanese model and an African model of organizational ethics was justified by Dore for future research (Dore 1973: 418). In all these attempts, a privileged position of British capitalism is jettisoned. The horizons for non-hierarchical comparisons have expanded dramatically in the past half-century.

Although class positions matter, it must be remembered that people's social as well as personal attributes cannot be determined solely by their positions in class structures. There are several flaws in crude class reductionism. One concerns the political attitudes of the petty bourgeoisie which cannot be predicted only by its class position. In practical terms, students or the youth whose positions in society are yet to be determined may hold extremely polarized political creeds in the wake of their exposure to political events. The classic agrarian question has also been discussed, typically by Moore (1966), from the perspectives of varied and differentiated political attitudes of small- and medium-scale farmers, as well as landlords. These have something to do with a rule of thumb in twentieth-century politics: regardless of ideological sophistication, a political party that depreciates the role of the middle class cannot embrace victory.

The other point is that we are confronted with serious issues that cannot be explained appropriately only with class perspectives. In the major part of the twentieth century, traditional left movements largely ignored such issues as gender, disability, cultural identity, and the question of sustainability that was addressed as metabolism between humans and nature in *Grundrisse* by Marx. Even if a radical restructuring of economic system is realized, human injustices may last, and the danger of a systemic runaway in human–nature relationships will continue to haunt us. Without cumulative efforts to address these questions explicitly, a socialist millennium cannot fix them.

Several parts of this essay discuss the role of the youth in social transformation. In terms of class categories, university students are petty bourgeois, filled with future possibilities. The old and new petty bourgeoisie combined may become a distinctive social force through fascist parties, as discussed by Nicos Poulantzas (1970), or otherwise may transform themselves into a social force committed to the liberatory cause if they succeed in 'class suicide', as argued by Amilcar Cabral (1969). In the following sections, I try to juxtapose the narratives presented in the vortex of Japanese social protests in the 1970s with the narratives of their contemporaneous Black Consciousness Movement in South Africa, where some perceptive white citizens betrayed their race/class positions and joined the liberation struggle during the heyday of apartheid, though this fact is now brought into obscurity.

Setting the Scenes

Let us begin with the case of Japan. Reflecting renewed interest in '1968' as a symbol of simultaneous global political protest, a number of books and articles that review the political events in that year and thereafter have been published in Japan. Most of them are written by young scholar-activists who belong to the post-1968 generation, and the works include a voluminous chronology by Oguma (2009). Although the political radicalism of Japanese students was largely influenced by sectarian 'leftist' politics, young activists were also exposed to fresh voices of formerly disempowered sections of people, as described below.

As vividly depicted in the novels of Hiroshi Noma, Kazumi Takahashi and others, a queer feeling of having incidentally survived World War II captured the mind of the war generation. Then, the core generation of Japan's 1968 protest, which did not have direct memories of the war, grew up in the process of post-war economic recovery and rapid urbanization. A new wave of student activism that started with the occupation of university campuses in 1968 enjoyed broad popular support, possibly broader than its European counterparts at the time (Otake 2007), due to the rapid expansion of tertiary education in the post-war period. The 18-year-old population increased from 1.6 million in 1953 to a record high of 2.5 million in 1968, while university enrolment almost tripled from 0.13 million in 1955 to 0.33 million in 1968. As the post-war baby boomers entered the universities, the young masses started to form a broad support base of militant activists identified as the New Left. Occupation of university campuses in 1968 was ignited by the discontent of students over an increase in tuition fees and other campus-specific issues. After a series of showdown, battles with riot police, the campuses became normalized, but the frustrated activists wanted to continue mobilizing students around broader social and political issues.

From 1955 to 1973, the Japanese economy maintained an average annual growth rate of more than 10 per cent, although the distribution of wealth was far from equitable. Some students felt that they would betray their home communities and possibly their parents with lower education by stepping up the ladder of the social hierarchy and pursuing their own personal interests and careers. Then, after a strange peace was restored on campuses, people formerly deprived of their voices started to raise critical voices in numerous gatherings and print media, inspired by the direct action of students in the preceding years. They were women, foreigners, people with disabilities, underclass workers and other socially marginalized groups of people. Their messages caught the heart of young activists and made them waver between embarrassment, guilt and defiance. For elite students who had lived lives segregated from social realities, the encounter was a rude shock, forcing some of them to change the course of lives and abandon their entitlements.

In many respects, the significance of this unexpected event in Japan was in parallel with the impact brought by the Black Consciousness Movement in South Africa at exactly the same time. The collection of political writings of Steve Biko (1946–77), *I Write What I Like*, was translated into Japanese and read in the context of Japanese social movements (to be described in the following section). While Japanese and South African political activists did not exert visible mutual influence, activists from both countries occasionally communicated face-to-face since the early 1960s. Throughout the Cold War, the anti-apartheid movement had a certain influence and mobilization base in Japan as well, though this fact is not widely known in the west, or in Africa (Makino 2018).

Biko, enrolled in the non-white section of the medical school of the University of Natal in 1966, organized the South African Students' Organization (SASO) with his comrades in 1968, and was banned in 1973, before being brutally killed in police custody in 1977. At that time, South African universities were racially segregated, and student organizations were dominated by white students. Biko and his friends' provocation and articulated criticism of the control of movements by 'good-will' whites were not welcomed by the public initially, but the straightforward message began to attract widespread support not only from the black masses but also a small number of serious 'converts' of white dissidents, as vividly recorded in Woods (1979) and the subsequent film, *Cry Freedom* (1987).

Negation and Self-Negation

Back in the late 1960s, Biko delivered fierce indignation to the indecisive attitude of 'white liberals' in his article entitled 'Black Souls in

White Skins?', an apparent adaptation from *Black Skin, White Masks* by Frantz Fanon (1967). At that time, white activist students were liberal democrats who wanted to remove irrational colour-bars, or a few clandestine communists. Biko describes their positions as follows:

> If you ask him to do something like stopping to use segregated facilities or dropping out of varsity to work at menial jobs like all blacks or defying and denouncing all provisions that make him privileged, you always get the answer – 'but that's unrealistic!' While this may be true, it only serves to illustrate the fact that no matter what a white man does, the colour of his skin – his passport to privilege – will always put him miles ahead of the black man. Thus in the ultimate analysis no white person can escape being part of the oppressor camp. (Biko [1970] 1979: 22–23)[2]

Here, Biko highlighted the awkwardness of persons who were not part of the oppressed, spoke eloquently for justice on their behalf and went back to their safe urban home segregated from black areas. The same logic of rejecting complacent 'friends of natives' was presented by the Kaseito (Kakyo Seinen Toso Iinkai [Chinese Youth Struggle Committee]), a group of young Chinese activists in Japan imbued with Maoist thinking and the ethos of the Cultural Revolution.

After the occupation of campuses was violently suppressed in 1968, Japanese New Left factions with all sorts of Marxist creeds started to compete with each other and seek out a fresh issue for mass mobilization. They eventually tried to seize control of a new wave of the movement against xenophobia as a means of political manoeuvring. At one of the rallies in 1970, Kaseito decisively broke away from the New Left parties in protest against their predator behaviour. Eventually, the New Left leaders were forced to make bitter self-criticism in front of their own supporters, while the indicter group, Kaseito, disbanded in despair. In a document, Kaseito referred to the Great Kanto Earthquake in 1923, when thousands of Koreans and anarchists were brutally killed by Japanese vigilante groups instigated by the security police and the army:

> Now that the authorities conspire to restage the abhorrent massacre of Koreans that occurred at the time of Great Kanto Earthquake, we cannot help but feel great fear. Japanese can secure an escape route, as long as they are Japanese, by taking a self-satisfied position of non-commitment. We, however, cannot even take refuge due to the fact that we are Koreans or Chinese. As long as we are treated as potential criminals, being forced to carry alien registration cards, even passive Japanese

> bystanders are criminals in our eyes, not to mention those Japanese who identify with imperialists.[3] (Kaseito 1970: n.p.)

The above two narratives were expressed in the same year, 1970. While Biko and his comrades challenged white student activists to drop out from universities (Biko himself dropped out of medical school in 1972), Kaseito asserted that Japanese citizen 'bystanders' belonged to the oppressor camp. In those days, some participants in the student movement in Japan, especially from elite national universities such as Tokyo and Kyoto Universities, favoured the discourse of 'self-negation' and cried out slogans such as 'Down with Imperial Universities!'. Although class suicide could not become a main theme of the popular movement, the self-reflective mindset was shared by the best part of the student community and made their leaders receptive to criticisms such as those raised by Kaseito.

A student of Hiroshima University, Shuji Funamoto (1945–75), quit the university and lurked in *yoseba* (urban communities of homeless people; literally, this term means 'places where people are gathered') as a maverick revolutionary. Typically, day labourers were people who emigrated from the countryside, lost touch with their families and engaged in heavy labour on daily contract in city construction sites. The largest *yoseba*, called Kamagasaki, is located in the south of Osaka City. Funamoto eloquently articulates 'self-negation' in his own way as follows:

> 'Self-negation' means to deny the present real state of self. For labourers, self-negation is not to be elevated from the status of labourers to that of recruiters, but to negate their own way of living in surrender and despair, being obedient under the thumb of the white pigs – being fussed over when young and healthy, then exploited, and once their bodies are worn to rags with age, thrown out on the streets, dying like dogs, and eventually used as specimens for dissection in medical universities. . . . The basis of our organizing principle is not to organize indebtedness on the part of the 'strong' but to organize humiliation and grudges on the part of the 'weak'. . . . If you are the guardian of a weapon (i.e. knowledge), you should either direct this weapon against the state, or hand it over quietly to the 'weak' who know the best usage of the weapon. (Funamoto 1973: n.p.)

Funamoto was born in Manchuria, the northeastern part of China that Japan colonized. Even if it was uncommon, there were always a number of students like Funamoto who 'disappeared' from campuses and got immersed in underclass communities. After engaging in the radicalization of the movement of day labourers for the liberation of *yoseba*, he immolated himself in Okinawa in political protest, in 1975. Today, Kamagasaki, where he hid himself, has undergone gentrification and attracts young international tourists who seek relatively cheap accommodation.

Contradictions among the People

The strategy of Black Consciousness was to withdraw from a would-be multi-racial, inclusive organization dominated by a group of privileged elites, and to organize their own group that would grow at their own pace and under their own responsibility. As the unity of the oppressed was prioritized, those who flirted with people on the side of establishment were considered dangerous elements, as described by Biko:

> They have been made to feel inferior for so long that for them it is comforting to drink tea, wine or beer with whites who seem to treat them as equals. This serves to boost up their own ego to the extent of making them feel slightly superior to those blacks who do not get similar treatment from whites. These are the sort of blacks who are a danger to the community. (Biko [1970] 1979: 23)

Similarly, in the indictment by Kaseito, Chinese activists warned against their compatriotic 'selfish upstarts' or 'clever men' who plead for better treatment from the Japanese, 'crying "Please help me, at the least", in the delusive information technology age' (Kaseito 1970). However, even if they are dangerous, are persons who drink together with opponents really the enemy of the community?

The same question of cooptation, collaboration and betrayal was asked by Mitsu Tanaka (1943–), the most influential leader of Japanese post-war radical feminism at its inception. Radicalized by the student movement around 1968, Tanaka questioned why female student-activists always prepared meals for their male counterparts who passionately discussed about the revolutionary army and the emancipation of the human race only amongst themselves and stepped out to clash with the police. Female students were expected to serve for these boys from behind and keep clean the home-base, exactly as their mothers did in the division of labour in bourgeois, petty-bourgeois as well as traditional society.

The term 'women's lib [liberation]' spread rapidly in the 1970s, as the writings of Tanaka were read widely and their movement gained momentum. Some vigorously campaigned for legal reforms in favour of women's rights, while others set up women's collectives. Tanaka's *For Women of Life* still enjoys a wide readership as a manifesto of 'women's lib' and contemporary Japanese feminism. She currently runs an acupuncture clinic in Tokyo. Here, she describes the dynamics of solidarity in women's liberation:

> 'The enemy of "lib" is also women, isn't it?', some men say. Sure, those women who should not feel humiliation about 'being women' are the enemy. Those women who zip their lips about women who were forced to commit infanticide are the enemy. Those women who assume their *neutrality* and say smoothly, 'You ladies in the camp of women's liberation', are the enemy. However, I never condone men calling those women out as our enemy, because those who have changed sides are still *the enemy within the boundary of friendship*. We never sell them out, even if they sell us out. (Tanaka [1972] 2010: 185)

Tanaka underlined that 'lib' should be firmly anchored in women's own sufferings. She asked, 'Why do the voices raised by Koreans and Chinese in Japan bear such an essential importance? This is because those people are the agents of the struggle based on their own pains' (ibid.: 253). For her, the division between women was basically a contradiction among the people (Mao [1957] 2007), while the divide between men and women could be an antagonistic contradiction.

If the enemy is concentrated in the oppressor camp, it is easy to stay out of touch with him. It is possible to avoid direct contact with a person of the other sex. However, it is not an easy task to cut ties with one's own mother, from whose womb a boy or a girl was born. But what if your mother attempts to kill you because of the very fact that you are alive?

Koichi Yokozuka (1935–78) was born with cerebral palsy (CP) and eventually became a leading figure in an organization of persons with disability called the Society of Green Lawn. Notably, this organization campaigned against a popular petition that called for a reduction in sentence for a mother who killed her child with severe disability. If this kind of homicide was justified, the right to life of people with disabilities would be denied categorically, as noted by Yokozuka:

> When a mother rises from her slumber after delivery and sees her baby for the first time, she tries to confirm if all of its limbs and fingers are fine. But I think this has grave implications to we people who live with cerebral palsy. How is it if the baby has physical defects? How is it if it is born with cerebral palsy? After birth, we are treated as those who appear to deviate from normalcy, or more precisely, as beings that should not have existed. This is when the struggle between parents and people with cerebral palsy (their children) starts. . . . Because the cause

> of our movement, the Society of Green Lawn, is to bring into the open the real state of people with cerebral palsy, it boils down to calling for our liberation from our parents. Even with running tears, even with apologies for our unfilial attitudes, we are destined to kick over parental affection. (Yokozuka [1970] 2007: 24, 27)

Return to the Source

Biko delivered a powerful statement: the 'most potent weapon in the hands of the oppressor is the mind of the oppressed' (Biko [1970] 1979: 92). With the objective of escaping from this control, one needs to keep a certain unwavering point of reference in one's mind, which may fundamentally discord with conventional social norms.

Yokozuka asked, '[i]n this world, is there any person who leads a life wishing to be understood day and night in the first place?' (Yokozuka [1970] 2007: 65), while Tanaka wrote, '[p]ersons who are suffering at the moment do not have the luxury to explain lucidly about their pains. Because the expression of true feelings based on one's own pains emanates from one's very existence, it is no use replying to those who want to demand words from us' (Tanaka [1972] 2010: 88–89). Thus, the unshakeable ground may not be a sound theory of the social sciences but inexplicable affection or emotion emanating from one's own existence.

When cultural hegemony is in contestation, the core belief against manipulation of mind by the powerful can be the collective, indigenous memory of the past or hidden places where the influence of the conquerors has not reached. For Cabral, it was the African countryside where imperialist penetration was still partial and the authentic African way of life was preserved (Cabral 1973). In apartheid South Africa, Biko and his contemporary activists considered a sort of 'Africanness' the source of emancipatory inspiration. While Biko envisioned 'a colourless and non-exploitative egalitarian society' in which the Black Consciousness approach would be irrelevant, he believed that this synthesis would be achieved only after a protracted battle was settled between the industrial and military values of the west and the spiritual and humanistic values of Africa, with the triumph of the latter. This would become a sort of clash between hard power and soft power, as the power of Africa lies in the modalities of contextual and intimate communication:

> One of the most fundamental aspects of our culture is the importance we attach to Man. Ours has always been a Man-centred society. Westerners have on many occasions been surprised at the capacity we have for talking to each other – not for the sake of arriving at a particular conclusion

> but merely to enjoy the communication for its own sake. Intimacy is a term not exclusive for particular friends but applying to a whole group of people who find themselves together. (Biko [1970] 1979: 41)

However, preserving cultural authenticity and returning home become impracticable in some colonial and post-colonial situations. While many of the first-generation Koreans and Chinese in Japan were forcibly uprooted from their home nations before and during World War II, the subsequent generations had a tough time making a living in Japanese environments. For the latter generations, the question was not necessarily one of physically returning to their original home nations; there was a large-scale campaign for Koreans to 'return to North Korea' from the 1950s with unpleasant and even tragic outcomes awaiting the returnees. Kaseito noted some of the challenges the Korean and Chinese diasporas faced in Japan:

> More than a half of 600,000 Koreans and 50,000 Chinese [at that time] grew up as the postwar generation. While our parents think in their mother languages, speak them, and live in an inconvenient Japanese language environment, we of the second and the third generations forget these languages. Here we face enormous contradictions. The first generation feels loneliness and bleakness with which they have to bury their agony and joy into the land of the alien country. If we end up being uprooted, we may not be able to draw on the nourishment of our national soul forever from the land on which our parents treaded. To restore national culture is not to repossess what has been lost, but to build something anew and create what has not been there. (Kaseito 1970: n.p.)

For Kaseito activists, paying respect to the historical experience of their parents and ancestors was indispensable, but this practice did not contradict their attempt to create a new identity in this alien land where they were born. The Kaseito document signified that wandering in liminal spaces and taking resolute action would not be incompatible for a single person in quest of an identity base.

Funamoto found that *yoseba* was the urban shore of drifters. Like his contemporary radical intellectuals including Biko, Funamoto was affected by the influence of the Hegelian master–slave dialectic. However, he must have marvelled at the diversity of workers on the ground in the *yoseba* when he chose to live there in his twenties. 'Buraku' in the following text are the communities of Japanese outcast minorities entrenched during the feudal era. Funamoto argues:

> For the *Anko* (day labourers), Kamagasaki is the node of a circuit of migrants from agricultural villages, fishing villages, unliberated Buraku, Korean communities and Okinawa, as well as from abandoned mines. After very hard work, villages are scrapped, and people are fired on the pretext of industrial restructuring, 'forcibly recruited' from Okinawa, or driven out of Buraku due to discrimination or destitution. Kamagasaki is a relay point of their wandering. As long as their struggles remain in an individual, pre-reflective state, these are destined to be mutually segregated and buried forever. Our principle is to make these discrete struggles of the *Anko* develop into the struggle of all people, and to develop the partial reason to the universal reason. (Funamoto 1973: n.p.)

As discussed by Cabral and Biko, cultural dignity matters. And the concept of dignity has something to do with communication because dignity is related to the ways of *expressing* one's respect to the intrinsic values of other human beings. Tanaka's remarks about men's language of enlightenment and women's language of existence seem to correspond to the distinction between low-context and high-context cultures 'discovered' by anthropologists (Hall 1976). In her manifesto of Japanese feminism, Tanaka reinstated the value of irrationality:

> Around us, so many people espouse the value of words. One who relies on words in communication tries to varnish one's blunt body with words. The language flying out of men's neatly sorted drawers is a lifeless language, of enlightenment, which leans toward the dominant side. Modern rationalism separates words from bodies, expelling insanity from bodies. As such, women's confusion, or words spoken with confusion, has something to do with regenerating our bodies, to reinstate insanity. While men speak about insanity with their words, women speak about insanity through their existence. Confusion is the most beautiful weapon of women, the soul of women itself. (Tanaka [1972] 2010: 167)

Yokozuka thinks that the people with serious disabilities embody the universality of human beings precisely because of the fact that disabled people have been a target for elimination by their fellow humans. If people who consider themselves to be normal continue to murder those who are perceived as different, the planet will become empty sooner or later. By implication, Yokozuka's discussion attests to the absurdity of racism:

> Power always excludes certain minorities from society, thereby implanting a superiority complex and discriminatory consciousness in the mind of the majority. From the viewpoint of those who are in power, discard-

> ing deficient descendants is 'a procedure deemed to be necessary for the progress of the humankind'. . . . Many people may be convinced by such words, or become quiet if not convinced, because they unconsciously side with those in power, namely, those who would discard and eliminate 'defective children', or at least because they assume that they are not on the side of being eliminated. However, if the one in last place is eliminated, the next appear one after another, and the process will continue until a time when only one remains in the world. I don't care about whatever 'wonderful society' emerges after I am eliminated as a 'defective person', because I will be non-existent by then. (Yokozuka [1972] 2007: 132)

Although relationships between the oppressors and the oppressed are thus deeply entangled and complex, the activist narratives point to their common quest for autonomy as an individual or as a group in the hope that freed individuals seek for larger frames of solidarity based on pains and sufferings of self and others with irreplaceably unique attributes of individual persons.

Conclusion

The emancipatory thoughts and discourses presented in the previous sections have been revived for varying degrees in respective national contexts. In South Africa, on the one hand, the Black Consciousness Movement almost vanished after fierce repression, and many of its activists joined the African National Congress (ANC) and other parties in the 1980s. After the demise of apartheid, frustrated young black students started to read Biko's texts for the first time, though mostly in fragmented ways. By 2017, enrolment of university students in South Africa had surpassed 1 million, rising from 0.47 million in 1993. Nowadays, black students are becoming dominant, assertive and defiant in most campuses. In Japan, on the other hand, the Japanese texts cited in this essay were almost forgotten by the turn of the century, but some of them have been reprinted for activist or academic purposes, or because of curiosity about past social activism.

There were diverging patterns in the trajectories of social movements in Japan and South Africa since the early 1970s. In the age of the anti-apartheid struggle in South Africa, social issues faced by individual persons were merged with, or subordinated to, the cause of national liberation, and the Black Consciousness discourse galvanized the emancipatory mass movement when the ANC and other liberation movements were totally banned. Given the collusive relationship between apartheid and racial capitalism, it was assumed that all serious discrimination would be buried forever when the apartheid regime collapsed. The millenarian rhetoric prevailed even though the mainstream leadership espoused the two-step theory of National Democratic Revolution (NDR).

Indeed, the abolition of institutional apartheid only marked the first step in overcoming various forms of oppression including ethnocentrism and xenophobia. In South Africa, some of the contemporary writings aspiring for ultimate cosmopolitan freedom shift towards criticism of African nationalism and single agency that aimed to wield power by means of progressive capture of the state apparatuses. Ivor Chipkin (2007) criticizes the male-centric aspect of the Black Consciousness discourse on the liberation of 'Man', as well as the nation-centric agenda of the NDR, although he totally disregards, deliberately, the historical contexts in which black students spoke 'with a greater sense of urgency than whites' (Biko [1970] 1979: 22). The abolition of apartheid was a major achievement of humanity. The baseline is to recognize that the agency of black African nationalism eventually triumphed in South Africa, and yet there remain multiple issues beyond race and class.

In Japan, in contrast, the New Left and social movements failed to constitute a single political agency for change. Some of the issues discussed in Japanese narratives in the preceding sections persisted over the long term – may have been so since the birth of humankind – but were rendered invisible in the era of rapid economic growth, until the new generation of activists tried to place the issues on the explicit agenda of the 1970s. However, since then, Japanese progressive forces have not succeeded in uniting themselves both in and out of parliamentary politics. Brutal infighting among New Left political factions devastatingly alienated their sympathizers in the 1970s. More fundamentally, critical discourses at the time underscored the fact that power relations are deeply embedded in society and can be transformed only by changing the quality of everyday life through self-reflection and self-transformation (Ando 2014). As an unintended consequence, however, the critical social movement gradually became depoliticized and its scope was more or less reduced to the question of moral attitudes of individual persons in the intimate spheres. In contemporary Japan, there is a wide diversity of civil protests which have very limited influence on people's voting behaviour.

Despite such an eventual divergence, South African and Japanese emancipatory politics in the 1970s shared an important pattern of events: exposure of individuals in the oppressor camp to the lived realities of the oppressed people. In the visionary classic *Pedagogy of the Oppressed*, Paulo Freire (1970) set forth a new form of educational process in which both the oppressed and the oppressors regain humanity through dialogue by way of subverting the one-way teacher–student relationship. 'Converts' should not behave like the executors of the transformation by assuming that they monopolize correct knowledge, but trust people, their wisdom and their own transforming power (ibid.). In some discourses presented in this essay, the oppressed raise voices to the oppressors, whilst in others, they talk to their fellow-oppressed. The exception is the narrative of Funamoto who resolutely parted with his original student position and expressed indignation on behalf of the oppressed. In any case, it must be remembered that the process of humanization always begins with initial exposure as an eye-opening encounter with fellows and others.

The major activist generation of the 1970s is on the cusp of 'retirement'. Even though their political battles may have been lost, the legacy of initiatives they took still remains here and there. Albert O. Hirschman once described this dynamism as the 'principle of conservation and mutation of social energy'. After quitting political activism, people may launch different collective ventures whose characters have some links to the formerly espoused ideals. In the Latin American contexts, Hirschman paid attention to the bottom–up rise of entrepreneurship and consolidation of social capital, which were expected to counteract and perhaps eventually overwhelm authoritarian neoliberalism by functioning as a 'Trojan Horse' (Hirschman 1984: 42–44, 99).

Mutation of energy may take place several times in the same lifetime of a person, but a critical moment of learning, or a radical exposure to realities of which privileged people were not conscious, may not happen again. Every encounter should be treasured. The conclusion of this essay is thus very simple. We emphasize the significance of listening to the voices of the oppressed and of providing spaces where deliberation to find fundamental solutions flourishes. And importantly, such spaces should continue to be set up for younger generations, especially in the contemporary contexts of gentrification, gated communities and land-grabbing that reproduce themselves without legal segregation and colonial annexation. Cabral's class suicide 'cannot be attained merely by one-off volition of individuals but must involve a protracted process full of trials and errors' (Moyo and Mine 2016: 28).

In this sense, the challenges of the 1970s will never end. The emancipatory narratives presented here do not hide anger and frustration, but seek for conversation and dialogue as opposed to monologue. If we went awry, this was because we replied in wrong ways. Let us rewind and listen to people's original voices once more.

Notes

[1] An earlier version of this essay appeared in *Thread*, a South African web magazine: www.threadjournal.org/issue-one/an-entanglement/, accessed 17 August 2019.

[2] The writings in this text had been earlier published, mostly in the form of articles in mimeographed newsletters, in different years and different places. The same applies to the writings in Mao (2007), Yokozuka (2007) and Tanaka (2010) as well.

[3] The translations of Japanese texts in this essay are by the author.

References

Ando, T. (2014), *Japan's New Left Movements: Legacies for Civil Society*, Abingdon, Oxon: Routledge.

Biko, S. ([1970] 1979), *I Write What I Like: Selected Writings*, edited by Aelred Stubbs C.R., London: Heinemann.

Cabral, A. (1969), *Revolution in Guinea: Selected Texts*, New York: Monthly Review Press.

——— (1973), *Return to the Source: Selected Speeches*, New York: Monthly Review Press.

Chipkin, I. (2007), *Do South Africans Exist? Nationalism, Democracy and the Identity of 'the People'*, Johannesburg: Wits University Press.

Dore, R. (1973), *British Factory, Japanese Factory: The Origins of National Diversity in Industrial Relations*, Berkeley: University of California Press.

Fanon, F. (1967), *Black Skin, White Masks*, New York: Grove Press.

Freire, P. (1970), *Pedagogy of the Oppressed*, New York: Continuum.

Funamoto, S. (1973), 'Jakusha no tatakaikata ni manabi, "jakusha" no seikatsushiso wo taitoku shi, "jakusha" no kakumeishiso wo kochiku suru tameni' (To Learn from the Way of Struggle of the 'Weak', to Capture the Living Thought of the 'Weak', and to Forge a Revolutionary Thought of the 'Weak'), mimeo, n.p.

Hall, E.T. (1976), *Beyond Culture*, Garden City, NY: Anchor Press.

Hirschman, A.O. (1984), *Getting Ahead Collectively: Grassroots Experiences in Latin America*, New York: Pergamon Press.

Kaseito (Kakyo Seinen Toso Iinkai [Overseas Chinese Youth Struggle Committee]) (1970), 'Nyukan toso wo tatakau nakakara minzoku no tamashii no fukken wo' (Restore the national soul through the struggle against the immigration control)', mimeo, n.p.

Makino, K. (2018), 'Travelling for Solidarity: Japanese Activists in the Transnational Anti-Apartheid Movement', in S. Cornelissen and Y. Mine, eds, *Migration and Agency: Afro-Asian Encounters*, London: Palgrave: 247–70.

Mao, T. ([1957] 2007), *On Practice and Contradiction*, London: Verso.

Moore Jr., B. (1966), *Social Origins of Dictatorship and Democracy: Lord and Peasant in the Making of the Modern World*, Boston: Beacon Press.

Moyo, S. and Y. Mine (2016), 'Introduction', in S. Moyo and Y. Mine, eds, *What Colonialism Ignored: African Potentials for Resolving Conflicts in Southern Africa*, Cameroon: Langaa RPCIG: 1–34.

Oguma, E. (2009), *1968*, 2 vols, Tokyo: Shin-yo-sha.

Otake, H. (2007), *Shinsayoku no isan: Nyu refuto kara posutomodan he* (The Legacy of Shinsayoku: From New Left to Post-Modern), Tokyo: The University of Tokyo Press.

Pomeranz, K. (2000), *The Great Divergence: China, Europe, and the Making of the Modern World Economy*, Princeton, NJ: Princeton University Press.

Poulantzas, N. (1970), *Fascisme et Dictature: La IIIe Internationale Face au Fascisme*, Paris: Maspero.

Tanaka, M. ([1972] 2010), *Inochi no onnatachi he: Torimidashi uman ribu ron* (For the Women of Life: Confusion and Women's Liberation), New Edition, Tokyo: Gendai Shokan.

Yokozuka, K. ([1970] 2007), *Haha yo korosuna!* (Mother, Don't Kill!), New Edition, Tokyo: Seikatsu Shoin.

Woods, D. (1979), *Biko*, Harmondsworth: Penguin.

Contributors

Dinesh Abrol is former Chief Scientist, Council of Scientific and Industrial Research–National Institute of Science, Technology and Development Studies (CSIR–NISTADS), New Delhi, India.

Kojo S. Amanor is Professor, Institute of African Studies, University of Ghana, Legon.

Samir Amin (1931–2018) was Director, Third World Forum, in Dakar, Senegal; co-founder of the World Forum for Alternatives; and Director, United Nations African Institute for Economic Development and Planning.

Arindam Banerjee is Associate Professor in Economics, School of Liberal Studies, Ambedkar University Delhi, New Delhi, India.

Sandeep Chachra is Co-Chair, World Urban Campaign of UN-HABITAT; Executive Director, ActionAid Association, New Delhi, India; and managing editor, *Agrarian South: Journal of Political Economy*.

Walter Chambati is Executive Director, Sam Moyo African Institute for Agrarian Studies, Harare, Zimbabwe; and associate editor, *Agrarian South: Journal of Political Economy*.

C.P. Chandrasekhar is retired Professor, Centre for Economic Studies and Planning, School of Social Sciences, Jawaharlal Nehru University, New Delhi, India.

Jayati Ghosh is Professor, Centre for Economic Studies and Planning, School of Social Sciences, Jawaharlal Nehru University, New Delhi, India.

Smita Gupta is an independent economist who advised the All India Kisan Sabha and Left Parliamentarians on several drafts of The Land Acquisition and Resettlement and Rehabilitation Bills that the UPA government introduced between 2006 and 2013.

Praveen Jha is Professor of Economics, Centre for Economic Studies and Planning, Adjunct Professor, Centre for Informal Sector and Labour Studies, Jawaharlal Nehru University, New Delhi, India; and editor of *Agrarian South: Journal of Political Economy.*

Lau Kin Chi is Vice President, World Forum for Alternatives; founding member, Global University for Sustainability, Hong Kong; and Associate Professor, Department of Cultural Studies, Lingnan University, Hong Kong, China.

Gladys T. Lechini is Professor of International Relations, National University of Rosario, Argentina; and former Coordinator, South–South Programme, Latin American Council of Social Sciences, 2003–07.

William G. Martin is Professor of Sociology, Binghamton University, State University of New York, USA.

Yoichi Mine is Professor, Graduate School of Global Studies, Doshisha University, Japan.

Tendai Murisa is Executive Director, SIVIO Institute, Harare, Zimbabwe, a research organization focused on public policy working across southern Africa.

Lyn Ossome is Senior Research Fellow, Makerere Institute of Social Research, Makerere University, Uganda; and associate editor, *Agrarian South: Journal of Political Economy.*

Prabhat Patnaik is Emeritus Professor, Centre for Economic Studies and Planning, School of Social Sciences, Jawaharlal Nehru University, New Delhi, India.

Utsa Patnaik is Emeritus Professor, Centre for Economic Studies and Planning, School of Social Sciences, Jawaharlal Nehru University, New Delhi, India.

Archana Prasad is Professor, Centre for Informal Sector and Labour Studies, School of Social Sciences, Jawaharlal Nehru University, New Delhi, India; and associate editor, *Agrarian South: Journal of Political Economy*.

Anamitra Roychowdhury is Assistant Professor, Centre for Informal Sector and Labour Studies, Jawaharlal Nehru University, New Delhi, India.

Ian Scoones is Professor, Institute of Development Studies, University of Sussex, Brighton, United Kingdom.

Issa G. Shivji is retired Professor of Public Law and the first Nyerere Professor of Pan-African Studies, University of Dar es Salaam, Tanzania; and editor, *Agrarian South: Journal of Political Economy*.

Wen Tiejun is Executive Dean, Institute of Advanced Studies for Sustainability, Renmin University of China, Beijing; Executive Dean, Institute of Rural Reconstruction of China, Southwest University, Chongqing; and Executive Dean, Institute of Rural Reconstruction of the Straits, Fujian Agriculture and Forestry University, Fuzhou, China.

Dzodzi Tsikata is Research Professor, Institute of Statistical, Social and Economic Research and Director, Institute of African Studies, University of Ghana, Legon; editor, *Agrarian South: Journal of Political Economy*; and former president, Council for the Development of Social Science Research in Africa (CODESRIA).

Sit Tsui is Associate Professor, Institute of Rural Reconstruction of China, Southwest University, Chongqing, China.

Erebus Wong is Senior Researcher, Kwan Fong Cultural Research and Development Programme, Lingnan University, Hong Kong, China.

Paris Yeros is Professor of International Economics and Coordinator of the Postgraduate Programme in World Political Economy, Federal University of ABC, São Paulo, Brazil; and editor, *Agrarian South: Journal of Political Economy*.